The Illustrated Collector's Guide To
Led Zeppelin
(CD Edition- Volume 2)

Robert Godwin

We acknowledge the financial support of the Government of Canada through the Book Publishing Industry Development Program for our publishing activities.
Published by Collector's Guide Publishing Inc., Box 62034, Burlington, Ontario, Canada, L7R 4K2
Printed and bound in Canada by Webcom Ltd of Toronto
The Illustrated Collector's Guide To Led Zeppelin (Sixth edition)
ISBN 1-896522-42-4
Cover Art - Robert Godwin

The
Illustrated
Collector's Guide To
Led Zeppelin
(CD Edition - Volume 2)

CONTENTS

Introduction

This latest edition is a compilation of material not to be found in the previous book editions. Some of the material did appear on the CDROM (the one we call the 5th edition), however since many people own Apple computers and were not able to use the CDROM, the bulk of that information has been reproduced here. This leads to some absurd number of new titles approaching six or seven hundred.

As the CDROM featured everything that was available up until 1995 it seemed appropriate to include a color tribute to the first 25 years of Led Zeppelin bootleg cover art.

You may notice that the dreaded "n/a" symbol appears more often than I would like. It has become increasingly difficult to determine all of the information on many releases, also some pictures may be a bit rough on quality but we do what we can!

Acknowledgements

Many people have contributed to the six editions of this book. As clichéd as it may sound, they are too many to mention (or remember!). However, some do stand out because they have for many years provided a wealth of information.

◉ Rick Barrett of Merit Adventures, has been an uncompromising supporter of this book for nearly fifteen years. He frequently has turned up gems for my use and continues to do so to this day. If anyone has a real interest in collecting ephemera from the legit side of things, contact Rick at his Houston office c/o Merit Adventures, Box 66262, Houston, Texas, 77266-6262. Rick doesn't sell bootlegs.

◉ Bob Walker of Hot Wacks publishing has often and frequently loaned me the more expensive items to photograph and document, his Hot Wacks books are undoubtedly the world's best on the subject of bootleg collecting.

◉ Art, wherever you are, thank you for taking over the nurturing of the monster and thanks to Tony for being the delivery man.

◉ Ross Halfin for photographing his collection.

◉ My wife Pat and my kids Dayne and Emily for enduring years of me rambling on.

◉ All the gang at CG Publishing who had to once again listen to weeks of Led Zeppelin (Hey! You should have paid me for the privilege!).

◉ Brad Tolinski at Guitar World, Howard Kramer at the Rock & Roll Hall Of Fame, Tom Kaniewski at VH1, the crew at Muchmusic, Jeff Woods at Q107, Mike Hardy at Power 97, all the folks in Tokyo including Masato Kato, Ikumi Numata, Eric Sachs and Hiroki Hayakawa. Muneo Imamura and Ronald Girouard for providing the really cool rare stuff. And to the many people who over the years have (sometimes unknowingly) provided material for this book:

◉ Red Robinson, Hugh Jones, Dave Lewis, Grant Burgess, Howard Mylett, Chris Welch, Eric Romano, David Borgonovo, Benoit Pascal, Bruce Deerhake, Dan O'Connor, Brad Lauchor, Sam Katenjian, and Taj Mahal.

◉ Finally, to Led Zeppelin for turning a blind eye and letting me do this book for fifteen years, to Jonesy for saying nice things about me, and to Bonzo, wherever you are.

Bootlegs - thirty years on and still going....

It's been three years since the CDROM version of this book and four since the last print edition. Things have certainly changed in that time. The hatchet men have all but exterminated the European and American bootleggers. The Australians have (as predicted) passed draconian new laws to stamp out the dreaded scourge. Which leaves us with third world pirates and ...... gee I wonder who else?

Unbelievably the world's bootleg production has not shifted to Israel or Brazil or even South Africa but is centred almost entirely in Japan.

Almost everything in this book which has been released over the last four years is Japanese. It seems incomprehensible that after doing everything short of thumb screws and hot pokers the RIAA haven't done a damn thing about Japan. Could it be that they don't care, or is it that they have little or no influence on the Japanese parliament? Regardless of what is happening it would seem that for now they are not doing anything about it. In Tokyo you can find at least a dozen stores that have their own in-house label which they promote with everything from monthly color catalogs to pictures of the proprietor with the artists hanging in the window.

Meanwhile the legitimate music business in North America is undergoing a lengthy and painful restructuring. As of this writing hundreds of independent labels are finding themselves without distribution since the debacle forced upon them by the budget CD wars. Chains such as "Best Buy" and "Circuit City" moved into the CD game with a vengeance. One of the goals they accomplished was to establish an in-depth catalog of imports and indie titles. The result of this was a price war which almost obliterated the Ma and Pa record shop from the American music scene. However the amount of returns which were then foisted upon the majors and indies alike ultimately brought about the demise of massive distributors such as the Alliance who filed for Chapter 11 protection in early 1998. Alliance had been on a massive growth cycle for the better part of three years and had positioned themselves to be *the* distributor for hundreds of indies. When the shit hit the fan, the indies were left without a distributor and the Ma and Pa's (that were still in business) had hardly anywhere to buy product. Through all this the independent shops found themselves in a situation where their traditional ace card, the import, was now no longer drawing clientele. Let's face it if you can buy an import at "Best Buy" for a dollar or two over cost you're not going to hunt out the poor Ma and Pa that can only offer it to you at $30. Consequently more of these small retailers briefly shifted to carrying bootlegs.

Then it got ugly. The RIAA armed with new legislation (and new enthusiasm from state Attorney Generals keen to be seen on television, this was an election year) raided many of these stores and dropped the hammer on them. To really make it all hilariously ironic the companies that were bringing in the imports were then slapped down as well, forcing many of them to go underground while others simply went out of business. Let's not forget that these imports were being bought from the major labels foreign divisions who knew damn well what was happening to the product.

End result....the big chains are now back to selling washing machines. The major labels are desperately casting about for a way to get the public enthusiastic about the "next big thing". The Ma and Pa's are either dead or licking their wounds. Some of the biggest importer/distributors in America are gone. Hundreds of indie labels are earnestly in search of distribution and thousands of upcoming musicians are not getting into the stores at all. Bootleg production has all but sequestered itself in the Far East. The American public has had a huge percentage of the world's music denied to them (legit and bootleg). But.....

Along came....CDR and MP3.

In the late 1990's the bulk of the world's music is owned by the huge entertainment conglomerates such as Sony/CBS, BMG, Time Warner, MCA/Universal etc. These same companies are gradually allying themselves more and more with the big software companies and hardware manufacturers. While the left hand is bitching about piracy and bootlegging the right hand is selling tonnage of the hardware and software to make CD's to anyone who wants to. A CD recorder can now be purchased for as little as $250 and the blank

discs are down to $1. Meanwhile some bright spark figured out that audio files could be compressed down to a manageable size and then shot anywhere in the world via the Internet. The process was christened "MP3". Am I the only one who sees the humour in this??

While these new technologies have almost certainly sounded the death knell for mass pro-duced bootlegging as we have known it for the last thirty years, they have simultaneously opened the door to home bootlegging on a scale that has surely already surpassed even the hey days of the early seventies.
One minor victory that this turn of events has given the RIAA is that a CDR has little or no intrinsic collectible value. The average bootleg collector is attracted by the collecting process (i.e. the hunt, the catch, the showing off to their friends). They are also drawn to the more obvious virtues (besides the music) such as the imaginative packaging (much of which was spawned by the bootleg industry before being appropriated by the legit biz). To most collectors, a CDR is nothing more than a fancy tape recording and thus easily dupli-cated. While the RIAA and it's international equivalents would have the world believe that bootlegs are bought solely because the customer has been hoodwinked, the reality is that a lot of bootlegs are bought because they encapsulise a moment in time and, at their best, put historical audio and pictorial documents in one nice neat tidy package. This type of bootleg will now undoubtedly go the way of the Dodo thanks to CDR and MP3, however the problem the RIAA now faces will be truly unstoppable as more and more burners find their way into everyday life. No doubt they already have a blank CD tax pending, it makes you wonder who will actually get *that* money. It sure as hell won't be the musicians.

In the midst of all this somewhere lies the music. Most of this material would never have survived had it not been for the bootleggers: that handful of people who dared to actual-ly want to take the music home with them and didn't settle for a hazy memory and a ripped ticket stub. How many of those 15,000 odd people at the LA Forum in September 1970 have since forgotten that night? Probably most of them, but thousands of others have experienced the magic of hearing Led Zeppelin in full flight, pounding out of their home stereo system thanks to "Blueberry Hill". Not just any old concert slapped together from three or four nights in 1973, but the real magic.

The managers and agents and record execs often condemn the process, they say that the bootlegger thinks of himself as Robin Hood, while to them he is just a common thief, not giving anything back to the musician or the industry which invests so much time and money in the artist. This is such a politically convenient stereotype. It gives them the abil-ity to slap one another on the back and then sleep at night knowing that they have moral-ity on their side. It's also dead wrong.

Like it or not bootlegging is a part of modern life. I'm not talking about the wholesale pira-cy and counterfeiting of movies or CDs or software, I'm talking about someone pressing up a concert that doesn't exist in commercial circulation. These are historic snapshots. They are the very essence of a moment in time. At their best they can transport a person back to that moment and let them relive it in living color. In a hundred years from now there will probably be very few people who will care who owns the rights to most of the music. Let's face it Michael Jackson owns the Beatles' publishing, does anyone really think that his heirs will still own it in a hundred years? It will get bought and sold by business men. Each and every one of them will carve off their slice of the pie. Some of them may even have earned the right to make a living from some poor dead rock star, but will the real magic survive? Will history and posterity have been served. Will people in a hundred years listen to "Stairway To Heaven" and marvel at Jimmy Page's virtuosity or will some-one dig out a recording of "Listen To This Eddie" and be totally amazed. No studio tricks and multi-tracking to hide behind, no possibility of some session man sneaking in and doing the hard bits. No Milli-Vanilli syndrome, just a master musician exercising his craft in front of 15,000 spellbound acolytes.

Bootleggers are not like Robin Hood - I wouldn't insult anyone by saying that they are not motivated by profit, many surely are. A far less flattering analogy would be to compare

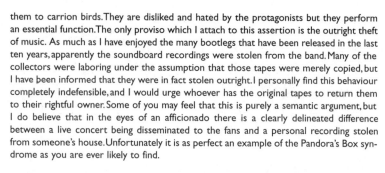

them to carrion birds. They are disliked and hated by the protagonists but they perform an essential function. The only proviso which I attach to this assertion is the outright theft of music. As much as I have enjoyed the many bootlegs that have been released in the last ten years, apparently the soundboard recordings were stolen from the band. Many of the collectors were laboring under the assumption that those tapes were merely copied, but I have been informed that they were in fact stolen outright. I personally find this behaviour completely indefensible, and I would urge whoever has the original tapes to return them to their rightful owner. Some of you may feel that this is purely a semantic argument, but I do believe that in the eyes of an afficionado there is a clearly delineated difference between a live concert being disseminated to the fans and a personal recording stolen from someone's house. Unfortunately it is as perfect an example of the Pandora's Box syndrome as you are ever likely to find.

This brings us back to CDR. As much as I love the damn things I can't see any purpose in listing them in this book. For fifteen years this book has served as a guideline for collectors who want to know what they're buying from their local supplier of black market music. During that time well over a thousand Led Zeppelin bootlegs have hit record shows and indie shops around the world. As long as this supply continued (pre-crackdown) there seemed to be some purpose in identifying these items and helping people from being deceived by often inaccurate cover art.

Very few CDR's will be distributed on the scale of a mass produced CD. For example if someone in San Francisco decides to knock out 25 CDR copies of a tape they made the night before, what chance does a collector have of acquiring that item in London? Who would even want to? Consequently, as I have been predicting for the better part of the last three or four years, CDR will surely be the end of bootleg collecting as we know it. Inevitably this may also mean the end of this book. Six editions are probably enough anyway!

It has been extremely gratifying to have spent the last fifteen years watching the network of Led Zeppelin afficionados grow. Back when I wrote the first edition there were only 114 Led Zeppelin bootlegs, 10 albums and 38 singles. Since then those numbers have grown to well over a thousand bootlegs, dozens of legit solo, radio, foreign pressings and other obscurities and a whole book (or two) written about just the singles. Led Zeppelin have surpassed the Beatles, Stones, Dylan, Floyd and everyone else to become easily the most bootlegged band on Earth. The last time anyone actually counted, the Beatles were in second place but were at least 20% behind. What an astounding accomplishment for the band. As much as they almost certainly don't approve and probably don't want this particular accolade it is a tribute to them that so many people crave their music that they have even surpassed the Beatles. Supply and demand you know...people wouldn't make 'em if people didn't buy 'em.

When Led Zeppelin split up, their story was almost a complete mystery. Not being happy to deal with the usual trappings of success they deliberately shrouded themselves from the public, creating a veil of secrecy which remained unbroken for years. In 1998 thanks to the Internet, fanzines, bootleggers, historians and fans around the world the secrets have slowly revealed themselves. Many of the things we now take for granted would have been inconceivable twenty years ago. Now we have books and videos and soundboard tapes and Page & Plant performing on TV.

I am grateful that I have had the chance to participate in some small way towards lifting that veil of secrecy. I am particularly grateful to the band for not dropping the hammer on this book (which I suppose they could have done) and I am indebted to the thousands of people who have bought it. I'm glad to see that all the research has been of some use and that it has inspired others to seek out more information. I still receive several messages a week from people who have enthusiastically uncovered another gem of information. Keep up the good work, maybe one day the importance of all of this data will be recognised. Someday someone will look back and see that the greatest rock band of this century deserve to be remembered in the same way that the Beatles inevitably will be.

The trainspotter turns critic....

Wednesday March 25th 1998 Shepherd's Bush London England

It's bloody freezing - about 45 degrees. Nearly two hundred people are clutching themselves tightly, looking earnestly at a handful of security guards pacing around in leather jackets. It's only 6.30 and a scalper just chased my car the length of the sidewalk as my lift tried to pull up in front of the hall. I don't have a ticket but I tell him to get stuffed when he asks for two hundred quid. It's the first clear sign that I'm in the right place. The old devils are back - at least that's what the front cover of *Uncut* magazine proclaims. Inside this grubby looking old theatre about a thousand or two of the faithful are about to witness an event.

On the previous Saturday an innocuous advert in Time Out announced that Robert Plant and Jimmy Page along with their cohorts would be playing a one nighter on home turf. Naturally enough the thousand or so tickets sell out in about half a second. By the time I roll into London on business and find out about the gig I'm at least four days too late. Fortunately someone "in-the-know" tells me that if I get down to the Empire by 7.00 on the night I should be able to get one of a hundred tickets held back. This brings me back to telling the scalper to f**k off.

Leaning dejectedly against the iron railings outside the Empire are a couple of students from Vermont. I ask them which line is for buying tickets, only to find out that both lines are for people who already have them. I conclude that this explains why they are looking miserable and not in either line. I share my secret with them and watch their faces light up. I ask one of the burly guards. "Where do you think they will be selling tickets?" "They're not!" he replies and points at the *Sold-Out* signs on every door. "Well if you were going to put some tickets on sale, where would you sell them?" I meekly enquire. "Well if it was me mate I'd stand right there," he says pointing at the ticket window and winking.

It's only 6.45 and the show is at least two hours away. I join the ranks of the people huddling against the wall for shelter. Twenty five years have gone by since the last time I did this.
"Have you seen them before?" I ask the students and they all shake their heads. "But it's going to be great! What a way to finish March break!" retorts one of them. I decide it would be impolite to ask why he thinks that if he hasn't seen the boys before, but I know it would be a stupid question. They subsequently set themselves up for an earful when they ask me if I've ever seen them before.
In an instant they find the chatty old bastard more interesting. "Are they playing any Zep stuff?" they ask. Rising to the occasion I rattle off a pretty inaccurate approximation of the set list (way off...). On discovering that one of them actually owns a copy of one of my books their intellectual credentials skyrocket. "Oh it was nothing...." etc etc - (display of false modesty as I inwardly beam from ear to ear). By now it's past 8.00 and I'm numb with cold and asking myself whether this is going to be worth it, then I hear the rush of enthusiasm from the people up front as they all push for the ticket window. An audible stream of curses comes from the scalpers as they start telling everyone that they have *really* good seats for only £50. Ahh....the sweet taste of revenge....god bless ya P & P.

After snagging a floor ticket we are shuffled over to the ticket holders line where I overhear some guys talking about the gig in Istanbul. I have a sneaky suspicion that I know one of them. After inquiring it turns out I have met him before and within a few seconds I start seeing all kinds of people I vaguely recognise. Finally legendary Zep scholar and all round loony Dave Lewis appears and throws himself at me. "What the f**k are you doin' 'ere?" he inquires with all the sincerity he can muster while his friends take the piss out of both of us about our various Zep tomes. Odd this — I'm four thousand miles from home and I feel like I just nipped down to the corner pub.
"Got any cameras or cell-phones?" asks one of the guards. "Wrong question," says someone as they rush in and pull out the tape deck.

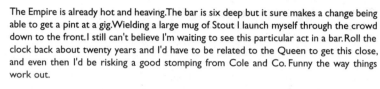

The Empire is already hot and heaving. The bar is six deep but it sure makes a change being able to get a pint at a gig. Wielding a large mug of Stout I launch myself through the crowd down to the front. I still can't believe I'm waiting to see this particular act in a bar. Roll the clock back about twenty years and I'd have to be related to the Queen to get this close, and even then I'd be risking a good stomping from Cole and Co. Funny the way things work out.

The lights go out and after a quick intro straight out of *Sinbad* a decidedly healthy looking Jimmy Page stalks out all trimmed down and raring to go. The place goes completely bonkers. Out from the shadows swaggers Percy Plant his seamed appearance disguised by the darkness. Ten seconds and then *The Wanton Song* — scorched earth here gang. These guys are definitely not taking any prisoners tonight. Plant is bobbing up and down like a nineteen year old while Page just hangs his head and gets down to business. No mistakes to speak of, he is barely recognisable as the same guy I saw at Madison Square Gardens in May 1988. This is a strangely renovated version of the Earl's Court maestro, different hair but no mistaking what I'm hearing, f**king brilliant.

Can't take my eyes off the two of them to the point where I almost feel guilty that I have barely noticed Lee and Jones solidly pounding it out at the back. These two are not just a cartoon parody of the other legendary defensive line. No, they know what to do and when to do it, thundering along like a bloody division of Centurion tanks. Straight into *Bring It On Home* more swagger and stagger. Page unleashes a blinding string of pearls from the Les Paul, firing them out at the front of the crowd like some blood-crazed commando. Plant stretches and contorts the lyrics to fit, having some difficulty getting up into the original stratospheric realms of the album. It's barely noticeable given the fact that he's just so damned interesting to watch and since he's leading the attack with so much gusto you feel that should he blow a whistle and shout "Over the top!" the entire crowd would storm the stage like a herd of berserking Vikings.

A quick millisecond's pause and then Page lays out the blistering intro to *Heartbreaker*. A furtive glance above and behind me reveals the entire audience from the floor right up to the last seat on the second balcony is bobbing up and down like corks in a storm. A lot of smiling faces. Page flawlessly rips through the middle solo and flicks the pick-up switch before launching the final offensive. As Percy bellows the last few words Page duckwalks forward until his machine-heads threaten to poke out the eyes of the front row. This is really intimate stuff folks - half of the legendary heavier than air machine is back and IN YOUR FACE.

Plant waves and smiles at the incredibly noisy roar from the crowd and then Page slips out the beginnings of *Ramble On*. The two of them lean together in that patented pose that so many others just can't make work. Even with his hair shorn, Page just has that *look,* and leaning into Plant's improbable curls it *just works*. Each shift of the guitar's sound is flawless, with Page sliding effortlessly from verse to chorus to solos as though someone has dared him to prove he can play it perfectly.

Next up is a new one, the title track from the album *Walking Into Clarksdale*. It starts slowly but quickly has Page blistering the paint on the walls with another of his unmistakeable blitzkrieg riffs. Can't make out what Percy is crooning about but he seems to know so why should I care? I just close my eyes and immerse myself — interesting.

Out of the twilight comes the distinctive shimmering sound of the synth intro to *No Quarter*. A keyboard no bigger than a kitchen sink is manned by someone I've never seen before. Seems a bit of an odd choice to play, having been a showcase piece for John Paul Jones, but who the hell am I to judge. The sound is luxuriant and when Charley Jones steps out with his synthesised wardrobe and punches out the coolest rolling bass sounds - I can feel the hair standing up on my neck. Plant is flanged and distorted all to hell and my eyes are closed again. This one always takes me back to that f**king scary bit in *Lord Of The Rings*. Page peels off the solo with as much flare as Earl's Court in '75 but he limits it to just about the exact length of the studio version, really tasty and just about the best bit so far.

Into *When I Was A Child* from the new album. I can't figure this one out at all. Way too lethargic for me at this point. Out come the kitchen chairs and mandolins and then it's into *Going To California*. The finger-picking is impeccable, and Percy delivers his usual emotional take. At the end of this one the crowd seems to go really daft. Plant mentions that they were going to drop this song from the set and he seems to be genuinely surprised by the sheer depth of feeling from the crowd. Suddenly we're hearing *Tangerine* in all it's glory. Don't know if I'm right but I seem to think this is the first time this has been done for bloody ages. The mystery keyboard man, now introduced as Phil Andrews, picks the solo on a mandolin. I'm so surprised, it's over before I've really figured out what's what.

Since it's revival in 1995 *Gallow's Pole* has become an anthem. No disappointment tonight. If Plant was perched in the stands at Molyneux watching Wolves win the European Cup he wouldn't have seen as many truly supportive faces. The audience at this point is really impressing me with their stamina. Some have been bouncing up and down for an hour without even sliding to the bar for a refill, in fact the bartenders are distinctly idle. Page is throwing around his acoustic double-neck like a lunatic.

Next is another new one *Burning Up*. This one sounds like some kind of fifties thing. Again I can't make out a bloody word Plant is saying. He clings to the mike-stand with both hands, eyes closed, veins bulging in his neck and arms. Looks like he's been working out. Every so often he does one of those little shimmies that makes him look like he ought to be per-manently locked up in the harem, no doubt a good idea in his books.

He introduces the next one as a folk song and Page gently picks out the beginning of *Babe I'm Gonna Leave You*. It sounds exactly like the original except instead of sounding like a nineteen year old who's just figured out he won't get laid tonight Percy sways and croons like a guy who just got left in the rain by his one true love. Page bleeds out an emotional and moody solo before he propels the band back into the riff only to finally conclude with an incongruous snippet of *Stairway*.

By now the crowd is primed to be launched into orbit by *How Many More Times*. Plant calls it jazz but no jazz band ever swung like this juggernaut. This is pure bravado. Page perfect-ly recreates the blistering wah-wah attack and sounds of thirty years ago. No denying it —
he really is absolutely on the top of his form playing better than all those interim years, pushing in and out of the solos and verses with effortless ease. Then he grabs the bow and just etches his mark into every single memory with those searing licks that we all know and love. Meanwhile it's no mere wall of sound from the back, Jones and Lee methodical-ly build an entire friggin' coliseum with Page weaving in and out like a slalom skier going for the gold. Just as everyone waits for that "Oh Rosie" from Plant they switch the engine into reverse and start trudging through *In The Light*. Startling effect which may have been a mercy given the fact that Percy has eschewed the upper octaves for most of the evening.

Any doubting Thomases have now well and truly had their hands thrust into the fire —
yeah....that burns. The winding intro of the new single *Most High* meanders it's way out of the thirty foot stack four feet to my right. It's bloody loud - and at times it sounds like more than a few coils have already been torched. No going back now though, out comes *Whole Lotta Love*, big and nasty. Oddly this one seems a bit out of place to me, even more than *No Quarter*. When Page shifts into the boogie riff which they had inaugurated at Knebworth I just keep looking up and expecting to see Bonzo, although Lee is exemplary, I just can't shake the ghost in my head. Then Page goes into sorcerer mode and begins his theramin duel with Plant, concluding with a very passable high register wail before going back into the riff. Nice —but a bit spooky.

Well, that was it. Off they go back into the shadows like a bunch of marauders into the fog, nothing but the echoes and war cries left behind. Not a chance that they were getting away that easily. The audience splits down the middle, half surging towards the stage the other half storming the bar but all in full voice. No fifteen minute delay like Earl's Court, no Plant apologising for the delay while he has a cup of tea. They're back and Lee pounds into another new one *House Of Love*. People near me gasp for breath, at the time I assumed

that this meant that they hadn't expected this particular choice for the encore. It's all funk and bluster as they complete the track and Page blurts out a vaguely familiar chord sequence, it's *Crossroads*. Yeah - that thing Cream made so famous. Very unexpected this. Plant belts it out in his own unique style and Page ejects a staccato flow of lightning fast licks that would make Clapton cringe in a corner. And off they go again all smiles and hugs.

And then back again for an emotional rendering of *Thank You* , a brief respite before finally searing the last vestiges of resistance with a stunning *Rock And Roll* with Plant actually nailing the key successfully.

I'm out on the street. It's still bloody cold and my ears are ringing. "Good show mate?" asks the taxi driver. "Yeah." I can't bring myself to elaborate any further. I just have to think it over for a while. Did I just see Led Zeppelin in a place the size of my local? Bloody nearly. Although Jones and Bonzo weren't there in person, their shadow loomed large over everything. For some reason I have a picture in my mind of Bonzo throwing Michael Lee a banana.

The never ending concert itinerary...

Thanks to the tenacious research of the Francophone contingent, Benoit Pascal has turned up details of several dates which were either unknown or in need of confirmation:

Tous En Scene Television Appearance in Paris France confirmed as June 19th 1969 by photographers at the show. The band also made a quick French appearance at L'Ecole Centrale in Chatenay- Malabry in the suburbs of **Paris** on December 6th 1969, this has apparently been confirmed by people who attended.

My suspicions of a Dutch tour in late 1969 have now been confirmed by at least one date in **Haarlem Holland** on October 13th 1969.

Special thanks to Benoit for sharing this info, readers are advised to check out his excellent book, Led Zeppelin - Hexagonal Experiences, in which Benoit has unearthed some amazingly rare information and pictures about the band's French escapades. It is available from Benoit Pascal - 14bis, rue de la Cavee Boudin - 27000 Evreux - France

My assumptions about **Raleigh 1970** have also been borne out. The gig was on April 8th 1970 and not April 7th as had been previously thought.

Another date which had been left to conjecture after my last book was the band's possible appearance in **Salt Lake City** in 1969, this has now been confirmed by David Borgonovo who says that they appeared at the Terrace Ballroom on July 30th 1969 with Vanilla Fudge supporting. David also had an encounter with someone who claimed to see Zeppelin and Vanilla Fudge in Vancouver in 1968, with the benefit of this information I managed to track down an advert for the show (unfortunately Zep aren't mentioned but Vancouver Radio personality and local oracle Red Robinson confirmed that Led Zeppelin certainly did the gig and that promoter Gary Switlow didn't realise that they would become so famous so he neglected to mention them in his advertising.) This would make this their first Canadian appearance. Bill Bates, a Vanilla Fudge expert, was kind enough to also provide details of the rest of the year. Zeppelin parted company with the Fudge the next day, 29 December. The Fudge went on to headline at the New Capital Theatre, NY, and the Charles Lloyd Quintet were the opening act. On the 31 December: Vanilla Fudge headlined a New Years Eve show with Richie Havens, The Youngbloods & Cold Blood at the Fillmore West, San Francisco. Although I haven't seen any positive proof of Zeppelin in Spokane on 30th December conventional wisdom still places them there. This leaves the 29th as the only remaining 1968 mystery. Page mentions a gig in Portland with Vanilla Fudge in a 1970 interview, it was always presumed that this was on the 31st although Richard Cole clearly places them at Seattle airport on New Years Eve, so maybe Portland was the 29th.

New Legitimate Releases

New Legitimate Releases

You may notice that the bulk of the Led Zeppelin catalog does not appear on the next few pages. That is because it was in the last edition of this book.

The BBC Sessions

Recorded between March 1969 and April 1971 at the BBC studios, Paris Theatre London and Playhouse Theatre London. Compilation and mastering by Jimmy Page. Released November 18th 1997.
Atlantic CD83061(USA) East West AMCY 24012 (Japan)
Finally the BBC sessions get an official release, although the 1971 material is edited.

D1:
You Shook Me (5.14)
I Can't Quit You (4.22)
Communication Breakdown (3.12)
Dazed & Confused (6.39)
The Girl I Love She Got Long Black Wavy Hair (3.00)
What Is & What Should Never Be (4.20)
Communication Breakdown (2.40)
Travelling Riverside Blues (5.12)
Whole Lotta Love (6.09)
Somethin' Else (2.06)
Communication Breakdown (3.05)
I Can't Quit You (6.21)
You Shook Me (10.19)
How Many More Times (11.51)
D2:
Immigrant Song (3.20)
Heartbreaker (5.16)
Since I've Been Loving You (6.56)
Black Dog (5.17)
Dazed & Confused (18.36)
Stairway To Heaven (8.49)
Going To California (3.54)

That's The Way (5.43)
Whole Lotta Love Medley (Inc. Boogie Chillen - Fixin' To Die - That's Alright Mama - A Mess Of Blues) (13.45)
Thank You (6.37)

The BBC Sessions (Promo CD)

The Girl I Love (3.00) - Whole Lotta Led (Historical Medley)
Atlantic promo PRCD 8351 featuring a lengthy and surely pointless medley which includes a snippet of every song they ever did. The liner notes are also wrong listing that The Girl I Love is from April 1st 1971 when it is from June 1969.

The Girl I Love/ Whole Lotta Love

Atlantic PRCD8376-2 promo enhanced CD. Features one audio track and the promo video of Whole Lotta Love for playing on a CDROM drive. Picture disc.

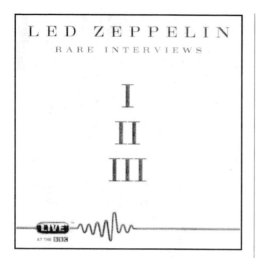

BBC Sessions Rare Interviews

Atlantic 830742 USA In store bonus CD available at Best Buy Discount stores. Features three rare interviews one with Page and Plant from June 1969, one with Page from November 1976 and finally the interviews with Page, Plant and Jones from the Remasters CD box set.

Whole Lotta Love (4.50) - Baby Come On Home (4.29) - Travelling Riverside Blues (5.09)

Atlantic 7567 84014-6 CD single USA - AT0013CD UK, gatefold digipak, Australia in jewel case on gold disc (7567-84014-2)

Stairway To Heaven - Good Times Bad Times - Kashmir
Atlantic 95289 French promo CD Single

Communication Breakdown - The Girl I Love - Whole Lotta Love
Atlantic PRCD 923 (UK) Promo CD Sampler

BBC In-Store Sampler
Atlantic PRCD8401 (USA) 14 Track sampler featuring, You Shook Me - I Can't Quit You - Communication Breakdown - Dazed & Confused - What Is & What Should Never Be - Communication Breakdown - Travelling Riverside Blues - Something Else - Communication Breakdown - I Can't Quit You - You Shook Me - How Many More Times

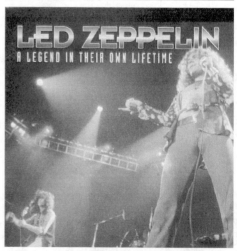

A Legend In Their Own Lifetime
UK Rockview RVCD 204 Interview CD

Superstar Concert Series 95-30

Westwood One two CD concert set air date July 17th
1995 featuring live versions of Immigrant Song -
Heartbreaker - Dazed & Confused - Black Dog - Going
To California - That's The Way - What Is & What Should
Never Be - Stairway To Heaven - Whole Lotta Love -
Communication Breakdown - I Can't Quit You

The Song Doesn't Remain The Same

USA Westwood One Show 95-19 95-20 Eight CD set
for radio broadcast featuring The Girl I Love and
Something Else plus many other rare BBC live tracks.

BBC Classic Tracks

USA A2H00300A Westwood One radio promo disc for
airdate March 25th 1991. Includes live versions of You
Shook Me, Whole Lotta Love, What Is & What Should
Never Be - Heartbreaker - Immigrant Song

Baby Come On Home - Travelling
Riverside Blues - White Summer -
Black Mountain Side -
Hey Hey What Can I Do

Germany Atlantic PRCD 27 Promo CD single

Encomium A Tribute To

Led Zeppelin Sampler

USA Atlantic PRCD 6117-2

Featuring Plant with Tori Amos

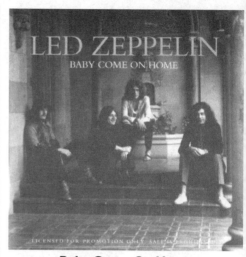

Baby Come On Home
Germany Atlantic PRCD3 Promo CD single

Client: ATLANTIC RECORDS
Title: *ENCOMIUM* - A TRIBUTE TO LED ZEPPELIN
Master #: EQ'd CD - TEST PRESSING

PRCD 6132

Encomium

USA Atlantic PRCD 6132-2 Test Pressing Promo

It's Been A Long Time - A Tribute To
John Bonham
USA Discovery Systems 9UFO300A Westwood One
radio show, 6CD set for airdate August 31 - September
3rd 1990. 35 Zeppelin studio tracks, four Yardbird tracks,
two Page solo tracks, one Plant solo track, eight live BBC
tracks, three Jason Bonham tracks, one Honeydripper
track, two live Zeppelin tracks from Zurich 1980, one
live track from Atlantic 40th birthday party.

Plant & Page

Walking Into Clarksdale

Atlantic CD 83092 (USA) Mercury 558324-2 (UK)

Mercury PHCR1591 (Japan)

Recorded at Abbey Road Studios London, mixed by

Steve Albini, produced by Jimmy Page & Robert Plant.

Released April 1998. Japanese edition includes "Whisky

In The Glass."

Shining In The Light

When The World Was Young

Upon A Golden Horse

Blue Train

Please Read The Letter

Most High

Heart In Your Hand

Walking Into Clarksdale

Burning Up

When I Was A Child

House Of Love

Sons Of Freedom

TBA

Mercury ADV982 (UK) Promo CD
Early UK advance promo of Walking Into Clarksdale
with the title yet unchosen, thus "TBA".

Most High - Upon A Golden Horse - The Window
Mercury (UK CD single) 568 751-2

Most High (Radio Mix) - Most High (Album Mix)
Mercury (UK promo CD single) PPMHR1

Battle Of Evermore
Fontana PPCDJ4 French Promo CD single

Gallow's Pole - Four Sticks - What Is & What Should Never Be
UK Fontana PPDD2 CD single in digipak

Gallow's Pole - City Don't Cry - The Rain Song
Australia Fontana 856-421-2 CD single with slipcase

Kashmir - When The Levee Breaks
France Fontana PY 901 CD single

Gallow's Pole - City Don't Cry - The Rain Song - What Is & What Should Never Be
Japan Fontana PHCR 8316 CD single

No Quarter - Unledded
USA Atlantic 82706-2 Also PHCR 1952 (Japan) in sleeve. Nobody's Fault But Mine - Thank You - No Quarter - Friends - Yallah - City Don't Cry - Since I've Been Loving You - Battle Of Evermore - Wonderful One - That's The Way - Gallow's Pole - Four Sticks - Kashmir

No Quarter - Unledded

UK Fontana 526 362-2

Nobody's Fault But Mine - Thank You - No Quarter -
Friends - Yallah - City Don't Cry - Since I've Been Loving
You - Battle Of Evermore - Wonderful One - Wah Wah -
That's The Way - Gallow's Pole - Four Sticks - Kashmir

No Quarter - Unledded

Australia Fontana 526-362-2 Limited edition slipcase
from Virgin Record stores. Track listing is the same as the
UK edition of the album.

**Gallow's Pole - Four Sticks - What Is &
What Should Never Be**

Holland Fontana 856541-2 CD single with Phone Card

**Gallow's Pole - City Don't Cry -
The Rain Song**

Holland Fontana 856-421-2 CD single with Phone Card

**Gallow's Pole - City Don't Cry -
The Rain Song**

UK Fontana PPCD2 CD single

Gallow's Pole
USA Atlantic PRCD 5921-2 Promo CD single

Conversations With
Jimmy Page & Robert Plant
USA Atlantic PRCD 5987-2 Promo interview CD

Jimmy Page & Robert Plant
A Songwriting Legacy
USA Atlantic PRCD 6061-2 promo CD 10 track CD
sampler of Zeppelin and P&P.

Jimmy Page & Robert Plant
A Songwriting Legacy
USA Atlantic PRCD 6094-2 Miller beer promo CD

Kashmir (P&P) - Good Times Bad Times - Whole Lotta
Love - That's The Way - When The Levee Breaks - No
Quarter - Custard Pie - Tea For One -
Southbound Saurez - Poor Tom -
Wonderful One (P&P) - Gallow's Pole (P&P)

Jimmy Page & Robert Plant
A Songwriting Legacy
USA Atlantic PRCD 6095-2 Miller beer promo CD same
as above piece but with different cover.

Kashmir (P&P) - Good Times Bad Times - Whole Lotta
Love - That's The Way - When The Levee Breaks - No
Quarter - Custard Pie - Tea For One - Southbound
Saurez - Poor Tom - Wonderful One (P&P) - Gallow's
Pole (P&P)

Thank You - Gallow's Pole -

When The Levee Breaks

Holland Mercury - Fontana 852-019 CD single

**Nobody's Fault But Mine -
Gallow's Pole**

USA Atlantic PRCD 5954 Promo CD single

Wonderful One (Edit) - Wonderful One

- What Is & What Should Never Be -

When The Levee Breaks

USA Atlantic 85591-2 CD single

Catch Up 5

Mercury BDCP 9035 Japan Promo CD sampler featuring
"Most High" and tracks by multiple other artists.

Yardbirds

Over Under Sideways Down

Raven Records (Australia RVCD-12)
28 track compilation including nine Page tracks.
A really excellent compilation which features most of
the band's hits from all eras.

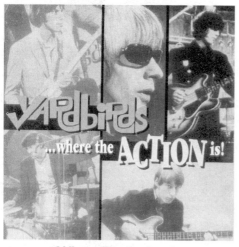

Where The Action Is

New Millenium Communications PILOT 10 (UK). Double
CD set including 13 Page tracks. This set includes the
Yardbirds radio broadcast from Stockholm Sweden in
1967. This is the first official release of this concert
which featured Page on guitar (no Beck). Eight tracks of
previously unavailable Page era Yardbirds, the balance of
the set is the BBC Yardbirds sessions.

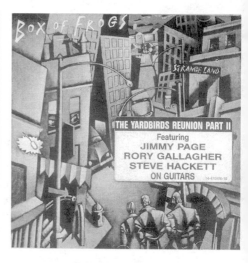

Box Of Frogs - Strange Land

Sony EPC 475976-2 (UK) Yardbirds reunion CD under
the name "Box Of Frogs" with Dreja, McCarty, Samwell-
Smith, Page and assorted other luminaries including Rory
Gallagher, Steve Hackett, Ian Dury, and Graham
Gouldman.

Sessions

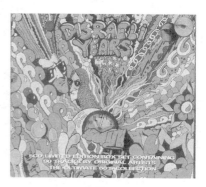

Disraeli Years

Dressed To Kill DTKBOX69. Five CD budget compilation
which includes various Page sessions including Chris
Farlowe, Clapton-Page, Marianne Faithful, John Mayall, etc.

In Search Of Space

Dressed To Kill DTKBOX73. (UK) Three CD budget compilation featuring Page on "Loving Up A Storm" as well as various unrelated material by Chicago, Tim Rose, Hawkwind, Jimi Hendrix, Yardbirds, etc.

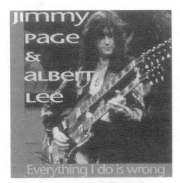

Jimmy Page & Albert Lee - Everything I Do Is Wrong

Reissue of the album "No Introduction Necessary".

Robert Plant - Up Close

Radio CD - Neer Perfect Productions 9447 1994 two CD set.

Godzilla - The Album

Sony EK 69338-2 soundtrack featuring Jimmy Page with Puff Daddy performing a variation of Kashmir.

Alexis Korner - On The Move

Castle Communications CCSCD 809 UK CD featuring a previously unreleased track with Robert Plant from 1968 "Steal Away".

Various Artists -

Anthology Of British Blues Volume One

Immediate CSL 6037(UK) Featuring several Page sessions

Various Artists -

Anthology Of British Blues Volume Two

Immediate CSL 6038(UK) Featuring several Page sessions

Various Artists -

The British Invasion Volume Five

USA Rhino R2 70323 Featuring several Page sessions

Various Artists - Pop Inside The Sixties
Volume 2 1963 - 1967

UK See For Miles SEECD 399 (UK)
Featuring John Paul Jones session

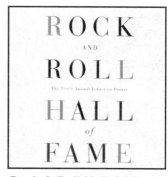

Rock & Roll Hall Of Fame

USA DPRO 19969 Tenth Annual Induction Dinner promotional CD includes Whole Lotta Love and Black Dog

Roy Harper - HQ

UK Science Friction HUCD019 featuring John Paul Jones

Various Artists - Immediate Hit Singles
UK Immediate CSL 6039 Featuring Various Page Sessions

P.J. Proby - Rough Velvet
UK EMI 07777 80544-29
Featuring Jones and Page sessions

The Pretty Things - Get The Picture
UK Fontana TL 5280 featuring Page session

The Pretty Things
Get A Buzz -
The Best Of The Fontana Years
UK Fontana 314 512446-2
Featuring Page
session

British Percussion par
Le London All Star
France Barclay. This early French album has recently been bootlegged in Japan. It features several sessions by Jimmy Page along with Bobby Graham from the mid-sixties. The difference with this particular one is that it mentions Jimmy in depth on the cover including several song-writing credits. Songs which he wrote include "Stop The Drums", "Drum Stomp" and "Lord Byron Blues". Originally only on vinyl the Japanese bootleg is a CD and has both front and back cover reproduced making it a counterfeit.

Page & Plant
Bootlegs

Plant & Page Bootlegs

Another Evening In Sydney
Venue: Sydney
Date: 2/25/96
Cover: D4C
Recording: 8
Source: St - Aud
Company: Two Symbols
Matrix #: TS014AB
Place Of Origin: Japan
Total Disc Time: 68:15 - 71:07

D1:
Babe I'm Gonna Leave You
Celebration Day
Ramble On
Heartbreaker
No Quarter
The Song Remains The Same
The Rain Song
Since I've Been Loving You
Whole Lotta Love Medley (Inc. In The Light - Season Of
The Witch - Break On Through - Dazed And Confused)
D2:
Hurdy Gurdy Solo
Gallows Pole
Four Sticks
Yallah
In The Evening - Carouselambra
Dancing Days
Kashmir
Thank You
Black Dog
Rock And Roll

Back To Blueberry Hill
Venue: Los Angeles
Date: 5/16/95
Cover: D4C
Recording: 7
Source: St - Aud
Company: n/a
Matrix #: n/a
Place Of Origin: Japan

D1:
Thank You
Bring It On Home
Ramble On
Shake My Tree
Lullaby
No Quarter
Gallow's Pole
Hurdy Gurdy Solo
Nobody's Fault But Mine
Hey Hey What Can I Do
Song Remains The Same
Since I've Been Loving You
D2:
Friends
Calling To You
Four Sticks
In The Evening
Black Dog
Kashmir

Back To Kindergarten

Venue: Melbourne - Sydney*
Date: 2/29/96^ - 3/1/96 - 2/25/96*
Cover: D4C
Recording: 9
Source: St - Aud
Company: Red Hot
Matrix #: n/a
Place Of Origin: Australia

D1:
Babe I'm Gonna Leave You
Heartbreaker
Ramble On
Going To California
Hurdy Gurdy Solo
Gallow's Pole
Song Remains The Same
Rain Song^
Since I've Been Loving You^
Whole Lotta Love^
D2:
Yallah^
In The Evening^
Four Sticks^
Kashmir^
Black Dog^
Rock & Roll^
Rain Song*
Thank You^

Break On Through

Venue: Tacoma - New Orleans^ - Chicago*
Date: 3/25/95 - 3/11/95^ - 4/29/95*
Cover: D4C
Recording: 7
Source: St - Aud
Company: n/a
Matrix #: n/a
Place Of Origin: Japan

D1:
Thank You
Bring It On Home
Ramble On
Shake My Tree
Lullaby
No Quarter
Gallow's Pole
Hurdy Gurdy Solo
When The Levee Breaks
Hey Hey What Can I Do
Song Remains The Same
Since I've Been Loving You
Friends (cut)
D2:
Friends
Calling To You Medley (Inc. Down By The Seaside - Break
On Through - Dazed & Confused)
Four Sticks
In The Evening
Black Dog
Kashmir
House Of The Rising Sun Medley (Inc. Good Times Bad
Times - Bring It On Home - Celebration Day)
That's The Way
Whole Lotta Love*

JIMMY PAGE & ROBERT PLANT

Bring It To Rio

Venue: Rio De Janeiro

Date: 1/27/96

Cover: D4C

Recording: 9

Source: St - SB

Company: Blizzard

Matrix #: n/a

Place Of Origin: Japan

D1:

The Wanton Song

Bring It On Home

Ramble On

No Quarter

Gallow's Pole

Since I've Been Loving You

Song Remains The Same

Going To California

Babe I'm Gonna Leave You

D2:

Whole Lotta Love

Four Sticks

Kashmir

Black Dog

Rock & Roll

Broadcasts

Venue: New Orleans - Glastonbury* - Luneberg^

Date: 3/95 - 6/25/95* - 6/95^

Cover: D4C

Recording: 8

Source: St -SB

Company: Two Symbols

Matrix #: TS004

Place Of Origin: Japan

Total Disc Time: 65.09

D1:

In The Evening

Black Dog

Four Sticks

In The Evening^

Calling To You Medley^ (Inc. Break On Through, Dazed & Confused)

Four Sticks*

In The Evening*

Kashmir*

Since I've Been Loving You*

Candy Store Rock
(Return To Electric Magic Vol 2)
Venue: London
Date: 7/26/95
Cover: D4C
Recording: 7
Source: St - Aud
Company: Two Symbols
Matrix #: TS002 A-B
Place Of Origin: Japan
Total Disc Time: 66.20 - 54.59

D1:
Introduction
Immigrant Song - Wanton Song
Bring It On Home
Ramble On
Thank You
No Quarter
Battle Of Evermore
Hurdy Gurdy Solo
Gallows Pole
Since I've Been Loving You
The Song Remains The Same
Going To California
Friends
D2:
Four Sticks
Whole Lotta Love
In The Evening
Candy Store Rock, Black Dog
Kashmir

Celebrating Fifth & Sixth Days (The)
Venue: Tokyo
Date: 2/12/96 - 2/13/96
Cover: D4C
Recording: 8
Source: St - Aud
Company: n/a
Matrix #: n/a
Place Of Origin: Japan
D1:
Immigrant Song - The Wanton Song
Bring It On Home - Heartbreaker
Ramble On
No Quarter
Hurdy Gurdy Solo
Gallows Pole
Tea For One
The Song Remains The Same
D2:
Going To California
That's The Way
Babe I'm Gonna Leave You - Stairway To Heaven
Whole Lotta Love Medley (Inc. Bring It On Home -
Break On Through - Dazed And Confused)
Yallah
Four Sticks
Kashmir
Rock And Roll
D3:
Thank You
Custard Pie
Out On The Tiles - Black Dog
In My Time Of Dying -Tangerine
Hurdy Gurdy Solo - Gallows Pole
Tea For One
The Song Remains The Same
Going To California
D4:
Babe I'm Gonna Leave You – Stairway To Heaven
Whole Lotta Love (Inc. I'm A King Bee - Break On
Through - Dazed And Confused - Friends)
Yallah
Four Sticks
Kashmir

Celebrating First & Second Days (The)

Venue: Tokyo
Date: 2/5/96 - 2/6/96
Cover: D4C
Recording: 8
Source: St - Aud
Company: n/a
Matrix #: n/a
Place Of Origin: Japan
D1:
Immigrant Song - The Wanton Song -
Bring It On Home - Heartbreaker
Ramble On
No Quarter
Hurdy Gurdy Solo - Gallows Pole
Since I've Been Loving You
The Song Remains The Same
Going To California
D2:
Babe I'm Gonna Leave You - Stairway To Heaven
Whole Lotta Love Medley (Inc. White Rabbit - Break
On Through - Dazed And Confused)
Yallah
Four Sticks
Kashmir
Out On The Tiles - Black Dog
In My Time Of Dying
Rock And Roll
D3:
Babe I'm Gonna Leave You - Stairway To Heaven
Bring It On Home - Heartbreaker
Thank You
Gallows Pole
Hurdy Gurdy Solo - Nobody's Fault But Mine
Going To California
Since I've Been Loving You
Dancing Days
D4:
Yallah
Four Sticks
Egyptian Pharaohs- In The Evening (Inc. Carouselambra)
Kashmir
Tangerine
Whole Lotta Love Medley (Inc. In The Light - Break On
Through To The Other Side - Dazed And Confused)
Rock And Roll

Celebrating Seventh & Ninth Days (The)

Venue: Osaka
Date: 2/15/96
Cover: D4C
Recording: 7 - 8
Source: St - Aud
Company: n/a
Matrix #: n/a
Place Of Origin: Japan
D1: Custard Pie - Bring It On Home
Heartbreaker
What Is And What Should Never Be
Hurdy Gurdy Solo - Gallows Pole
Wonderful One
Going To California
Ten Years Gone
Babe I'm Gonna Leave You - Stairway To Heaven
D2: Whole Lotta Love Medley (Inc. You Shook Me -
Break On Through - Dazed And Confused)
Tea For One
Friends
Yallah
Four Sticks
Kashmir
Out On The Tiles - Black Dog - In My Time Of Dying
Rock And Roll
D3: Celebration Day
Bring It On Home - Heartbreaker
What Is And What Should Never Be
Tangerine
Thank You
Hurdy Gurdy Solo - Gallows Pole
Nobody's Fault But Mine
The Song Remains The Same
Since I've Been Loving You
D4: Whole Lotta Love Medley (Inc. It's All Over Now -
Break On Through - Dazed And Confused)
Egyptian Pharaohs - In The Evening (Inc. Carouselambra)
Four Sticks
Kashmir
Can You Feel It - Black Dog - In My Time Of Dying
Rock And Roll

Celebrating Third & Fourth Days
Venue: Tokyo
Date: 2/8/96 - 2/9/96
Cover: D4C
Recording: 8
Source: St - Aud
Company: n/a
Matrix #: n/a
Place Of Origin: Japan
D1:
Celebration Day - Bring It On Home - Heartbreaker
What Is And What Should Never Be
The Rain Song (take 1 and 2)
Hurdy Gurdy Solo - When The Levee Breaks
Gallows Pole
Tea For One
The Song Remains The Same
Babe I'm Gonna Leave You - Stairway To Heaven
D2:
Whole Lotta Love Medley (Inc. Down By The Seaside -
Break On Through - Dazed And Confused)
Yallah (cut)
Egyptian Pharaohs - In The Evening (Inc. Carouselambra)
Four Sticks
Kashmir
Black Dog - In My Time Of Dying
Rock And Roll
D3:
The Rain Song
No Quarter
Babe I'm Gonna Leave You - Stairway To Heaven
Immigrant Song - The Wanton Song
Heartbreaker - Ramble On
Hurdy Gurdy Solo - Gallows Pole
Whole Lotta Love Medley (Inc. Spoonful - Break On
Through - I Want To Take You Higher - Dazed And
Confused)
D4:
Tea For One
Dancing Days
Yallah
Four Sticks
Egyptian Pharaohs - In The Evening (Inc. Carouselambra)
Kashmir
Out On The Tiles - In My Time Of Dying
Rock And Roll

Celebration Day
Venue: Orlando
Date: 3/7/95
Cover: D4C
Recording: 8
Source: St -Aud
Company: n/a
Matrix #: n/a
Place Of Origin: Japan
Total Disc Time: 65.11 - 70.15

D1:
Intro
Wanton Song
Bring It On Home
Celebration Day
Thank You
Dancing Days
Shake My Tree
Lullaby
No Quarter
Wonderful One
Gallows Pole
Nobody's Fault But Mine
Song Remains The Same
D2:
Since I've Been Loving You
Friends
Calling To You (Inc. The Hunter - Dazed And Confused)
Four Sticks
In The Evening
Hey Hey What Can I Do
Black Dog
Kashmir

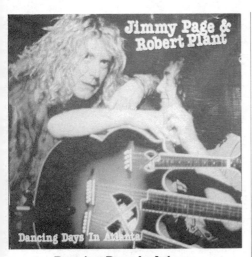

Dancing Days In Atlanta

Venue: Atlanta
Date: 3/1/95
Cover: D4C
Recording: 8
Source: St - Aud
Company: n/a
Matrix #: JR001-2
Place Of Origin: Japan
Total Disc Time: 65.13 - 60.09

D1:
Immigrant Song-Wanton Song
Bring It On Home
Celebration Day
Thank You
Dancing Days
Don't Shake My Tree
Spider
No Quarter
Wonderful One
Gallows Pole
Nobody's Fault But Mine
The Song Remains The Same
D2:
Since I've Been Loving You
Friends
Calling You Medley (Inc. Riders On The Storm -Dazed
And Confused)
Four Sticks
In The Evening
Black Dog
Kashmir

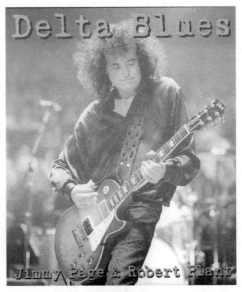

Delta Blues

Venue: Salt Lake City
Date: 10/10/95
Cover: D4C
Recording: 7
Source: St - Aud
Company: Two Symbols
Matrix #: TS
Place Of Origin: Japan

D1:
The Wanton Song
Bring It On Home
Ramble On
Thank You
No Quarter
That's The Way
Hurdy Gurdy Solo
Gallows Pole
Since I've Been Loving You
The Song Remains The Same
Going To California
D2:
Babe I'm Gonna Leave You
Four Sticks
In The Evening
Whole Lotta Love
Black Dog
Kashmir

Eternal Burning

Venue: Fukuoka
Date: 2/20/95
Cover: D4C
Recording: 8
Source: St - Aud
Company: Magnum
Matrix #: 005-6
Place Of Origin: Japan

D1:
Babe I'm Gonna Leave You - Stairway To Heaven
Ramble On
Custard Pie
Heartbreaker
Wonderful One
The Song Remains The Same
The Rain Song
Celebration Day
Hurdy Gurdy Solo
Gallows Pole
Since I've Been Loving You
D2:
Whole Lotta Love Medley (Inc. Going Down - Break On
Through - Dazed And Confused)
In the Evening
Four Sticks
Kashmir
Black Dog
Rock And Roll

Evening Custard

Venue: Tokyo
Date: 2/12/96
Cover: D4C
Recording: 9
Source: St - Aud
Company: Pore The Sole
Matrix #: PTS024-25
Place Of Origin: Japan

D1:
Introduction - Immigrant Song
The Wanton Song
Bring It On Home - Heartbreaker
Ramble On
No Quarter
Hurdy Gurdy Solo
Gallows Pole
Tea For One
The Song Remains The Same
Going To California
That's The Way
Babe I'm Gonna Leave You (Inc. Stairway To Heaven)
D2:
Whole Lotta Love Medley (Inc. Bring It On Home -
Break On Through - Dazed And Confused)
Yallah
Four Sticks
Kashmir
Custard Pie
Rock And Roll

15 Years On

Venue: San Jose
Date: 5/20/95
Cover: D4C
Recording: 9
Source: St - SB
Company: Hawk
Matrix #: n/a
Place Of Origin: Europe
Total Disc Time: 71.31 - 50.01

D1:
Intro
Thank You
Bring It On Home
Ramble On
Celebration Day
Lullaby
No Quarter
Gallow's Pole
Hurdy Gurdy Solo
Nobody's Fault But Mine
Hey Hey What Can I Do
Song Remains The Same
Since I've Been Loving You
Friends
D2:
Calling To You Medley (Inc. Break On Through - Dazed & Confused)
Four Sticks
In The Evening
Black Dog
Kashmir

Fifth Show At TFOB (The)

Venue: Tokyo
Date: 2/12/96
Cover: D4C
Recording: 9
Source: St - Aud
Company: Real Dragon
Matrix #: n/a
Place Of Origin: Japan

D1:
The Wanton Song
Bring It On Home
Heartbreaker
No Quarter
Ramble On
Hurdy Gurdy Solo
Gallows Pole
Tea For One
The Song Remains The Same
Going To California
That's The Way
Babe I'm Gonna Leave You
D2:
Whole Lotta Love
Yallah
Four Sticks
Kashmir
Custard Pie
Rock & Roll

First Day (The)

Venue: Tokyo
Date: 2/5/96
Cover: D4C
Recording: 8
Source: St - Aud
Company: Cobra
Matrix #: n/a
Place Of Origin: Japan

D1:
Immigrant Song Intro - The Wanton Song -
Bring It On Home
Heartbreaker
Ramble On
No Quarter
Hurdy Gurdy Solo
Gallows Pole
Since I've Been Loving You
The Song Remains The Same
Going To California
Babe I'm Gonna Leave You (Inc. Stairway To Heaven)
D2:
Whole Lotta Love Medley (Inc. White Rabbit - Break
On Through - Dazed And Confused)
Yallah
Four Sticks
Kashmir
Black Dog
Rock And Roll

First Night In Japan 96

Venue: Tokyo
Date: 2/5/96
Cover: D4C
Recording: 8
Source: St - Aud
Company: Pore The Sole
Matrix #: PTS016-17
Place Of Origin: Japan
Total Disc Time: 62.16 - 55.54

D1:
Introduction - Immigrant Song Intro -
The Wanton Song - Bring It On Home
Heartbreaker
Ramble On
No Quarter
Nigel Eaton's Hurdy Gurdy Solo
Gallows Pole
Since I've Been Loving You
The Song Remains The Same
Going To California
Babe I'm Gonna Leave You (Inc. Stairway To Heaven)
D2:
Whole Lotta Love Medley (Inc. White Rabbit - Break
On Through - Dazed And Confused)
Yallah
Four Sticks
Kashmir
Black Dog
Rock And Roll

2/05/1996
The First Show At The Famous Old Building

First Show At The Famous Old Building (The)

Venue: Tokyo
Date: 2/5/96
Cover: D4C
Recording: 9
Source: St - Aud
Company: Real Dragon
Matrix #: RD 019-020
Place Of Origin: Japan

D1:
Eastern
Immigrant Song (Intro) - The Wanton Song
Bring It On Home
Heartbreaker
Ramble On - What Is And What Should Never Be
No Quarter
Hurdy Gurdy Solo
Gallows Pole
Since I've Been Loving You
The Song Remains The Same
Going To California
Babe I'm Gonna Leave You - Stairway To Heaven
D2:
Whole Lotta Love Medley (Inc. Guitar Solo - White
Rabbit - Break On Through - Dazed & Confused)
Yallah
Four Sticks
Kashmir
Out On The Tiles (Intro) - Black Dog
Rock And Roll

Fourth Night Live (The)

Venue: Tokyo
Date: 2/9/96
Cover: D2C
Recording: 8
Source: St - Aud
Company: Pore The Soul
Matrix #: PTS 022-23
Place Of Origin: Japan
Time Of Disc: 71.11 - 57.22

D1:
The Rain Song
No Quarter
Babe I'm Gonna Leave You - Stairway To Heaven
Immigrant Song Intro - The Wanton Song
Heartbreaker - Ramble On
Nigel Eaton's Hurdy Gurdy Solo
Gallows Pole
Whole Lotta Love Medley (Inc. Spoonful - Break On
Through - I Want To Take You Higher - Dazed And
Confused)
Tea For One
D2:
Dancing Days
Yallah
Four Sticks
In The Evening (Inc. Carouselambra)
Kashmir
Out On The Tiles Intro - Black Dog
Rock And Roll

Forth Show At The Famous Old Building (The)

Venue: Tokyo
Date: 2/9/96
Cover: D4C
Recording: 9
Source: St - Aud
Company: Real Dragon
Matrix #: RD021-22
Place Of Origin: Japan

D1:
The Rain Song
No Quarter
Babe I'm Gonna Leave You - Stairway To Heaven
Immigrant Song (Intro) - The Wanton Song
Heartbreaker
Ramble On -
What Is And What Should Never Be
Nigel Eaton's Hurdy-Gurdy Solo
Gallows Pole
Whole Lotta Love Medley (Inc. Spoonful - Break On Through - Dazed And Confused)
Tea For One
D2:
Dancing Days
Yallah
Four Sticks
Egyptian Pharaohs
In The Evening (Inc. Carouselambra)
Kashmir
Out On The Tiles (Intro) - Black Dog -
In My Time Of Dying
Rock And Roll

Gamble On

Venue: Las Vegas
Date: 5/12/95
Cover: D4C
Recording: 8
Source: St - Aud
Company: Ride The Tiger
Matrix #: n/a
Place Of Origin: Japan

D1:
Thank You
Bring It On Home
No Quarter
Gallow's Pole
Nobody's Fault But Mine
Hey Hey What Can I Do
Song Remains The Same
Friends
Calling To You
Four Sticks
In The Evening
Black Dog

Get Rid Of The Smoke

Venue: Glastonbury - Glasgow* - Sheffield^ - St Austell** - Poole^^ - Birmingham#† - London‡ - Boston††

Date: 6/25/95 - 7/12/95* - 7/13/95^ - 7/15/95** - 7/16/95^^ - 7/22/95# - 7/23/95† - 7/25/95‡ - 7/26/95‡‡ - 10/23/95††

Cover: D4C

Recording: 8

Source: St - Aud

Company: n/a

Matrix #: n/a

Place Of Origin: Japan

Total Disc Time: 47.21 - 41.55 - 50.52 - 61.45 - 47.27 - 65.20 - 51.07 - 61.21 - 50.20 - 44.00 - 57.22 - 68.41 - 52.49 - 62.31 - 56.55 - 63.06 - 57.11 - 62.03 - 59.47 - 74.27

DI:
Immigrant Song
Wanton Song
Bring It On Home
Thank You
No Quarter
Hurdy Gurdy Solo
Gallows Pole

Since I've Been Loving You
The Song Remains The Same
Friends
D2:
Calling To You Medley (Inc. Smokestack Lightening - Break On Through - Dazed And Confused)
Four Sticks
In The Evening
Kashmir
D3:
Intro
Wanton Song
Bring It On Home
Ramble On
No Quarter
Gallows Pole
Hurdy Gurdy Solo
When The Levee Breaks
Yallah (with Orchestra)
Since I've Been Loving You
The Crunge
The Song Remains The Same
D4:
Whole Lotta Love Medley (Inc. Guitar Solo - Down By The Seaside - Break On Through - Dazed And Confused -You Need Love)
Friends
Four Sticks
Kashmir
Black Dog
In The Evening
D5:
Egyptian Violin Intro
Wanton Song
Bring It On Home
Ramble On
No Quarter
Gallows Pole
Hurdy Gurdy
Solo
Yallah
Since I've Been Loving You - Tea For One
The Song Remains The Same
D6:
Whole Lotta Love Medley (Inc. Smokestack Lightening - Break On Through - Dazed And Confused - You Need Love)
Friends
Four Sticks
Kashmir
Louis Louis
Black Dog
In The Evening
D7:
Egyptian Intro
Whole Lotta Love
Bring It On Home
Ramble On
No Quarter

Gallows Pole
Hurdy Gurdy Solo
Yallah
Since I've Been Loving You
The Song Remains The Same
D8:
Friends
Calling You
What Is And What Should Never Be
Unknown Jam - Break On Through
Four Sticks
Kashmir
Blue Jean Baby
Black Dog
In The Evening
D9:
Egyptian Intro
Thank You
Bring It On Home
Whole Lotta Love
No Quarter
Gallows Pole
Hurdy Gurdy Solo
Yallah
Since I've Been Loving You - Tea For One
The Song Remains The Same
D10:
Dancing Days
Four Sticks
Kashmir
Black Dog
In The Evening
D11:
Egyptian Intro
Wanton Song
Bring It On Home
Ramble On
Thank You
No Quarter
Battle Of Evermore
Hurdy Gurdy Solo
Gallows Pole
Since I've Been Loving You
The Song Remains The Same
D12:
Going To California
Friends
Four Sticks
Whole Lotta Love (Inc. Smokestack Lightening - Break
On Through - Dazed And Confused)
Kashmir
Black Dog
In The Evening
D13:
Egyptian Intro
Wanton Song
Bring It On
Home
Thank You

No Quarter
Battle Of Evermore
Hurdy Gurdy Solo
Gallows Pole
Since I've Been Loving You
The Song Remains The Same
D14:
Going To California
Friends
Four Sticks
Whole Lotta Love (Inc. Porl Solo – Jimmy Page Solo)
Kashmir
Black Dog
In The Evening
D15:
Egyptian Intro
Wanton Song
Bring It On Home
Ramble On
Thank You
No Quarter
Battle Of Evermore
Hurdy Gurdy Solo
Gallows Pole
Since I've Been Loving You
The Song Remains The Same
D16:
Going To California
Friends
Four Sticks
Whole Lotta Love
Calling To You
Kashmir
Black Dog
In The Evening
D17:
Egyptian Intro
Wanton Song
Bring It On Home
Ramble On
Thank You
No Quarter
Battle Of Evermore
Hurdy Gurdy Solo
Gallows Pole
Since I've Been Loving You
The Song Remains The Same
D18:
Going To California
Friends
Four Sticks
Whole Lotta Love Medley (Inc. Smokestack Lightning -
Calling To You - Dazed And Confused)
In The Evening
Candy Store Rock Jam
Black Dog
Kashmir
D19:
Egyptian Intro

Wanton Song
Heartbreaker
What Is And What Should Never Be
Thank You
No Quarter
Tangerine
Hurdy Gurdy Solo
Gallows Pole
Since I've Been Loving You
The Song Remains The Same
D20:
Going To California
Babe I'm Gonna Leave You
Whole Lotta Love Medley (Inc. It's A Man's World -
Break On Through - Dazed And Confused)
Dancing Days
In The Evening
Black Dog
Kashmir

Glastonbury
Venue: Glastonbury
Date: 6/25/95
Cover: D4C
Recording: 10
Source: St - SB
Company: Kiss The Stone
Matrix #: KTS462
Place Of Origin: Europe
Total Disc Time: 65.09

D1:
Gallows Pole
Since I've Been Lovin' You
The Song Remains The Same
Friends
Calling To You (Inc. Break On Through - Dazed And
Confused)
Four Sticks
In The Evening
Kashmir

Going Down To South
Venue: Fukuoka
Date: 2/20/96
Cover: D4C
Recording: 7
Source: St - Aud
Company: Pore The Sole
Matrix #: PTS
Place Of Origin: Japan

D1:
Babe I'm Gonna Leave You
Ramble On
Custard Pie
Heartbreaker
Wonderful One
Song Remains The Same
Rain Song
Gallow's Pole
Since I've Been Loving You
D2:
Whole Lotta Love
In The Evening
Four Sticks
Kashmir
Black Dog
Rock & Roll

Good Times Bad Times

Venue: New Orleans
Date: 3/11/95
Cover: D4C
Recording: 8
Source: St - Aud
Company: Tarantura
Matrix #: NO 1-2
Place Of Origin: Japan
Total Disc Time: 66.49 - 66.44

D1:
The House Of The Rising Sun
Good Times Bad Times
Bring It On Home
Celebration Day
Thank You
Dancing Days
Shake My Tree
Lullaby
No Quarter
That's The Way
Gallows Pole
When The Levee Breaks
Ramble On
D2:
The Song Remains The Same
Since I've Been Loving You
Friends
Calling To You (Inc. Dazed And Confused)
Four Sticks
In The Evening
Black Dog
Kashmir

Have Mercy Osaka

Venue: Osaka
Date: 10/19/96
Cover: D4C
Recording: 8
Source: St - AUd
Company: Pore The Sole
Matrix #: PTS
Place Of Origin: Japan

D1:
Celebration Day
Bring It On Home
Heartbreaker
What Is & What Should Never Be
Tangerine
Thank You
Hurdy Gurdy Solo
Gallow's Pole
Nobody's Fault But Mine
Song Remains The Same
Since I've Been Loving You
Whole Lotta Love
D2:
Dancing Days
In The Evening
Four Sticks
Kashmir
Black Dog
Rock & Roll

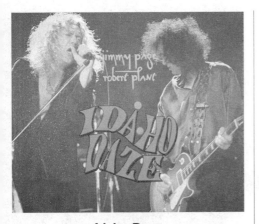

Idaho Daze

Venue: Boise
Date: 10/9/95
Cover: D4C
Recording: 8
Source: St - Aud
Company: Two Symbols
Matrix #: TS 009 A-B
Place Of Origin: Japan
Total Disc Time: 61.44 - 64.18

D1:
Immigrant Song - Wanton Song
Bring It On Home
Ramble On
Thank You
No Quarter
Tangerine
Hurdy Gurdy Solo
Gallows Pole
Since I've Been Loving you
The Song Remains The Same
Going To California
D2:
Babe I'm Gonna Leave You - Stairway To Heaven
Friends
Four Sticks
Whole Lotta Love Medley (Inc. Light My Fire - For What
It's Worth - Break On Through - Dazed And Confused)
In The Evening - Carouselambra
Kashmir

It's Flyin' Time Again

Venue: Atlanta
Date: 2/28/95
Cover: D4C
Recording: 7
Source: St - Aud
Company: OZS
Matrix #: 001-002
Place Of Origin: Europe

D1:
Celebration Day
Dancing Days
Shake My Tree
Since I've Been Loving You
Lullaby
Achilles Last Stand
No Quarter
Wonderful One
Gallows Pole
When The Levee Breaks
D2:
Friends
Calling To You Medley (Inc. Season Of The Witch - Dazed
And Confused)
Four Sticks
In The Evening
Black Dog
Kashmir

Journey To The Past (A)

Venue: Tacoma

Date: 5/25/95

Cover: D4C

Recording: 7

Source: St - Aud

Company: n/a

Matrix #: n/a

Place Of Origin: Japan

D1:

Thank You

Bring It On Home

Ramble On

Shake My Tree

Lullaby

When The Levee Breaks

Hey Hey What Can I Do

Song Remains The Same

Since I've Been Loving You

Friends

Calling To You

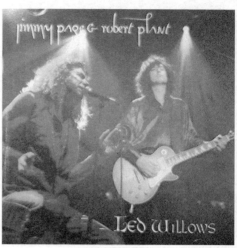

Led Willows

Venue: Nagoya

Date: 2/17/96

Cover: D4C

Recording: 8

Source: ST - Aud

Company: Victory

Matrix #: n/a

Place Of Origin: Japan

D1:

Heartbreaker

Bring It On Home

Custard Pie

Ramble On

Tangerine

Thank You

Hurdy Gurdy Solo

Gallow's Pole

Rain Song

Song Remains The Same

Tea For One

D2:

Dancing Days

In The Evening

Four Sticks

Kashmir

Celebration Day

Black Dog

Rock & Roll

Light My Fire
Venue: Pittsburgh
Date: 3/25/95
Cover: D4C
Recording: 7
Source: St - Aud
Company: n/a
Matrix #: n/a
Place Of Origin: Japan
Total Disc Time: 66.15 - 57.39

D1:
Intro
Wanton Song
Bring It On Home
Ramble On
Thank You
Shake My Tree
Lullaby
No Quarter
Gallows Pole
Nobody's Fault But Mine
Song Remains The Same
Since I've Been Loving You
D2:
Friends
Calling You (Inc. Light My Fire - Dazed And Confused)
Four Sticks
In The Evening
Black Dog
Kashmir

Light My Fire American Tour 1995
Venue: Indianapolis
Date: 4/26/95
Cover: D4C
Recording: 8
Source: St -Aud
Company: Sonic Zoom
Matrix #: SZ 2011-2012
Place Of Origin: Japan
Total Disc Time: 57.24 - 69.17

D1:
Tales Of Bron
Thank You
Bring It On Home
Ramble On
Shake My Tree
Lullaby
No Quarter
Gallows Pole
Hurdy-Gurdy solo
When the Levee Breaks
Hey Hey What Can I Do
The Song Remains the Same
D2:
Since I've Been Loving You
Friends
Calling To You
Light My Fire (Inc. Dazed & Confused)
Four Sticks
In the Evening (Inc. Carouselambra)
Out On The Tiles intro
Black Dog
Kashmir

Little Jimmy

Venue: Nagoya
Date: 2/17/96
Cover: D2C
Recording: 8
Source: St - Aud
Company: Pore The Soul
Matrix #: PTS 026-027
Place Of Origin: Japan

D1:
Introduction - Heartbreaker
Bring It On Home
Custard Pie
Ramble On
Tangerine
Thank You
Nigel Eaton's Hurdy Gurdy Solo
Gallows Pole
The Rain Song
The Song Remains The Same
Tea For One
D2:
Dancing Days
In The Evening
Four Sticks
Kashmir
Celebration Day
Black Dog
Rock And Roll

Live At The Shark Tank

Venue: San Jose
Date: 5/20/95
Cover: D4C
Recording: 9
Source: St - SB
Company: Swinging Pig
Matrix #: TSP 197-2
Place Of Origin: Europe
Total Disc Time: 56.08 - 62.42

D1:
Thank You
Bring It On Home
Ramble On
Shake My Tree
Lullaby
No Quarter
Gallows Pole
Hurdy Gurdy Solo
Nobody's Fault But Mine
Hey Hey What Can I Do
The Song Remains The Same
D2:
Since I've Been Loving You
Friends
Calling To You
Four Sticks
In The Evening
Black Dog
Kashmir

Live Legend Japan Tour 1996

Venue: Tokyo - Osaka* - Nagoya^ - Fukuoka**
Date: 2/5/96 - 2/6/96 - 2/8/96 - 2/9/96 - 2/12/96 -
2/13/96 - 2/15/96* - 2/17/96^ - 2/19/96* - 2/20/96**
Cover: D2C
Recording: 7-9
Source: St - Aud
Company: Black Moon
Matrix #: PP BOX 01
Place Of Origin: Japan

FIRST SHOW
D1:
Eastern Introduction - Immigrant Song
Intro - The Wanton Song -
Bring It On Home - Heartbreaker
Ramble On
No Quarter
Nigel Eaton's Hurdy Gurdy Solo
Gallows Pole
Since I've Been Loving You
The Song Remains The Same
Going To California
D2:
Babe I'm Gonna Leave You (includes
Stairway To Heaven)
Whole Lotta Love Medley (Inc. White Rabbit - Break
On Through - Dazed And Confused)
Yallah
Four Sticks
Kashmir
Out On The Tiles - Black Dog
In My Time Of Dying
Rock And Roll
SECOND SHOW
D3:
Babe I'm Gonna Leave You - Stairway To Heaven
Bring It On Home - Heartbreaker
Thank You

Gallows Pole
Hurdy Gurdy Solo
Nobody's Fault But Mine
Going To California
Since I've Been Loving You
Dancing Days
D4:
Yallah
Four Sticks
Egyptian
Pharaohs
In The Evening (Inc. Carouselambra)
Kashmir
Tangerine
Whole Lotta Love Medley (Inc. In The Light - Break On
Through To The Other Side - Dazed And Confused)
Rock And Roll
THIRD SHOW
D5:
Eastern Introduction - Celebration Day
Bring It On Home - Heartbreaker
What Is And What Should Never Be
The Rain Song (take 1 and 2)
Hurdy Gurdy Solo
When The Levee Breaks
Gallows Pole
Tea For One
The Song Remains The Same
Babe I'm Gonna Leave You - Stairway To Heaven
D6:
Whole Lotta Love Medley (Inc. Down By The Seaside -
Break On Through (To The Other Side) - Dazed And
Confused)
Yallah (cut)
Egyptian Pharaohs
In The Evening (Inc. Carouselambra)
Four Sticks
Kashmir
Black Dog - In My Time Of Dying
Rock And Roll
FOURTH SHOW
D7:
The Rain Song
No Quarter
Babe I'm Gonna Leave You - Stairway To Heaven
Immigrant Song - The Wanton Song
Heartbreaker - Ramble On
Hurdy Gurdy Solo
Gallows Pole
Whole Lotta Love Medley (Inc. Spoonful - Break On
Through (To The Other Side) - I Want To Take You
Higher - Dazed And Confused)
D8:
Tea For One
Dancing Days
Yallah
Four Sticks
Egyptian Pharaohs
In The Evening (Inc. Carouselambra)

Kashmir
Out On The Tiles - In My Time Of Dying
Rock And Roll
FIFTH SHOW
D9:
Eastern Introduction - Immigrant Song - The Wanton
Song
Bring It On Home
Heartbreaker
Ramble On
No Quarter
Hurdy Gurdy Solo
Gallows Pole
Tea For One
The Song Remains The Same
D10:
Going To California
That's The Way
Babe I'm Gonna Leave You - Stairway To Heaven
Whole Lotta Love Medley (Inc. Bring It On Home -
Break On Through - Dazed And Confused)
Yallah
Four Sticks
Kashmir
Rock And Roll
SIXTH SHOW
D11:
Thank You
Custard Pie
Out On The Tiles - Black Dog
In My Time Of Dying -Tangerine
Hurdy Gurdy Solo
Gallows Pole
Tea For One
The Song Remains The Same
Going To California
D12:
Babe I'm Gonna Leave You – Stairway To Heaven
Whole Lotta Love (Inc. I'm A King Bee - Break On
Through - Dazed And Confused - Friends)
Yallah
Four Sticks
Kashmir
SEVENTH SHOW
D13:
Eastern Introduction
Custard Pie/
Bring It On Home
Heartbreaker
What Is And What Should Never Be
Hurdy Gurdy Solo
Gallows Pole
Wonderful One
Going To California
Ten Years Gone
Babe I'm Gonna Leave You - Stairway To Heaven
D14:
Whole Lotta Love Medley (Inc. You Shook Me - Break
On Through (To The Other Side) - Dazed And

Confused)
Tea For One
Friends
Yallah
Four Sticks
Kashmir
Out On The Tiles - Black Dog - In My Time Of Dying
Rock And Roll
EIGHTH SHOW
D15:
Intro Heartbreaker - Bring It On Home
Custard Pie
Ramble On
Tangerine
Thank You
Hurdy Gurdy Solo
Gallows Pole
The Rain Song
The Song Remains The Same
Tea For One
D16:
Dancing Days
Egyptian Pharaohs
In The Evening (Inc. Carouselambra)
Four Sticks
Kashmir
Celebration Day
Black Dog - In My Time Of Dying
Rock And Roll
NINTH SHOW
D17:
Eastern Introduction
Celebration Day
Bring It On Home - Heartbreaker
What Is And What Should Never Be
Tangerine
Thank You
Hurdy Gurdy Solo
Gallows Pole
Nobody's Fault But Mine
The Song Remains The Same
Since I've Been Loving You
D18:
Whole Lotta Love Medley (Inc. It's All Over Now -
Break On Through - Dazed And Confused)
Egyptian Pharaohs
In The Evening (Inc. Carouselambra)
Four Sticks
Kashmir
Can You Feel It - Black Dog - In My Time Of Dying
Rock And Roll
TENTH SHOW
D19:
Babe I Gonna Leave You - Stairway To Heaven
Ramble On
Custard Pie
Heartbreaker
Wonderful One
The Song Remains The Same

Rain Song
Celebration Day
Hurdy Gurdy Solo
Gallows Pole
Since I've Been Loving You
D20:
Whole Lotta Love (Inc. Baby Let Me Follow You Down -
Going Down - Break On Through - Dazed And
Confused)
Egyptian Pharaohs
In The Evening (Inc. Carouselambra)
Four Sticks
Kashmir
Out On The Tiles - Black Dog - In My Time Of Dying
Rock And Roll

Memphis Daze

Venue: Memphis
Date: 3/4/95
Cover: D4C
Recording: 8
Source: St - Aud
Company: n/a
Matrix #: n/a
Place Of Origin: Japan

D1:
Wanton Song
Bring It On Home
Celebration Day
Thank You
Dancing Days
Shake My Tree
Lullaby
No Quarter
Wonderful One
Hey Hey What Can I Do
Gallow's Pole
Hurdy Gurdy Solo
Nobody's Fault But Mine
D2:
The Song Remains The Same
Since I've Been Loving You
Friends
Calling To You
Four Sticks
In The Evening
Black Dog
Kashmir

Live '95

Venue: New York
Date: 1/12/95
Cover: D4C
Recording: 10
Source: St - SB
Company: KTS Of Australia
Matrix #: 010A
Place Of Origin: Australia

D1:
The Rockline Interview (52.27)
John Paul Jones Interview (1.59)
Induction Speech (3.56)
Bring It On Home (3.17)
No Matter How You Treat Me -
Baby Please Don't Go (8.00)
When The Levee Breaks - For What It's Worth (8.30)

Most High

Venue: London
Date: 3/25/98
Cover: D4C
Recording: 8
Source: St - Aud
Company: n/a
Matrix #: n/a
Place Of Origin: Europe
Total Disc Time: n/a

N.B. This show was doomed to be bootlegged. I was at this show on the Thursday night and by Sunday morning I was buying the CD in London at a flea market. Recorded at the Shepherd's Bush Empire Theatre. Also available as the title "Queuing by the Sick".

D1:
The Wanton Song
Bring It on Home
Heartbreaker
Ramble On
Walking into Clarksdale
No Quarter
When I Was a Child
Going to California
Tangerine
Gallow's Pole
D2:
Burning Up
Babe I'm Gonna Leave You
How Many More Times
Most High
Whole Lotta Love
House of Love
Crossroads
Thank You
Rock and Roll

Night Flight Of The Swan

Venue: Melbourne
Date: 3/1/96
Cover: D4C
Recording: 8
Source: St - Aud
Company: Two Symbols
Matrix #: TS 00
Place Of Origin: Japan

D1:
Babe I'm Gonna Leave You
Bring It On Home
Heartbreaker
Ramble On
Going To California
Hurdy Gurdy Solo
Gallows Pole
Song Remains The Same
Rain Song
Since I've Been Loving You
Whole Lotta Love
D2:
Yallah
Four Sticks
In The Evening (Inc. Carouselambra)
Kashmir
Wonderful One
Black Dog
Rock And Roll

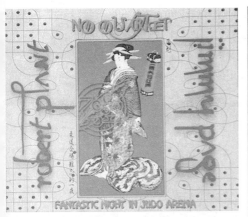

No Quartet - Fantastic Night In Judo Arena

Venue: Tokyo
Date: 2/6/96 - 2/5/96*
Cover: D4C
Recording: 8
Source: St - Aud
Company: Oiran
Matrix #:AMP25001
Place Of Origin: Japan
Total Disc Time: 65.21 - 62.40

D1:
Babe I'm Gonna Leave You
Bring It On Home
Heartbreaker
Thank You
Gallows Pole
Nigel Eaton's Hurdy Gurdy Solo
Nobody's Fault But Mine
Going To California
Since I've Been Loving You
Dancing Days
Yallah
Four Sticks
D2:
In The Evening (Inc. Carouselambra)
Kashmir
Tangerine
Whole Lotta Love Medley (Inc. In The Night - Break On
Through - Dazed And Confused)
Rock And Roll
No Quarter*
Black Dog*

On Tor

Venue: Glastonbury - San Jose*
Date: 6/25/95 - 5/20/95*
Cover: D4C
Recording: 10
Source: St - SB
Company: n/a
Matrix #: n/a
Place Of Origin: Japan
Total Disc Time: 77.58

D1:
Gallows Pole
Since I've Been Loving You
Song Remains The Same
Calling To You (Inc. Smokestack Lightning, Break On
Through, Dazed And Confused)
Four Sticks
In The Evening
Kashmir
Thank You*
Black Dog

PP
Venue: Dublin
Date: 7/19/95 - 7/20/95
Cover: D4C gatefold sleeve
Recording: 8
Source: St - Aud
Company: Tarantura
Matrix #: IRE 001-004
Place Of Origin: Japan
Total Disc Time: 51.33 - 70.03 - 46.14 - 59.21
D1:
Thank You - Bring It On Home - Ramble On
Whole Lotta Love
No Quarter
Gallows Pole
Yallah
Since I've Been Loving You
D2:
Song Remains The Same
Dancing Days
Calling To You Medley (Inc. Light My Fire - Break On
Through - Dazed And Confused)
Four Sticks
Kashmir
Black Dog
In The Evening
D3:
Celebration Day - Bring It On Home
Custard Pie
No Quarter
Going To California
Battle Of Evermore
Gallows Pole
Since I've Been Loving You (Inc. Tea For One)
D4:
Whole Lotta Love Medley (Inc. All Of My Love - What Is
& What Should Never Be - Break On Through - Dazed
And Confused)
Friends
Four Sticks
Kashmir
Black Dog
Song Remains The Same

Paris '95
Venue: Paris
Date: 6/6/95
Cover: D2C
Recording: 8
Source: St - Aud
Company: Silver Rarities
Matrix #: SIRA 183/184
Place Of Origin: Europe
Total Disc Time: 66.39 - 65.02

D1:
Introduction
Thank You
Bring It On Home
Ramble On
Shake My Tree
Lullaby
No Quarter
Gallows Pole
Hurdy Gurdy Intro, Nobody's Fault But Mine
Hey Hey What Can I Do
The Song Remains The Same
Since I've Been Loving You
D2:
Dancing Days (with orchestra)
Calling You
Four Sticks
In the Evening
Black Dog
Kashmir

Presence Now

Venue: Toronto - New York*
Date: 3/27/95 - 1/12/95*
Cover: D4C
Recording: 9
Source: St - Aud
Company: Rain
Matrix #: n/a
Place Of Origin: Europe
Total Disc Time: 67.32 - 72.33

D1:
Wanton Song
Bring It On Home
Celebration Day
Thank You
Dancing Days
Shake My Tree
Lullaby
No Quarter
Gallow's Pole
Nobody's Fault But Mine
The Song Remains The Same
Since I've Been Loving You
Friends
D2:
Dazed And Confused Medley
Four Sticks
In The Evening
Black Dog
Kashmir
Bring It On Home*
Long Distance Call Blues*
Baby Please Don't Go*
When The Levee Breaks - For What It's Worth*

Presence Now 2

Venue: San Jose - London*
Date: 5/20/95 - 11/1/94*
Cover: D4C
Recording: 9
Source: St - Aud
Company: Rain
Matrix #: n/a
Place Of Origin: Europe

D1:
Thank You
Bring It On Home
Ramble On
Shake My Tree
Lullaby
No Quarter
Gallow's Pole
Nobody's Fault But Mine
Hey Hey What Can I Do
Song Remains The Same
Since I've Been Loving You
D2:
Friends
Yallah
Dazed & Confused
Four Sticks
In The Evening
Black Dog
Kashmir
No Quarter*
Gallow's Pole*
Wonderful One*
Four Sticks*

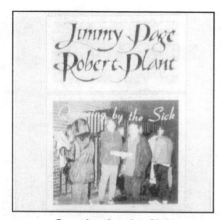

Queuing by the Sick

Venue: London
Date: 3/25/98
Cover: D4C
Recording: 8
Source: St - Aud
Company: Broken Jam
Matrix #: n/a
Place Of Origin: Europe
Total Disc Time: n/a

N.B. This was doomed to be bootlegged. I was at this show on the Thursday night and by Sunday morning I was buying the CD in London at a flea market. Recorded at the Shepherd's Bush Empire Theatre. Also available as the title "Most High".

D1:
The Wanton Song
Bring It on Home
Heartbreaker
Ramble On
Walking into Clarksdale
No Quarter
When I Was a Child
Going to California
Tangerine
Gallow's Pole
Burning Up
D2:
Babe I'm Gonna Leave You
How Many More Times
Most High
Whole Lotta Love
House of Love
Crossroads
Thank You
Rock and Roll

Ramble On Into The 90's

Venue: San Diego
Date: 5/13/95
Cover: D4C
Recording: 8
Source: St - Aud
Company: Two Symbols
Matrix #: TS 003A-B
Place Of Origin: Japan
Total Disc Time: 57.27 - 65.36

D1:
Intro
Thank You
Bring It On Home
Ramble On
Shake My Tree
Lullaby
No Quarter
Gallows Pole
Hurdy Gurdy Solo
Nobody's Fault But Mine
Hey Hey What Can I Do
Song Remains The Same
D2:
Since I've Been Loving You
Friends
Calling To You Medley (Inc. Down By The Seaside - Break On Through - Dazed And Confused)
Four Sticks
In The Evening
Black Dog
Kashmir

Return To Electric Magic Vol 1
Venue: London
Date: 7/25/95
Cover: D4C
Recording: 7
Source: St - Aud
Company: Two Symbols
Matrix #: TS001 A-B
Place Of Origin: Japan
Total Disc Time: 61.04 - 60.50

D1:
Introduction
Immigrant Song, Wanton Song
Bring It On Home
Ramble On
Thank You
No Quarter
Battle Of Evermore
Hurdy Gurdy Solo
Gallows Pole
Since I've Been Loving You
The Song Remains The Same
Going To California
D2:
Friends
Four Sticks
Whole Lotta Love
Kashmir
Black Dog
In The Evening

Rise Of The Phoenix
Venue: Phoenix
Date: 5/10/95
Cover: D4C
Recording: 7
Source: St - Aud
Company: Two Symbols
Matrix #: TS 006 A-B
Place Of Origin: Japan
Total Disc Time: 70.07 - 61.59

D1:
Intro
Wanton Song
Bring It On Home
Ramble On
Thank You
Shake My Tree
Lullaby
No Quarter
Gallows Pole
Hurdy Gurdy Solo
When The Levee Breaks
Hey Hey What Can I Do
The Song Remains The Same
Since I've Been Loving You
D2:
Friends
Calling To You Medley (Inc. Down By The Seaside - Break
On Through - Dazed And Confused)
Four Sticks
In The Evening
Black Dog
Kashmir

Rock & Roll Hall Of Fame

Venue: New York - London* - Denhaag^

Date: 1/12/95 - 11/1/94* - 6/26/93^

Cover: D4C

Recording: 9

Source: St - SB

Company: Kiss The Stone

Matrix #: KTS 404

Place Of Origin: Europe

Total Disc Time: 56.32

D1:

Bring It On Home

Long Distance Call Blues

Baby Please Don't Go

When The Levee Breaks - For What It's Worth

Wonderful One*

When The Levee Breaks*

29 Palms^

What Is And What Should Never Be^

Ship Of Fools^

Whole Lotta Love^

Royal Orleans

Venue: New Orleans - Tokyo*

Date: 3/10/95 - ?/96*

Cover: D4C

Recording: 8

Source: St - Aud

Company: Real Live

Matrix #: PP 953101

Place Of Origin: Japan

Total Disc Time: 55.14 - 68.02

D1:

Intro

Wanton Song

Bring It On Home

Celebration Day

Thank You

Dancing Days

Shake My Tree

Lullaby

No Quarter

Hey Hey What Can I Do

Gallows Pole

Nobody's Fault But Mine

D2:

Song Remains The Same

Since I've Been Loving You

Friends

Calling To You Medley (Inc. White Rabbit - Dazed And Confused)

Four Sticks

In The Evening

Black Dog

Kashmir

Stairway To Heaven (acoustic version)*

San Jose

Venue: San Jose - Amsterdam*
Date: 5/20/95 - 6/26/93*
Cover: D4C
Recording: 9
Source: St - SB
Company: Tuff Bites
Matrix #: n/a
Place Of Origin: Europe
D1:
Thank You - Bring It On Home
Shake My Tree
Lullaby
No Quarter
Gallow's Pole
Hurdy Gurdy Solo
Nobody's Fault But Mine
Hey Hey What Can I Do
Song Remains The Same
Since I've Been Loving You
Friends
D2:
Calling To You Medley (Inc. Break On Through - Dazed &
Confused)
Four Sticks
In The Evening
Black Dog
Kashmir
29 Palms*
What Is & What Should Never Be*
Ship Of Fools*
Whole Lotta Love*

Second Coming (The)

Venue: Glastonbury
Date: 6/26/95
Cover: D4C
Recording: 10
Source: St - SB
Company: Octopus

Matrix #: OCTO 195
Place Of Origin: Europe
D1:
Gallows Pole (4:52)
Since I've Been Loving You (8:33)
The Song Remains The Same (6:31)
Friends (4:20)
Calling To You Medley (Inc. Guitar Solo - Break On
Through - Dazed And Confused) (13:48)
Four Sticks (5:13)
In The Evening (9:05)
Kashmir (14:16)

Second Day (The)

Venue: Tokyo
Date: 2/6/96
Cover: D4C
Recording: 7
Source: St - Aud
Company: Cobra
Matrix #: n/a
Place Of Origin: Japan
D1:
Babe I'm Gonna Leave You
Bring It On Home - Heartbreaker
Thank You
Gallows Pole
Hurdy Gurdy Solo
Nobody's Fault But Mine
Going To California
Since I've Been Loving You
Dancing Days
Yallah
D2:
Four Sticks
In The Evening
Kashmir
Tangerine
Whole Lotta Love
Rock & Roll

Shake My Tree

Venue: Philadelphia

Date: 4/4/95

Cover: D4C

Recording: 7

Source: St - Aud

Company: Party Line

Matrix #: PLCD 020/1

Place Of Origin: Japan

Total Disc Time: 55.59 - 58.28

D1:

Wanton Song

Bring It On Home

Celebration Day

Thank You

Shake My Tree

Lullaby

No Quarter

Wonderful One

Hurdy Gurdy Solo

Nobody's Fault But Mine

The Song Remains The Same

D2:

Since I've Been Loving You

Friends

Yallah

Four Sticks

In The Evening

Black Dog

Kashmir

Simple Truth

Venue: San Jose

Date: 5/20/95

Cover: D2C

Recording: 9

Source: St - SB

Company: Kiss The Stone

Matrix #: KTS 450/51

Place Of Origin: Europe

Total Disc Time: 57.17 - 63.05

D1:

Intro

Thank You

Bring It On Home

Ramble On

Shake My Tree

Intro

Lullaby

No Quarter

Gallows Pole

Hurdy Gurdy Solo

Nobody's Fault But Mine

Hey Hey What Can I Do

The Song Remains The Same

D2:

Intro

Since I've Been Loving You

Friends

Calling To You Medley (Inc. Dazed And Confused - Break

On Through)

Four Sticks

In The Evening

Black Dog

Kashmir

Page & Plant
Since We've Been Loving Them

Since We've Been Loving Them

Venue: San Jose
Date: 5/20/95
Cover: D4C
Recording: 9
Source: St - SB
Company: Alfa
Matrix #: 13018
Place Of Origin: Italy

D1:
Thank You
Bring It On Home - Ramble On
Shake My Tree
Lullaby
No Quarter
Gallow's Pole
Hurdy Gurdy Solo
Nobody's Fault But Mine
Hey Hey What Can I Do
Song Remains The Same
Since I've Been Loving You
D2:
Friends
Calling To You Medley
(Inc. Break On Through - Dazed & Confused)
Four Sticks
In The Evening
Black Dog

Sixth Show At TFOB (The)

Venue: Tokyo
Date: 2/13/96
Cover: D4C
Recording: 9
Source: St - Aud
Company: Real Dragon
Matrix #: n/a
Place Of Origin: Japan

D1:
Thank You
Custard Pie
Black Dog
Tangerine
Hurdy Gurdy Solo
Gallows Pole
Tea For One
The Song Remains The Same
Going To California
Babe I'm Gonna Leave You
D2:
Whole Lotta Love
Friends
Yallah
Four Sticks
Kashmir
What Is & What Should Never Be
Rock & Roll

Song Still Remains (The)

Venue: New York
Date: 10/27/95 - 10/26/95
Cover: D4C
Recording: 7
Source: St - Aud
Company: Real Live
Matrix #: 951027
Place Of Origin: Europe

D1:
Intro
Immigrant Song - Wanton Song
Bring It On Home
Heartbreaker
Ramble On
No Quarter
Tangerine
Hurdy Gurdy Solo
Gallow's Pole
Since I've Been Loving You
Song Remains The Same
Going To California
What Is & What Should Never Be*
That's The Way*
D2:
Babe I'm Gonna Leave You - Stairway To Heaven
Whole Lotta Love Medley (Inc. When The Levee Breaks -
Break On Through - Dazed & Confused)
Four Sticks
In The Evening - Carouselambra
Black Dog
Kashmir
Rock & Roll

Story So Far (The)

Venue: New York - Buxton* -
Amsterdam^ - New York**
Date: 1/12/95 - 4/17/94*- 12/20/93^ - 10/5/88**
Cover: D4C
Recording: 9
Source: St - SB - St - Aud
Company: Octopus
Matrix #: OCTO 162
Place Of Origin: Europe

D1:
Bring It On Home (3:32)
You've Been Smart (3:46)
Baby, Please Don't Go (4:01)
You Gotta Move (8:43)
Intro, Baby Please Don't Go (4:08)*
I Can't Quit You Babe (7:03)*
I've Been Down So Long (3:28)*
That's Why I Love You (4:26)*
Train Kept A Rollin' (4:22)*
Thank You (6:39)^
Whole Lotta Love (8:08)^
Over The Hills And Far Away (5:34)^
Custard Pie - Black Dog (4:04)**
Stairway To Heaven (9:17)**

Supreme Theater

Venue: San Jose - New York*
Date: 5/20/95 - 3/27/95^ - 1/12/95*
Cover: D4C
Recording: 9
Source: St - SB
Company: Planet X
Matrix #: PLAN 060-2
Place Of Origin: Europe

D1:
Intro
Thank You
Bring It On Home
Shake My Tree
Lullaby
No Quarter
Gallow's Pole
Hurdy Gurdy Solo
Nobody's Fault But Mine
Hey Hey What Can I Do
Song Remains The Same
Since I've Been Loving You
D2:
Friends
Calling To You Medley (Inc. Break On Through - Dazed & Confused)
Four Sticks
In The Evening
Black Dog
Kashmir
Immigrant Song - Wanton Song^
Dancing Days^
Bring It On Home*
Long Distance Call*
Baby Please Don't Go*

Sydney Can You Feel It

Venue: Sydney
Date: 2/24/96 - 2/25/96*
Cover: D4C
Recording: 9
Source: St - Aud
Company: Red Hot
Matrix #: n/a
Place Of Origin: Australia

D1:
The Wanton Song
Bring It On Home
Heartbreaker
Ramble On
Going To California
Hurdy Gurdy Solo
Gallows Pole
The Song Remains The Same
The Rain Song
Since I've Been Loving You
Whole Lotta Love
D2:
Yallah
In The Evening
Four Sticks
Kashmir
Black Dog
Rock & Roll
Babe I'm Gonna Leave You*
Since I've Been Loving You*
Dancing Days*

Tangerine
Venue: Landover
Date: 3/23/95
Cover: D4C
Recording: 7
Source: St - Aud
Company: n/a
Matrix #: n/a
Place Of Origin: Japan
Total Disc Time: 66.19 - 64.04

D1:
Intro
Wanton Song
Bring It On Home
Ramble On
Thank You
Dancing Days
Shake My Tree
Lullaby
Tangerine
Hey Hey What Can I Do
Gallows Pole
When The Levee Breaks
Song Remains The Same
D2:
Since I've Been Loving You
Friends - Calling To You (Inc. Dazed And Confused)
Four Sticks
In The Evening
Black Dog
Kashmir

10 Days
Venue: Tokyo - Osaka - Nagoya - Fukuoka
Date: 2/5 - 6- 8 - 9 - 12 - 13 - 15 - 17 - 19 - 20/96
Cover: D4C
Recording: 7 - 9
Source: St - Aud
Company: n/a
Matrix #: n/a
Place Of Origin: Japan

Complete Japanese tour. Limited edition box set, 250 numbered silver box then re-issued as 250 in gold box. All track listings not available. Extremely limited edition.

Thank You
Venue: Pensacola - Auburn Hills*
Date: 2/26/95 4/1/95*
Cover: D4C
Recording: 9
Source: St - SB
Company: Kiki Overrun
Matrix #: n/a

Place Of Origin: Japan
Total Disc Time: 50.03 - 46.21

D1:
Yallah (cut)
Bring It On Home
Celebration Day
Dancing Days (cut)
Gallows Pole (cut)
Hurdy Gurdy solo
Nobody's Fault But Mine (cut)
Friends (cut) - Ramble On*
Thank You*
Hey Hey What Can I Do*
Four Sticks*
In the Evening (Inc. Carouselambra)*
D2:
Since I've Been Loving You
Bring It On Home (no vocals)**
Celebration Day (no vocals)**
Dancing Days (no vocals)**
Robert Plant interview (not broadcast)**

Today, Yesterday And Some Years Ago
Venue: London - Madrid* - New York^
Date: 11/1/94 - 6/19/93* - 5/14/88^
Cover: D4C
Recording: 9
Source: St - SB
Company: Kobra
Matrix #: HRCR001
Place Of Origin: Japan
Total Disc Time: 66.18

D1:
Gallows Pole
Wonderful One
Four Sticks
Hoochie Coochie Man*

29 Palms - Thank You*
I Believe*
Tears I Cry - Light My Fire*
Kashmir^
Heartbreaker - Whole Lotta Love^
Misty Mountain Hop^
Stairway To Heaven^

Together Again
Venue: Buxton - Cologne - Brixton - Birmingham
Date: 4/17/94 - 6/4/93* - 7/16/93^ - 11/21/88**
Cover: D4C
Recording: 7 - 8
Source: St -Aud
Company: n/a
Matrix #: OP94PPB
Place Of Origin: Europe

D1:
Baby Please Don't Go
I Can't Quit You
I've Been Down So Long
That's Why I Love You
Train Kept A Rollin'
Ramble On*
Going To California*
What Is & What Should Never Be^
You Shook Me^
Custard Pie- Black Dog **
Train Kept A Rollin'**
Stairway To Heaven**

Together Again II

Venue: Sydney - Sydney* - London+ - Tokyo@ -
Bombay^

Date: 11/16/94 - 11/16/94* - 11/8/94+ - 11/10/94@ -
5/72^

Cover: D4C

Recording: 8 - 8,7*

Source: St - SB

Company: n/a

Matrix #: n/a

Place Of Origin: Europe

D1:

Mega Mix (2.17)

No Quarter (3.08)

Black Dog Rehearsal (9.01)*

Black Dog (2.45)*

Interview (1.21)*

Sun Arise (1.51)*

Gallow's Pole (4.16)+

Wonderful One (4.35)+

Four Sticks (5.10)+

Stairway To Heaven (3.03)@

Four Sticks (5.00)^

Friends (4.51)^

Friends (4.30)^

Four Sticks (2.30)^

Together Again III

Venue: Miami

Date: 3/6/95

Cover: D4C

Recording: 9

Source: St - Aud

Company: n/a

Matrix #: n/a

Place Of Origin: Japan

Total Disc Time: 61.25 - 61.02

D1:

Opening

Immigration Intro - Wanton Song

Black Dog Intro - Bring It On Home

Celebration Day

Thank You

Dancing Day

Shake My Tree - Guitar Solo

Lullaby

No Quarter

Wonderful One

Hey Hey What Can I Do

Gallows Pole

Hurdy Gurdy Intro

Nobody's Fault But Mine

D2:

Song Remains The Same

Since I've Been Loving You

Egyptian Intro - Friends

Calling To You Medley (Inc. Dazed And Confused - The
Hunter)

Four Sticks

Egyptian Intro,

In The Evening - Carouselambra

Black Dog

Kashmir (cut)

Together Again IV

Venue: Los Angeles
Date: 5/17/95
Cover: D4C
Recording: 7
Source: St - Aud
Company: JR Music
Matrix #: TRH 4-1-2
Place Of Origin: Japan
Total Disc Time: 62.05 - 71.56

D1:
Introduction
Immigrant Song
Bring It On Home
Ramble On
Thank You
Shake My Tree
Lullaby
No Quarter
Gallows Pole
Hurdy Gurdy Intro
When The Levee Breaks
The Song Remains The Same
D2:
Since I've Been Loving You
Dancing Days (with orchestra)
Calling To You Medley (Inc. Down By The Seaside - Break
On Through - Dazed And Confused)
Four Sticks
In The Evening
Black Dog
Kashmir

Together Again V

Venue: London - Buxton* - New Orleans^ - Atlanta**
- Pensacola^^ - Miami†
Date: 1/25/95 - 4/17/94* - 3/11/95^ - 2/28/95** -
2/26/95^^ - 3/6/95†
Cover: D4C
Recording: 8
Source: St - Aud - St - SB
Company: n/a
Matrix #: n/a
Place Of Origin: Europe

D1:
Black Dog
I Can't Quit You Baby*
Shake My Tree^
In The Evening^
Out On The Tiles Intro - Black Dog
Kashmir^
Achilles Last Stand^
House Of The Rising Sun Medley**
(Inc. Good Times Bad Times)
That's The Way**
Yallah (The Truth Explodes)^^
Kashmir†

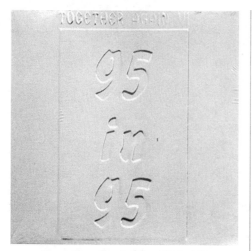

Together Again VI - 95 In 95
Venue: New York
Date: 10/27/95
Cover: D4C metallic box
Recording: 7
Source: St - Aud
Company: n/a
Matrix #: n/a
Place Of Origin: Japan
Total Disc Time: 50.36 - 79.01

D1:
Intro
Wanton Song
Bring It On Home
Heartbreaker
Ramble On
No Quarter
Tangerine
Hurdy Gurdy Solo
Gallow's Pole
Since I've Been Loving You
The Song Remains The Same
D2:
Going To California
Babe I'm Gonna Leave You
Whole Lotta Love Medley (Inc. In The Light - Break On
Through - Dazed And Confused)
Four Sticks
In The Evening
Black Dog
Kashmir
Rock And Roll

Together Again VII - Goin' South
Venue: Rio De Janeiro
Date: 1/27/96
Cover: D4C
Recording: 8
Source: St - SB
Company: n/a
Matrix #: n/a
Place Of Origin: Europe

D1:
The Wanton Song
Bring It On Home
Heartbreaker
Ramble On
No Quarter
Hurdy Gurdy Solo
Since I've Been Loving You
Song Remains The Same
Going To California
D2:
Babe I'm Gonna Leave You
Whole Lotta Love
Friends
Kashmir
Black Dog
Rock & Roll

Together Again VIII - Soundbites & More

Venue: Irvine - Hartford* - German TV^ - Eurorocken Festival** - Dublin^^ - Mexico†‡
Date: 10/3/95 - 10/21/95* - ?/95^ - ?/95** - 7/20/95^^ - 9/23/95† - 9/24/95‡
Cover: D4C
Recording: n/a
Source: n/a
Company: n/a
Matrix #: n/a
Place Of Origin: Europe

D1:
Intro
Immigrant Song
Wanton Song
Bring it On Home
Song Remains The Same
Going To California
Four Sticks
Black Dog*
Four Sticks^
In The Evening^
Black Dog**
Custard Pie^^
Heartbreaker†
Rock & Roll†
Tie Dye On The Highway‡

Tour Over Europe

Venue: Milan
Date: 6/10/95
Cover: D4C
Recording: 6
Source: St - Aud
Company: Two Symbols
Matrix #: TS 008 A-B
Place Of Origin: Japan
Total Disc Time: 42.15 - 42.05

D1:
Wanton Song
Bring It On Home - Heartbreaker - Black Dog
Thank You
No Quarter
Gallows Pole
Yallah
Since I've Been Loving You
D2:
The Song Remains The Same
Calling To You Medley (Inc. When The Levee Breaks - Break On Through - Dazed And Confused)
Dancing Days
Four Sticks
In The Evening - Carouselambra

Truth Explodes (The)
Venue: Atlanta
Date: 2/28/95
Cover: D4C
Recording: 8
Source: St - Aud
Company: Two Symbols
Matrix #: TS 00
Place Of Origin: Japan

D1:
Yallah
Bring It On Home
Celebration Day
Shake My Tree
Since I've Been Loving You
Lullaby
Achilles Last Stand
No Quarter
Wonderful One
D2:
Gallow's Pole
Hurdy Gurdy Solo
When The Levee Breaks
Friends
Calling To You
In The Evening
Black Dog
Kashmir

Two Days In Osaka
Venue: Osaka
Date: 2/15/96 - 2/19/96*
Cover: D4C
Recording: 9
Source: St - Aud
Company: Real Dragon
Matrix #: n/a
Place Of Origin: Japan
D1:
Custard Pie - Bring It On Home- Heartbreaker
What Is & What Should Never Be
Hurdy Gurdy Solo - Gallow's Pole
Wonderful One
Going To California
Ten Years Gone
Babe I'm Gonna Leave You
Whole Lotta Love
D2:
Tea For One
Friends
Yallah
Four Sticks
Kashmir
Black Dog
Rock & Roll
D3:
Celebration Day - Bring It On Home - Heartbreaker
What Is & What Should Never Be
Tangerine
Thank You
Hurdy Gurdy Solo - Gallow's Pole
Nobody's Fault But Mine
Song Remains The Same
Since I've Been Loving You
Whole Lotta Love
D4:
Dancing Days
In The Evening
Four Sticks
Kashmir
Black Dog
Rock & Roll

Two Swans On A Century Lake
Venue: Nagoya* - Tokyo - Osaka† - Fukuoka‡
Date: 2/17/96* - 2/5/96 - 2/6/96 - 2/12/96 - 2/13/96 -
2/19/96† - 2/20/96‡
Cover: D4C
Recording: 8
Source: St - Aud
Company: Real Dragon
Matrix #: RD 031/32/33/34
Place Of Origin: Japan
Total Disc Time: 64.57 - 60.09 - 66.12 - 71.19
D1:
Heartbreaker*- Bring It On Home* - Custard Pie*
Ramble On*
What Is And What Should Never Be - Tangerine*
Thank You*
Hurdy-Gurdy Solo* - Gallows Pole*
The Rain Song*
The Song Remains The Same*
Tea For One*
D2:
Dancing Days*
Egyptian Pharaohs* - In The Evening (Inc.
Carouselambra)*
Four Sticks*
Kashmir*
Celebration Day*
Black Dog - In My Time Of Dying *
Rock And Roll*
D3:
(2/5/96) Immigrant Song - The Wanton Song
Bring It On Home - Heartbreaker
Ramble On - What Is And What Should Never Be
What Is And What Should Never Be†
(2/9/96) No Quarter
(2/13/96) Going To California
(2/12/96) That's The Way
Babe I'm Gonna Leave You - Stairway To Heaven
(2/6/96) Hurdy-Gurdy Solo - Nobody's Fault But Mine
Wonderful One‡
(2/13/96) Yallah
D4:
Friends

Since I've Been Loving You
(2/15/96) Ten Years Gone
Whole Lotta Love Medley (Inc. In The Light - Break On
Through - Dazed And Confused)
(2/6/96) Whole Lotta Love
(2/8/96) Bonus: The Rain Song (intro) - The Rain Song
Nigel Eaton's Hurdy-Gurdy Solo
When The Levee Breaks
Tea For One (intro) - Tea For One
Yallah (cut)

(Two Symbols)
Venue: Knoxville
Date: 3/3/95
Cover: D4C box
Recording: 8
Source: St - Aud
Company: Tarantura
Matrix #: KNOX 3-4 1,2
Place Of Origin: Japan
D1:
Immigrant Song - Wanton Song
Bring It On Home
Celebration Day
Thank You
Dancing Days
Shake My Tree
Lullaby
No Quarter
Wonderful One
Gallow's Pole
Nobody's Fault But Mine
D2:
Song Remains The Same
Since I've Been Loving You
Friends
Calling To You Medley (Inc. Dazed & Confused)
Four Sticks
In The Evening
Black Dog
Kashmir

Unledded Live 1996

Venue: Tokyo
Date: 2/6/96
Cover: D4C
Recording: 8
Source: St - Aud
Company: Pore The Soul
Matrix #: 0
Place Of Origin: Japan

D1:

Babe I'm Gonna Leave You
Bring It On Home
Heartbreaker
Thank You
Gallow's Pole
Hurdy Gurdy Solo
Nobody's Fault But Mine
Going To California
Since I've Been Loving You
Dancing Days
Yallah
D2:
Four Sticks
In The Evening
Kashmir
Tangerine
Whole Lotta Love
Rock & Roll

We're Gonna Groove

Venue: Mountain View
Date: 10/7/95
Cover: D4C
Recording: 7
Source: St - Aud
Company: Two Symbols
Matrix #: n/a
Place Of Origin: Japan

D1:

Wanton Song
Bring It On Home
Ramble On
Thank You
No Quarter
That's The Way
Battle Of Evermore
Hurdy Gurdy Solo
Since I've Been Loving You
Song Remains The Same
Going To California
D2:
Babe I'm Gonna Leave You
Friends
Four Sticks
Whole Lotta Love
Heartbreaker
Kashmir

Welcome To The Rehearsals

Venue: Tokyo

Date: 2/8/96

Cover: D4C

Recording: 7 -8

Source: St - Aud

Company: Pore The Soul

Matrix #: PTS 020/1

Place Of Origin: Japan

Total Disc Time: 67.30 - 66.06

D1:

Intro

Celebration Day - Bring It On Home - Heartbreaker

What Is And What Should Never Be

The Rain Song (take 1 And 2)

Hurdy Gurdy Solo

When The Levee Breaks

Gallows Pole

Tea For One

The Song Remains The Same

Babe I'm Gonna Leave You - Stairway To Heaven

D2:

Whole Lotta Love Medley (Inc. Down By The Seaside -

Break On Through - Dazed And Confused)

Yallah

Four Sticks

Kashmir

Black Dog

Rock And Roll

What Is And Will Always Be

Venue: Denver

Date: 9/30/95

Cover: D4C

Recording: 8

Source: St - Aud

Company: Two Symbols

Matrix #: n/a

Place Of Origin: Japan

D1:

Bring It On Home

What Is & What Should Never Be

The Wanton Song

Thank You

No Quarter

That's The Way

Hurdy Gurdy Solo

Gallow's Pole

Since I've Been Loving You

Song Remains The Same

Going To California

D2:

Babe I'm Gonna Leave You

Friends

Four Sticks

Whole Lotta Love

Kashmir

Whole Lotta Love

Venue: Rotterdam

Date: 6/15/95

Cover: D4C

Recording: 8

Source: St - Aud

Company: Sonic Zoom

Matrix #: SZ2013/2014

Place Of Origin: Japan

D1:

The Wanton Song

Bring It On Home

Whole Lotta Love

Thank You

Lullaby

No Quarter

Gallow's Pole

Yallah

Since I've Been Loving You

Song Remains The Same

D2:

Friends

Calling To You

Four Sticks

In The Evening

Black Dog

Kashmir

Whole Lotta Zep

Venue: San Jose

Date: 5/20/95

Cover: D4C

Recording: 9

Source: St - SB

Company: Octopus

Matrix #: OCTO 182/3

Place Of Origin: Europe

D1:

Intro, Thank You (8:26)

Bring It On Home - Ramble On (6:30)

Shake My Tree (8:32)

Lullaby (6:30)

No Quarter (5:20)

Gallows Pole (5:13)

Nobody's Fault But Mine (6:23)

Hey, Hey What Can I Do (4:26)

Song Remains The Same (5:55)

D2:

Since I've Been Lovin' You (9:18)

Friends (5:11)

Calling To You Medley (Inc. Guitar Solo - Break On Through - Dazed And Confused) (12:42)

Four Sticks (5:16)

In the Evening (9:24)

Black Dog (6:05)

Kashmir (16:18)

Solo Bootlegs

Jimmy Page Bootlegs

Arms Benefit

Venue: London
Date: 9/20/83
Cover: D4C
Recording: 9
Source: St - SB
Company: n/a
Matrix #: n/a
Place Of Origin: Japan

D1:
Clapton Interview
Everybody Oughta Make A Change
Lay Down Sally
Wonderful Tonight
Ramblin' On My Mind
Have You Ever Loved A Woman
Rita Mae
Cocaine
Women Are Smarter
Slowdown Sundown
Take Me To The River
Gimme Some Lovin'
D2:
Star Cycle
The Pump
Out Of A Book
Led Boots
People Get Ready
Hi Ho Silver Lining
Prelude
Who's To Blame
City Sirens
Tulsa Time
Bye Bye Baby
Layla
Goodnight Irene

Checks & Chops

Venue: Tokyo - Osaka* - Nagoya^
Date: 12/17/93 - 12/20/93* - 12/22/93^
Cover: D4C
Recording: 9
Source: St - SB
Company: n/a
Matrix #: n/a
Place Of Origin: Japan
Total Disc Time: 67.14

D1:
Theramin Solo
For Your Life
Nobody's Fault But Mine
Jam
Dazed & Confused
Jam
In My Time Of Dying
Dancing Days*
Bron-y-Aur Stomp*
Black Country Woman*
Jam*
In My Time Of Dying*
White Summer*
Whole Lotta Love*
Communication Breakdown*
Acoustic Jam - Stairway To Heaven*
Jam^
Whole Lotta Love^
Jam^

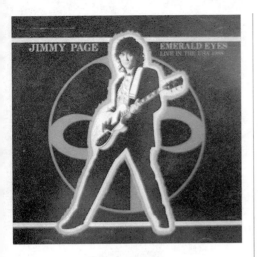

Emerald Eyes

Venue: n/a

Date: n/a

Cover: D4C

Recording: 9

Source: St - SB

Company: Silver Glitters

Matrix #: n/a

Place Of Origin: Japan

Total Disc Time: 70.15

D1:

Who's To Blame

Prelude

Over The Hills & Far Away

Writes Of Winter

Tear Down The Walls

Emerald Eyes

Midnight Moonlight

In My Time Of Dying

Prison Blues

Wasting My Time

Custard Pie - Black Dog

Train Kept A Rollin'

Stairway To Heaven

Final Stage (Coverdale - Page)

Venue: Nagoya

Date: 12/22/93

Cover: D4C

Recording: 8

Source: St - Aud

Company: n/a

Matrix #: n/a

Place Of Origin: Japan

D1:

Absolution Blues

Slide It In

Rock & Roll

Over Now

Kashmir

Pride & Joy

Take A Look At Yourself (Acoustic)

Take Me For A Little While

In My Time Of Dying

D2:

Here I Go Again

White Summer - Black Mountain Side

Don't Leave Me This Way

Shake My Tree

Still Of The Night

Out On The Tiles - Black Dog

The Ocean - Wanton Song - Feeling Hot

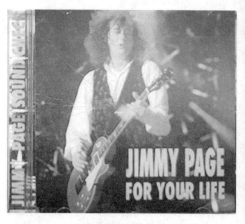

First Stage (The) (Coverdale - Page)

Venue: Tokyo

Date: 12/14/93

Cover: D4C

Recording: 8

Source: St - Aud

Company: n/a

Matrix #: CP001/2

Place Of Origin: Japan

D1:

Absolution Blues

Slide It In

Rock & Roll

Over Now

Kashmir

Pride & Joy

Take A Look At Yourself (Acoustic)

Take Me For A Little While

In My Time Of Dying

D2:

Here I Go Again

White Summer - Black Mountain Side

Don't Leave Me This Way

Shake My Tree

Still Of The Night

Out On The Tiles - Black Dog

The Ocean - Wanton Song - Feeling Hot

For Your Life

Venue: Tokyo

Date: 12/18/93

Cover: D4C

Recording: 9

Source: St - SB

Company: Red River

Matrix #: n/a

Place Of Origin: Japan

D1:

The Ocean

Wanton Song

Feelin' Hot

Whole Lotta Love

For Your Life

For Your Life

Nobody's Fault But Mine

Absolution Blues

Dazed & Confused

In My Time Of Dying

Guitar Solo

For Zeppelin Fans Only

Venue: New York

Date: 10/22/88

Cover: D4C

Recording: 9

Source: St -SB

Company: n/a

Matrix #: n/a

Place Of Origin: Japan

D1:

Who's To Blame

Prelude

Over The Hills & Far Away

Writes Of Winter

Tear Down The Walls

Emerald Eyes

Midnight Moonlight

In My Time Of Dying

Prison Blues

Wasting My Time

Custard Pie - Black Dog

Train Kept A Rollin'

Stairway To Heaven

Hanging Out (Coverdale - Page)

Venue: n/a

Date: n/a

Cover: D4C

Recording: n/a

Source: n/a

Company: n/a

Matrix #: n/a

Place Of Origin: Japan

D1:

Absolution Blues

Slide It In

Rock & Roll

Over Now

Kashmir

Pride & Joy

Take A Look At Yourself (Acoustic)

Take Me For A Little While

In My Time Of Dying

D2:

Here I Go Again

White Summer - Black Mountain Side

Don't Leave Me This Way

Shake My Tree

Still Of The Night

Out On The Tiles - Black Dog

The Ocean - Wanton Song - Feeling Hot

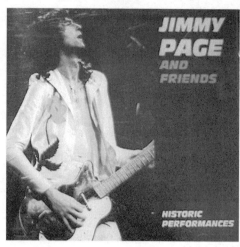

Hat Off To Jimmy Page

Venue: Battersea - London*

Date: 7/29/84 - 1/21/84*

Cover: D4C

Recording: 8 - 9*

Source: St - Aud ,St - SB*

Company: Fire Power

Matrix #: FP05

Place Of Origin: Japan

D1:

Short & Sweet

Referendum

Highway Blues

True Story

The Game

Studio Jam*

Jimmy Page & Friends

Venue: Various

Date: Various

Cover: D4C

Recording: 7 - 9

Source: St - Aud

Company: Asian Trading

Matrix #: n/a

Place Of Origin: Hong Kong

Total Disc Time: 61.55

D1:

Shake Your Moneymaker (Santana)

The Lemon Song (Led Zeppelin)

Think About It (Yardbirds)

I'm Down (Yes)

It'll Be Me (Led Zeppelin)

Blues Jam (Jaco Pastorious)

Barbara Ann (Beach Boys)

Fun Fun Fun (Beach Boys)

Roll Over Beethoven (Eric Clapton)

Jimmy Page & More Friends

Venue: Various

Date: Various

Cover: D4C

Recording: 7 - 9

Source: St - Aud

Company: Asian Trading

Matrix #: n/a

Place Of Origin: Hong Kong

Total Disc Time: 61.46

D1:

CommunicationBreakdown (Ron Wood)

Going Down (Jeff Beck)

Still Of The Night (David Coverdale)

Rock Me Baby (Bad Company)

Lucille (Beach Boys)

Further On Up The Road (Eric Clapton)

Cocaine (Eric Clapton)

White Summer (Julie Felix TV)

Stairway To Heaven (Led Zeppelin)

Jimmy Page's Firm

Venue: Los Angeles

Date: n/a

Cover: D4C

Recording: 8

Source: St - Aud

Company: BM

Matrix #: 029

Place Of Origin: Japan

D1:

Closer

City Sirens

Make Up Or Break Up

Morning After

Together

Long Black Cadillac

Prelude

Money Can't Buy

Radioactive

Live In Peace

Midnight Moonlight

Lovin Feelin

Full Circle

Boogie Mama

Everybody Needs Somebody To Love

Last Rave-Up In L.A. (The Yardbirds)

Venue: Los Angeles
Date: 5/31/68
Cover: D4C
Recording: 6
Source: M - Aud
Company: Glimpses
Matrix #: GR001 CD1/2
Place Of Origin: Japan

D1:
Train Kept A Rollin
You're A Better Man Than I
Heart Full Of Soul
Dazed & Confused
Shapes Of Things
I'm A Man
White Summer
Smokestack Lightning
Becks Bolero
I'm Waiting For The Man
D2:
Bye Bye Bird
Drinking Muddy Water
Happenings Ten Years Time Ago
New York City Blues
I Wish You Would
Hey Gyp
I Ain't Done Wrong
Over Under Sideways Down

Legendary Rockers

Venue: Tokyo
Date: 12/17/93
Cover: D4C
Recording: 8
Source: St - Aud
Company: n/a
Matrix #: n/a
Place Of Origin: Japan

D1:
Absolution Blues
Slide It In
Rock & Roll
Over Now
Kashmir
Pride & Joy
Take A Look At Yourself (Acoustic)
Take Me For A Little While
In My Time Of Dying
Here I Go Again
D2:
White Summer - Black Mountain Side
Don't Leave Me This Way
Shake My Tree
Still Of The Night
Out On The Tiles - Black Dog
Feeling Hot

Legendary Rockers - 18th December 1993

Venue: Tokyo
Date: 12/18/93
Cover: D4C
Recording: 8
Source: St - Aud
Company: n/a
Matrix #: n/a
Place Of Origin: Japan

D1:
Absolution Blues
Slide It In
Rock & Roll
Over Now
Kashmir
Pride & Joy
Take A Look At Yourself (Acoustic)
Take Me For A Little While
In My Time Of Dying
Here I Go Again
D2:
White Summer - Black Mountain Side
Don't Leave Me This Way
Shake My Tree
Still Of The Night
Out On The Tiles - Black Dog
Feeling Hot
Rock & Roll

Live Yardbirds

Venue: New York - Various*
Date: ?/68 - 1965-68*
Cover: D4C
Recording: 9
Source: St - SB
Company: n/a
Matrix #: n/a
Place Of Origin: Japan

D1:
Train Kept A Rollin'
You're A Better Man Than I
Heart Full Of Soul
I'm Confused
My Baby
Over Under Sideways Down
Drinking Muddy Water
Shapes Of Things
White Summer
I'm A Man
D2:
Psycho Daisies*
Shapes In My Mind*
I Wish You Would*
Keep Moving*
I'm A Man*
Blues Sands*
She Just Satisfies*
Hang On Sloopy*
Pafff....Bum*
Heart Full Of Soul*
Shapes In My Mind*
Shapes Of Things*
For Your Love*
I Wish You Would*
Questa Volta*

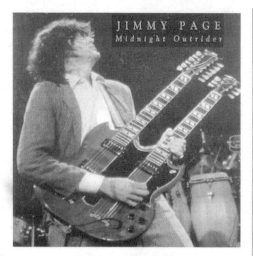

Midnight Outrider

Venue: Studio

Date:

Cover: D4C in case

Recording: 7-8, 6*

Source: St - SB

Company: Red Sun Music

Matrix #: RSMCD1-2

Place Of Origin: Germany

Total Disc Time: 43.24 - 45.41

N.B. Good quality outtakes from the Outrider sessions. The overall sound is a bit muddy compared to the tape. The second disc says "Midnight Moonlight sessions" but I believe this may be the recording which was rumoured to have been made in the seventies under the title "Swansong". It unquestionably did end up as Midnight Moonlight. Originally released under the title Dangerous Relation by Tarantura.

D1:

Wasting My Time (4.28)

Wanna Make Love (5.30)

Judas Touch (6.10)

Hummingbird (5.23)

Prison Blues #1 (7.08)

Prison Blue #2 (7.16)

Train Kept A Rollin (3.31)

Blues Anthem (3.27)

D2:

Swansong acoustic rehearsals Takes 1 - 17

New York City Blues (The Yardbirds)

Venue: New York

Date: 3/30/68

Cover: D3C

Recording: 7

Source: M -Aud

Company: Last Stand

Matrix #: n/a

Place Of Origin: Japan

D1:

Train Kept A Rollin (Soundcheck)

Train Kept A Rollin

You're A Better Man Than I

Dazed & Confused

My Baby

Over Under Sideways Down

Drinking Muddy Water

Shapes Of Things

White Summer

I'm A Man

One More Zep

Venue: Tokyo
Date: 12/14/93
Cover: D4C
Recording: 9
Source: St - Aud
Company: n/a
Matrix #: n/a
Place Of Origin: Japan

D1:
Absolution Blues
Slide It In
Rock & Roll
Over Now
Kashmir
Pride & Joy
Take A Look At Yourself (Acoustic)
Take Me For A Little While
In My Time Of Dying
D2:
Here I Go Again
White Summer - Black Mountain Side
Don't Leave Me This Way
Shake My Tree
Still Of The Night
Out On The Tiles - Black Dog
The Ocean - Wanton Song - Feeling Hot

Over Now (Coverdale - Page)

Venue: London
Date: ?/93
Cover: D4C
Recording: 9
Source: St - SB
Company: Banzai
Matrix #: BZCD
Place Of Origin: Japan

D1:
Absolution Blues
Slide It In
Rock & Roll
Over Now
Kashmir
Pride & Joy
Take A Look At Yourself
Take Me For A Little While
In My Time Of Dying
D2:
Here I Go Again
Don't Leave Me This Way
Feelin' Hot
Still Of The Night
Whisper A Prayer
Black Dog
Shake My Tree

Radioactive (The Firm)

Venue: London

Date: 5/22/85

Cover: D4C

Recording: 8

Source: St - SB

Company: Tailfin Music Co.

Matrix #: n/a

Place Of Origin: Japan

DI:

Closer

City Sirens

Make Or Break

The Morning After

Together

Prelude

Money Can't Be Love

D2:

Radioactive

Live In Peace

Midnight Moonlight

You've Lost That Loving Feeling

The Chase

I Just Wanna Make Love

Someone To Love

Mama Boogie

Everybody Needs Somebody To Love

Royal Darkness

Venue: Montreal

Date: ?/85

Cover: D4C

Recording: 7

Source: St - Aud

Company: Buccaneer

Matrix #: n/a

Place Of Origin: Japan

DI:

Intro

Fortune Hunter

Found Somebody

Make Up Or Break Up

Prelude

Money Can't Buy

Satisfaction Guaranteed

Radioactive

All The King's Horses

Long Black Cadillac

You've Lost That Loving Feeling

Midnight Moonlight

Tear Down The Walls

Live in Peace

Session Man Into The 80's To The Future

Venue: Various
Date: Various
Cover: D4C
Recording: n/a
Source: n/a
Company: Patriot
Matrix #: n/a
Place Of Origin: Japan

D1:
Shake Your Maker (Santana)
Going Down (Jeff Beck)
Further On Up The Road
Cocaine
Roll Over Beethoven
Match Box
Goodnight Irene (Phil Collins & Eric Clapton)
I'm Down (Yes)
Unknown (Jaco Pastorius)
D2:
Unknown (Les Paul)
Lucille
Surfin USA
Barbara Ann (Beach Boys)
Bad News (Brian May & Bad News)
Train Kept A Rollin
Good Golly Miss Molly - Long Tall Sally
With A Little Help From My Friends (Bon Jovi)
Train Kept A Rollin
Walk This Way (Aerosmith)
Surfin USA
Barbara Ann (Beach Boys)
Think About It
Red House
Immigrant Song (Aerosmith)
Shapes Of Things
Happenings Ten Years Time Ago (Yardbirds)

Something Eles (The Firm)

Venue: Philadelphia - Studio
Date: 5/11/85 - ?/84*
Cover: D4C
Recording: 7 - 9
Source: St - SB
Company: Rag Doll
Matrix #: n/a
Place Of Origin: Japan

D1:
Closer
City Siren
Make Or Break
The Morning After
Together
Cadillac
Prelude
Money Can't Buy Love
Radioactive
Live In Peace
Midnight Moonlight
You've Lost That Loving Feeling
The Chase
D2:
The Chase
I Just Wanna Make Love
Someone To Love
Everybody Needs Somebody To Love
I Just Wanna Make Love*
A Girl Possessed*
Someone To Love*

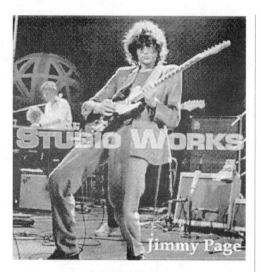

Studio Works

Venue: Sol Studio

Date: ?/82

Cover: D4C

Recording: 7

Source: St - SB

Company: Countdown Factory

Matrix #: CDF 942001A/B

Place Of Origin: Japan

D1:

Prelude

Carol's Theme

The Chase

Hypnotizing Ways (Oh Mama)

The Chase

Sax, And Violence

Shadow In The City

Hotel Rats

Shadow In The City

Jam Sandwich #1

Jam Sandwich #2

Jam Sandwich #3

Orchestra Tracks

The Fiesta

Fiesta Too

The Restaurant

Western Daze (Coverdale - Page)

Venue: Osaka
Date: 12/20/93 - 12/21/93*
Cover: D4C
Recording: 8
Source: St - Aud
Company: n/a
Matrix #: n/a
Place Of Origin: Japan
D1:
Absolution Blues
Slide It In
Rock & Roll
Over Now
Kashmir
Pride & Joy
Take A Look At Me Now
Take Me For A Little While
In My Time Of Dying
D2:
Here I Go Again
White Summer - Black Mountain Side
Don't Leave Me This Way
Shake My Tree
Still Of The Night
Out On The Tiles - Black Dog
The Ocean - Feelin' Hot
D3:
Absolution Blues*
Slide It In*
Rock & Roll*
Over Now*
Kashmir*
Pride & Joy*
Take A Look At Me Now*
Take Me For A Little While*
In My Time Of Dying*
D4:
Here I Go Again*
White Summer - Black Mountain Side*
Don't Leave Me This Way*
Shake My Tree*
Still Of The Night*
Out On The Tiles - Black Dog*
The Ocean - Feelin' Hot*

You Never Close Your Eyes (The Firm)

Venue: Costa Mesa
Date: 3/16/85
Cover: D4C
Recording: 8
Source: St - SB
Company: Midas Touch
Matrix #: MD 95521-95522
Place Of Origin: Japan

D1:
Closer
City Sirens
Make Or Break
The Morning After
Together
Cadillac
Prelude
Money Can't Buy Love
Radioactive
Live In Peace
Midnight Moonlight
D2:
You've Lost That Loving Feeling
The Chase
I Just Wanna Make Love
Someone To Love
Mama Boogie
Everybody Needs Somebody To Love

John Bonham Bootleg

John Henry Bonham Session Man

Venue: Various
Date: Various
Cover: D4C
Recording: 9
Source: St - SB
Company: RSR International
Matrix #: RSR 112CD
Place Of Origin: Japan

D1:
Wailing Sounds
Cause I Love You
Flashing Lights
Keep Your Hands On The Wheel
Jim's Blues
(Inc George Wallace Is Rolling In This Morning)
Thumping Beat
Union Jack Car
So Glad To See You Here
Baby Come Back
Rockestra Theme

John Paul Jones Counterfeit

Scream For Help Soundtrack

Venue: Studio (Counterfeit)
Date: Various
Cover: D4C
Recording: 10
Source: St - SB
Company: n/a
Matrix #: n/a
Place Of Origin: Japan

D1:
Spaghetti Junction
Bad Child
Silver Train
Crackback
Chilli Sauce
Take It Or Leave It
Christie
When You Fall In Love
Here I Am

Robert Plant Bootlegs

Forbidden Planet

Venue: London
Date: 2/3/88
Cover: D4C sleeve
Recording: n/a
Source: n/a
Company: Tarantura
Matrix #: MC001
Place Of Origin: Japan

D1:
Little By Little
Other Arms
Billy's Revenge
In The Evening
Big Log
Messin With The Mekon
Heaven Knows
Dimples
Heartbreaker
Trampled Underfoot
Tall Cool One
Custard Pie
Misty Mountain Hop
Break On Through

STEREO SOUNDBOARD • 2CD SET

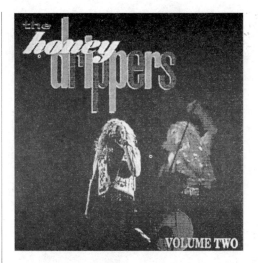

The Honeydrippers Blue Note Club

Venue: Nottingham

Date: 4/21/81

Cover: D4C

Recording: 7

Source: St - Aud

Company: Midas Touch

Matrix #: n/a

Place Of Origin: Japan

Dl:

Little Sister

Hey Mae

Lotta Lovin

You True Love

Deep In The Heart Of Texas

Honky Tonk

Cross Cut Saw

Bring It On Home

I Can't Be Satisfied

D2:

Treat Me Right

Born Under A Bad Sign

Keep On Loving Me Babe

What Can I Do

Tell Me How

Queen Of The Hop

She She Little Sheila

Got My Mojo Working

The Honeydrippers Volume Two

Venue: Nottingham

Date: 4/21/81

Cover: D4C

Recording: 7

Source: St - Aud

Company: n/a

Matrix #: n/a

Place Of Origin: Japan

Dl:

Little Sister

Hey Mae

Lotta Lovin

You True Love

Deep In The Heart Of Texas

Honky Tonk

Cross Cut Saw

Bring It On Home

I Can't Be Satisfied

D2:

Treat Me Right

Born Under A Bad Sign

Keep On Loving Me Babe

What Can I Do

Tell Me How

Queen Of The Hop

She She Little Sheila

Got My Mojo Working

In The Moonlight

Venue: Brighton

Date: 12/17/83

Cover: D4C

Recording: 9

Source: St - Aud

Company: Midas Touch

Matrix #: 95321-22

Place Of Origin: Europe

D1:

In The Mood

Pledge Pin

Messin With The Mekon

Worse Than Detroit

Thru WIth The Two Step

Other Arms

D2:

Horizontal Departure

Moonlight In Samosa

Wreckless Love

Slow Dancer

Like I've Never Been Gone

Let The Good Times Roll
Venue: Knebworth
Date: 6/30/90
Cover: D4C
Recording: 8
Source: St - SB
Company: n/a
Matrix #: n/a
Place Of Origin: Europe
Total Disc Time: 47.00

D1:
Hurting Kind (4.30)
Immigrant Song (3.37)
Tye Dye On The Highway (6.06)
Liar's Dance (4.14)
Going To California (4.18)
Nirvana (5.28)
Tall Cool One (5.18)
Misty Mountain Hop (5.04)
Wearing & Tearing (5.22)
Rock & Roll (3.28)

Midnight Rehearsals
Venue: Vancouver
Date: 6/9/85
Cover: D4C
Recording: 9
Source: St - SB
Company: Midas Touch
Matrix #: MS 61611
Place Of Origin: Japan
D1:
In The Mood (8:26)
Pledge Pin (5:17)
Pink And Black (5:13)
Doo Doo A Do Do (8:31)
Little By Little (8:46)
Burning Down One Side (4:06)

Rockin' At Midnight (4:36)

Young Boy Blues (7:07)

Once I Had A Girl (5:26)

Mellow Saxaphone (4:58)

Sea Of Love (3:36)

Honey Hush (7:05)

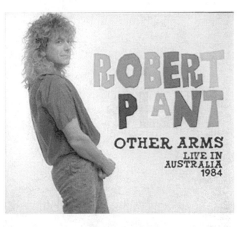

Misty Dancer

Venue: Cincinnatti - San Bernadino*

Date: ?/85 - ?/88*

Cover: D4C

Recording: n/a

Source: n/a

Company: Beech Morton

Matrix #: BM 075

Place Of Origin: Europe

D1:

In The Mood (8.24)

Little By Little (9.11)

Sea Of Love (2.57)

Burning Down One Side (4.56)

Big Log (7.07)

Pledge Pin (5.02)

Good Rockin' At Midnight (5.02)

Tall Cool One*

Trampled Underfoot*

Misty Mountain Hop*

Other Arms

Venue: Newcastle Australia

Date: 11/8/84

Cover: D4C

Recording: n/a

Source: n/a

Company: Midas Touch

Matrix #: 61721-22

Place Of Origin: Japan

D1:

In The Mood

Pledge Pin

Messin With The Mekon

Moonlight In Samosa

Fat Lip

Thru With The Two Step

Other Arms

D2:

Horizontal Departure

Wreckless Love

Slow Dancer

Like I've Never Been Gone

Past & Present

Venue: Philadelphia

Date: ?/84

Cover: D4C

Recording: 9

Source: St - SB

Company: Observation

Matrix #: OB 011

Place Of Origin: Europe

D1:

Heaven Knows (5.46)

In The Evening (8.54)

In The Mood (8.50)

Black Country Woman (5.10)

Ship Of Fools (5.56)

Dimples (6.35)

Trampled Underfoot (5.35)

Misty Mountain Hop (5.10)

Tall Cool One (6.54)

Promised Land

Venue: Perugia Blues Festival

Date: ?/93

Cover: D4C

Recording: 5

Source: St - Aud

Company: Insect

Matrix #: INT 19

Place Of Origin: Japan

D1:

Ramble On

I Believe

29 Palms

Bluebird

If I Were A Carpenter

Going To California

Promised Land

Calling To You

What Is And What Should Never Be

Ship Of Fools

Whole Lotta Love

29 Palms and I Plant

Venue: Amsterdam - London*

Date: 2/13/93 - 11/1/94*

Cover: D4C

Recording: 8

Source: St - SB

Company: Hammejack

Matrix #: HJ014

Place Of Origin: Europe

D1:

Interview

29 Palms

Thank You

In The Mood

Whole Lotta Love

Hurting

Kind

Ship Of Fools

If I Were A Carpenter

Going To California

Babe I'm Gonna Leave You

I Believe*

Ramble On

Venue: Montreux - Glastonbury*

Date: n/a

Cover: D4C

Recording: 9

Source: St - SB

Company: Why Not

Matrix #: n/a

Place Of Origin: Europe

D1:

Ramble On (5.28)

29 Palms (5.07)

Going To California (3.57)

If I Were A Carpenter (2.38)

Whole Lotta Love (4.45)

Calling To You (5.45)

Promised Land (8.05)

29 Palms (5.49)

Ship Of Fools (7.35)

Whole Lotta Love (7.40)

Led Zeppelin
Bootlegs

A15

Venue: Rotterdam
Date: 3/11/73
Cover: D4C
Recording: n/a
Source: M - Aud
Company: Diagrams of Led Zeppelin
Matrix #: Vol. 062
Place Of Origin: Japan
Total Disc Time: n/a
N.B. Recorded live at the Ahoyhalle in Rotterdam.

D1:
Rock and Roll
Over the Hills and Far Away
Black Dog
Misty Mountain Hop
Since I've Been Loving You
Dancing Days
Bron-y-Aur Stomp
Song Remains the Same
The Rain Song
D2:
Dazed and Confused
Stairway to Heaven
D3:
Whole Lotta Love
Heartbreaker
What Is and What Should Never Be

Acoustically

Venue: Melbourne
Date: 2/20/72
Cover: D4C
Recording: 5-7
Source: M - Aud
Company: Diagrams of Led Zeppelin
Matrix #: Vol 047
Place Of Origin: Japan
Total Disc Time: 53.08 - 39.22
N.B. Another nice package from Diagrams of Led Zeppelin. This particular piece borrows its cover art from the Australian 45. A superior version of the tape.

D1:
Immigrant Song
Heartbreaker
Black Dog
Since I've Been Loving You
Stairway to Heaven
Going to California
That's the Way
Tangerine
Bron-y-Aur Stomp
D2:
Dazed and Confused
Rock and Roll
Whole Lotta Love

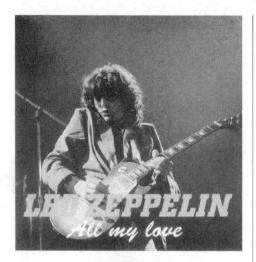

All My Love

Venue: Rotterdam

Date: 6/21/80

Cover: D4C in case

Recording: 8

Source: St - SB

Company: Pipeline

Matrix #: PPL 512

Place Of Origin: Italy

Total Disc Time: 64.55

N.B. A straight knock off of "Live in Rotterdam 1980" by Neutral Zone.

D1:

The Rain Song (8.00)

Hot Dog (3.45)

All My Love (5.51)

Trampled Underfoot (7.50)

Since I've Been Loving You (9.03)

Achilles Last Stand (9.15)

Kashmir (10.32)

Rock & Roll (4.15)

Heartbreaker (6.53)

All My Love

Venue: Polar Studios

Date: 11/?/78

Cover: D4C sleeve with inner sleeve

Recording: 8

Source: St - SB

Company: Tarantura

Matrix #: NO.16000

Place Of Origin: Japan

Total Disc Time: 70.38

N.B. Limited edition of 300 with fifty of each of six different inner sleeves.

D1:

Carouselambra

Untitled

Wearing And Tearing

Fool In The Rain

Hot Dog

In The Evening

South Bound Saurez

Darlene

Fool In The Rain

Carouselambra

All My Love

All My Love

All That Jazz

Venue: Montreux
Date: 3/7/70
Cover: D4C
Recording: 7-8
Source: M - Aud
Company: Diagram's of Led Zeppelin
Matrix #: TDOLZ 339701/339702
Place Of Origin: Japan
Total Disc Time: 44.04 - 45.16

N.B. Just another reissue of the well circulated Montreux tape. Previously available as the titles We're Gonna Groove, Feel All Right, and Dark Tower. This tape seems to have been subjected to many different problems with pitch control. Some of these titles either run too fast or too slow. Once again the cover incorrectly lists this as being from the 14th.

D1:
We're Gonna Groove
I Can't Quit You
White Summer/Black Mountain Side
Dazed and Confused
Heartbreaker
Since I've Been Loving You
D2:
Thank You
What Is and What Should Never Be
Moby Dick
How Many More Times (Cut)

American Accents

Venue: Raleigh
Date: 4/8/70
Cover: D4C
Recording: 4-6
Source: M - Aud
Company: Baby Face
Matrix #: 9663
Place Of Origin: Japan
Total Disc Time: n/a

N.B. Previously available as the title Fearsome Four Live Onstage. The cover incorrectly lists this as being from the seventh of April. It has recently been confirmed that this show took place on the eighth.

D1:
We're Gonna Groove
Dazed and Confused
Heartbreaker
Bring It on Home
White Summer-Black Mountain Side
Since I've Been Loving You
Thank You
What Is and What Should Never Be
Moby Dick

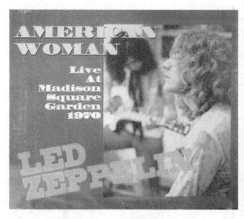

American Woman

Venue: New York

Date: 9/19/70

Cover: D4C Sleeve

Recording: 5

Source: M -Aud

Company: Diagrams Of Led Zeppelin

Matrix #: TDOLZ 18/19

Place Of Origin: Japan

Total Disc Time: n/a

N.B. Another new show on bootleg. Not a very good recording. Actually a combination of two different tapes. Part of this show was released as "Maui Wowie".

American Beauty

Venue: San Francisco

Date: 4/27/69

Cover: D4C Sleeve

Recording: 9

Source: St- SB

Company: Tarantura

Matrix #: SFSB-1,2.

Place Of Origin: Japan

Total Disc Time: 66:25 - 33:34

N.B. Another re-issue of the San Francisco tape.

D1:

Train Kept A Rollin' (3.00)

I Can't Quit You (6.15)

As Long As I Have You (Inc. Fresh Garbage-Shake-Cat's Squirrel-Cadillac, No Money Down-I'm A Man) (20.01)

You Shook Me (9.50)

How Many More Times

(Inc. Feel So Bad-The Hunter-Mulberry Bush) (19.44)

Killing Floor (7.35)

D2:

Babe I'm Gonna Leave You (7.11)

Sitting And Thinking (7.48)

Dazed And Confused (13.13)

Communication Breakdown (5.22)

D1:

Immigrant Song

Heartbreaker

Dazed And Confused

Bring It On Home

That's The Way

Bron-y-Aur

Since I've Been Loving You

Thank You

What Is And What Should Never Be

D2:

Moby Dick

Whole Lotta Love

Communication Breakdown Medley

(Inc. American Woman)

Another IV Symbols

Venue: Headley Grange

Date: 1/?/71

Cover: D4C gatefold sleeve with hot foil

Recording: 8

Source: St - SB

Company: Tarantura

Matrix #: TCD-4

Place Of Origin: Japan

Total Disc Time: 43.30

N.B. Another re-issue of the Headley Grange rehearsals for the fourth album.

D1:

Stairway To Heaven (Instrumental)

Untitled Instrumental

Untitled Instrumental

Black Dog

No Quarter

Stairway To Heaven (Instrumental)

Untitled Instrumental

Stairway To Heaven

Stairway To Heaven

Another Trip

Venue: Studio[1] - London[2,5,6,7,16] - Staines[3] - San Francisco[4] - Los Angeles[8] - Toronto[10] - Osaka[11] - Olympic Studio[12] - Island Studio[9] - Chicago[13] - New York[14] - Dallas[15] - Cleveland[17] - Knebworth[18] - Rotterdam[19] - Nuremburg[20] - Zurich[21] - Frankfurt[22] - Berlin[23]

Date: 9/27/68[1] - 3/3/69[2] - 3/25/69[3] - 4/27/69[4] - 6/16/69[5] - 6/24/69[6] - 3/?/70[7] - 9/4/70[8] - 9/4/71[10] - 9/29/71[11] - 5/?/72[12,9] - 7/6/73[13] - 7/29/73[14] - 3/4/75[15] - 5/24/75[16] - 4/27/77[17] - 8/4/79[18] - 6/21/80[19] - 6/27/80[20] - 6/29/80[21] - 6/30/80[22] - 7/7/80[23]

Cover: D4C boxset

Recording: 7 - 10

Source: St - SB, St - Aud, M - SB

Company: Big Music

Matrix #: BIG BX 007 - 4023 4024 4025 4026 4027

Place Of Origin: Italy

Total Disc Time: 74.16 - 74.57 - 74.14 - 78.02 - 78.38

N.B. A mish-mash of studio and live material in a very nicely presented package.

D1:

Gotta Find My Baby (Demo '67) (3:50)

You Shook Me (7:31) [1]

Communication Breakdown (2:58) [2]

Dazed And Contused (7.38) [3]

Train Kept A Rollin' (2:54) [4]

I Can't Quit You Baby (5:58) [4]

How Many More Times (19:23) [4]

Babe I'm Gonna Leave You (7:30) [4]

Sittin' And Thinkin' (7:00) [4]

The Girl I Love (2:59) [5]

Something Else (2:06) [5]

What Is And What Should Never Be (4:24) [6]
D2:

White Summer-Black Mountain Side (5:04) [7]

John Paul Jones Organ Improvisation (6:00) [8]

Out On The Tiles (4:07) [8]

Blueberry Hill (3:17) [8]

Bring It On Home (9:47) [8]

Whole Lotta Love Medley (17:13) [8]
(Inc. Boogie Chillen - Movin' On - I've Got A Girl -
Some Other Guy - Think it Over - The Lemon Song)

Moby Dick (15:34) [10]

Friends (5:21) [11]

The Rover (1:03) [12]

No Quarter (7:27) [9]
D3:

Schooldays (2:42) [13]

Nadine (1:02) [13]

Round And Round (3:03) [13]

Move On Down The Line (2:06) [13]

Shakin' All Over (2:31) [13]

Rock And Roll (4:02) [14]

Celebration Day (3:26) [14]

Black Dog (6:43) [14]

Over The Hills And Far Away (6:56) [14]

Misty Mountain Hop (4:56) [14]

Since I've Been Loving You (8:46) [14]

No Quarter (13:38) [14]

The Song Remains The Same (5:29) [14]

The Rain Song (8:49) [14]
D4:

Sick Again (5:35) [15]

Kashmir (9:44) [15]

Trampled Underfoot (8:11) [15] Tangerine (6:26) [16]

That's The Way (8:47) [16]

Ten Years Gone (6:13) [16]

Battle Of Evermore (6:00) [17]

Black Country Woman (2:35) [17]

Bron Y Aur Stomp (5:00) [17]

Jimmy Page Guitar Solo (9:51) [17]

Achilles Last Stand (9:37) [17]
D5:

Hot Dog (3:11) [18]

All My Love (5:39) [19]

Nobody's Fault But Mine (6:21) [20]

Black Dog (6:35) [20]

In The Evening (10:46) [21]

Stairway To Heaven (11:47) [21]

Heartbreaker (9:59) [21]

Money (5:19) [22]

Whole Lotta Love (18:59) [23]

Arabesque & Baroque
Venue: London
Date: 5/17/75
Cover: D4C sleeve
Recording: 7
Source: M -Aud
Company: Antrabata
Matrix #: ARM 170575
Place Of Origin: Europe
Total Disc Time:

D1:
Intro,
Rock And Roll,
Sick Again,
Over The Hills And Far Away,
In My Time Of Dying,
The Song Remains The Same,
The Rain Song,
Kashmir
D2:
No Quarter,
Tangerine,
Going To California,
That's The Way,
Bron-Y-Aur Stomp,
Trampled Underfoot
D3:
Moby Dick,
Dazed And Confused,
Stairway To Heaven,
Whole Lotta Love,
Black Dog

Arabesque & Baroque /
The Second Night

Venue: London
Date: 5/18/75
Cover: D4C sleeve
Recording: 7
Source: M -Aud
Company: ANTRABATA
Matrix #: ARM 180575
Place Of Origin: Europe
Total Disc Time:
N.B. Limited edition of 325 numbered copies

D1:
Rock And Roll,
Sick Again,
Over The Hills And Far Away,
In My Time Of Dying,
The Song Remains The Same,
The Rain Song,
Kashmir
D2:
No Quarter
D3:
Tangerine,
Going To California,
That's The Way,
Bron-Y-Aur Stomp,
Trampled Underfoot,
Moby Dick
D4:
Dazed And Confused,
Stairway To Heaven,
Whole Lotta Love,
Black Dog

Arabesque & Baroque /
The Third Night

Venue: London
Date: 5/23/75
Cover: D4C sleeve
Recording: 7
Source: M -Aud
Company: ANTRABATA
Matrix #: ARM 250371
Place Of Origin: Europe
Total Disc Time: n/a
N.B. Limited edition of 325 numbered copies

D1:
Immigrant Song
Heartbreaker
Since I've Been Loving You
Black Dog
Dazed And Confused
Stairway To Heaven
D2:
Going To California
That's The Way
What Is And What Should Never Be
Whole Lotta Love
Thank You
Communication Breakdown

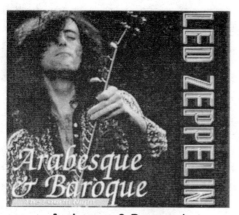

Arabesque & Baroque/
The Fourth Night

Venue: London - Bremen*
Date: 5/24/1975 - 6/23/1980*
Cover: D4C sleeve
Recording: 9
Source: St -SB
Company: Antrabata
Matrix #: ARM 200680/ARM230680
Place Of Origin: Europe
Total Disc Time: n/a
N.B. Limited edition of 325 numbered copies

DI:
Train Kept A Rollin'
Nobody's Fault But Mine
Black Dog
In The Evening
The Rain Song
Hot Dog
All My Love
Trampled Underfoot
Since I've Been Loving You
D2:
Achilles Last Stand
White Summer - Black Mountain Side - Kashmir
Stairway To Heaven
Rock And Roll
Whole Lotta Love
D3:
Train Kept A Rollin',
Nobody's Fault But Mine
Black Dog,
In The Evening
The Rain Song
Hot Dog
All My Love
Trampled Underfoot
Since I've Been Loving You
D4 :
Achilles Last Stand
White Summer - Black Mountain Side - Kashmir
Stairway To Heaven
Rock And Roll,
Communication Breakdown

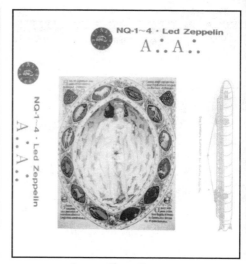

Argentium Astrum

Venue: London
Date: 5/18/75
Cover: D4C sleeve
Recording: 7
Source: M -Aud
Company: Tarantura
Matrix #: NQ 1~4
Place Of Origin: Japan
Total Disc Time: n/a
N.B. Another re-issue of this well circulated audience
recording in a beautifully packaged box sleeve.

DI:
Rock And Roll
Sick Again
Over The Hills And Far Away
In My Time Of Dying
The Song Remains The Same
The Rain Song
Kashmir
D2:
No Quarter
Tangerine
Going To California
That's The Way
Bron-Y-Aur Stomp
Trampled Underfoot
D3:
Moby Dick
Dazed And Confused
Stairway To Heaven
D4:
Whole Lotta Love
Black Dog

Art Disc

Venue: Studio

Date: n/a

Cover: D4C

Recording: 10

Source: St - SB

Company: Big Artist

Matrix #: ADC 1-8

Place Of Origin: Japan

Total Disc Time: n/a

N.B. A straight pirate knock off of various studio tracks.

D1:

Immigrant Song

Good Times Bad Times

Whole Lotta Love

Custard Pie

I Can't Quit You

Rock & Roll

Over The Hills & Far Away

Going To California

Royal Orleans

Black Dog

Stairway To Heaven

At The Beeb 1971

Venue: London

Date: 4/1/71

Cover: D4C in case

Recording: 9

Source: St - SB

Company: Cuttlefish

Matrix #: CFR 009

Place Of Origin: Japan

Total Disc Time: 64.14

N.B. Another re-issue of the edited BBC broadcast.

D1:

The Immigrant Song (3.29)

Heartbreaker (5.42)

Black Dog (5.40)

Going To California (4.34)

That's The Way (6.08)

What Is & What Should Never Be (4.31)

Communication Breakdown (5.34)

Stairway To Heaven (8.47)

Whole Lotta Love Medley (19.49)

(Inc. Boogie Chillen - Mess Of Blues - My Baby Left Me -

Mess Of Blues - The Lemon Song)

At The Beeb 1971

Venue: London

Date: 3/25/71

Cover: D4C

Recording: 9

Source: St - SB

Company: Cuttlefish

Matrix #: CFR 009

Place Of Origin: Europe

Total Disc Time: n/a

N.B. Another BBC reissue.

D1:

Immigrant Song

Heartbreaker

Black Dog

Going To California

That's The Way

What Is & What Should Never Be

Communication Breakdown

Stairway To Heaven

Whole Lotta Love Medley (Inc. Boogie Chillen - My Baby

Left Me - Mess Of Blues - Lemon Song)

Back To The Garden

Venue: New York

Date: 6/7/77

Cover: D4C

Recording: 7

Source: M - Aud

Company: Diagrams Of Led Zeppelin

Matrix #: TDOLZ 0025/26/27

Place Of Origin: Japan

Total Disc Time: 67:52 - 49:58 - 61:31

N.B. Another interesting new release from this prolific Japanese label.

D1;

The Song Remains The Same

The Rover intro.-Sick Again

Nobody's Fault But Mine

In My Time of Dying

Since I've Been Loving You

No Quarter

D2:

Ten Years Gone

The Battle of Evermore

Going to California

Black Country Woman

Bron-Y-Aur Stomp

White Summer - Black Mountain Side

Kashmir

D3:

Out on Tiles intro.-Moby Dick

Guitar Solo

Achilles Last Stand

Stairway to Heaven

Whole Lotta Love

Rock And Roll

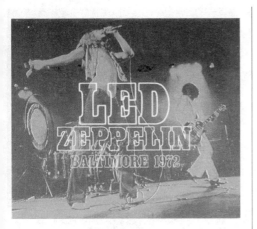

Baltimore 1972

Venue: Baltimore

Date: 6/11/72

Cover: D4C in double case

Recording: 4

Source: M - Aud

Company: Immigrant

Matrix #: IM 026 - 028

Place Of Origin: Japan

Total Disc Time: 55.57 - 68.30 - 36.42

N.B. Really poor audience recording.

D1:

Immigrant Song (4.15)

Heartbreaker (10.39)

Black Dog (6.45)

Since I've Been Loving You (9.10)

Stairway To Heaven (12.24)

Going To California (5.56)

That's the Way (6.48)

D2:

Tangerine (4.08)

Bron-y-Aur Stomp (6.13)

Dazed & Confused (23.36)

What Is & What Should Never Be (5.54)

Moby Dick (28.39)

D3:

Whole Lotta Love Medley (27.51)

(Inc. Boogie Chillen - I Need Your Love Tonight -

Hello Mary Lou - Heartbreak Hotel -

I'm Going Down - Going Down Slow)

Rock & Roll (4.38)

Communication Breakdown (4.13)

BBC

Venue: London **Date:** 6/16/69-3/3/69-6/24/69-4/26/70-6/27/69-3/25/71 **Cover:** D4C **Recording:** 8-9 **Source:** M-SB, St-SB **Company:** Last Stand Disc **Matrix #:** LSD 05/06/07/08 **Place Of Origin:** Japan **Total Disc Time:** n/a **N.B.** Although I haven't heard this piece personally, I suspect that if the quality is as good as it should be then this may actually be better than the official release, mainly because it is apparently the complete broadcasts. It even includes the Jimmy Page appearance on the Julie Felix show.

D1: Interview with Chris Grant

The Girl I Love

Communication Breakdown

What Is and What Should Never Be

Something Else

You Shook Me

I Can't Quit You

Communication Breakdown

Dazed and Confused

What Is and What Should Never Be

Whole Lotta Love

Communication Breakdown

White Summer-Black Mountain Side

D2: Communication Breakdown

I Can't Quit You

Dazed and Confused

White Summer-Black Mountain Side

You Shook Me

How Many More Times

D3: Introduction

Immigrant Song

Heartbreaker

since I've Been Loving You

Black Dog

Dazed and Confused

Stairway to Heaven

Going to California

That's the Way

D4: What Is and What Should Never Be

Whole Lotta Love

Thank You

Communication Breakdown

BBC Zep

Venue: London

Date: 3/25/1971

Cover: D4C sleeve

Recording: 8

Source: St - SB

Company: Antrabata

Matrix #: ARM 250371

Place Of Origin: Europe

Total Disc Time: n/a

N.B. Another re-issue of the BBC concerts. Nothing special

D1:

Immigrant Song,

Heartbreaker,

Since I've Been Loving You,

Black Dog,

Dazed And Confused,

Stairway To Heaven

D2:

Going To California,

That's The Way,

What Is And What Should Never Be,

Whole Lotta Love,

Thank You,

Communication Breakdown

BBC Zep Original Master

Venue: London

Date: 4/1/71

Cover: D4C sleeve

Recording: 9

Source: St - SB

Company: Tarantura

Matrix #: T2 - CD 7 1,2

Place Of Origin: Japan

Total Disc Time: n/a

N.B. Just another of the (hopefully) now redundant BBC tapes. If there's any justice in the world now that the band have released this show (changed somewhat) we won't see anymore bootlegs of it.

D1:

Immigrant Song (3:25)

Heartbreaker (5:25)

Since I've Been Loving You (7:20)

Black Dog (5:02)

Dazed And Contused (19:35)

Stairway To Heaven (8:21)

D2:

Going To California (4:23)

That's The Way (6:12)

What Is And What Should Never Be (4:12)

Whole Lotta Love Medley: (21:35) (Inc. Boogie Chillen - Truckin' Little Mama - Fixin' To Die - That's Alright - For What's It's Worth - Mess Of Blues - Honey Bee - Lemon Song)

Thank You (7:23)

Communication Breakdown (5:30)

Beast Of Toronto

Venue: Toronto

Date: 11/2/69

Cover: DBW in case

Recording: 5 -6

Source: M - Aud

Company: Immigrant

Matrix#: IM043

Place Of Origin: Japan

Total Disc Time: 68.11

N.B. A quite nice previously unreleased recording   replete with photos on the cover from the period. The band perform an unusually daring mixture of improvisations.

D1:

Good Times Bad Times -

Communication Breakdown (4.46)

I Can't Quit You (7.23)

Heartbreaker (5.37)

Dazed & Confused (18.27)

White Summer/ Black Mountain Side (12.50)

Babe I'm Gonna Leave You (6.57)

Moby Dick (12.11)

Berdu

Venue: San Bernadino

Date: 6/22/72

Cover: D4C sleeve

Recording: 5 -6

Source: M - Aud

Company: Cobra

Matrix#: 010

Place Of Origin: Japan

Total Disc Time: n/a

N.B. A knock off of the vinyl title.

D1:

Immigrant Song (4.00)

Heartbreaker (7.11)

Since I've Been Loving You (8.32)

Stairway To Heaven (9.48)

Dazed And Confused (28.12)

(Inc. The Crunge - Route 66 - Born To Be Wild)

Going To California (7.18)

D2:

That's The Way (6.45)

Tangerine (3.08)

Bron-Y-Aur Stomp (4.48)

What Is And What Should Never Be (4.30)

Moby Dick (12.11)

Whole Lotta Love Medley (22.04) (Inc. Boogie Chillen -

Let's Have A Party - Mary Lou - Going Down Slow)

Rock And Roll (4.32)

Best Of Artist Selection

Venue: Studio

Date: n/a

Cover: D4C

Recording: 10

Source: St - SB

Company: Golden Age Of Popular

Matrix #: CA 10041

Place Of Origin: Japan

Total Disc Time: n/a

N.B. A straight pirate knock off of various studio tracks.

D1:

Lemon Song

That's The Way

Bring It On Home

Tangerine

Thank You

Living Loving Maid

Whole Lotta Love

Immigrant Song

Since I've Been Loving You

Heartbreaker

Friends

Celebration Day

Black Dog

Rock & Roll

Stairway To Heaven

Good Times Bad Times

The Best Vibes In Frisco

Venue: San Francisco

Date: 6/2/73

Cover: D4C

Recording: 7

Source: M -Aud

Company: Jerry Roll

Matrix #: JR04/05

Place Of Origin: Japan

Total Disc Time: n/a

N.B. Not many details available on this title at press time.

D1:

Rock & Roll

Celebration Day

Black Dog

Over The Hills & Far Away

Misty Mountain Hop

Since I've Been Loving You

No Quarter

Song Remains The Same

Rain Song

Dazed & Confused

D2:

Stairway To Heaven

Moby Dick(cut)

Heartbreaker

Whole Lotta Love

Communication Breakdown

The Ocean

Birth Of The Gods

Venue: San Francisco - Kansas City*

Date: 1/11/69 - 11/5/69*

Cover: D4C in case

Recording: n/a

Source: n/a

Company: Balboa

Matrix#: BP 0001

Place Of Origin: Japan

Total Disc Time: n/a

N.B. All details are not available but this certainly includes the newly found tape from Kansas City.

Billboard Hits USA

Venue: Studio

Date: n/a

Cover: D4C

Recording: 10

Source: St - SB

Company: Billboard Hits

Matrix #: B 0017

Place Of Origin: Japan

Total Disc Time: n/a

N.B. A straight pirate knock off of various studio tracks in a cardboard long box.

D1:

Black Dog

Rock & Roll

Whole Lotta Love

Immigrant Song

Tangerine

Living Loving Maid

Stairway To Heaven

Heartbreaker

Lemon Song

Thank You

Since I've Been Loving You

That's The Way

D1:

I Can't Quit You

Dazed & Confused

You Shook Me

How Many More Times

Communication Breakdown*

I Can't Quit You*

Heartbreaker*

Dazed & Confused*

How Many More Times*

Bizarre

Venue: London-Clearwell Castle-Hollywood

Date: ?/1974-5/78-9/75

Cover: D4C

Source: n/a

Recording: n/a

Company: Tarantura

Matrix #: RH001

Place Of Origin: Japan

Total Disc Time: n/a

N.B. Interesting that this tape should suddenly appear. It makes you wonder where it came from. Don't know whether it's sound board or audience but the material from Clearwell Castle is recorded live in the rehearsal room. The first three trackjs are from the performance at the Rainbow theatre in London where Roy Harper appeared with amongst others three members of Led Zeppelin and Keith Moon.

D1:

Male Chauvinist Pig Blues

Too Many Movies

Home

Untitled

Carouselambra

Carouselambra

Carouselambra

Carouselambra

Untitled Blues Jam

Blaze

Venue: Baton Rouge

Date: 2/28/75

Cover: D2C

Recording: 6 - 7

Source: St -Aud

Company: Immigrant

Matrix #: 040 - 042

Place Of Origin: Japan

Total Disc Time: n/a

N.B. Another reissue of the Baton Rouge show. Also available as "Bon Soir Baton Rouge", "Freeze", and "Led Astray".

D1:

Rock & Roll - Sick Again (10.07)

Over The Hills & Far Away (7.37)

In My Time Of Dying (11.42)

The Song Remains The Same (5.24)

The Rain Song (8.26)

Kashmir (9.06)

D2:

No Quarter (19.27)

Trampled Underfoot (10.32)

Moby Dick (27.00)

D3:

Dazed & Confused (

Stairway To Heaven (12.42)

Whole Lotta Love - Black Dog (14.02)

Blow Up

Venue: San Francisco

Date: 11/6/69

Cover: D4C

Recording: n/a

Source: n/a

Company: Immigrant

Matrix #: IM 029 - 030

Place Of Origin: Japan

Total Disc Time: n/a

N.B. All track information not available at press time. Previously unreleased show.

D1:
Opening (1.28)
Good Times Bad Times (0.34)
Communication Breakdown (3.13)
I Can't Quit You (7.19)
Heartbreaker (5.36)
Dazed & Confused (18.21)
White Summer/Black Mountain Side (13.03)
D2:
What Is & What Should Never Be (5.21)
Moby Dick (12.09)
How Many More Times Medley (22.18)
(Inc. The Hunter - Boogie Chillen -
Move On Down the Line - The Lemon Song)
C'mon Everybody (3.00)
Something Else (2.25)

Blueberry Hill

Venue: Los Angeles - Dusseldorf*

Date: 9/4/70 - 3/11/70*

Cover: D4C in double case

Recording :8, 6*

Source: St - Aud - M - Aud *

Company: Roundpin

Matrix#: LZCD 522/1

Place Of Origin: Luxembourg

Total Disc Time: 71.03 - 57.21

N.B. A re-issue of the tape used for the Tarantura piece "Live On Blueberry Hill" with the addition of a track from the tape which is currently credited to Dusseldorf.

D1:
Immigrant Song (3.25)
Heartbreaker (6.27)
Dazed & Confused (cut) (16.42)
Bring It On Home (9.30)
That's The Way (7.05)
Bron-y-Aur (5.36)
Since I've Been Loving You (6.58)
Organ Improvisation (5.57)*
Thank You (7.02)*
What Is & What Should Never Be (cut) (4.29)
D2:
Whole Lotta Love Medley (cut) (17.24)
(Inc. Boogie Chillen- Movin On- I've Got A Girl- Some
Other Guy- Think It Over- The Lemon Song)
Communication Breakdown Medley (10.12)
(Inc. Good Times Bad Times-For What It's Worth-
I Saw Her Standing There)
Out On The Tiles (3.30)
Blueberry Hill (3.55)
How Many More Times Medley (20.57)*
(Inc. Bolero - The Hunter -
High Flying Mama - The Lemon Song)

Blue Box

Venue: Various

Date: n/a

Cover: D2C

Recording: 10

Source: St -SB

Company: Atlantic

Matrix #: 7567-80516-2

Place Of Origin: Japan

Total Disc Time: n/a

N.B. A compilation of the second third and fourth

albums. Could be legit.

Bonham Sessions (The)

Venue: Studio - London
Date: Various - 4/1/71
Cover: D4C in case
Recording: 9 - 10
Source: St - SB
Company: Hammerjack
Matrix #: HJ-013
Place Of Origin: Italy
Total Disc Time: 78.52

N.B. A CD version of the bootleg LP "John Henry Bonham - Session Man" but with some bonus tracks taken from various Zeppelin tapes. Tracks 1-3,7 & 8 from Lord Sutch and Heavy Friends, track 4 from Roy Wood's album "On the Road Again", tracks 5 & 6 from PJ Proby album "Three Week Hero", tracks 9 & 10 from the Wings "Back To The Egg", track 11 from the album "Concert For The People Of Kampuchea", tracks 12 & 13 from May 1970 rehearsal, tracks 14-21 from Headley Grange rehearsal 1974 and track 22 from 4/1/71 BBC session.

D1:
Wailing Sounds (2:37)
Cause I Love You (2:45)
Flashing Lights (3:11)
Keep Your Hands On The Wheel (4:20)
Jim's Blues (3:41)
George Wallace Is Rolling' In This Morning(2:22)
Thumping Beat (3:07)
Union Jack Car (3:00)
So Glad To See You Here (3:33)
Baby Come Back (2:33)
Rockestra Theme (4:23)
Immigrant Song (2:42)
Out On The Tiles (3:38)
Custard Pie (4:47)
The Rover (2:05)
In My Time Of Dying (7:12) Trampled Underfoot (3:52)
In The Light (5:22)
The Wanton Song (3:32)
Sick Again (3:38)
Hots On For Nowhere (4:08)
Going To California (3:48)

Bon Soir Baton Rouge

Venue: Baton Rouge

Date: 2/28/75

Cover: D4C in double slimline case

Recording: 6 - 7

Source: St - Aud

Company: Capricorn

Matrix #: CR 2028-29

Place Of Origin: Australia

Total Disc Time: 71.54 - 64.16

N.B. The cover says limited to 1000 numbered copies.

D1:

Rock & Roll - Sick Again (10.07)

Over The Hills & Far Away (7.37)

In My Time Of Dying (11.42)

The Song Remains The Same (5.24)

The Rain Song (8.26)

Kashmir (9.06)

No Quarter (19.27)

D2:

Trampled Underfoot (10.32)

Moby Dick (27.00)

Stairway To Heaven (12.42)

Whole Lotta Love - Black Dog (14.02)

Bonzo's Birthday Party

Venue: Los Angeles

Date: 5/31/73

Cover: D4C sleeve

Recording: 5 - 8

Source: M - Aud

Company: Cobra Standard

Matrix #: 002

Place Of Origin: Japan

Total Disc Time: n/a

N.B. A more complete tape than the original vinyl release of this title.

D1:

Rock & Roll

Celebration Day

Black Dog

Over The Hills & Far Away

Misty Mountain Hop (4.50)

Since I've Been Loving You

No Quarter (12.15)

D2:

The Song Remains The Same (5.23)

The Rain Song (9.03)

Dazed & Confused

Stairway To Heaven

D3:

Moby Dick

Happy Birthday - Heartbreaker (7.25)

Whole Lotta Love (12.12) (Incl. Boogie Chillen)

Communication Breakdown

The Ocean (5.04)

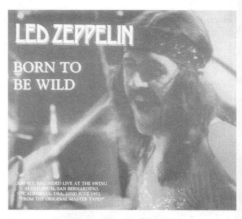

Bonzo's 25th Birthday

Venue: Los Angeles

Date: 5/31/73

Cover: D4C in double case

Recording: n/a

Source: n/a

Company: ARMS

Matrix #: ARMS 31 32 33

Place Of Origin: Japan

Total Disc Time: n/a

N.B. All track information not available at press time.

DI:

Rock And Roll (3.59)

Celebration Day (3.25)

Black Dog (6.48)

Over The Hills And Far Away (6.22)

Misty Mountain Hop (4.43)

Since I've Been Loving You (7.55)

No Quarter (13.12)

The Song Remains The Same (5.35)

The Rain Song (8.36)

D2:

Dazed And Confused (28.35)

Stairway To Heaven (9.25)

D3:

Moby Dick (16.14)

Happy Birthday (0.35)

Heartbreaker (6.25)

Whole Lotta Love (11.27)

The Ocean (4.16)

Born To Be Wild

Venue: San Bernadino

Date: 6/22/72

Cover: D4C in double case

Recording: 4 - 5

Source: M - Aud

Company: Whole Lotta Live

Matrix #: WLL 018 - 019

Place Of Origin: Italy

Total Disc Time: 58.56 - 73.07

N.B. A straight knock off of the Tarantura title "Route 66" discs one and two.

DI:

Immigrant Song (4.00)

Heartbreaker (7.11)

Black Dog (5.32)

Since I've Been Loving You (8.32)

Stairway To Heaven (9.48)

Going To California (7.18)

That's The Way (6.45)

Tangerine (3.08)

Bron-Y-Aur Stomp (4.48)

D2:

Dazed And Confused (28.12)

(Inc. The Crunge - Route 66 - Born To Be Wild)

What Is And What Should Never Be (4.30)

Moby Dick (12.11)

Whole Lotta Love Medley (22.04)

(Inc. Boogie Chillen - Let's Have A Party -

Mary Lou - Going Down Slow)

Rock And Roll (4.32)

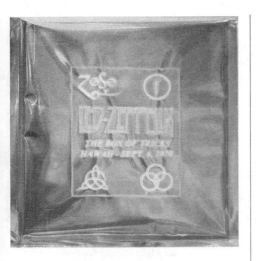

The Box Of Tricks

Venue: Honolulu

Date: 9/6/70

Cover: B&W sleeve in foil bag

Recording: 6

Source: M - Aud

Company: RED HOT

Matrix #: RH-023

Place Of Origin: Japan

Total Disc Time: 74.50

N.B. Excellent package with a gold foil bag covering a deluxe sleeve. Limited to 750 numbered copies.

D1:

Immigrant Song

Dazed And Confused

Heartbreaker

Since I've Been Loving You

What Is And What Should Never Be

Moby Dick

Whole Lotta Love

Communication Breakdown

Bradford UK 1973

Venue: Bradford

Date: 1/18/73

Cover: D4C sleeve

Recording: 4

Source: M - Aud

Company: Diagrams Of Led Zeppelin

Matrix #: TDOLZ 209701/2

Place Of Origin: Japan

Total Disc Time: n/a

N.B. A new tape. A poor recording of the Bradford gig.

D1:

Rock & Roll

Over The Hills & Far Away

Black Dog

Misty Mountain Hop

Since I've Been Loving You

Dancing Days

Bron-y-Aur Stomp

Song Remains The Same

Rain Song

Dazed & Confused

D2:

Stairway To Heaven

Whole Lotta Love

Heartbreaker

Bremen 1980

Venue: Bremen
Date: 6/23/80
Cover: D4C gatefold
Recording: 9
Source: St - SB
Company: Tarantura
Matrix #: 1980-9,10
Place Of Origin: Japan
Total Disc Time: n/a

N.B. Part of the deluxe set "1980" and also available separately as this two CD set. Nothing special it is the well documented soundboard tape.

D1:
Train Kept A Rollin'
Nobody's Fault But Mine
Black Dog
In The Evening
Rain Song
Hot Dog
All My Love
Trampled Underfoot
D2:
Since I've Been Loving You
Achilles Last Stand
White Summer - Black Mountain Side
Kashmir
Stairway To Heaven
Rock & Roll
Communication Breakdown

Bring It On Home

Venue: Tampa - Hamburg*
Date: 4/9/70 - 3/12/70*
Cover: D4C in double case
Recording: n/a
Source: n/a
Company: POT
Matrix #: POT 008-009
Place Of Origin: Japan
Total Disc Time: n/a

N.B. All track information not available at press time. First release of the Hamburg material on CD.

D1:
Since I've Been Loving You (7.01) *
White Summer/Black Mountain Side (10.38)*
Dazed & Confused (18.56)*
Intro - Bring It On Home (2:42 (Cut)
White Summer (5:44)
Black Mountain She (6:34)
Since I've Been Loving You (7:12)
D2:
Organ Solo (3:34) - Thank You (5:45)
What Is And What Should Never Be (1 :44 cut)
Moby Dick (18:12)
How Many More Times Medley: (22:18)
(Inc. Ravels Bolero - The Hunter - Boogie Chillen -
Trucking Little Mama - Mess Of Blues -
My Baby Don't Love Me - Lemon Song)
Whole Lotta Love (7:44)

Broken Fingers

Venue: Stoke

Date: 1/15/73

Cover: D4C

Recording: 8

Source: St -SB

Company: Image Quality

Matrix #: IQ 001/2

Place Of Origin: Japan

Total Disc Time: n/a

N.B. Another re-issue of the Stoke soundboard.

D1:

Rock & Roll (4.13)

Over The Hills & Far Away (5.57)

Black Dog (6.20)

Misty Mountain Hop (4.54)

Since I've Been Loving You (8.16)

Dancing Days (4.32)

Bron-y-Aur Stomp (6.28)

Song Remains The Same (5.06)

Rain Song (7.15)

D2:

Dazed & Confused (29.49)

(Inc. The Crunge - San Francisco)

Stairway To Heaven (9.47)

Whole Lotta Love Medley (15.23)

(Inc. Everybody Needs Someone To Love - Boogie

Chillen - Baby I Don't Care - Let's Have A Party)

Brussels 1980

Venue: Brussels

Date: 6/20/80

Cover: D4C sleeve

Recording: 9

Source: St - SB

Company: Tarantura

Matrix #: n/a

Place Of Origin: Japan

Total Disc Time: n/a

N.B. Another re-issue of the Brussels soundboard.

D1:

Train Kept A Rollin',

Nobody's Fault But Mine,

Black Dog,

In The Evening,

The Rain Song,

Hot Dog ,

All My Love,

Trampled Underfoot

D2:

Since I've Been Loving You,

Achilles Last Stand,

White Summer -Black Mountain Side,

Kashmir,

Stairway To Heaven,

Rock And Roll,

Whole Lotta Love

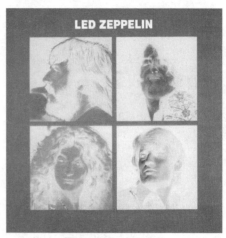

Brutal Artistry

Venue: Headley Grange
Date: ?/1973 - ?/1974
Cover: D4C
Recording: 9
Source: St - SB
Company: Midas Touch
Matrix #: 72731-2-3
Place Of Origin: Japan
Total Disc Time: n/a

N.B. Another reissue of the amazing studio out takes from Physical Graffiti. I believe that this was one of the first ones to feature this material.

D1:
The Wanton Song One
The Wanton Song Two
Take Me Home
In the Morning Take One
Trampled Underfoot
In the Morning Take Two
Sick Again
The Rover (acoustic version)
Untitled Instrumental
In My Time of Dying (Various Versions)
D2:
Swan Song (Full Version)
D3:
Ten Years Gone (Jimmy Page Demo)
The Wanton Song (alternative version)
Trampled Underfoot (alternate mix different vocal track)
Kashmir (instrumental version)
Custard Pie (Alternative Full Version with Different Harmonica Solo)
In the Light (Different Lyrics)
Swan Song Segment 1
Swan Song Segment 2

Brutal Artistry II

Venue: Olympic Studios** – SIR Studio^^ – Clearwell Castle^ – Island Studio*
Date: 11/74** - 11/75^^ - 5/78^ - 5/78*
Cover: D4C sleeve
Recording: 9
Source: St - SB
Company: Midas Touch
Matrix #: 72811
Place Of Origin: Japan
Total Disc Time: 50.24 – 31.35

N.B. Another of those releases that must be considered essential to most collectors. This is a collage of amazing quality recordings taken straight from the studio. Parts of this have certainly never been out before but I believe all of it is the best quality I have heard. The version of Custard Pie is worth the price of admission. Also it is amazing to finally hear the track Swansong which Page talked about many times in the seventies. It undoubtedly finally became "Midnight Moonlight" when it was finally released by the Firm but this version indicates just how much Page had already worked out ten years before. It's also a revelation to hear Bonham playing it.

As for the live versions of "Carouselambra" from Clearwell Castle – well it's just an incredible shame we never got to see them do it on stage. The sources are clearly defined on the cover but they may be open to speculation.

D1:
Boogie With Stu (6.07)**
Night Flight (14.32)**
Royal Orleans Instrumental (0.19)^^
Tea For One (2.41)^^
Don't Start Me Talking – All My Loving (4.56)^^
Instrumental (Hotel Rats & Photostats) (5.01)
Fire (4.19)^
Carouselambra (three takes) (12.29)^
D2:
Trampled Underfoot (5.41)*
Kashmir (Instrumental) (8.51)*
Custard Pie (4.19)*
In The Light (7.27)*
Swan Song (Midnight Moonlight) (1.26)*
Swan Song (Midnight Moonlight) (3.51)*

Buck Rogers

Venue: London
Date: 5/25/75
Cover: D4C sleeve
Recording: 7
Source: M -Aud
Company: Tarantura
Matrix #: 75EARL 1-4
Place Of Origin: Japan
Total Disc Time: 54.19 - 60.09 - 63.25 - 28.59

N.B. Another nice package from Tarantura in a deluxe color sleeve. The tape is the one which has been circulating for years.

D1:
Rock & Roll
Sick Again
Over The Hills & Far Away
In My Time Of Dying
Song Remains The Same
Rain Song
Kashmir
D1:
No Quarter
Tangerine
Going To California
That's The Way
Bron-y-Aur Stomp
Trampled Underfoot
D3:
Moby Dick
Dazed & Confused
Stairway To Heaven
D4:
Whole Lotta Love - Black Dog
Heartbreaker
Communication Breakdown

Budokan Oct 2.1972

Venue: Tokyo
Date: 10/2/72
Cover: D4C
Recording: 7
Source: M -Aud
Company: Patriot
Matrix #: n/a
Place Of Origin: Japan
Total Disc Time: 73.39 - 52.25

N.B. Another release of the Budokan tape although it claims on the cover to be better quality I couldn't tell.

D1:
Introduction
Rock & Roll
Over The Hills & Far Away
Black Dog
Misty Mountain Hop
Since I've Been Loving You
Dancing Days
Bron-y-Aur Stomp
Song Remains The Same
Rain Song
D2:
Stairway To Heaven
Whole Lotta Love
Heartbreaker
Immigrant Song
Communication Breakdown

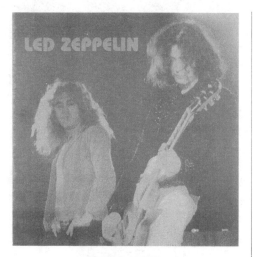

Buffalo 1973

Venue: Buffalo - Chicago*

Date: 7/15/73 - 7/7/73*

Cover: D4C in case

Recording: 8

Source: M - SB

Company: VIP

Matrix #: VIP 008

Place Of Origin: Italy

Total Disc Time: 71.16

N.B. A knock off of "And It Makes Me Wonder".

D1:

Rock & Roll   (3.46)

Celebration Day   (3.32)

Black Dog (5.48)

Over The Hills & Far Away   (5.57)

Misty Mountain Hop   (4.43)

Since I've Been Loving You   (8.13)

No Quarter   (12.30)

The Song Remains The Same   (5.17)

The Rain Song   (7.50)

Stairway To Heaven   (10.41)*

Bursting Night

Venue: Los Angeles

Date: 6/25/77

Cover: D4C sleeve

Recording: 7-8

Source: St - Aud

Company: Diagrams of Led Zeppelin

Matrix #: Vol 053

Place Of Origin: Japan

Total Disc Time: n/a

N.B. Just another reissue of one of the forum tapes.

D1:
Song Remains the Same
Sick Again
Nobody's Fault but Mine
In My Time of Dying
Since I've Been Loving You
No Quarter
D2:
Ten Years Gone
The Battle of Ever More
Going to California
Black Country Woman
Bron-y-Aur Stomp
White Summer
Black Mountain Side
Kashmir
Trampled under Foot
D3:
Moby Dick
Guitar Solo
Achilles Last Stand
Stairway to Heaven
Whole Lotta Love

Communication Breakdown

Cabala

Venue: London[1,2] - San Francisco[3,4] - Raleigh[5] - Headley Grange[6] - Bron -y-Aur[7] - Bombay[8] - Los Angeles [9,10] - Chicago [11] - Dallas [12,13] - Polar Studios [14] - Cleveland [15] - Frankfurt [16] - Rotterdam [17] - Zurich [18] - Brussels [19] - Berlin [20] - New York [21]- Olympic Studio [22] - Fort Worth [23] - Essen [24]

Date: 6/16/69[1] - 4/1/71[2] - 1/9/69[3] - 4/27/69[4] - 4/7/70[5] - 5/70[6,7] - 3/72[8] - 6/3/73[9] - 6/25/77 [10] - 7/6/73 [11] - 8/31/69 [12] - 3/4/75 [13] - 11/78 [14] - 4/27/77 [15] - 6/30/80 [16] - 6/21/80 [17] - 6/29/80 [18] - 6/20/80 [19] - 7/7/80 [20] - 5/14/88 [21] - 5/72 [22] - 5/19/73 [23] - 3/22/73 [24]

Cover: D4C box set **Recording:** 8 - 9
Source: St - SB **Company:** CD Company srl
Matrix #: OSOZ 001-008 **Place Of Origin:** Italy
Total Disc Time: 77.46 - 79.23 - 77.20 - 75.45 - 79.02 - 76.13 - 77.18 - 78.01

N.B. This is a nicely executed package from Italy. Eight CD's a video and a lengthy book. The book includes the entire content of a special issue of Goldmine magazine which included several articles by yours truly and others. Although it's nice to see the stuff re-printed again I'm not sure that inside a high-profile boot-leg was the place I had in mind! The sources for this piece are many and varied. Disc one includes material from the Yardbirds Anderson Theatre album, various Yardbirds tracks featuring Page and several Plant CBS solo singles from the sixties. Track 19 is not Lulu doing "Surprise Surprise", it escapes me who it is. There is also material from PJ Proby's "Three Week Hero" album as well as some Zep BBC studio stuff which continues onto disc two. Disc two track three is "Killing Floor" and track eight is from the Fillmore not from Newport Jazz. Disc five includes the dubious Lucifer Rising tape I still don't believe this is Page. Disc six is from the Chicago 1973 soundcheck not Minneapolis 1975. The material which is not clearly identified on the cover is a mix-ture of stuff from Essen and Fort Worth and the songs marked Tokyo 1979 (!) are from Zurich 1980.

D1:

I'm Confused (6.21) Yardbirds
Train Kept A Rollin (3.09) Yardbirds
She Just Satisfies (1.59) Page
Keep Movin' (3.24) Page
You Better Run (2.26) Plant
Everybody's Gonna Say (2.10) Plant
Our Song (2.30) Plant
Long Time Coming (2.29) Plant
I've Got A Secret (3.08) Plant
Goodnight Sweet Josephine (2.45) Yardbirds
Think About It (3.45) Yardbirds
Hey Hey What Can I Do (3.55) Led Zeppelin
Psycho Daisies (1.48) Yardbirds
Happenings Ten Years Time Ago (2.55) Yardbirds
Stroll On (2.42) Yardbirds
My Baby Left Me (1.59) Dave Berry
A Certain Girl (2.17) The First Gear
Leave My Kitten Alone (2.18) The First Gear
Little By Little (2.23) ???
How Do You Feel (2.20) The Primitives
Jim's Blues (5.59) P J Proby
Traveling Riverside Blues (5.11) [1]
You Shook Me (5.11) [1]
The Girl I Love (2.59) [1]

D2:

Whole Lotta Love (6.04) [1]
Something Else (2.03) [1]
Killing Floor (7.00) [3]
Babe I'm Gonna Leave You (7.03) [3]
Pat's Delight (13.02) [3]
How Many More Times Medley (21.12) [12]
(Inc. The Hunter - Suzie Q - The Lemon Song - Eyesight To The Blind - Boogie Chillen
Communication Breakdown (4.22) [12]
As Long As I Have You Medley (17.49) [4]
(Inc. Fresh Garbage - The Lemon Song - Cat's Squirell - I'm A Man - Cadillac No Money Down)

D3:

Organ Solo - Thank You (10.29) [5]
Bring It On Home (8.58) [5]
Friends (7.03) [8]
Friends (12.36) [8]
That's The Way (3.38) [7]
Friends (3.14) [7]
Hey Hey What Can I Do (1.51) [7]
Instrumental Jam (2.58) [7]
Immigrant Song (3.26) [2]
Heartbreaker (5.14) [2]
Black Dog (5.26) [2]
Stairway To Heaven (8.52) [2]
Going To California (4.04) [2]

D4:

That's The Way (6.03) [2]
What Is & What Should Never Be (4.20) [2]
That's The Way (5.35) [6]
Blues Medley (Hat's Off To Harper) (6.34) [6]
Since I've Been Loving You (6.54) [6]
No Quarter (7.47) [22]
No Quarter (7.22) [22]
Dazed & Confused (28.48) [23]
Celebration Day (3.51) [23]

D5:
Whole Lotta Love Medley (22.30) [24]
(Inc. Baby I Don't Care - Lets Have A Party -
I Can't Quit You - The Lemon Song)
Dancing Days (4.25) [9]
The Song Remains The Same (5.17) [23]
The Rain Song (7.31) [23]
Lucifer Rising Part One (4.23) Page? Part Two (6.17)
Page? Part Three (6.00) Page? Part Four (1.52) Page?
Part Five (1.53) Page? Part Six (3.08) Page?
Part Seven (13.58) Page? Part Eight (10.40) Page?
D6:
Schooldays (Long Live Rock & Roll) (2.43) [11]
Nadine (1.03) [11]
Round & Round (3.16) [11]
Move On Down The Line (2.17) [11]
Love Me Like A Hurricane (2.43) [11]
Move It (1.26) [11]
Dynamite (1.10) [11]
Shakin All Over (2.52) [11]
Hungry For Love (1.59) [11]
I'll Never Get Over You (2.20) [11]
Reelin & Rockin (2.07) [11]
Strawberry Jam #1 (3.01) [11]
Strawberry Jam #2 (1.40) [11]
The Wanton Song (2.23) [11]
The Rover #1 (3.50) [11]
The Rover # (1.54) [11]
Night Flight #1 (0.58) [11]
Night Flight #2 (1.52) [11]
Night Flight #3 (2.20) [11]
Rock And Roll (1.58) [13]
Sick Again (5.28) [13]
Over The Hills & Far Away (7.31) [13]
In My Time Of Dying - Rip It Up (11.43) [10]
D7:
All My Love (7.50) [14]
Since I've Been Loving You (8.24) [15]
Ten Years Gone (9.25) [15]
Black Country Woman (2.29) [15]
Bron-y-Aur Stomp (5.11) [15]
White Summer (3.59) [18]
Kashmir (6.19) [18]
Trampled Underfoot (8.12) [18]
Achilles Last Stand (9.05) [18]
Money (5.26) [16]
Hot Dog (3.29) [17]
Train Kept A Rollin (3.25) [18]
Nobody's Fault But Mine (5.26) [18]
D8:
Whole Lotta Love (9.31) [19]
Kashmir (7.13) [19]
Heartbreaker (3.16) [21]
Whole Lotta Love (5.55) [21]
Misty Mountain Hop (3.49) [21]
Stairway To Heaven (9.57) [21]
Black Dog (6.24) [20]

In The Evening (9.33) [20]
The Rain Song (8.54) [20]
Since I've Been Loving You (9.38) [20]
Rock And Roll (4.56) [20]

California 69

Venue: San Francisco
Date: 1/12/69 - 4/25/69*
Cover: D4C sleeve
Recording: 7
Source: M -Aud
Company: Lemon Song
Matrix #: LS7206-7
Place Of Origin: Japan
Total Disc Time: 57.56 - 44.28
N.B. Another digpak package from Japan.
Nothing else notable about this piece.
The tapes have been around for ages.

D1:
As Long As I Have You Medley (Inc. Fresh Garbage)
I Can't Quit You
Dazed & Confused
Babe I'm Gonna Leave You
Communication Breakdown
You Shook Me
White Summer
Train Kept A Rollin
Pat's Delight
D2:
How Many More Times Medley (Inc. The Hunter)
Killing Floor
Train Kept A Rollin'*
You Shook Me*
Communication Breakdown*
As Long As I Have You Medley (Inc. Fresh Garbage)*

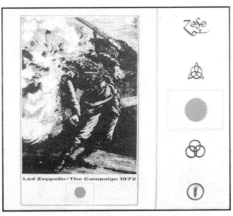

California Mystery Train

Venue: San Diego
Date: 6/19/77
Cover: D4C
Recording: 7
Source: St - Aud
Company: Blimp
Matrix #: n/a
Place Of Origin: Japan
Total Disc Time: n/a

N.B. Just another reissue of the San Diego audience recording. The cover claims that it has been digitally remastered from the master tapes. This seems to be the claim of the week. This exact same piece was previously available on the Silver Rarities label.

D1:
Song Remains the Same
Sick Again
Nobody Fault but Mine
In My Time of Dying
Since I've Been Loving You
No Quarter
D2:
Ten Years Gone
The Battle of Ever More
Going to California
Mystery Train
Black Country Woman
Bron-Y-Aur Stomp
White Summer-Black Mountain Side
Kashmir
D3:
Guitar Solo
Achilles Last Stand
Stairway to Heaven
Whole Lotta Love
Rock and Roll

Campaign

Venue: Kyoto - Osaka^ - Tokyo* - Nagoya^^
Date: 10/10/72 - 10/9/72^ - 10/4/72** - 10/2/72* -
10/3/72# - 10/5/72^^
Cover: D4C box set **Recording:** 5 - 8
Source: M - Aud **Company:** Tarantura
Matrix #: 1972 -5 –1 -12 **Place Of Origin:** Japan
Total Disc Time: n/a

N.B. A super rare box set from Tarantura featuring fourteen CD's and including good versions of the various tapes involved. These titles were released individually by Tarantura as "No Use Greco", "2nd Night In A Judo Arena", "Dancing Geisha", "Cherry Blossom", "Live", "Last Campaign", and "The Campaign" although I have never seen "Last Campaign" or "Cherry Blossom" individually.

D1:
Introduction*
Rock & Roll*
Over The Hills & Far Away*
Black Dog*
Misty Mountain Hop*
Since I've Been Loving You*
Dancing Days*
Bron-y-Aur Stomp*
Song Remains The Same*
Rain Song*
D2:
Dazed & Confused*
Stairway To Heaven*
Whole Lotta Love*
Heartbreaker*
Immigrant Song*
Communication Breakdown*
D3:
Introduction#
Rock & Roll#
Black Dog#
Over The Hills & Far Away#
Misty Mountain Hop#
Since I've Been Loving You#
Dancing Days#
Bron-y-Aur Stomp#

Song Remains The Same#
Rain Song#
D4:
Dazed & Confused#
Stairway To Heaven#
Whole Lotta Love#
Immigrant Song#
The Ocean#
D5:
Rock & Roll**
Black Dog**
Over The Hills & Far Away**
Misty Mountain Hop**
Since I've Been Loving You**
Dancing Days**
Bron-y-Aur Stomp**
Song Remains The Same**
Rain Song**
D6:
Dazed & Confused**
Stairway To Heaven**
Whole Lotta Love**
Heartbreaker**
Immigrant Song**
D7:
Rock & Roll^^
Black Dog^^
Misty Mountain Hop^^
Since I've Been Loving You^^
Dancing Days^^
Bron-y-Aur Stomp^^
Song Remains The Same^^
Rain Song^^
D8:
Dazed & Confused^^
Stairway To Heaven^^
Whole Lotta Love^^
Cherry Blossom^^
Thank You^^
D9:
Rock & Roll^
Black Dog^
Over The Hills & Far Away^
Misty Mountain Hop^
Since I've Been Loving You^
Dancing Days^
Song Remains The Same^
Rain Song^
Dazed & Confused^
D10:
Stairway To Heaven^
Moby Dick^
Whole Lotta Love^
Stand By Me^
Immigrant Song^
D11:
Rock & Roll
Black Dog
Misty Mountain Hop

Since I've Been Loving You
Song Remains The Same
Rain Song
Dazed & Confused
D12:
Stairway To Heaven
Over The Hills & Far Away
Whole Lotta Love
Immigrant Song
D13:
Rock & Roll*
Over The Hills & Far Away*
Black Dog*
Since I've Been Loving You*
Dancing Days*
Bron-y-Aur Stomp*
Song Remains The Same*
Rain Song*
Dazed & Confused*
D14:
Stairway To Heaven*
Whole Lotta Love*
Heartbreaker*
Immigrant Song*
Communication Breakdown*

Canada Dry
Venue: Vancouver
Date: 7/18/73
Cover: D4C sleeve
Recording: 7
Source: M - Aud
Company: Tarantura
Matrix #: CD 001
Place Of Origin: Japan
Total Disc Time: 48.32
N.B. Typical colour package from Tarantura. Dazed is chopped right off. Really ambient recording, distant but with a good live sound to it.

D1:
Rock &Roll (3.56)
Celebration Day (3.42)
Black Dog (4.14)
Over The Hills &Far Away (7.29)
Misty Mountain Hop (6.13)
Since I've Been Loving You (8.28)
No Quarter (14.02)
Dazed &Confused (0.28) (cut)

Canadian Graffiti

Venue: Montreal
Date: 2/6/75
Cover: D4C
Recording: 5
Source: St - Aud
Company: Black Rose
Matrix #: BR 001-2
Place Of Origin: Japan
Total Disc Time: 40.51 - 49.52
N.B.A re-issue of the annoying audience recording from
the Montreal Forum.

D1:
Rock & Roll
Sick Again
Over The Hills & Far Away
In My Time Of Dying
Song Remains The Same
Rain Song
D2:
Dazed & Confused
Stairway To Heaven
Whole Lotta Love
Black Dog
Heartbreaker

Can't Take Your Evil Ways

Venue: New York
Date: 2/12/75
Cover: D4C gatefold sleeve
Recording: 8
Source: St - Aud
Company: Diagrams Of Led Zeppelin
Matrix #: TDOLZ 019
Place Of Origin: Japan
Total Disc Time: n/a
N.B.A re-issue of the recording which originally
appeared on the Rock Solid vinyl titles "In Person" and
"In Concert".

D1:
Rock & Roll - Sick Again (8.16)
Over The Hills & Far Away (7.22)
In My Time Of Dying (10.44)
Song Remains The Same - Rain Song (12.41)
Kashmir (7.46)
D2:
No Quarter (16.15)
Trampled Underfoot (7.33)
Moby Dick (cut)
D3:
Dazed & Confused (30.20)
Stairway To Heaven (11.26)
Whole Lotta Love - Black Dog (6.57)
Heartbreaker - That's Alright (8.19)

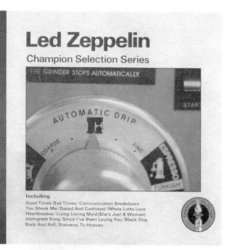

Champion Selection Series

Venue: Studio

Date: n/a

Cover: D4C

Recording: 10

Source: St - SB

Company: Champion Selection

Matrix #: n/a

Place Of Origin: Japan

Total Disc Time: n/a

N.B. A straight pirate knock off of various studio tracks.

D1:

Good Times Bad Times

Communication Breakdown

You Shook Me

Dazed & Confused

Whole Lotta Love

Heartbreaker

Living Loving Maid

Immigrant Song

Since I've Been Loving You

Black Dog

Rock & Roll

Stairway To Heaven

Check It Out

Venue: Chicago - Southampton - Los Angeles

Date: 7/6/73 - 1/22/73 - 6/25/72

Cover: D4C sleeve

Recording: 9

Source: St -SB

Company: Antrabata

Matrix #: 8

Place Of Origin: Europe

Total Disc Time: 62.09

N.B. This piece is one of many compilations put together by Antrabata. Most of these discs were put together in a rare deluxe box set (see "Led Zeppelin 10 CD Box Set") Nothing special about the material. I've long ago given up trying to figure out whether this comes from Southampton or Chicago....does it matter??

D1:

The Wanton Song (5.51)

The Rover (5.06)

Night Flight (Various takes) (2.39)

School Days (8.21)

Nadine (11.03)

Round & Round (3.10)

Move On Down The Line (1.02)

Love Me Like A Hurricane (3.25)

C'mon Pretty Baby (2.53)

Shakin' All Over (2.43)

Hungry For Love (3.03)

I'll Never Get Over You (2.50)

Reelin & Rockin' (2.27)

Surrender (2.12)

Checkpoint Charlie

Venue: Berlin

Date: 7/12/70

Cover: D4C sleeve

Recording: 5

Source: M - Aud

Company: Immigrant

Matrix #: IM 050-051

Place Of Origin: Japan

Total Disc Time: 41.03 - 42.59

N.B. The rest of the Berlin show.

Not previously available.

D1:

Immigrant Song

Heartbreaker

Dazed & Confused

Bring It On Home

Since I've Been Loving You

D2:

Thank You

What Is & What Should Never Be

Whole Lotta Love Medley

(Inc. Boogie Chillen - I've Got A Girl -

Hoochie Coochie Man - Lemon Song)

Moby Dick

Cherry Blossom

Venue: Nagoya

Date: 10/5/72

Cover: D4C sleeve

Recording: 5

Source: M - Aud

Company: Tarantura

Matrix #: 1972-7/8

Place Of Origin: Japan

Total Disc Time: 50:20 - 64:36

N.B. 1972 Second Japanese Tour.

Cover says strictly limited to 300 sets.

D1:

Rock And Roll

Black Dog

Misty Mountain Hop

Since I've Been Loving You

Dancing Days

Bron-Y-Aur Stomp

The Song Remains The Same

The Rain Song

D2:

Dazed And Confused

Stairway To Heaven

Whole Lotta Love

Organ Solo (Inc. Cherry Blossom)

Thank You

Chien Noir

Venue: Brussels - Bremen*
Date: 6/20/80 - 6/23/80*
Cover: D4C in double case
Recording: 8 - 9 **Source:** St - SB
Company: Antrabata **Matrix #:** ARM 200-230680
Place Of Origin: Japan
Total Disc Time: 60.27 - 58.46 - 55.56 - 44.06
N.B. A nicely packaged Japanese re-issue of the sound-
board tapes. Limited to 325 copies.

D1:
The Train Kept A Rollin' (3.22)
Nobody's Fault But Mine (5.30)
Black Dog (5.15)
In The Evening (7.55)
The Rain Song (6.31)
Hot Dog (2.57)
All My Love (5.49)
Trampled Underfoot (7.56)
Since I've Been Loving You (9.20)
D2:
Achilles Last Stand (9.30)
White Summer- Black Mountain Side (9.29)
Kashmir (8.22)
Stairway To Heaven (11.25)
Rock & Roll (3.48)
Whole Lotta Love (9.37)
D3:
The Train Kept A Rollin' (2.53)*
Nobody's Fault But Mine (5.53)*
Black Dog (6.21)*
In The Evening (8.17)*
The Rain Song (8.06)*
Hot Dog (3.48)*
All My Love (6.11)*
Trampled Underfoot (4.52)*
Since I've Been Loving You (9.29)*
D4:
Achilles Last Stand (10.42)*
White Summer -
Black Mountain Side (7.45)*
Kashmir (9.26)*
Stairway To Heaven (9.01)*
Rock And Roll (4.26)*
Communication Breakdown (2.40)*

Cincinnati Kids

Venue: Cincinnati

Date: 4/19/77

Cover: D2C slick

Recording: n/a

Source: n/a

Company: H & Y

Matrix #: HY 001

Place Of Origin: Japan

Total Disc Time: n/a

N.B. All track information not available at press time.

First release of this show limited to 500 numbered

copies.

D1:

The Song Remains The Same

Sick Again

Nobody's Fault But Mine

Since I've Been Loving You

No Quarter

Ten Years Gone

Cleveland 1969

Venue: Cleveland

Date: 7/20/69

Cover: D4C

Recording: 4

Source: M - Aud

Company: Diagrams Of Led Zeppelin

Matrix #: TDOLZ 029

Place Of Origin: Japan

Total Disc Time: n/a

N.B. The famous show performed the night of Neil Armstrong's walk on the moon. For some time speculation placed this show on the 16th July but thanks to recently unearthed artifacts my original estimation proved correct. In fact the Rock and Roll Hall of Fame mentions this show in their promotional literature, claiming that the band had to cut the set short so that people could go and watch that "One Small Step....".

D1:

Train Kept A Rollin' (3.01)

I Can't Quit You Baby (7.32)

Dazed & Confused (14.28)

White Summer - Black Mountain Side (7.15)

You Shook Me (11.58)

How Many More Times Medley

(Inc. the Hunter - Lemon Song) (17.21)

Coded

Venue: Studio Pirate

Date: Various

Cover: D4C case

Recording: 10

Source: St - SB

Company: Chelsea

Matrix #: CFC 016

Place Of Origin: Italy

Total Disc Time: 73.58

N.B. Bizarre re-mixing of various studio tracks. The perpetrators have made a series of the ever-popular mega-mixes presumably for playing in Italian night clubs where they seem to have an affinity for such things. Strangely enough there are a few tracks which I couldn't help but like. A curiosity for the die-hard. The last track has not been terminated correctly and it runs for an additional 13 minutes of total silence.

D1:

The Immigrant Song (7.39)

In The Light (7.15)

Nobody's Fault But Mine (6.50)

Misty Mountain Hop (8.26)

No Quarter (12.14)

Stairway To Heaven (5.39)

Black Dog (2.43)

Spirit Of The City (4.17)

Crackback (4.05)

Cologne 1980

Venue: Cologne

Date: 6/18/80

Cover: D4C sleeve

Recording: 8

Source: St - SB

Company: Diagrams of Led Zeppelin

Matrix #: Vol 061

Place Of Origin: Japan

Total Disc Time: n/a

N.B. A nice reproduction of the original vinyl bootleg cover artwork. However this one is from the sound board tape.

D1:
Train Kept a Rolling
Nobody's Fault but Mine
Black Dog
In the Evening
The Rain Song
Hot Dog
All My Love
Trampled Underfoot
Since I've Been Loving You
D2:
Achilles Last Stand
White Summer-Black Mountain Side
Kashmir
Stairway to Heaven
Rock and Roll
Communication Breakdown

Come Back To Boston

Venue: Boston

Date: 9/9/70

Cover: D4C

Recording: 4

Source: M - Aud

Company: Holy

Matrix #: SH 001A

Place Of Origin: Japan

Total Disc Time: n/a

N.B. Another re-issue of the Boston tape which partially emerged years ago on the vinyl titles "207.19" Also available as "No License No Festival".

D1:
Introduction (3.11)
Immigrant Song (5.41)
Heartbreaker (6.29)
Dazed & Confused (16.42)
Bring It On Home (9.20)
That's The Way (7.14)
Bron-y-Aur (5.03)
Since I've Been Loving You (12.15)
D2:
Thank You (11.03)
What Is & What Should Never Be (4.48)
Moby Dick (12.40)
Whole Lotta Love Medley (18.27)
(Inc. Boogie Chillen - Ramble On - For What It's Worth - Some Other Guy - Honey Bee - The Lemon Song)
Communication Breakdown (5.44)

Complete Dancing Days

Venue: Tokyo - Dusseldorf*
Date: 10/2/72 - 3/11/70*
Cover: D4C
Recording: 7
Source: M -Aud
Company: n/a
Matrix #: n/a
Place Of Origin: Japan
Total Disc Time: n/a

N.B. Another reissue of the Budokan gig. Again with the bonus tracks from Germany 1970 tagged on the end. Exactly the same as the title "Dancing Days"

D1:
Rock & Roll
Over The Hills & Far Away
Black Dog
Misty Mountain Hop
Since I've Been Loving You
Dancing Days
Bron-y-Aur Stomp
Song Remains The Same
Rain Song
Dazed & Confused
D2:
Stairway To Heaven
Whole Lotta Love Medley (Inc Boogie Chillen - My Baby
Left Me - Lemon Song - I Can't Quit You)
Heartbreaker
Immigrant Song
Communication Breakdown
How Many More Times Medley (Inc. Boogie Chillen -
Some Other Guy - Killing Floor)*

Complete Knebworth '79

Venue: Knebworth
Date: 8/4/79 - 8/11/79*
Cover: D4C sleeve
Recording: 7
Source: St -Aud
Company: ZOSO'S Company
Matrix #: ZE-210/220/230
Place Of Origin: Japan
Total Disc Time: 67:16 - 55:52 - 34:27

N.B. All details not known at press time.

D1:
The Song Remains The Same
Celebration Day
Black Dog
Nobody's Fault But Mine
Over The Hills And Far Away
Misty Mountain Hop
Since I've Been Loving You
No Quarter
Hot Dog
The Rain Song
D2:
White Summer - Black Mountain Side
Kashmir
Trampled Underfoot
Sick Again *
Achilles Last Stand
Guitar Solo - In The Evening
Ten Years Gone
D3:
Stairway To Heaven
Rock And Roll
Whole Lotta Love (Inc. Boogie Chillen)
Communication Breakdown *
Heartbreaker

Complete Performance In Minnesota

Venue: St. Paul
Date: 7/9/73
Cover: D4C
Recording: 5
Source: M - Aud
Company: Diagram's of Led Zeppelin
Matrix #: TDOLZ 439701/439702/439703
Place Of Origin: Japan
Total Disc Time: 50.24 - 47.16 -60.45

N.B. A recently surfaced recording from the St. Paul civic center. This particular recording first appeared on CDR. To be honest there are so many good recordings from the 1973 tour that why anyone would want to listen to this is beyond me. Not very good quality.

D1:
Rock and Roll
Celebration Day
Black Dog
Over the Hills and Far Away
Misty Mountain Hop
Since I've Been Loving You
No Quarter
D2:
Song Remains the Same
The Rain Song
Dazed and Confused
D3:
Stairway to Heaven (Cut)
Moby Dick
Heart Breaker
Whole Lotta Love (Inc. Boogie Chillen)
Communication Breakdown

Complete Rockpile Show

Venue: Toronto
Date: 8/18/69
Cover: D2C
Recording: 5 - 7
Source: M-Aud
Company: The Symbols
Matrix #: n/a
Place Of Origin: Japan
Total Disc Time: n/a

N.B. A compilation of two tapes from the Toronto Rockpile gig. The afternoon and evening shows. One is considerably better than the other.

D1:
Train Kept A Rolling
I Can't Quit You
Dazed & Confused
White Summer
Black Mountain Side
You Shook Me
How Many More Times Medley
(Inc. Feel So Fine - The Hunter - Trucking Little Mama
- Needle Blues - The Lemon Song)
D2:
Communication Breakdown
Train Kept A Rolling
I Can't Quit You
Dazed & Confused
You Shook Me
How Many More Times Medley
(Inc. The Hunter - The Lemon Song)

Complete Tapes (The) (1970/71 - Vol 1)
Venue: Montreux - Raleigh* - Bron Y-Aur^ - Los
Angeles† - London‡ - Copenhagen# - Tokyo+
Date: 3/7/70 - 4/7/70* - 5/?/70^ - 9/4/70† - 4/1/71‡ -
5/3/71# - 9/23/71+ **Cover:** D4C boxset
Recording: 7 - 9 **Source:** St - SB, M-Aud
Company: Tintagel **Matrix #:** TIBX 000043-5
Place Of Origin: Europe
Total Disc Time: 62.27 - 64.28 - 58.03
N.B. Intelligently thought out "best of" from Italy. A
compilation of common material with a booklet.
D1:
We re Gonna Groove (2.58)
Dazed And Contused (15.11)
Heartbreaker (6.11)
How Many More Times (9.57) (cut)
Bring It On Home (8.48) *
I Wanna Be Her Man (2.01)^
Down By The Seaside (5.24)^
That's The Way (4.24)^
Friends (3.08)^
Poor Tom (2.46)^
Hey Hey What Can I Do (1.39)^
D2:
Immigrant Song (3.31) †
What Is And What Should Never Be (4.29)†
Moby Dick (12.21)†
Communication Breakdown Medley (10.15)† (Inc. Good
Times Bad Times - For What It's Worth - I Saw Her
Standing There)
That's The Way (7.05)†
Blueberry Hill (3.53)†
Whole Lotta Love Medley (17.21)† (Inc. Boogie Chillen -
I'm Movin On - I've Got A Girl - Some Other Guy -
Think It Over - The Lemon Song)
Bron-Y-Aur Stomp (5.32)†
D3:
Since I ve Been Loving You (7.05)‡

Black Dog (6.55)‡
Stairway To Heaven (8.47)‡
Going To California (4.05)‡
Thank You (6.34)‡
Four Sticks (6.33)#
Gallows Pole (5.51)#
Misty Mountain Hop (5.34)#
Rock And Roll (4.10)#
Celebration Day (4.03)+

Complete Tapes (The) (1968/69 - Vol 2)
Venue: Stockholm - San Francisco*† -
Copenhagen^ - London‡#+§
Date: 3/14/69 - 1/10/69* - 3/17/69^ - 4/27/69† -
6/16/69‡ - 6/24/69# - 10/12/69+ - 11/?/69§
Cover: D4C boxset
Recording: 7 - 9
Source: St - SB, M-Aud
Company: Tintagel
Matrix #: TIBX 000032-34
Place Of Origin: Europe
Total Disc Time: 52.42 - 51.40 - 44.20
N.B. Intelligently thought out "best of" from Italy. A
compilation of common material with a booklet.
D1:
I Can't Quit You (6:29)
I Gotta Move (3:04)
Dazed And Confused (10:42)
How Many More Times (2:00)
For Your Love (5:40)*
As Long As I Have You Medley (12:06) ^
(Inc. Fresh Garbage - Shake - I Just Wanna Make Love)
You Shook Me (7:44) ^
Communication Breakdown (4:52) ^
D2:
Train Kept A Rollin' (2:58)†
How Many More Times Medley (19:21)†
(Inc The Hunter - The Mulberry Bush)
Killing Floor (7:36) †
Babe I'm Gonna Leave You (7:30) †
Sitting And Thinking (6:56) †
Pat's Delight (7:19) †
D3:
The Girl I Love (3:14) ‡
Something Else (2:15) ‡

What Is And What Should Never Be (4:29) #
Traveling Riverside Blues (3:16) (cut) #
Good Times, Bad Times (2:57) +
Heartbreaker (5:02)+
Jenning's Farm Blues (takes 1 to 10) (16:48) §
Jenning's Farm Blues (take 11) (6:19) §

Condition Breakdown

Venue: Indianapolis
Date: 1/25/75
Cover: D4C
Recording: 4
Source: St -Aud
Company: Holy
Matrix #: SH006A
Place Of Origin: Japan
Total Disc Time: n/a

N.B. A new tape surfaces on bootleg. The tape has been trading for years and hardly bears mentioning. Lots of cuts and bits missing.
One of the few rare performances of The Wanton Song.

Compositions

Venue: Charlotte
Date: 6/9/72
Cover: D4C sleeve
Recording: n/a
Source: M - Aud
Company: Tarantura
Matrix #: CC001-002
Place Of Origin: Japan
Total Disc Time: n/a
N.B. Full details of this title were not available at press time.

D1:
Immigrant Song
Heartbreaker
Celebration Date
Black Dog
since I've Been Loving You
Stairway to Heaven
Going to California
That's the Way
Tangerine
Bron-y-Aur Stomp
D2:
Dazed and Confused
What Is and What Should Never Be
Moby Dick
Whole Lotta Love
Rock and Roll
Communication Breakdown

D1:
Rock & Roll (4.09)
Sick Again (5.59)
Over The Hills & Far Away (7.11)
Song Remains The Same (3.56)
Rain Song (7.03)
Kashmir (8.33)
Wanton Song (5.15)
No Quarter (13.54)
D2:
Trampled Underfoot (8.12)
Moby Dick (4.16) (cut)
How Many More Times (5.41) (cut)
Stairway To Heaven (11.20)
Whole Lotta Love - Black Dog (9.11)

Confusion

Venue: Oakland
Date: 7/23/77*
Cover: D4C
Recording: 8
Source: M -Aud
Company: n/a
Matrix #: LZ 72377 A - B
Place Of Origin: Japan
Total Disc Time: n/a

N.B. Another new show debuts on bootleg. Surprising that this one hadn't surfaced before.

DI:
Song Remains The Same
Sick Again
Nobody's Fault But Mine
Over The Hills & Far Away
Since I've Been Loving You
No Quarter
Ten Years Gone
Battle Of Evermore
Going To California
D2:
Black Country Woman
Bron-y-Aur Stomp
Trampled Underfoot
White Summe - Black Mountain Side
Kashmir
Achilles Last Stand
Stairway To Heaven
Whole Lotta Love
Rock & Roll
Black Dog

Connexion

Venue: Osaka
Date: 10/4/72
Cover: D4C
Recording: 4 -5
Source: M -Aud
Company: Amsterdam
Matrix #: AMS 9612-2
Place Of Origin: Japan
Total Disc Time: n/a

N.B. Also available as "Dancing Geisha" and"Stand By Me" "Second Daze". Part of the 6CD box set "Osaka Tapes".

DI:
Rock & Roll
Black Dog
Over The Hills & Far Away
Misty Mountain Hop
Since I've Been Loving You
Dancing Days
Bron-y-Aur Stomp
Song Remains The Same
Rain Song
D2:
Dazed & Confused
Stairway To Heaven
Whole Lotta Love
Heartbreaker
Immigrant Song

Copenhagen Warm Ups

Venue: Copenhagen
Date: 7/23/79 – 7/24/79*
Cover: D2C **Recording:** 8
Source: St - SB **Company:** ZOSO
Matrix #: CWU 2301-4
Place Of Origin: Europe
Total Disc Time: 71.40 – 57.36 – 67.18 – 74.07
N.B. A really nice compilation of the two shows in Copenhagen.
As good quality as I have heard. The cover is just
green and white with no readily identifiable company.

D1:
Intro (2.16)
Song Remains The Same (5.32)
Celebration Day (3.45)
Black Dog (6.06)
Nobody's Fault But Mine (6.09)
Over The Hills & Far Away (6.13)
Misty Mountain Hop (5.07)
Since I've Been Loving You (9.01)
No Quarter (14.56)
Hot Dog (4.14)
The Rain Song (8.21)
D2:
White Summer - Black Mountain Side (5.02) - Kashmir (9.47)
Trampled Underfoot (6.39)
Achilles Last Stand (10.21)
Guitar Solo (4.56) - In The Evening (6.43)
Stairway To Heaven (9.50)
Rock & Roll (4.18)
D3:
Song Remains The Same (6.19)
Celebration Day (3.57)
Black Dog (5.40)
Nobody's Fault But Mine (5.48)
Over The Hills & Far Away (5.54)
Misty Mountain Hop (5.11)
Since I've Been Loving You (9.21)
No Quarter (13.14)
Ten Years Gone (8.04)
Hot Dog (3.50)
D4:
The Rain Song (8.23)
White Summer - Black Mountain Side (4.48) - Kashmir (9.05)
Trampled Underfoot (6.40)
Sick Again (5.53)
Achilles Last Stand (9.03)
Guitar Solo (5.03)
In The Evening (7.51)
Stairway To Heaven (9.54)
Whole Lotta Love (7.27)

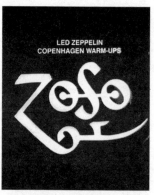

Copenhagen Warm-Ups

Venue: Copenhagen **Date:** 7/23/79 - 7/24/79*
Cover: D4C **Recording:** 8 **Source:** St -Aud
Company: Last Stand Disc **Matrix #:** LSD-01/02/03/04
Place Of Origin: Japan **Total Disc Time:** n/a
N.B. Apparently the cover claims "DIGITALLY REMASTERED
DIRECTLY FROM THE ORIGINAL TAPES. 23 BIT MASTERING
NO EQUALIZING". Never heard of 23 bit mastering but I bet it
sounds just like 32 bit.

D1:
Introduction (2.14)
The Song Remains The Same (5.36)
Celebration Day (3.17)
Black Dog (6.00)
Nobody's Fault But Mine (6.44)
Over The Hills And Far Away (6.18)
Misty Mountain Hop (4.40)
Since I've Been Loving You (9.06)
No Quarter (14.29)
Hot Dog (4.33)
The Rain Song (8.46)
D2:
White Summer / Black Mountain Side (5.04) - Kashmir (9.47)
Trampled Underfoot (6.04)
Achilles Last Stand (10.19)
Guitar Solo (5.33) - In The Evening (6.36)
Stairway To Heaven (9.35)
Rock And Roll (4.43)
D3:
The Song Remains The Same (6.21)*
Celebration Day (3.17)*
Black Dog (6.12)*
Nobody's Fault But Mine (5.49) *
Over The Hills And Far Away (6.00)*
Misty Mountain Hop (4.39)*
Since I've Been Loving You (9.44) *
No Quarter (11.08)*
Ten Years Gone (4.43)*
Hot Dog (4.22)*
D4:
The Rain Song (8.12) *
White Summer / Black Mountain Side (5.01)* - Kashmir (9.05)*
Trampled Underfoot (6.21) *
Sick Again (5.40)*
Achilles Last Stand (9.35) *
Guitar Solo (5.04)* - In The Evening (7.03)*
Stairway To Heaven (9.57)*
Whole Lotta Love (8.20)*

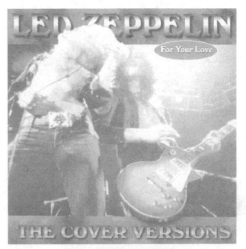

Copenhagen Warm Ups

Venue: Copenhagen **Date:** 7/23/79 - 7/24/79*
Cover: D4C sleeve **Recording:** 7 - 8
Source: St -Aud **Company:** Tarantura
Matrix #: T4 CD 2 **Place Of Origin:** Japan
Total Disc Time: 58.45 - 61.25 - 63.41 - 66.54
N.B. Nicely packaged set from Japan of both warm up shows in
Denmark.
D1: Opening (2:09)
The Song Remains The Same (5:39)
Celebration Day (3:12)
Black Dog (5:55)
Nobody's Fault But Mine (6:12)
Over The Hills And Far Away (6:12)
Misty Mountain Hop (4:25)
Since I ve Been Loving You (8:26) No Quarter (14:11)
Hot Dog (3:15)
D2:
The Rain Song (8:50)
White Summer, Black Mountain Side (4:51) - Kashmir (8:50)
Trampled Underfoot (5:48)
Achilles Last Stand (8:35)
Guitar Solo (5:31) - In The Evening (6:33)
Stairway To Heaven (8:54)
Rock And Roll (3:28)
D3:
The Song Remains The Same (5:34) *
Celebration Day (3:09) *
Black Dog (5:62) *
Nobody s Fault But Mine (6:05) *
Over The Hills And Far Away (6:16) *
Misty Mountain Hop (4:24)*
Since I ve Been Loving You (8:08) *
No Quarter (13:55) *
Ten Years Gone (7:04) *
Hot Dog (3:14) *
D4:
The Rain Song (7:28) *
White Summer, Black Mountain Side (4:48) * - Kashmir (8:53) *
Trampled Underfoot (5:42) *
Sick Again (4:42) *
Achilles Last Stand (8:43) *
Guitar Solo (5:25) * - In The Evening (6:22) *
Stairway To Heaven (8:15) *
Whole Lotta Love (6:36) *

The Cover Versions

Venue: Stockholm - Frankfurt - Chicago+ - Los
Angeles# - London^ - San Francisco~++ -
Osaka** - Olympic Studios## - Dallas^^
Date: 3/14/69 - 6/30/80* - 7/6/73+ - 3/25/75# -
6/16/69^ - 4/27/69~ - 10/9/72** -
1/10/69++ - 5/70## - 8/31/69^^
Cover: D4C in case
Recording: Various
Source: Various
Company : Fancy Pantry
Matrix#: FP006
Place Of Origin: Taiwan
Total Disc Time: 73.55
N.B. Amazing that no one has put this stuff all together
on one disc like this before. A variety of sound quality
from multiple different mono and stereo sources.
Generally good quality. Manufactured in Taiwan probably
for the European market.

D1:
I Gotta Move (3.14)
Money (4.19)*
Shakin' All Over (4.06)+
Sex Machine (6.21)#
Something Else (2.06)^
Sitting & Thinking (6.57)~
Stand By Me (6.17)**
The Girl I Love (3.01)^
For Your Love (5.29)++
Blues Medley (6.28)##
(Inc. Fixin' To Die - That's Alright)
Bye Bye Baby (10.32)^^
As Long As I Have You Medley (15.05)~ (Inc. Fresh
Garbage - Killing Floor - Cat's Squirrel - I'm A Man -
Cadillac No Money Down - You Shook Me)

Crazed Attack

Venue: Dublin

Date: 3/6/71

Cover: D4C

Recording: 4

Source: M -Aud

Company: n/a

Matrix #: CRA-7103CD-1/2

Place Of Origin: Japan

Total Disc Time: 56.34 - 53.15

N.B. Another new tape debuts on bootleg. Not a great recording but the band are in fine form.

D1:

Immigrant Song (4.54)

Heartbreaker (6.57)

Since I've Been Loving You (10.00)

Black Dog (6.29)

Stairway To Heaven (9.49)

Dazed & Confused (18.26)

D2:

Going To California (2.00)

What Is & What Should Never Be (1.22) (cut)

Moby Dick (14.31)

Whole Lotta Love Medley (25.57)

(Inc. Boogie Chillen - Suzie Q - Some Other Guy - Lemon Song - That's Alright)

Rock & Roll (2.28) (cut)

Custard Pie

Venue: Offenburg - London *

Date: 3/24/73 - 5/17/75*

Cover: D4C sleeve

Recording: 8, 6*

Source: St - Aud, M -Aud*

Company: Cobra Standard

Matrix #: 001

Place Of Origin: Japan

Total Disc Time: 73:53 / 53:48

N.B. First release of this legendary show on CD.

D1:

Rock & Roll (3.44)

Over The Hills & Far Away (5.21)

Black Dog (5.00)

Misty Mountain Hop (4.40)

Since I've Been Loving You (8.05)

Bron-y-Aur Stomp (4.47)

Song Remains The Same (5.15)

The Rain Song (7.55)

Dazed & Confused (21.10)

D2:

Stairway To Heaven (9.50)

Dazed & Confused (4.54)

Whole Lotta Love Medley (25.52)

(Inc. Everybody Needs Someone To Love - Boogie Chillen - Baby I Don't Care - Let's Have A Party - I Can't Quit You - The Lemon Song)

Heartbreaker (6.48)

Kashmir (8.14)*

Dallas 1975

Venue: Dallas

Date: 3/4/75

Cover: D4C

Recording: 8

Source: M - SB

Company: Last Stand Disc

Matrix #: LSD 20/21

Place Of Origin: Japan

Total Disc Time: n/a

N.B. Another reissue from Japan of the 1975 Memorial Auditorium board tape. Cover claims that it is digitally re-mastered directly from the original mastered tapes. Somehow I doubt it.

D1:

Rock and Roll

Sick Again

Over the Hills and Far Away

In My Time of Dying

The Song Remains the Same

The Rain Song

D2:

Kashmir

No Quarter

Trampled under Foot

Moby Dick

Dallas 1975

Venue: Dallas

Date: 3/4/75

Cover: D2C

Recording: 8

Source: M - SB

Company: Blimp

Matrix #: n/a

Place Of Origin: Japan

Total Disc Time: n/a

N.B. Just another re-issue of the well -circulated Dallas soundboard tape

D1:

Rock and Roll

Sick Again

Over the Hills and Far Away

In My Time of Dying

The Song Remains the Same

The Rain Song

D2:

Kashmir

No Quarter

Trampled Underfoot

Moby Dick

Dallas Second Night

Venue: Dallas

Date: 3/5/75

Cover: D4C

Recording: 6

Source: M - Aud

Company: n/a

Matrix #: n/a

Place Of Origin: Japan

Total Disc Time: n/a

N.B. Also available as "Live In Dallas". A decent enough audience recording of the second night.

D1:

Rock & Roll

Sick Again

Over The Hills & Far Away

In My Time Of Dying

Song Remains The Same

Rain Song

Kashmir

D2:

No Quarter

Trampled Underfoot

Moby Dick

Dazed & Confused

Dancing Bears

Venue: Amsterdam

Date: 5/27/72

Cover: D4C

Recording: 4

Source: M -Aud

Company: Tarantura

Matrix #: BEAR 001/2

Place Of Origin: Japan

Total Disc Time: 70.04 - 52.23

N.B. Previously available as the title "Running Bear". This show had barely been out in trading circles at all when it appeared on CD.

D1:

Immigrant Song (3.38)

Heartbreaker (6.45)

Black Dog (5.05)

Since I've Been Loving You (7.32)

Celebration Day (4.08)

Stairway To Heaven (cut) (7.16)

Bron - y - Aur Stomp (4.03)

Dazed & Confused (23.36)

D2:

What Is & What Should Never Be (4.51)

Moby Dick (11.36)

Whole Lotta Love Medley (22.10)

(Inc. Boogie Chillen - Mary Lou - Running Bear - That's Alright Mama - Hoochie Coochie Man - Shape I'm In - Going Down Slow)

Rock And Roll (3.51)

Communication Breakdown (3.37)

Dancing Geisha

Venue: Osaka
Date: 10/4/72
Cover: D4C box
Recording: n/a
Source: n/a
Company: Tarantura
Matrix #: n/a
Place Of Origin: Japan
Total Disc Time: n/a

N.B. All track information not available at press time.

D1:
Rock & Roll (3.57)
Black Dog (5.11)
Over The Hills & Far Away (5.26)
Misty Mountain Hop (5.05)
Since I've Been Loving You (7.12)
Dancing Days (4.02)
Bron-y-Aur Stomp (5.30)
The Song Remains The Same (5.12)
The Rain Song (7.09)
D2:
Dazed & Confused (24.09)
Stairway To Heaven (9.55)
Whole Lotta Love Medley (22.37)
(Inc. Everybody Needs Some To Love - Boogie Chillen -
Got A Lot Of Livin To Do - Let's Have A Party - You
Shook Me - The Lemon Song)
Heartbreaker (7.45)
Immigrant Song (3.46)

Dancing with the Snow Queen

Venue: Copenhagen
Date: 2/28/70
Cover: D4C
Recording: 5-6
Source: M - Aud
Company: Baby Face
Matrix #: 9602
Place Of Origin: Japan
Total Disc Time: n/a

N.B. Nothing new about this recording. This one has
been available before as the titles "Riot Going On", and
"The Nobs".

D1:
Dazed and Confused
Heart Breaker
White Summer/Black Mountain Side
Since I've Been Loving You
Thank You
Moby Dick
D2:
How Many More Times Medley (Inc. The Hunter - Move
on down the Line - Trucking Little Mama)
Whole Lotta Love
Communication Breakdown
Come On Everybody
Something Else
Bring It On Home
Long Tall Sally

Dazed & Confused

Venue: London

Date: 3/3/69 - 6/24/69*

Cover: D4C in case

Recording: 8

Source: M - SB

Company: Joker

Matrix #: JOK 008C

Place Of Origin: Australia

Total Disc Time: 31.57

N.B. A very short disc of extremely common material.

D1:

You Shook Me (5.22)

Communication Breakdown (3.03)

I Can't Quit You (4.31)

Dazed & Confused (6.48)

What Is & What Should Never Be (4.26)*

Communication Breakdown (2.47)*

Whole Lotta Love   (6.15)*

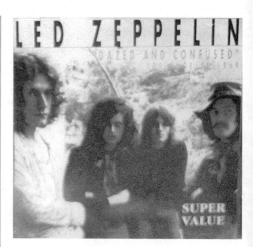

Dazed & Confused

Venue: San Francisco

Date: 4/27/69

Cover: D4C

Recording: 8

Source: St - SB

Company: Discomagic

Matrix #: n/a

Place Of Origin: Italy

Total Disc Time: n/a

N.B. A thinly disguised version of the ubiquitous Fillmore tape. The cover trys to pass it off as Los Angeles and then throws in a repro of the UC Irvine poster for good measure.

D1:

How Many More Times (4.00)

The Hunter (4.30)

Mulberry Bush (1.21)

Train Kept A Rollin' (3.52)

Babe I'm Gonna Leave You (5.40)

Dazed & Confused (12.19)

Definitive Kingdom (The)

Venue: Los Angeles
Date: 8/22/71
Cover: D4C double case
Recording: 3 - 5
Source: M -Aud
Company: Whole Lotta Live
Matrix #: WLL 020 - 021
Place Of Origin: Italy
Total Disc Time: 69.41 - 67.45
N.B. A straight knock off of the Immigrant title "Walk Don't Run".

D1:
Rhumba (Walk Don't Run) (2.17)
Immigrant Song (4.03)
Heartbreaker (6.23)
Since I've Been Loving You (7.11)
Black Dog (5.32)
Dazed And Confused (20.13)
Stairway To Heaven (9.05)
Celebration Day (3.36)
That's The Way (6.44)
D2:
What Is And What Should Never Be (4.16)
Moby Dick (17.52)
Whole Lotta Love Medley (23.42) (Inc. Boogie Chillen - Think I'm Crazy - Take It Easy - My Baby Left Me - Mess Of Blues - You Shook Me)
Communication Breakdown (7.37)
Organ Solo (5.19)
Thank You (7.47)

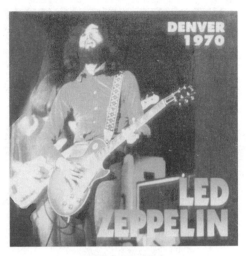

Denver 1970

Venue: Denver
Date: 3/25/70
Cover: D4C
Recording: 5
Source: M - Aud
Company: Diagrams of Led Zeppelin
Matrix #: Vol 045
Place Of Origin: Japan
Total Disc Time: n/a
N.B. First release of a new tape. This one from the Denver Coliseum. Average quality but always interesting to hear a new tape from that era.

D1:
We're Gonna Groove
I Can't Quit You
Dazed and Confused
Heartbreaker
Since I've Been Loving You
Thank You
D2:
Moby Dick
How Many More Times (Inc. Ramble On –Ravel''s Bolero -Boogie Chillen - Move on Down the Line -Going Down South - The Lemon Song)
Whole Lotta Love

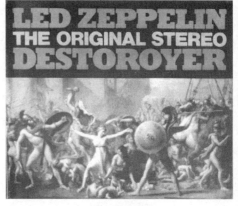

Destoroyer

Venue: Cleveland

Date: 4/28/77

Cover: D4C in double case

Recording: n/a

Source: n/a

Company: POT

Matrix #: POT 001-002

Place Of Origin: Japan

Total Disc Time: n/a

N.B. Total track information not available at press time.

D1:

The Song Remains The Same (6.12)

Sick Again (6.00)

Nobody's Fault But Mine (6.14)

In My Time Of Dying (9.39)

Surrender (0.10)

Since I've Been Loving You (8.30)

No Quarter (21.05)

Ten Years Gone (8.33)

D2:

Battle Of Evermore (5.29)

Going To California (4.26)

Black Country Woman (2.15)

Bron-y-Aur Stomp (5.00)

White Summer (cut) (5.45)

Kashmir (8.38)

Moby Dick (17.15)

Guitar Solo (9.31)

Achilles Last Stand (9.26)

Rock & Roll (4.00)

Trampled Underfoot (6.30)

Destroyer (The)

Venue: Cleveland

Date: 4/27/77

Cover: D4C

Recording: 8

Source: n/a

Company: Last Stand Disc

Matrix #: LSD 16/17/18

Place Of Origin: Japan

Total Disc Time: n/a

N.B. I'm not sure if this is the audience or the sound board recording. All track details were not available at press time.

D1:

The Song Remains the Same

Sick Again

Nobody Fault but Mine

In My Time of Dying

Since I've Been Loving You

No Quarter

D2:

Ten Years Gone

The Battle of Ever More

Going to California

Bron-y-Aur Stomp

White Summer-Black Mountain Side

Kashmir

D3:

Moby Dick

Guitar Solo

Achilles Last Stand

Stairway to Heaven

Rock and Roll

Trampled Underfoot

Destroyer - Final Edition

Venue: Cleveland
Date: 4/27/77
Cover: D4C sleeve
Recording: 9
Source: St - SB
Company: Cobra Standard
Matrix #: 004
Place Of Origin: Japan
Total Disc Time: n/a
N.B. All details not available.

D1:
The Song Remains The Same (cut)(3.38)
Sick Again (6.10)
Nobody's Fault But Mine (6.35)
In My Time Of Dying (10.54)
Since I've Been Loving You (8.24)
No Quarter (19.56)
D2:
Ten Years Gone (9.25)
Battle Of Evermore (6.43)
Going To California (4.51)
Black Country Woman-
Bron-y-Aur Stomp (7.39)
White Summer- Kashmir (12.41)
D3:
Moby Dick
Guitar Solo- Achilles Last Stand (19.45)
Stairway To Heaven (10.13)
Rock & Roll (3.23)
Trampled Underfoot (6.57)

[handwritten annotation: The groupings plus 2 CDS No Moby D.]

The Destroyer Gold

Venue: Cleveland
Date: 4/27/77
Cover: D4C
Recording: 9
Source: St -SB
Company: Tarantura
Matrix #: TUDCD-004/006
Place Of Origin: Japan
Total Disc Time: 55:20 - 41:28 - 56:23
N.B. Another reissue of the Soundboard.

D1:
The Song Remains The Same
The Rover Intro / Sick Again
Nobody's Fault But Mine
In My Time Of Dying
Since I've Been Loving You
No Quarter
D2:
Ten Years Gone
The Battle Of Evermore
Going To California
Black Country Woman
Bron-Y-Aur Stomp
White Summer
Black Mountain Side
Kashmir
D3:
Out On The Tiles / Moby Dick
Guitar Solo (Inc. Star Spangled Banner)
Achilles Last Stand
Stairway To Heaven
Rock And Roll
Trampled Underfoot

Destroyer II

Venue: Cleveland
Date: 4/28/77
Cover: D4C in double case
Recording: 6
Source: M - Aud
Company: Silver Rarities
Matrix #: SIRA 197/198/199
Place Of Origin: Europe
Total Disc Time: 58.10 - 40.57 - 58.04
N.B. The audience recording of the second night in Cleveland. Nowhere near as good as the well known Destroyer from the first night but still not a bad version of this well circulated tape. It appears to be the whole show.

D1:
The Song Remains The Same (6:17)
Sick Again (6:06)
Nobody's Fault But Mine (6.20)
In My Time Of Dying (9.51)
Since I've Been Loving You (8:36)
No Quarter (21.01)
D2:
Ten Years Gone (8.51)
Battle Of Evermore (5.45)
Going To California (4.31)
Black Country Woman (2.13)
Bron-y-Aur Stomp (5:03)
White Summer - Black Mountain Side (5.47)
Kashmir (8.47)
D3:
Moby Dick (17.29)
Guitar Solo (9.38)
Achilles Last Stand (9:33)
Stairway To Heaven (10.31)
Rock & Roll (4.09)
Trampled Underfoot (6.44)

The Destroyer - Storongest Edition

Venue: Cleveland
Date: 4/28/77
Cover: D4C sleeve
Recording: 8
Source: M - Aud
Company: Diagrams Of Led Zeppelin
Matrix #: TDOLZ0015/16/17
Place Of Origin: Japan
Total Disc Time: 61:27 - 43:54 - 61:54
N.B. A newly surfaced audience recording of this over bootlegged show. Not sure whether I prefer this to the soundboard.

D1:
The Song Remains The Same
The Rover intro.-Sick Again
Nobody's Fault But Mine
In My Time of Dying
Since I've Been Loving You
No Quarter
D2:
Ten Years Gone
The Battle of Evermore
Going to California
Black Country Woman
Bron-Y-Aur Stomp
White Summer
Black Mountain Side
Kashmir
D3:
Out on Tiles intro.-Moby Dick
Guitar Solo/Achilles Last Stand
Stairway to Heaven
Rock And Roll
Trampled Underfoot

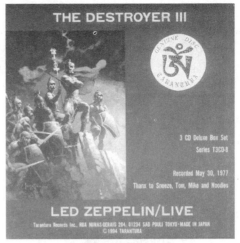

Destroyer 1969

Venue: Cleveland

Date: 7/20/69

Cover: D4C

Recording: 4

Source: M - Aud

Company: Tarantura

Matrix #: TDOLZ VOL.012

Place Of Origin: Japan

Total Disc Time: 61.14

N.B. Another nicely packaged and unique show from

Tarantura. The date is wrong this show was on July 20th

1969 not the 16th as the cover suggests.

D1:

Train Kept A Rollin' (3.03)

I Can't Quit You (6.35)

Dazed And Confused (15.08)

White Summer/Black Mountain Side (7.33)

You Shook Me (11.21)

How Many More Times (17.34)

Destroyer III

Venue : Largo

Date: 5/30/77

Cover: D4C slip case

Recording: 5

Source: M - Aud

Company: Tarantura

Matrix #: T3 CD -8 1 - 3

Place Of Origin: Japan

Total Disc Time : 69.25 - 46.39 - 56.02

N.B. Consistent sound throughout. Comes with a poster

D1:
The Song Remains The Same (6:33)
Sick Again (6:23)
Nobody's Fault But Mine (7:16)
In My Time Of Dying (11:05)
Since I've Been Loving You (7:35)
No Quarter (19:44)
D2:
Ten Years Gone (8:18)
The Battle Of Evermore (6:24)
Going To California (4:35)
Black Country Woman (2:33)
Bron-Y-Aur Stomp (5:54)
White Summer (5:17)
Black Mountain Side (1:44)
Kashmir (8:34)
D3:
Out On The Tiles,
Moby Dick (cut) (14:43)
Guitar Solo - Star Spangled Banner (11:12)
Achilles Last Stand (9:45)
Stairway To Heaven (10:44)
Whole Lotta Love - Rock And Roll (4:32)

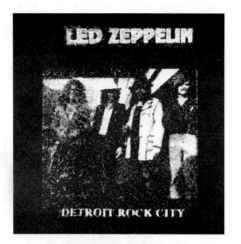

Detroit Rock City

Venue: Detroit

Date: 7/12/73

Cover: D4C

Recording: 6

Source: M - Aud

Company: Lemon Song

Matrix #: LS-7218/19/20

Place Of Origin: Japan

D1:

Rock and Roll

Celebration Day

Black Dog

Over the Hills and Far Away

Misty Mountain Hop

Since I've Been Loving You

No Quarter

Song Remains the Same

The Rain Song

D2:

Dazed and Confused

Stairway to Heaven

Moby Dick

Heart Breaker

Whole Lotta Love

Communication Breakdown

The Ocean

Different Mixed Coda

Venue: Studio
Date: Various
Cover: D4C in double case
Recording: 7
Source: St - SB
Company: POT
Matrix #: POT 010 011
Place Of Origin: Japan
Total Disc Time: n/a

N.B. All track information not available at press time.
More of the completely unconfirmable "remixes" from
Coda.

D1:
We're Gonna Groove (2.41)
Poor Tom (3.07)
I Can't Quit You (4.07)
Walter's Walk (4.23)
Ozone Baby (3.31)
Darlene (4.55)
Bonzo's Montreux (4.15)
Wearing & Tearing (5.25)
Sugar Mama (2.50)
Poor Tom (Instrumental) (3.13)
Walter's Walk (Instrumental) (4.31)
D2:
We're Gonna Groove (2.41)
Poor Tom (3.07)
I Can't Quit You (4.07)
Walter's Walk (4.23)
Ozone Baby (3.31)
Darlene (4.55)
Bonzo's Montreux (4.15)
Wearing & Tearing (5.25)
Sugar Mama (2.50)
Poor Tom (Instrumental) (3.13)
Walter's Walk (Instrumental) (4.31)

Discover America

Venue: Dallas - New York* +
Date: 5/18/73 - 7/27/73* - 7/28/73+
Cover: D4C sleeve
Recording: 8 - 9
Source: St - SB
Company: Tarantura
Matrix #: T3 CD 10
Place Of Origin: Japan
Total Disc Time: n/a
N.B. Another nice package from Tarantura
of the commonly found sound board tapes.

D1:
Rock And Roll (3:44)
Celebration Day (3:26)
Bring On Home Intro (:17)
Black Dog (5:02)
Over The Hills And Far Away (6:23)
Misty Mountain Hop (4:55)
Since I ve Been Loving You (7:12)
No Quarter (14:34)
D2:
The Song Remains The Same (5:38)
The Rain Song (7:54)
Dazed And Contused (27:23)
Stairway To Heaven (10:45)
D3:
Moby Dick (26:34)*
Heartbreaker (7:23)*
Whole Lotta Love (13:55)*
The Ocean (4:23)+

Dixie

Venue: Birmingham
Date: 5/18/77
Cover: D4C sleeve over double case
Recording: 8 - 9
Source: St - SB
Company: Antrabata
Matrix #: ARM 180577
Place Of Origin: Japan
Total Disc Time: 63.18 - 67.35 - 45.57
N.B. Includes a certificate of authenticity.
Limited edition of 325.
Nice packaging with hot foil stamped logo.

D1:
The Song Remains The Same (8.12)
Sick Again (6.23)
Nobody s Fault But Mine (7.34)
In My Time Of Dying (11.30)
Since I ve Been Loving You (8.54)
No Quarter (20.40)
D2:
Ten Years Gone (12.53)
The Battle Of Evermore (6.21)
Going To California (5.49)
Black Country Woman (1.46)
Bron-Y-Aur Stomp (5.42)
White Summer - Black Mountain Side (5.50)
Kashmir (9.01)
Moby Dick (20.07)
D3:
Guitar Solo - Dixie - Guitar Solo (19.26)
Achilles Last Stand (10.34)
Stairway To Heaven (11.37)
Rock And Roll (4.18)

Don't Do It If You Don't Want To

Venue: Charlotte
Date: 6/9/72
Cover: D4C sleeve
Recording: n/a
Source: n/a
Company: Holy Grail
Matrix #: HGCD 105
Place Of Origin: Japan
Total Disc Time: n/a

N.B. All track information not available at press time. Some material available here for the first time.

D1:
Immigrant Song
Heartbreaker
Celebration Day
Black Dog
Since I've Been Loving You
Stairway To Heaven
Going To California
That's The Way (7.06)
Tangerine (3.34)
Bron-y-Aur Stomp (5.36)
D2:
Dazed & Confused (25.07)
What Is & What Should Never Be (4.56)
Moby Dick
Whole Lotta Love (7.46)
Rock & Roll (4.36)
Communication Breakdown (4.26)

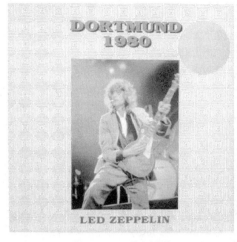

Dortmund 1980

Venue: Dortmund
Date: 6/17/80
Cover: D4C sleeve
Recording: 8
Source: St - SB
Company: Tarantura
Matrix #: 19801,2
Place Of Origin: Japan
Total Disc Time: n/a

N.B. Another reissue of the Dortmund board tape.

D1:
Train Kept a Rolling
Nobody's Fault But Mine
Black Dog
In the Evening
The Rain Song
Hot Dog
All My Love
Trampled Underfoot
Since I've Been Loving You
D2:
Achilles Last Stand
Whites Summer - Black Mountain Side
Kashmir
Stairway to Heaven
Rock and Roll
Whole Lotta Love
Heartbreaker

Double Clutch - Wild Weekend

Venue: Los Angeles

Date: 8/21/71

Cover: D4C

Recording: 6

Source: M - Aud

Company: Diagram's of Led Zeppelin

Matrix #: TDOLZ 389701/389702

Place Of Origin: Japan

Total Disc Time: 66.03 - 58.40

N.B. This is from the same source tape as the titles
"Walk Don't Run", and "Seventh American Tour".

D1:

Immigrant Song

Heart Breaker

Since I've Been Loving You

Black Dog

Dazed and Confused

Stairway to Heaven

That's the Way

Going to California

D2:

What Is and What Should Never Be

Whole Lotta Love (Inc. Boogie Chillen - I'm Moving on -
That's All Right Mama - Mess of Blues -Got A Lot Of
Living to Do - Honey Bee)

Weekend

Rock and Roll

Communication Breakdown

Thank You

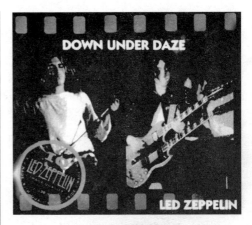

Down Under Daze

Venue: Melbourne

Date: 2/20/72

Cover: D4C

Recording: 5

Source: M - Aud

Company: Image Quality

Matrix #: IQ-038/039

Place Of Origin: Japan

Total Disc Time: n/a

N.B. Another reissue of the Melbourne Kooyong Tennis
Courts gig.

D1:

Immigrant Song (3.28)

Heartbreaker (7.04)

Black Dog (5.15)

Since I've Been Loving You (8.34)

Stairway to Heaven (8.40)

Going to California (5.53)

That's the Way (6.08)

Tangerine (2.47)

Bron-y-Aur Stomp (4.57)

D2:

Dazed and Confused (22.33)

Rock and Roll (3.40)

Whole Lotta Love Medley (12.54) (Inc. Boogie Chillen -
Let's Have a Party)

Drag Queen (The)

Venue: New Orleans

Date: 5/14/73

Cover: D4C sleeve

Recording: 9

Source: St - SB

Company: Tarantura

Matrix #: DG-001~3

Place Of Origin: Japan

Total Disc Time: n/a

N.B. A re-issue of the New Orleans soundboard.

D1:

Rock And Roll

Celebration Day

Black Dog

Over The Hills And Far Away

Misty Mountain Hop

Since I've Been Loving You

No Quarter

The Song Remains The Same

The Rain Song

D2:

Dazed And Confused,

Stairway To Heaven,

Moby Dick

D3:

Heartbreaker,

Whole Lotta Love,

Communication Breakdown

Earl's Court 75

Venue: London

Date: 5/25/75

Cover: D4C in double case

Recording: 7

Source: M - Aud

Company: Mud Dogs

Matrix #: 024 025 026

Place Of Origin: Japan

Total Disc Time: n/a

N.B. All track information not available at press time.

D1:

Rock & Roll

Sick Again

Over The Hills & Far Away

In My Time Of Dying

The Song Remains The Same

The Rain Song

No Quarter

D2:

Kashmir

Tangerine

Going To California

That's the Way

Bron-y-Aur Stomp Trampled Underfoot

Moby Dick

D3:

Dazed & Confused

Stairway To Heaven

Whole Lotta Love Medley (Inc. Black Dog)

Heartbreaker

Communication Breakdown

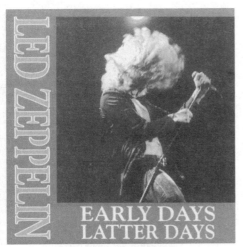

Early Days Latter Days

Venue: New York - Pittsburgh* - Chicago^# - Cincinnatti^
Date: 5/30/69 - 7/24/73* - 4/9/77# - 4/19/77^
Cover: D4C gatefold sleeve   **Recording:** 4,5*,6^,7#
Source: M - Aud^,St - Aud*# **Company:** Early Days
Matrix #: ED 30569 24773 19477 09477
Place Of Origin: Europe **Total Disc Time:** 65.29 - 55.00 -
59.56 - 62.37 **N.B.** Very nicely packaged compilation of previously unavailable material. The New York tape is very distorted and Plant is barely audible. Heartbreaker-Whole Lotta Love from Pittsburgh are soundboard and are considerably better than the rest of the tape.

D1: Train Kept A Rollin (3.30)
I Can t Quit You Babe (7.12)
Dazed & Confused (12.39)
You Shook Me (11.12)
White Summer, Black Mountain Side (9.58)
How Many More Times Medley (17.21) (Incl. The Hunter)
Communication Breakdown (3.37)
D2:
Rock And Roll (3.49)*
Celebration Day (3.25)*
Black Dog (6.34)*
Misty Mountain Hop (4.35)*
Since I've Been Loving You (8.44)*
Heartbreaker (7.09)*
Whole Lotta Love (16.27)*
The Ocean (4.17)*
D3:
The Song Remains The Same (7.15)#
Sick Again (6.33)#
Nobody s Fault But Mine (8.25)#
Since I've Been Loving You (8.56)#
No Quarter (19.52)#
Ten Years Gone (9.39)#
Robert Plant Announcement (0.40)#
Richard Cole Announcement (0.58)#
Richard Cole Announcement (0.58)#
D4:
The Song Remains The Same (5.57)^
Sick Again (7.08)^
Nobody's Fault But Mine (7.19)^
Since I've Been Loving You (8.29)^
No Quarter (23.59)^
Ten Years Gone (7.04)^

Elvis Presley Has Left The Building

Venue: Liverpool - Bradford* - Southampton+

Date: 1/14/73 - 1/18/73* - 1/20/73+

Cover: D4C in case

Recording: 7 - 8

Source: M - SB

Company: **Matrix #:** 6837-281

Place Of Origin: Europe

Total Disc Time: 76.25

N.B. Contains the well known board recordings.

D1:

Let's Have A Party (2.06)

I Can't Quit You-Going Down Slow (8.53)

Whole Lotta Love (1.47)

Heartbreaker (6.47)

The Ocean (4.03)

Dazed & Confused (23.25)

Whole Lotta Love Medley (23.35)*

(Inc. Everybody Needs Someone To Love - Boogie

Chillen - Baby I Don't Care - Blue Suede Shoes - Let's

Have A Party - I Can't Quit You - Going Down Slow)

Treat Me Like A Fool - Frankfurt Special (1.55)+

King Creole (1.44)+

Treat Me Like A Fool (1.01)+

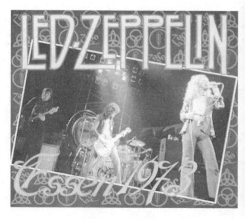

End Of 69 (The)

Venue: San Francisco

Date: 11/6/69

Cover: D4C in double case

Recording: 5 - 6

Source: M - Aud

Company: Whole Lotta Live

Matrix #: WLL 007 - 008

Place Of Origin: Italy

Total Disc Time: 49.34 - 45.13

N.B. This would seem to be the tape which is purportedly from the 6th November not the 8th as suggested by the cover. Lots of clipping and drop-outs but nevertheless a new performance for CD.

D1:

Opening (1.28)

Good Times Bad Times (0.34)

Communication Breakdown (3.13)

I Can't Quit You (7.19)

Heartbreaker (5.36)

Dazed & Confused (18.21)

White Summer - Black Mountain Side (13.03)

D2:

What Is & What Should Never Be (5.21)

Moby Dick (12.09)

How Many More Times Medley (22.18)

(Inc. The Hunter - Boogie Chillen -

Move On Down the Line - The Lemon Song)

C'mon Everybody (3.00)

Something Else (2.25)

Essen 1973

Venue: Essen

Date: 3/22/73

Cover: D4C in double case

Recording: 7

Source: M - Aud

Company: Savege Beast Music

Matrix #: SBM73 1-2

Place Of Origin: Japan

Total Disc Time: 42.17- 46.45

N.B. The band sound unbelievably powerful on this recording. Recording is distant but you can at least hear all the instruments equally well.

D1:

Rock & Roll (4.01)

Over The Hills &Far Away (5.42)

Black Dog (7.26)

Misty Mountain Hop (5.52)

Since I've Been Loving You (8.13)

Dancing Days (4.45)

Bron-y-Aur Stomp(6.15)

D2:

The Song Remains The Same (5.26)

The Rain Song (8.43)

Dazed & Confused (30.11)

Stairway To Heaven (2.25) (cut)

Evergreen (The)
Venue: Seattle
Date: 6/19/72
Cover: D4C
Recording: 6-7
Source: M - Aud
Company: Diagram's of Led Zeppelin
Matrix #: TDOLZ 319701/319702/319703
Place Of Origin: Japan
Total Disc Time: 64.43 - 56.22 -62.18
N.B. Apart from some chatter during songs, this is a reasonably listenable document.

D1:
Immigrant Song
Heart Breaker
Black Dog
The Ocean
Since I've Been Loving You
Stairway to Heaven
Going to California
Black Country Woman
That's the Way
Tangerine
Bron-y-Aur Stomp
D2:
Dazed and Confused
What Is and What Should Never Be
Dancing Days
Moby Dick
D3:
Whole Lotta Love (Inc. Everybody Needs Somebody to Love - Boogie Chillen - Let's Have a Party - hello Mary Lou - Only the Lonely - Heart Break Hotel - Going Down Slow)
Rock and Roll
Organ Solo - Thank You
How Many More Times
Over the Hills and Far Away
Dancing Days

Everybody, Everybody
Venue: Hamburg
Date: 3/11/70
Cover: D4C
Recording: 6
Source: M - Aud
Company: Image Quality
Matrix #: IQ-053/054
Place Of Origin: Japan
Total Disc Time: n/a
N.B. Cover on this piece incorrectly lists this as being from 1971.

D1:
We're Going to Groove (4.08)
I Can't Quit You (8.08)
Dazed and Confused (18.38)
Heart Breaker (cut) (7.16)
White Summer-Black Mountain Side (cut) (14.16)
Since I've Been Loving You (6.58)
Thank You (9.42)
D2:
Moby Dick (16.58)
How Many More Times (30.41) (Inc. Ravels' Bolero - Needle Blues- Boogie Chillen- Trucking Little Mama- Long Distance Call Blues-Shake 'Em On Down-The Lemon Song)

Fabulous Four (The)

Venue: Liverpool

Date: 1/14/73

Cover: D2C gold sleeve

Recording: 8

Source: M - SB

Company: Tarantura

Matrix #: FF-1,2

Place Of Origin: Japan

Total Disc Time: n/a

N.B. A sizeable chunk of the performance in Liverpool. Most of this has not been out on bootleg before.

D1:

Over The Hills And Far Away (5.28)

Black Dog (5.52)

Misty Mountain Hop (5.00)

Since I've Been Loving You (7.36)

Dancing Days (4.24)

Bron-Y-Aur Stomp (6.02)

The Song Remans The Same (5.49)

The Rain Song (5.38)

Dazed And Confused (22.50)

D2:

Stairway To Heaven (10.51)

Whole Lotta Love Medley (Inc. Everybody Needs Someone To Love - Boogie Chillen - Baby I Don't Care - Shape I'm In) (23.20)

Heartbreaker (7.02)

The Ocean (4.29)

Farewell To LA

Venue: Los Angeles

Date: 6/27/77

Cover: D4C

Recording: 8

Source: M -Aud

Company: Rabbit

Matrix #: RR 001/002/003

Place Of Origin: Japan

Total Disc Time: n/a

N.B. A re-issue of the last night at the LA forum still in great quality.

D1:

Song Remains The Same

Sick Again

Nobody's Fault But Mine

Over The Hills & Far Away

Since I've Been Loving You

No Quarter

D2:

Ten Years Gone

Battle Of Evermore

Going To California

Going Down South

Black Country Woman

Bron-y-Aur Stomp

Dancing Days

White Summer

Black Mountain Side

Kashmir

Trampled Underfoot

D3:

Moby Dick

Guitar Solo

Achilles Last Stand

Stairway To Heaven

Whole Lotta Love

Rock & Roll

Feel All Right

Venue: Montreux

Date: 3/14/70

Cover: D4C sleeve

Recording: 8

Source: M -Aud

Company: Cobra

Matrix #: 003

Place Of Origin: Japan

Total Disc Time: n/a

N.B. Another Cobra title utilising the artwork and track listings from a vinyl bootleg. The usual source tape of this material. Nothing special.

D1:

We're Gonna Groove (4.16)

I Can't Quit You (6.20)

White Summer (4.53)

Black Mountain Side (6.33)

Dazed & Confused (16.43)

Heartbreaker (7.08)

D2:

Since I've Been Loving You (6.39)

Organ Solo (2.21)

Thank You (6.27)

What Is & What Should Never Be (4.54)

MobyDick (16.00)

How Many More Times (cut) (7.20)

56,800 In The Ocean

Venue: Tampa

Date: 5/5/73

Cover: D4C in double slimline case

Recording: n/a

Source: n/a

Company: Silver Rarities

Matrix #: SIRA 166 167

Place Of Origin: Europe

Total Disc Time: n/a

N.B. All information not available at press time.

D1:

Rock & Roll (3.50)

Celebration Day (3.28)

Black Dog (5.10)

Over The Hills & Far Away (5.30)

Misty Mountain Hop (5.49)

Since I've Been Loving You (8.03)

No Quarter (5.18)

The Song Remains The Same (4.36)

The Rain Song (7.55)

D2:

Dazed & Confused (26.51)

Stairway To Heaven (10.14)

Moby Dick (cut) (11.00)

Heartbreaker Medley (14.52)

(Inc. Whole Lotta Love - Boogie Chillen)

The Ocean (4.21)

Communication Breakdown (3.16)

56,700 Fans Gathered Together And Boogie

Venue: Tampa

Date: 5/5/73

Cover: D4C in case

Recording: 7

Source: M - Aud

Company: Rock Calendar

Matrix #: RC 2127-28

Place Of Origin: Luxembourg

Total Disc Time: 65.56 - 57.20

N.B. An OK recording of the complete show in Tampa.

D1:

Rock & Roll (3.50)

Celebration Day (3.28)

Black Dog (5.10)

Over The Hills & Far Away (5.30)

Misty Mountain Hop (5.49)

Since I've Been Loving You (8.03)

No Quarter (5.18)

Dazed & Confused (26.51)

D2:

Communication Breakdown (3.16)

The Song Remains The Same (4.36)

The Rain Song (7.55)

Stairway To Heaven (10.14)

Moby Dick (cut) (11.00)

Heartbreaker Medley (14.52)

(Inc. Whole Lotta Love - Boogie Chillen)

The Ocean (4.21)

Fillmore West

Venue: San Francisco

Date: 4/24/69+ - 4/27/69

Cover: D4C

Recording: 6+,8

Source: M -Aud+, M - SB

Company: Last Stand

Matrix #: LSD 09/10/11

Place Of Origin: Japan

Total Disc Time: n/a

N.B. The umpteenth re-issue of this show along with some extracts from the rarer night of the 24th.

D1:

As Long As I Have You Medley (18.07)+ Incl. Fresh Garbage - Shake - Suzie Q

Killing Floor (6.58)+

White Summer-Black Mountain Side (11.07)+

Babe I'm Gonna Leave You (6.18)+

Pat's Delight (11.04)+

D2:

Train Kept A Rollin (2.52)

I Can't Quit You (7.43)

As Long As I Have You Medley (17.15)

(Inc. Fresh Garbage - Shake - Cat's Squirrel - Cadillac No Money Down - I'm A Man)

You Shook Me (9.11)

How Many More Times Medley (16.47)

(Inc. The Hunter - Mulberry Bush)

D3:

Killing Floor (6.46)

Babe I'm Gonna Leave You (6.35)

Sittin' & Thinking (6.44)

Dazed & Confused (11.00)

Communication Breakdown (5.02)

The Final Show in the Forum 1975

Venue: Los Angeles
Date: 3/27/75
Cover: D4C
Source: 7-8
Recording: St-Aud
Source: Jelly Roll
Matrix #: JR 012/13/14
Place Of Origin: Japan
Total Disc Time: n/a
N.B. Just another reissue of the well
circulated Forum tape.
Also available as the title "Tour De Force L.A. 1975".

D1:
Introduction
Rock and Roll
Sick Again
Over the Hills and Far Away
In My Time of Dying
The Song Remains the Same
The Rain Song
Kashmir
Since I've Been Loving You
D2:
No Quarter
Trampled Underfoot
Moby Dick
D3:
Dazed and Confused
Stairway to Heaven
Whole Lotta Love
Black Dog

Final Tour European Daze 1980

Venue: Zurich - Berlin*
Date: 6/29/80 - 7/7/80*
Cover: D4C
Recording: 9
Source: St - SB
Company: Patriot
Matrix #: 3-1/2
Place Of Origin: Japan
Total Disc Time: n/a
N.B. More re-issues of the old soundboard tapes. This a
combination of two shows.

D1:
Train Kept A Rollin' (3.24)
Nobody's Fault But Mine (5.30)
Black Dog (5.27)
In The Evening (9.01)
The Rain Song (8.53)
Hot Dog (4.02)
All My Love (6.13)
Trampled Underfoot (8.41)
Since I've Been Loving You (10.18)
Achilles Last Stand (9.56)
D2:
Stairway To Heaven (12.20)
Rock & Roll (4.04)
Heartbreaker (9.35)
Stairway To Heaven (14.12)*
Rock & Roll (3.39)*
Whole Lotta Love (16.35)*

The Final Statements
Venue: Los Angeles- New York* - Cleveland^
Date: 9/4/1970 - 7/28/1973* - 4/27/1977^
Cover: Hot foil stamped hard binder
Recording: 8
Source: M - Aud, St -SB*, St -Aud^
Company: Antrabata
Matrix #: ARM 040970, ARM 280773 ARM 270477
Place Of Origin: Europe
Total Disc Time: n/a
N.B. Another oddball rehash of very common material, this time in a very nice package. At this point rumour has it that Antrabata was deliberately attempting to rival Tarantura's packaging efforts.

D1:
Immigrant Song
Heartbreaker
Dazed And Confused
Bring It On Home
That's The Way
Bron-Y-Aur Stomp
Since I've Been Loving You
Organ Solo
Thank You
D2:
What Is And What Should Never Be
Moby Dick
Whole Lotta Love
Communication Breakdown
Out On The Tiles
Blueberry Hill
D3:
Rock And Roll *
Celebration Day *
Black Dog *
Over The Hills And Far Away *
Misty Mountain Hop *
Since I've Been Loving You *
No Quarter *
The Song Remans The Same *
The Rain Song *

D4:
Dazed And Confused *
Stairway To Heaven *
Moby Dick *
D5:
Heartbreaker *
Whole Lotta Love *
The Ocean *
D6:
The Song Remains The Same ^
The Rover intro.-Sick Again ^
Nobody's Fault But Mine ^
In My Time of Dying ^
Since I've Been Loving You ^
No Quarter ^
D7:
Ten Years Gone ^
The Battle of Evermore ^
Going to California ^
Black Country Woman ^
Bron-Y-Aur Stomp ^
White Summer ^
Black Mountain Side ^
Kashmir ^
Out on Tiles intro.-Moby Dick ^
D8:
Guitar Solo (Inc. Star Spangled Banner), ^
Achilles Last Stand, ^
Stairway To Heaven, ^
Rock And Roll, ^
Trampled Underfoot ^

Firecrackers Show
Venue: Los Angeles
Date: 3/24/75
Cover: D4C in case
Recording: 7
Source: M - Aud
Company: Diagrams Of Led Zeppelin
Matrix #: TDOLZ 0003/4/5
Place Of Origin: Japan
Total Disc Time: n/a
N.B. Just another re-issue of one of the Los Angeles

shows. The first track may be from a different show.

D1:
Rock & Roll (5.15)
Sick Again (4.59)
Over The Hills & Far Away (7.53)
In My Time Of Dying (11.33)
The Song Remains The Same (6.18)
The Rain Song (7.31)
Kashmir (9.06)
D2:
No Quarter (26.01)
Trampled Underfoot (7.38)
Moby Dick (21.22)
D3:
Dazed & Confused (34.33)
Stairway To Heaven (12.00)
Whole Lotta Love (9.06)
Black Dog (5.58)
Heartbreaker (8.24)

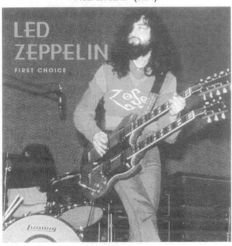

First Choice
Venue: Tampa
Date: 4/9/70 - 5/5/73*
Cover: D4C in case
Recording: 6,7*
Source: M - Aud
Company: Sugarcane
Matrix #: SC 52001/2
Place Of Origin: Italy
Total Disc Time: 55.25 - 58.56
N.B. An average compilation of two Tampa shows.
Nothing special.

D1:
Intro - Bring It On Home (2:42 Cut)
White Summer (5:44)
Black Mountain She (6:34)
Since I've Been Loving You (7:12)
Organ Solo(3:34)

Thank You (5:45)
What Is And What Should Never Be (1 :44 cut)
Moby Dick (18:12)
D2:
How Many More Times Medley:(22:18)
(Inc. Ravels Bolero - The Hunter - Boogie Chillen -
Trucking Little Mama - Mess O' Blues -
My Baby Don't Love Me - Lemon Song)
Whole Lotta Love (7:44)
Rock & Roll (3.49)
Celebration Day (3.23)
Black Dog (5.09)
Over The Hills & Far Away (5.31)
Misty Mountain Hop (4.35)
Since I've Been Loving You (4.36)

Five And A Half
Venue: Seattle
Date: 7/17/73
Cover: D4C
Recording: 8
Source: St - SB
Company: n/a
Matrix #: n/a
Place Of Origin: Japan
Total Disc Time: n/a
N.B. Another reissue of the Seattle board tape previ-
ously available as the same title but on Scorpio.

D1:
Rock And Roll (4.05)
Celebration Day (3.43)
Bring It On Home- Black Dog (5.54)
Over The Hills And Far Away (6.45)
Misty Mountain Hop (5.29)
Since I've Been Loving You (7.56)
No Quarter (13.54)
The Song Remains The Same (6.04)
The Rain Song (8.03)
D2:
Dazed And Confused (34.15)
Stairway To Heaven (10.54)

Flawless Performance

Venue: London
Date: 12/22/72
Cover: D4C
Recording: 5
Source: M - Aud
Company: Image Quality
Matrix #: IQ-013/014/015
Place Of Origin: Japan
Total Disc Time: 53.37 - 40.37 -48.37

N.B. Just another reissue of one of the tapes from the show at the Alexandra Palace. Parts of this show have previously been available as Riot House and Riot Show.

D1:
Introduction (0.42)
Rock & Roll (3.43)
Over The Hills & Far Away (6.10)
Black Dog (5.33)
Misty Mountain Hop (5.03)
Since I've Been Loving You (8.00)
Dancing Days (4.37)
Bron-y- Aur Stomp (5.34)
Song Remains The Same (5.25)
Rain Song (8.45)
D2:
Dazed & Confused (29.37)
Stairway To Heaven (10.59)
D3:
Whole Lotta Love Medley (27.03)
(Inc. Everybody needs Someone To Love -
Boogie Chillen - Let's Have A Party -
Heartbreak Hotel - I Can't Quit You)
Immigrant Song (3.54)
Heartbreaker (6.59)
Mellotron Solo - Thank You (10.58)

For Badge Holder's Only

Venue: Los Angeles
Date: 6/23/77
Cover: D2C sleeve
Recording: 8
Source: M - Aud
Company: Cobra
Matrix #: 017
Place Of Origin: Japan
Total Disc Time: 69:41 - 61:21 - 63:03

N.B. Another of Cobras re-issues of classic vinyl bootlegs but with better quality tapes.

D1:
The Song Remains the Same
Sick Again
Nobody Fault but Mine
Over the Hills and Far Away
Since I've Been Loving You
No Quarter
D2:
10 Years Gone
The Battle of Ever More
Going to California
Black Country Woman
Bron-y-Aur Stomp
White Summer-Black Mountain Side
Kashmir
Trampled under Foot
D3:
Moby Dick
Guitar Solo
Achilles Last Stand
Stairway to Heaven
Whole Lotta Love
Rock and Roll

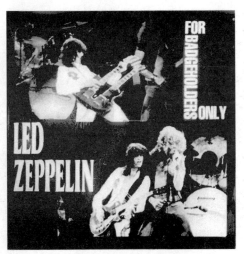

For Badge Holder's Only
Venue: Los Angeles
Date: 6/23/77
Cover: D4C sleeve
Recording: 6-7
Source: M - Aud
Company: Diagrams of Led Zeppelin
Matrix #: Vol 052
Place Of Origin: Japan
Total Disc Time: n/a
N.B. Just another re-issue of the forum tape. Killer version of No Quarter. Part of a series by Diagrams of Led Zeppelin reissuing the entire Los Angeles concert series.

D1:
The Song Remains the Same
Sick Again
Nobody Fault but Mine
Over the Hills and Far Away
Since I've Been Loving You
No Quarter
D2:
10 Years Gone
The Battle of Ever More
Going to California
Black Country Woman
Bron-y-Aur Stomp
White Summer-Black Mountain Side
Kashmir
Trampled under Foot
D3:
Moby Dick
Guitar Solo
Achilles Last Stand
Stairway to Heaven
Whole Lotta Love
Rock and Roll

For Badge Holders Only
Venue: Los Angeles - New York*
Date: 6/23/77 - 6/11/77*
Cover: n/a
Recording: n/a
Source: n/a
Company: Balboa
Matrix#: BP 95007/8/9
Place Of Origin: Japan
Total Disc Time: n/a
N.B. All details not available.

D1:
Since I've Been Loving You
No Quarter
Ten Years Gone
The Battle Of Evermore
Going To California
Black Country Woman
Bron-Y-Aur Stomp
D2:
White Summer
Black Mountain Side
Kashmir
Out On The Tiles Intro,
Moby Dick
Guitar Solo (includes Star Spangled Banner)
Achilles Last Stand
D3:
Stairway To Heaven
Whole Lotta Love
Rock And Roll
No Quarter *
Ten Years Gone *
The Battle Of Evermore *

For Badge Holders Only

Venue: Los Angeles
Date: 6/23/77
Cover: D4C in double case
Recording: n/a
Source: n/a
Company: ARMS
Matrix #: ARMS 28 29 30
Place Of Origin: Japan
Total Disc Time: n/a
N.B. All track information not available at press time.

D1:
The Song Remains The Same (6:18)
The Rover Intro, Sick Again (6:11)
Nobody's Fault But Mine (6:44)
Over The Hills And Far Away (6:03)
Since I've Been Loving You (7:56)
No Quarter (26:44)
D2:
Ten Years Gone (9:12)
Battle of Evermore (5:23)
Going To California (4:48)
Black Country Woman (1:39)
Bron-Y-Aur Stomp (6:50)
White Summer (7:28)
Black Mountain Side (2:07)
Kashmir (9:14)
D3:
Trampled Underfoot (8:44)
Out On The Tiles Intro, Moby Dick (17:43)
Guitar Solo (15:56)
Incl. Star Spangled Banner
Achilles Last Stand (8:55)
Stairway To Heaven (11:23)
Whole Lotta Love (1:25)
Rock And Roll (4:01)

For Badge Holders Only Part One

Venue: Los Angeles

Date: 6/23/77

Cover: D4C in case

Recording: 8

Source: St - Aud

Company: Continental Sounds

Matrix #: CD5 506

Place Of Origin: Italy

Total Disc Time: n/a

N.B. All track information not available at press time.

Actually the first release on CD of this legendary show.

D1:

Sick Again (6.04)

Nobody's Fault But Mine (6.49)

Over The Hills And Far Away (6.10)

Since I've Been Loving You (8.15)

No Quarter (28.15)

Ten Years Gone (8.57)

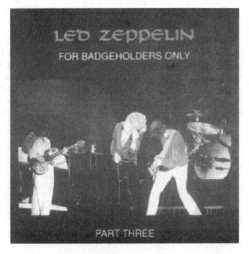

For Badge Holders Only Part Two

Venue: Los Angeles

Date: 6/23/77

Cover: D4C in case

Recording: 8

Source: St - Aud

Company: Continental Sounds

Matrix #: CD5 507

Place Of Origin: Italy

Total Disc Time: n/a

N.B. All track information not available at press time.

Actually the first release on CD of this legendary show.

D1:

Battle of Evermore (5:23)

Going To California (4:48)

Black Country Woman (1:39)

Bron-Y-Aur Stomp (6:50)

White Summer (7:28)

Black Mountain Side (2:07)

Kashmir (9:14)

Trampled Underfoot (8:44)

Out On The Tiles Intro, Moby Dick (17:43)

For Badge Holders Only Part Three

Venue: Los Angeles

Date: 6/23/77

Cover: D4C in case

Recording: 8

Source: St - Aud

Company: Continental Sounds

Matrix #: CD5 508

Place Of Origin: Italy

Total Disc Time: n/a

N.B. All track information not available at press time.

Actually the first release on CD of this legendary show.

D1:

Guitar Solo Includes Star Spangled Banner (15:56)

Achilles Last Stand (8:55)

Stairway To Heaven (11:23)

Whole Lotta Love (1:25)

Rock And Roll (4:01)

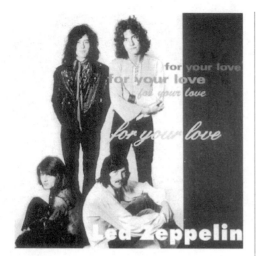

For Your Love

Venue: San Francisco

Date: 1/10/69

Cover: D4C in case

Recording: 7

Source: M- Aud

Company: SILVER RARITIES

Matrix #: SIRA 134135 2

Place Of Origin: Europe

Total Disc Time: 45.34 - 49.50

N.B. Good clear recording of the famous gig where they played the old Yardbirds hit "For Your Love".

D1:

The Train Kept A Rollin' (3:00)

I Can't Quit You Babe (6:04)

As Long As I Have You (10:50)

Dazed And Confused (11:09)

How Many More Times (14:33)

D2:

White Summer (7:15)

Killing Floor (4:39)

You Shook Me (8:35)

Pat's Delight (10:10)

Babe I'm Gonna Leave You (6:04)

Communication Breakdown (5:06)

For Your Love (8:02)

Freak Out

Venue: Los Angeles

Date: 8/22/71

Cover: D4C

Recording: 5

Source: M -Aud

Company: Diagrams Of Led Zeppelin

Matrix #: 039

Place Of Origin: Japan

Total Disc Time: 73.30 – 67.49

N.B. Another reissue of the second night at the Forum. Not great quality.

D1:

Walk Don't Run (2.21)

Immigrant Song (4.04)

Heartbreaker (6.38)

Since I've Been Loving You (8.13)

Black Dog (6.02)

Dazed & Confused (21.10)

Stairway To Heaven (9.29)

Celebration Day (3.41)

That's The Way (7.16)

What Is & What Should Never Be (4.36)

D2:

Moby Dick (18.34)

Whole Lotta Love Medley (Inc. Boogie Chillen – My Baby Left Me – Mess Of Blues –You Shook Me) (25.34)

Communication Breakdown (11.04)

Organ Solo – Thank You (12.37)

Led Zeppelin

25 Years Of Bootleg Cover Art.
1970 - 1995

LED ZEPPELIN
LISTEN ON THIS AGAIN VOL. 2

LISTEN TO THIS EDDIE
L.A. June 21 '77

LIGHTER THAN AIR

LED ZEPPELIN
LIVE AND LED LIVE PART 1

LED ZEPPELIN AGAIN
PART 2

LIMITED EDITION 24 Carat Gold DISC

LED ZEPPELIN
LIVE AND UNRELEASED

LED ZEPPELIN
LIVE AT BUDOKAN IN '72

IN JAP!

LED ZEP
LIVE AT THE BUDOKAN

LED ZEPPELIN LIVE!
ON BLUEBERRY HILL

LED ZEPPELIN

Live in Bremen, Stadthalle 23.6.80 (part 5)

LED ZEPPELIN

LIVE IN DALLAS, 1975

LED ZEPPELIN

LEDZEPPELIN
LIVE

LED ZEPPELIN
»Live«

»Live«

Led Zeppelin Live

I'VE BEEN LOVING YOU
DIDN'T QUIT YOU BABE

LED ZEPPELIN
LIVE!

Led Zeppelin

LED ZEPPELIN

LIVE AID

RUN DMC AID'S SOS GELDOF
THE LIVE AID TECHNOLOGY
FOR AFRICAN RHYTHMS ROAD

LIVE AID

LED ZEPPELIN LIVE:
ON BLUEBERRY HILL

LED ZEPPELIN LIVE
ON BLUEBERRY HILL

ON BLUEBERRY HILL

LED ZEPPELIN
PLATINUM

LED ZEPPELIN

LIVE IN DORTMUND, WEST GERMANY 1980

LED ZEPPELIN
LIVE FROM THE GOOD OLD DAYS

LEDZEPPELIN
LIVE

LED ZEPPELIN
LIVE ON THE LEVEE

LED ZEPPELIN

LIVE IN LONDON

LED ZEPPELIN
LIVE IN LONDON

LED ZEPPELIN

LIVE IN MADISON SQUARE GARDEN, PART ONE

LED ZEPPELIN

LIVE IN MADISON SQUARE GARDEN, PART TWO

LED ZEPPELIN
LIVE IN ENGLAND 1976

TAKRL 918

LED ZEPPELIN
LIVE IN ROTTERDAM

LED ZEPPELIN
LIVE IN ESSEN, W. GERMANY 1973 VOL. 1

LED ZEPPELIN
LIVE IN ESSEN, W. GERMANY 1973 VOL. 2

THE UNAUTHORISED LIVE RECORDINGS...
This live recording and its release has not been authorised by LED ZEPPELIN or their record company.

THE UNAUTHORISED LIVE RECORDINGS...
This live recording and its release has not been authorised by LED ZEPPELIN or their record company.

LED ZEPPELIN
UNAUTH LIVE VOL.1

LED ZEPPELIN
UNAUTH LIVE VOL.2

THIS SOUND RECORDING WAS RECORDED WITH AMATEUR EQUIPMENT AND WILL NOT BE OF THE SAME QUALITY AS AN AUTHORISED RELEASE

THIS SOUND RECORDING WAS RECORDED WITH AMATEUR EQUIPMENT AND WILL NOT BE OF THE SAME QUALITY AS AN AUTHORISED RELEASE

LED ZEPPELIN

Totally Tangible

LED ZEPPELIN
TROUBLE IN VANCOUVER

"TROUBLE IN VANCOUVER"

TOUR-DE-FORCE

LED ZEPPELIN

TRAMPLED   UNDERFOOT

RECORDED LIVE AT
MADISON SQUARE GARDEN
1975

LED ZEPPELIN

TULSA HILLBILLY

LED
ZEPPELIN

TWINIGHT
LED ZEPPELIN

LED·ZEPPELIN

Unburied Dead Zeppo's Grave
DEAD ZEPPELIN

Unburied Dead Zeppo's Grave
DEAD ZEPPELIN

THE UNOFFICIAL COLLECTION (1969-1971)

THIS IS AN
UNLICENSED
RECORDING OF
Led Zeppelin Live Vol. 2

IT HAS NOT BEEN LICENSED BY THE ARTISTS OR
THEIR RECORD COMPANY.

THIS IS A LIVE RECORDING, THE SOUND IS NOT THAT
OF A STUDIO MIXED RECORDING.

UNLICENSED

LED ZEPPELIN
UPWARDLY MOBILE

JIMMY PAGE U.S.A. 1988

VIENNA VOL.TWO

LED ZEPPELIN

LED ZEPPELIN

Radio Holders
Annual Meeting

LED ZEPPELIN

THE LEGEND OF THE END

LED ZEPPELIN

Senior
Citizens
15% OFF

That's Alright

LED ZEPPELIN

GOOD NIGHT, MOON LIGHT

COMPLETE BADGE HOLDERS

LED ZEPPELIN

OUT ON THE TILES

LED ZEPPELIN

OVER THE HILLS AND FAR AWAY

PAGE·COVERDALE
COME TO CLEVELAND

EARLS COURT

EARLS COURT

LED ZEPPELIN
We're Gonna Groove

LED ZEPPELIN
WE'RE GONNA GROOVE

LED ZEPPELIN
We're Gonna Groove

Led Zeppelin

Led Zeppelin
West Album State

Led Zeppelin
West Album State 1969

LEDZEPTOUR

LED ZEPPELIN
WHITE SUMMER

Led Zeppelin
White Summer

Led Zeppelin
WHITE SUMMER

LED ZEPPELIN
LIVE!

WHOLE LOTTA ROCK!

Above: Various bootleg videos, multiple CD sets and longboxes

Top: More bootleg videos and CD sets.
Bottom left: Swansong postcard, the only place
I have ever seen the unadulterated logo.
Bottom right: The highly collectible edition of
People Weekly magazine.

Robert Plant and John Paul Jones talk about

LED ZEPPELIN

PAST, PRESENT AND FUTURE

PROMOTIONAL USE ONLY
NOT FOR SALE

The Muneo Imamura Collection

The Muneo Imamura Collection

Merit Adventures/ Rick Barrett

Top left: Malaysian pressing of Physical Graffiti. Top right: Japanese Movie flyer. Centre: probably the rarest official Led Zeppelin record ever made. A Swansong interview promo. Only two copies are known to exist.
Right: Japanese Immediate Clapton-Page single.

NEW ROCK

BEST HIT SERIES

IMMEDIATE

IR-234

スネイク・ドライヴ

SNAKE DRIVE

TRIBUTE TO ELMORE

The Ronald Girouard Collection.

キョード―自主公演

LED ZEPPELIN

レッド・ツェッペリン特別公演

9/28 7:00 PM

特別席 ¥2,900

大阪フェスティバルホール

1階 7列 48番 主催＝FM大阪

【ご注意】

Feel
Better
with
Technics
テクニクス
ステレオ

Above: Poster for Osaka Japan show.
Left: Ticket from Bath Festival.

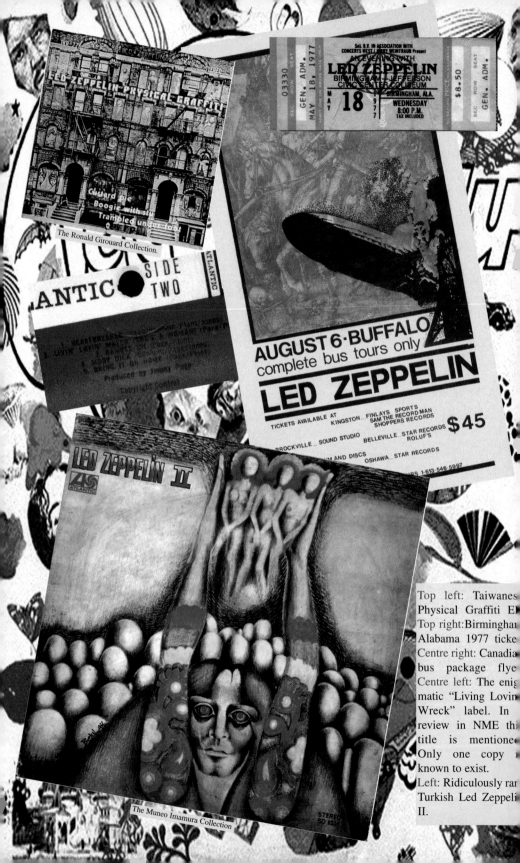

The Ronald Girourard Collection.

ANTIC SIDE TWO · ATLANTIC

1. HEARTBREAKER ... (Bonham/Jones/Plant/Page)
2. LIVIN LOVIN WRECK (SHE'S A WOMAN) (Page/Jones)
3. RAMBLE ON (Plant/Page)
4. MOBY DICK (Bonham/Jones/Page)
5. BRING IT ON HOME (Page/Plant)

Produced by Jimmy Page

Copyright Control

An evening with
LED ZEPPELIN
BIRMINGHAM · JEFFERSON
CIVIC CENTER COLISEUM
MAY 18 1977
WEDNESDAY
8:00 P.M.
TAX INCLUDED
$8.50

AUGUST 6 · BUFFALO
complete bus tours only
LED ZEPPELIN
$45

TICKETS AVAILABLE AT

KINGSTON... FINLAYS SPORTS
SAM THE RECORD MAN
SHOPPERS RECORDS

BROCKVILLE... SOUND STUDIO   BELLEVILLE... STAR RECORDS
ROLUF'S

...UM AND DISCS   OSHAWA... STAR RECORDS

...URS 1-613-546-5997

LED ZEPPELIN II · Atlantic

STEREO
SD 8-204

The Muneo Imamura Collection

Top left: Taiwanes
Physical Graffiti E
Top right:Birmingham
Alabama 1977 ticke
Centre right: Canadia
bus package flye
Centre left: The enig
matic "Living Lovin
Wreck" label. In
review in NME thi
title is mentioned
Only one copy
known to exist.
Left: Ridiculously rar
Turkish Led Zeppeli
II.

Above: Japanese tour poster 1972

Top: Japanese Led Zeppelin retail outlet. This is fairly typical of the kind of dedicated shop to be found in Tokyo.

Above left: The cover of Britain's Melody Maker following the 1975 Earl's Court concerts, a favourite of mine.

Centre right: A handbill from San Antonio Texas 1970

Right: Poster from Orlando 1971.

The Fuckin' PA System
Venue: Oklahoma City
Date: 4/3/77
Cover: D4C in case
Recording: 5
Source: M- Aud
Company: Tarantura
Matrix #: OK 001-003
Place Of Origin: Japan
Total Disc Time: 64:12 - 53:11 - 63:53
N.B. A pretty poor audience recording.

D1:
The Song Remains The Same
Sick Again
Nobody's Fault But Mine
In My Time Of Dying
Since I've Been Loving You
No Quarter
D2:
Ten Years Gone
The Battle Of Evermore
Going To California
Black Country Woman
Bron-Y-Aur Stomp
White Summer - Black Mountain Side
Kashmir
D3:
Out On The Tiles / Moby Dick
Guitar Solo
Achilles Last Stand
Stairway To Heaven
Rock And Roll
Trampled Underfoot

Fucking TY
Venue: Oklahoma - Tampa*
Date: 4/3/77 - 6/3/77*
Cover: D4C in double case
Recording: 4 - 6*
Source: M - Aud
Company: Tattytura
Matrix #: TAK 001 002 003
Place Of Origin: Europe
Total Disc Time: 75.21 - 61.24 - 63.07
N.B. Sound clears up a bit as it progresses but the over-all quality is almost unbearable. A lot of wasted time with chat and crowd noise at the beginning of disc two. The Tampa material is far superior. For those of you wondering about the title, this is the one which fired a shot across Tarantura's bows in response to a title they put out called Plays Pure Bob. It's such a shame the kids can't play nicely together.

D1:
Intro (1.38)
The Song Remains The Same (5:17)
Sick Again (6:42)
Nobody's Fault But Mine (7.18)
In My Time Of Dying (11.45)
Since I've Been Loving You (8:12)
No Quarter (19.26)
Ten Years Gone (10.08)
D2:
Chat - Battle Of Evermore (9.04)
Going To California (5:26)
Black Country Woman (3.01)
Bron-y-Aur Stomp (5:14)
White Summer - Black Mountain Side (7.56)
Kashmir (9.17)
Moby Dick (19.37)
D3:
Guitar Solo (8.57)
Achilles Last Stand (9:26)
Stairway To Heaven (10.56)
Rock & Roll (3.42)
Trampled Underfoot (7.46)

The Song Remains The Same (5.47)*
Sick Again (6.13)*
Nobody's Fault But Mine (6.24)*

Get Loose
Venue: San Diego
Date: 9/3/70
Cover: D4C sleeve
Recording: n/a
Source: n/a
Company: Holy Grail
Matrix #: HGCD 100
Place Of Origin: Japan
Total Disc Time: n/a

N.B. All track information not available at press time.

D1:
Immigrant Song
Heartbreaker
Dazed & Confused
Bring It On Home
That's The Way
Since I've Been Loving You
D2:
Organ Solo - Thank You
What Is & What Should Never Be
Moby Dick
Whole Lotta Love Medley (Inc. Boogie Chillen - I've Got
A Girl - Killing Floor - Two And One To Three - Crosscut
Saw - Honey Bee - The Lemon Song - Needle Blues -
Since My Baby's Been Gone - Lawdy Miss Claudie)
Communication Breakdown
Long Tall Sally

Going To California II
Venue: Berkeley
Date: 9/13/71
Cover: D4C in case
Recording: 5
Source: M - Aud
Company: Tarantura
Matrix #: T2CD 17-1,2
Place Of Origin: Japan
Total Disc Time: 74.02 - 55.45

N.B. This is seemingly the whole show. The quality
remains consistent but is never really good.
Available with two different colour covers,
blue and red — blue being the original.

D1:
Immigrant Song (4.33)
Heartbreaker (6.58)
Since I've Been Loving You (8.10)
Black Dog (5.55)
Dazed & Confused (21.40)
Stairway To Heaven (8.40)
Celebration Day (4.14)
That's The Way (6.36)
Going To California (4.55)
D2:
What Is & What Should Never Be (5.00)
Moby Dick (21.20)
Whole Lotta Love Medley (22.05)
Communication Breakdown (6.15)

Goin' Mobile

Venue: Mobile

Date: 5/13/73

Cover: D4C

Recording: 8

Source: St - SB

Company: MIDAS TOUCH

Matrix #: 61921/2

Place Of Origin: Japan

Total Disc Time: n/a

N.B. Another re-issue of the Mobile concert from the well circulated soundboard tape.

D1:

Rock And Roll (4.19)

Celebration Day (3.36)

Black Dog (6.17)

Over The Hills And Far Away (6.47)

Misty Mountain Hop (4.40)

Since I've Been Loving You (8.58)

No Quarter (11.34)

The Song Remains The Same (5.34)

The Rain Song (8.37)

D2:

Dazed And Confused (28.35)

Stairway To Heaven (11.09)

Moby Dick (15.54)

Golden Pop's Gallery (The)

Venue: Studio

Date: n/a

Cover: D4C

Recording: 10

Source: St - SB

Company: GPG

Matrix #: KDR017

Place Of Origin: Japan

Total Disc Time: n/a

N.B. A straight pirate knock off of various studio tracks. A strange pirate combination of Led Zeppelin and Chicago! Cover says made in Italy.

D1:

Black Dog

Whole Lotta Love

Immigrant Song

Stairway To Heaven

Heartbreaker

Thank You

Since I've Been Loving You

(Seven Chicago tracks follow)

Gonzaga '68

Venue: Spokane

Date: 12/30/68

Cover: D4C in case

Recording: 6

Source: M - Aud

Company: Capricorn

Matrix #: CR 2031E

Place Of Origin: Australia

Total Disc Time: 59.30

N.B. A very well cleaned up version of the earliest tape from the USA. A lot of effort has clearly gone into making this otherwise average tape sound good.

D1:

Train Kept A Rollin' (2.35)

I Can't Quit You (7.02)

As Long As I Have You Medley (9.12)

(Inc. Fresh Garbage - Mockingbird)

Dazed & Confused (9.52)

White Summer (6.59)

How Many More Times (16.11)

Pat's Delight (9.11)

Gonzaga '68

Venue: Spokane

Date: 12/30/68

Cover: D4C sleeve

Recording: 6

Source: M - Aud

Company: So Fucking What

Matrix #: n/a

Place Of Origin: Japan

Total Disc Time: n/a

N.B. The cover says that this is a limited edition of 300 numbered copies. The cover also lists the last track as being from Surrey University in October 1968. It certainly is not.

D1:

Train Kept a Rolling

I Can't Quit You

As Long As I Have You Medley

(Inc. Fresh Garbage – Shake – Hush)

Dazed and Confused

White Summer

How Many More Times

Pat's Delight

Dazed and Confused

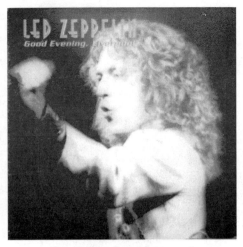

Good Evening Liverpool

Venue: Liverpool
Date: 1/14/73
Cover: D4C
Recording: 8
Source: M - SB
Company: Blizzard
Matrix #: n/a
Place Of Origin: Europe
Total Disc Time: n/a

N.B. The cover says made in Czechoslovakia. This tape is also available as "The Fabulous Four" and "Live In Liverpool".

D1:
Over The Hills & Far Away
Black Dog
Misty Mountain Hop
Since I've Been Loving You
Dancing Days
Bron-y-Aur Stomp
Song Remains The Same
Rain Song
Dazed & Confused (Part one)
D2:
Dazed & Confused (Part Two)
Stairway To Heaven
Whole Lotta Love Medley (Inc. Everybody Needs Someone To Love - Boogie Chillen - Baby I Don't Care - Shape I'm In)
Heartbreaker
The Ocean

Gracias

Venue: Hannover - Zurich*
Date: 6/24/80 - 6/29/80*
Cover: D4C
Recording: 9
Source: St - SB
Company: Antrabata
Matrix #: ARM 240680/ARM 290680
Place Of Origin: Europe
Total Disc Time: 49.13 - 56.13 - 52.53 - 65.30

N.B. Another compilation in very nice packaging from Antrabata. Nothing special about the source tapes which are all extremely overcirculated (if such a thing can be said without me being stoned by the Zepheads!)

D1:
Train Kept A Rollin'
Nobody's Fault But Mine
Black Dog
In The Evening
The Rain Song
Hot Dog
All My Love
Trampled Underfoot
D2:
Since I've Been Loving You
Achilles Last Stand
White Summer
Black Mountain Side
Kashmir
Stairway To Heaven
Rock And Roll
Communication Breakdown
D3:
Train Kept A Rollin' *
Nobody's Fault But Mine*
Black Dog*
In The Evening*
The Rain Song *
Hot Dog*
All My Love *
Trampled Underfoot *

D4:
Since I've Been Loving You *
Achilles Last Stand *
White Summer - Black Mountain Side *
Kashmir *
Stairway To Heaven*
Rock And Roll *
Communication Breakdown *

Graf Zeppelin Marsch
Venue: London
Date: 5/24/75
Cover: D4C
Recording: 8
Source: M - SB
Company: Tarantura
Matrix #: Ear 1-3
Place Of Origin: Japan
Total Disc Time: 58:33 - 57:40 - 63:35
N.B. Another gorgeous slipcase package from Tarantura.
The well circulated soundboard recording from the Earl's
Court show.

D1:
Rock And Roll
Sick Again
Over The Hills And Far Away
In My Time Of Dying
The Song Remains The Same
The Rain Song
Kashmir
D2:
No Quarter
Tangerine
Going To California
That's The Way
Bron-Y-Aur Stomp
Trampled Underfoot
D3:
Dazed And Confused
Stairway To Heaven
Whole Lotta Love
Black Dog

Graham's Superb Volume I
Venue: San Francisco
Date: 4/26/69
Cover: D4C
Recording: 7
Source: M-Aud
Company: Image Quality
Matrix #: IQ-059/060
Place Of Origin: Japan
Total Disc Time: 58:34 - 62:35
N.B. An above average recording from the Winterland
ballroom.

D1:
Communication Breakdown (5.46)
I Can't Quit You (6.57)
Dazed and Confused (15.52)
You Shook Me (10.51)
How Many More Times (19.06)
(Inc. Smokestack Lightning-
Roll Over Beethoven-The Hunter)
D2:
White Summer/Black Mountain Side (12.31)
Killing Floor Medley (9.01)
(Inc. The Lemon Song - That's All Right)
Babe I'm Gonna Leave You (7.22)
Pat's Delight (6.23)
As Long As I Have You Medley (18.24)
(Inc. Fresh Garbage – Shake)
Whole Lotta Love (8.51)

Graham's Superb Volume 2

Venue: San Francisco

Date: 4/27/69

Cover: D4C

Recording: 7

Source: M - Aud

Company: Image Quality

Matrix #: IQ-061/062

Place Of Origin: Japan

Total Disc Time: 61.34 - 61.50

D1:

The Train Kept a Rolling (3.15)

I Can't Quit You (8.09)

As Long As I Have You (18.36)

You Shook Me (9.43)

How Many More Times (21.48)

D2:

Killing Floor (8.59)

White Summer-Black Mountain Side (8.21)

Babe I'm Gonna Leave You (9.47)

Sitting and Thinking (7.44)

Pat's Delight (15.14)

Dazed and Confused (5.38) (cut)

Communication Breakdown (5.35)

Grandiloquence
Venue: Seattle - New York* - Chicago#
Date: 7/17/73 - 7/27/73* - 7/6/73#
Cover: Gatefold binder with pic discs
Recording: 7 -8
Source: St - SB
Company: Antrabata
Matrix #: ARM 17773
Place Of Origin: Europe
Total Disc Time: 52.01 - 51.53 - 74.57 - 66.24 - 49.07 - 58.28 -
60.15 - 40.47 - 53.42
N.B. All information not available at press time. A beautiful cloth
binder packaging with nine picture discs. Mostly previously avail-
able material.

D1:
Rock & Roll (3.57)
Celebration Day (3.53)
Black Dog (5.48)
Over The Hills & Far Away (6.28)
Misty Mountain Hop (4.59)
Since I've Been Loving You (8.35)
No Quarter (13.05)
D2:
The Song Remains The Same (5.40)
The Rain Song (cut) (8.20)
Dazed & Confused (35.12)
D3:
Stairway To Heaven (11.41)
The Ocean
D4:
Rock & Roll (3.57)
Celebration Day (3.53)
Black Dog (5.48)
Over The Hills & Far Away (6.28)
Misty Mountain Hop (4.59)
Since I've Been Loving You (8.35)
No Quarter (13.05)
The Song Remains The Same (5.40)
The Rain Song (cut) (8.20)
D5:
Dazed & Confused (35.12)
Stairway To Heaven (11.41)
D6:
Stairway To Heaven*
Moby Dick (26:34)*

Heartbreaker (7:23)*
Whole Lotta Love (13:55)*
The Ocean (4.16)*
D7:
Rock & Roll (4.23)#
Celebration Day (3.26)#
Black Dog (5.38)#
Over The Hills & Far Away (5.53)#
Misty Mountain Hop (4.36)#
Since I've Been Loving You (8.08)#
No Quarter (11.16)#
The Song Remains The Same (5.30)#
The Rain Song (7.32)#
D8:
Dazed & Confused (26.00)#
Stairway To Heaven (10.13)#
D9:
Moby Dick (6.23)#
Heartbreaker - Whole Lotta Love(18.00)#
Communication Breakdown (4.25)#

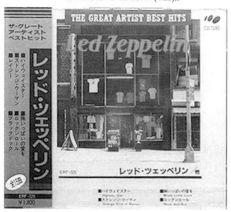

Great Artist Best Hits (The)
Venue: Studio
Date: n/a
Cover: D4C
Recording: 10
Source: St - SB
Company: Culture
Matrix #: ERF 026
Place Of Origin: Japan
Total Disc Time: n/a
N.B. A straight pirate knock off of various studio tracks.
Several Deep Purple tracks start the disc.

D1:
Whole Lotta Love
Stairway To Heaven
Rock & Roll
Black Dog
Immigrant Song
Good Times Bad Times
Heartbreaker
Living Loving Maid

Great Taste Last Night
Venue: London
Date: 5/25/75
Cover: D4C
Recording: 7
Source: M - Aud
Company: Image Quality
Matrix #: IQ-031/32/33/34
Place Of Origin: Japan
Total Disc Time: 56.10 - 63.37 -53.50 -43.22
N.B. One of the better tapes from this performance at
Earl's Court. Quite a bit of hiss on this one.
Not quite as good quality as the version on the title
"Earl's Court 1975".

D1:
Introduction (1.55)
Rock and Roll (3.45)
Sick Again (6.20)
Over the Hills and Far Away (8.33)
In My Time of Dying (13.17)
Song Remains the Same (5.14)
The Rain Song (7.33)
Kashmir (9.13)
D2:
No Quarter (27.24)
Tangerine (4.15)
Going to California (5.43)
That's the Way (8.45)
Bron-y-Aur Stomp (7.58)
Trampled under Foot (9.50)
D3:
Moby Dick (21.49)
Dazed and Confused (31.57)
D4:
Stairway to Heaven (18.29)
Whole Lotta Love Medley
(Inc.The Crunge -Black Dog (7.10)
Heartbreaker (10.52)
Communication Breakdown (8.15)

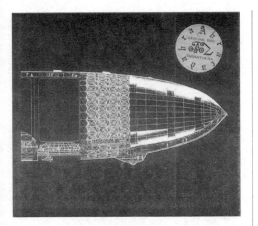

Groove

Venue: Raleigh

Date: 4/8/70

Cover: D4C in digipak and slipcase

Recording: 6

Source: M - Aud

Company: Tarantura

Matrix #: RAL-1,2

Place Of Origin: Japan

Total Disc Time: 49.05 - 39.11

N.B. The cover lists this show as the seventh of April but recent documentation puts it on the 8th of April at Dorten Auditorium.
Nice package again from Tarantura.

D1:

We're Gonna Groove (3.16)

Dazed And Confused(15.36)

Heartbreaker (7.06)

Bring It On Home (9.06)

White Summer - Black Mountain Side (14.01)

D2:

Since I've Been Loving You (7.23)

Thank You (10.19)

What Is And What Should Never Be (4.25)

Moby Dick (17.04)

Hamburg 1970

Venue: Hamburg

Date: 3/12/70

Cover: D4C in double slimline case

Recording: 3

Source: M - Aud

Company: Immigrant

Matrix #: IM 024-025

Place Of Origin: Japan

Total Disc Time: 61.53 - 57.52

N.B. An unusual but poor recording from the show in Hamburg. The date on the cover is incorrect. Strange intro to Heartbreaker.

D1:

We're Gonna Groove (4.10)

I Can't Quit You (6.17)

Dazed & Confused (18.12)

Heartbreaker (6.39)

White Summer - Black Mountain Side (13.05)

Since I've Been Loving You (6.55)

Organ Solo Thank You (6.26)

D2:

What Is & What Should Never Be (4.43)

Moby Dick (20.41)

How Many More Times (25.44)

Whole Lotta Love (6.44)

Hampton '71

Venue: Hampton Beach Coliseum
Date: 9/9/71
Cover: D4C sleeve
Recording: 8
Source: M - SB
Company: Theramin
Matrix #: 020971
Place Of Origin: Japan
Total Disc Time: n/a

N.B. This tape has surfaced in several different versions. The first inkling that a soundboard existed was a really dreadful mix with Jones entirely in one channel. Then a mono soundboard came out. My records show that this was on September 9th but the cover says the 2nd.

D1:
Immigrant Song
Heartbreaker
Since I've Been Loving You
Black Dog
Dazed And Confused
D2:
Stairway To Heaven
Celebration Day
That's The Way
Going To California
What Is And What Should Never Be
Moby Dick

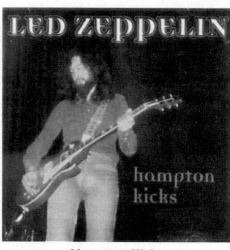

Hampton Kicks

Venue: Hampton - San Francisco** - Copenhagen*
Date: 9/9/71 - 1/11/69** - 3/16/69*
Cover: D4C
Recording: 5,8**,7*
Source: M – Aud, St- SB**, M – Aud*
Company: House of Elrond
Matrix #: AP-2001
Place Of Origin: Japan
Total Disc Time: n/a

N.B. A compilation of material from three different sources, all of which have been available before.

D1:
Immigrant Song
Heartbreaker
Since I've Been Loving You
Black Dog
Dazed and Confused
Stairway to Heaven
Celebration Day
That's the Way
D2:
Going to California
What Is and What Should Never Be
Moby Dick
I Can't Quit You**
Dazed and Confused**
You Shook Me**
I Can't Quit You*
I Gotta Move*
Dazed and Confused*
How Many More Times*

Hannover 1980

Venue: Hannover
Date: 6/24/80
Cover: D4C gatefold sleeve
Recording: 9
Source: St - SB
Company: Tarantura
Matrix #: 1980 11,12
Place Of Origin: Japan
Total Disc Time: n/a
N.B. Part of the deluxe set "1980" and also available
separately as this two CD set. Nothing special it is the
well documented soundboard tape.

D1:
Train Kept A Rollin'
Nobody's Fault But Mine
Black Dog
In The Evening
Rain Song
Hot Dog
All My Love
Trampled Underfoot
D2:
Since I've Been Loving You
Achilles Last Stand
White Summer - Black Mountain Side
Kashmir
Stairway To Heaven
Rock & Roll
Communication Breakdown

Hard Company

Venue: New York
Date: 9/3/71
Cover: D4C
Recording: 4
Source: M -Aud
Company: n/a
Matrix #: ZA 13/14
Place Of Origin: Japan
Total Disc Time: 71.07 – 67.56
N.B. Also available as "How've You Been".
A pretty poor recording from Madison Square Gardens.

D1:
Immigrant Song
Heartbreaker
Since I've Been Loving You
Black Dog
Dazed & Confused
Stairway To Heaven
Celebration Day
That's The Way
D2:
Going To California
What Is & What Should Never Be
Moby Dick
Whole Lotta Love Medley
(Inc. Boogie Chillen – My Baby Left Me –
That's Alright – Mess Of Blues – You Shook Me)
Communication Breakdown
Organ Solo - Thank You
Rock & Roll

Headley Grange

Venue: Headley Grange

Date: 12/?73 - 6/?/74

Cover: D2C in case

Recording: 8

Source: St - SB

Company: Immigrant

Matrix #: IM 008

Place Of Origin: USA

Total Disc Time: 67:24.

N.B. A very good version of the Physical Graffiti rehearsal tape.

D1:

The Rover (1.05)

In My Time Of Dying (8.19)

Trampled Underfoot (3.42)

In The Morning (take 1) (5.22)

The Wanton Song (take 1) (3.25)

Sick Again (3.37)

Hots On For Nowhere (3.02)

The Wanton Song (take 2) (0.49)

Take Me Home (5.55)

In The Morning (take 2) (5.58)

Trampled Underfoot (takes 1 to 6) (19.23)

The Rover (takes 1 to 3) (6.27)

Heartbeat

Venue: Bournemouth

Date: 12/2/71

Cover: D4C

Recording: 5 - 6

Source: M -Aud

Company: H Bomb

Matrix #: 9616

Place Of Origin: Japan

Total Disc Time: 65.00

N.B. The whole tape that has been circulating for years. A disjointed recording with various cuts and edits.

D1:

Immigrant Song

Heartbreaker

Black Dog

Bron-Y-Aur Stomp

Dazed And Confused

What Is And What Should Never Be

Rock And Roll

Whole Lotta Love Medley

(Inc. Just A Little Hideaway - Trucking Little Mama -

Boogie Woogie - Heartbeat - Hello Mary Lou -

Lawdy Miss Clawd -,I Can't Quit You)

Heaven Can Wait

Venue: n/a
Date: n/a
Cover: D4C triangular box set
Recording: n/a
Source: n/a
Company: n/a **Matrix #:** n/a
Place Of Origin: n/a
Total Disc Time: 72.11 - 76.14
N.B. Details not available at press time.
Probably one of the L.A. or Long Beach shows.
Limited to 300 numbered copies.

D1:
Rock And Roll (3.54)
Sick Again (5.13)
Over The Hills & Far Away (7.06)
In My Time Of Dying (11.22)
The Song Remains The Same (5.33)
The Rain Song (7.55)
Kashmir (8.44)
No Quarter (20.36)
D2:
Trampled Underfoot (7.20)
Moby Dick (21.52)
Dazed & Confused (22.17)
Stairway To Heaven (11.07)
Whole Lotta Love (7.15)
Black Dog (5.53)

Heineken

Venue: Berlin
Date: 7/7/80
Cover: D4C sleeve
Recording: 9
Source: St - SB
Company: Tarantura
Matrix #: LAST 1-2
Place Of Origin: Japan
Total Disc Time: n/a
N.B. Supposedly the last title from Tarantura
(Or possibly one of the last) which seems ironic as it
was the last title that Toasted did before folding.
Rumour has it that it may be one of only 100 copies.

D1:
Train Kept A Rollin'
Nobody's Fault But Mine
Black Dog
In The Evening
Rain Song
Hot Dog
All My Love
Trampled Underfoot
Since I've Been Loving You
D2:
Apology By Jimmy Page
White Summer
Black Mountain Side
Kashmir
Stairway To Heaven
Rock & Roll
Whole Lotta Love

Hello Pittsburgh

Venue: Pittsburgh

Date: 7/24/73

Cover: D4C

Recording: 5-6

Source: M - Aud

Company: Image Quality

Matrix #: IQ 057/058

Place Of Origin: Japan

Total Disc Time: n/a

N.B. An average recording from the Three Rivers Stadium.

D1:

Rock and Roll

Celebration Day

Black Dog

Over the Hills and Far Away

Misty Mountain Hop

Since I've Been Letting You

No Quarter

The Song Remains the Same

The Rain Song

D2:

Dazed and Confused

Heartbreaker

Whole Lotta Love (Inc. Boogie Chillen)

The Ocean

Historic BBC Presentation (The)

Venue: London

Date: 4/1/71

Cover: DBW Slipcase

Recording: n/a

Source: St- SB

Company: Antrabata

Matrix #: ARM 25371

Place Of Origin: Europe

Total Disc Time: n/a

N.B. Track times are not available at press time. Cover lists the date as March 25th.

D1:

Immigrant Song

Heartbreaker

Since I've Been Loving You

Black Dog

Dazed & Confused

Stairway To Heaven

D2:

Going To California

That's The Way

What Is & What Should Never Be

Whole Lotta Love Medley

Thank You

Communication Breakdown

Holiday In Waikiki

Venue: Honolulu

Date: 9/6/70

Cover: D4C

Recording: 6

Source: M -Aud

Company: Scorpio

Matrix #: n/a

Place Of Origin: USA

Total Disc Time: n/a

N.B. Also available as "Box Of Tricks".

A few minor cuts in the tape but overall a good atmospheric recording at the HIC. The disc is a gold CD but as far as I can tell it isn't a CDR.

D1:

Immigrant Song

Dazed And Confused

Heartbreaker

Since I've Been Loving You

What Is And What Should Never Be

Moby Dick

Whole Lotta Love

Communication Breakdown

Hot August Night

Venue: Fort Worth

Date: 8/23/71

Cover: D4C

Recording: 7

Source: M - SB

Company: Diagrams Of Led Zeppelin

Matrix #: TDOLZ 429701/2

Place Of Origin: Japan

Total Disc Time: 60.13 – 25.32

N.B. A whole slew of recently uncovered tapes from 1971 have been released in 97-98. The tapes from that year generally don't appear to have been very good. This could be as a direct result of Peter Grant's public statements concerning the bootlegging of Led Zeppelin immediately after the release of Blueberry Hill and Mudslide. This one however does manage to capture the band in reasonable quality. Recorded right after the two nights in Los Angeles. Nice to see a bootleg label still turning up new stuff worth having.

D1:

Dazed And Confused (18:40)

Stairway To Heaven (10:05)

Celebration Day (4:13)

That's The Way (7:26)

What Is And What Should Never Be (4:50)

Moby Dick (14:57)

D2:

Whole Lotta Love Medley (24:34)

(Inc. Truckin' Little Mama -

Mess O' Blues - You Shook Me)

Communication Breakdown (0:57) (cut)

Hot Rods In Pontiac
Venue: Pontiac
Date: 4/30/77
Cover: D4C sleeve
Recording: 7
Source: M -Aud
Company: Diagrams Of Led Zeppelin
Matrix #: TDOLZ 030/031/032
Place Of Origin: Japan
Total Disc Time: n/a
N.B. The complete tape of this show which has not been out previously on bootleg. An acceptable audience recording.

D1:
The Song Remains The Same
The Rover intro.-Sick Again
Nobody's Fault But Mine
In My Time of Dying
Since I've Been Loving You
No Quarter
D2:
Ten Years Gone
The Battle of Evermore
Going to California
Black Country Woman
Bron-Y-Aur Stomp
White Summer/Black Mountain Side
Kashmir
D3:
Out on Tiles intro.-Moby Dick,
Guitar Solo (Inc. Star Spangled Banner)
Achilles Last Stand
Stairway to Heaven
Rock And Roll
Trampled Underfoot

How've You Been
Venue: New York
Date: 9/3/71
Cover: D4C
Recording: 5
Source: M -Aud
Company: Diagrams Of Led Zeppelin
Matrix #: TDOLZ 020/021/022
Place Of Origin: Japan
Total Disc Time: n/a
N.B. Once more Diagrams gives us an unreleased show. Not the best recording but the best known tape to exist of this important show at MSG.

D1:
Immigrant Song
Heartbreaker
Since I've Been Loving You
Black Dog
Dazed & Confused
Stairway To Heaven
D2:
Celebration Day
That's The Way
Going To California
What Is & What Should Never Be
Moby Dick
D3:
Whole Lotta Love Medley
(Inc. Boogie Chillen – My Baby Left Me –
That's Alright – Mess Of Blues – You Shook Me)
Communication Breakdown
Organ Solo - Thank You
Rock & Roll

I Can't Get No Satisfaction

Venue: Stockholm
Date: 3/6/73
Cover: D4C
Recording: 4
Source: M - Aud
Company: Diagram's of Led Zeppelin
Matrix #: TDOLZ 369701/369702/369703
Place Of Origin: Japan
Total Disc Time: 59.35 - 41.30 - 40.03
N.B. A new recording from the Tennishallen.
Another one of those recordings probably
best left to completists although some
people consider it better quality than others.

D1:
Rock and Roll
Over the Hills and Far Away
Black Dog
Misty Mountain Hop
Since I've Been Loving You
Dancing Days
Bron-y-Aur Stomp
I Can't Get No Satisfaction - Song Remains the Same
The Rain Song
D2:
Dazed and Confused
Stairway to Heaven
D3:
Whole Lotta Love Medley
(Inc. Everybody Needs Somebody to Love -
Boogie Chillen - Baby I Don't Care -
Let's Have a Party -I Can't Quit You)
Heartbreaker
The Ocean

Image Club (The)

Venue: Miami
Date: 2/14/69
Cover: D4C in case
Recording: 4 - 5
Source: M - Aud
Company: Rag Doll
Matrix #: RDM 94002A-B
Place Of Origin: Japan
Total Disc Time: 43.15 - 44.34

N.B. Another re-issue of the show which first appeared
as "Snowblind". Not from January as previously thought.

D1:
Train Kept A Rollin' (3.14)
I Can't Quit You (5.38)
Dazed & Confused (11.22)
Killing Floor (5.54)
Babe I'm Gonna Leave You (6.36)
How Many More Times (11.36)
D2:
White Summer - Black Mountain Side (9.50)
As Long As I Have You Medley (13.15)
(Inc. Mockingbird)
You Shook Me (9.05)
Pat's Delight (11.59)

In A Daze

Venue: Toronto

Date: 9/4/71

Cover: D4C in double case

Recording: 5

Source: M - Aud

Company: Keep Out

Matrix #: 93103 93104

Place Of Origin: Japan

Total Disc Time: 57.45 - 57.49

N.B. The cover doesn't list That's The Way. A few cue stops are in the wrong places and the tape runs a bit slow. Also there is a much better recording of this out there.

D1:

Immigrant Song (3.50)

Heartbreaker (7.05)

Since I ve Been Loving You (7.05)

Black Dog (5.22)

Dazed And Confused (20.41)

Stairway To Heaven (9.00)

Celebration Day (4.20)

D2:

That's The Way (6.31)

Going To California (4.08)

What Is & What Should Never Be (4.20)

Moby Dick (14.52)

Whole Lotta Love Medley: (20.12)

(Inc. Boogie Chillen - My Baby Left Me -

Mess Of Blues - You Shook Me)

Communication Breakdown (7.31)

In Concert And Beyond

Venue: Buffalo

Date: 7/15/73

Cover: D4C

Recording: 8

Source: St - SB

Company: Diagrams Of Led Zeppelin

Matrix #: TDOLZ-0001/0002

Place Of Origin: Japan

Total Disc Time: 62:56 / 43:05

N.B. Another re-issue of the now well known Buffalo soundboard tape. Previously available as "Misty Mountain Crop", "And It Makes Me Wonder", "Outrageous Live", "Buffalo 1973".

D1:

Rock And Roll (4:56)

Celebration Day (3:27)

Bring It On Home - Black Dog (6:34)

Over The Hills And Far Away (7:04)

Misty Mountain Hop (4:45)

Since I've Been Loving You (9:06)

No Quarter (13:21)

The Song Remains The Same (5:24)

The Rain Song (8:19)

D2:

Dazed And Confused (Inc. San Francisco) (32:11)

Stairway To Heaven (10:54)

In Concert 1969 -1971

Venue: London

Date: 6/27/69 - 4/1/71*

Cover: DBW in double case

Recording: n/a

Source: n/a

Company: Liverpool

Matrix #: CDP-10002

Place Of Origin: Japan

Total Disc Time: n/a

N.B. All track information not available at press time.

Probably from the two BBC shows.

D1:

Communication Breakdown (3.22)

I Can't Quit You (6.16)

You Shook Me (10.13)

Immigrant Song (3.17)

Heartbreaker (5.07)

Dazed & Confused (16.19)

D2:

Going To California (4.03)

What Is & What Should Never Be (4.23)

Stairway To Heaven (8.43)

Black Dog (5.17)

Whole Lotta Love Medley (20.53)

(Inc. Boogie Chillen-Travelin Mama-

That's Alright- For What It's Worth-

Mess Of Blues- Honey Bee -The Lemon Song)

Inspired

Venue: Hampton Beach

Date: 9/9/71

Cover: D4C   sleeve

Recording: 8

Source: M- SB

Company: Antrabata

Matrix #: ARM 020971

Place Of Origin: Europe

Total Disc Time: 49.28 - 46.50

N.B. Limited edition of 325 numbered copies.

Recorded at Hampton Beach Coliseum.

Also available as "Hampton '71".

D1:

Immigrant Song (cut)

Heartbreaker

Since I've Been Loving You

Black Dog

Dazed And Confused (cut)

D2:

Stairway To Heaven

Celebration Day

That's The Way

Going To California

What Is And What Should Never Be

Moby Dick (cut)

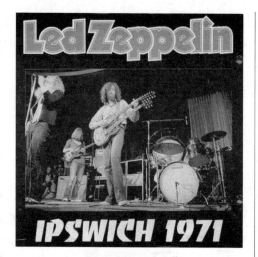

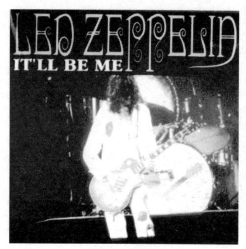

Ipswich 1971

Venue: Ipswich
Date: 11/16/71
Cover: D4C
Recording: 6
Source: M -Aud
Company: Diagrams Of Led Zeppelin
Matrix #: TDOLZ
Place Of Origin: 057
Total Disc Time: 62.38 - 60.50

N.B. Clear enough recording of the St Matthews Baths show. Recently surfaced.

D1:
Immigrant Song (4.42)
Heartbreaker (7.54)
Black Dog (6.49)
Since I've Been Loving You (8.17)
Rock & Roll (5.03)
Stairway To Heaven (10.26)
Going To California (5.35)
That's The Way (8.05)
Tangerine (5.47)
D2:
Dazed & Confused (28.33)
What Is & What Should Never Be (5.02)
Celebration Day (5.47)
Whole Lotta Love Medley (21.28)

It'll Be Me

Venue: Los Angeles
Date: 6/26/77
Cover: D4C sleeve
Recording: 7-8
Source: M - Aud
Company: Diagrams of Led Zeppelin
Matrix #: Vol 054
Place Of Origin: Japan
Total Disc Time: n/a

N.B. Just another reissue of one of the Forum tapes.

D1:
Song Remains the Same
Sick Again
Nobody Fault but Mine
Over the Hills and Far Away
Since I've Been Loving You
No Quarter
D2:
Ten Years Gone
The Battle of Evermore
Going to California
That's All Right - Black Country Woman -
Bron-Y-Aur Stomp
White Summer - Black Mountain Side
Kashmir
Moby Dick
D3:
Guitar Solo
Achilles Last Stand
Stairway to Heaven
It'll Be Me

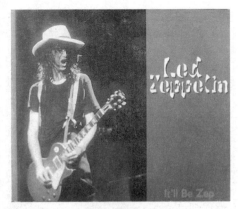

It'll Be Zep
Venue: Fort Worth
Date: 5/22/77
Cover: D4C in double case
Recording: 7-8
Source: St - Aud
Company: Silver Rarities
Matrix #: SIRA 171-172-173
Place Of Origin: Europe
Total Disc Time: n/a
N.B. Not all the information was available on this title
at press time.

D1:
The Song Remains The Same
The Rover Intro,
Sick Again
Nobody's Fault But Mine
Over The Hills And Far Away
Since I've Been Loving You
D2:
No Quarter
Ten Years Gone
Battle Of Evermore
Going To California
Black Country Woman
Bron-Y-Aur Stomp
White Summer - Black Mountain Side
Kashmir
D3:
Moby Dick (15.23)
Guitar Solo - Achilles Last Stand (20.24)
Stairway To Heaven (13.01)
Whole Lotta Love - Rock & Roll (6.59)
It'll Be Me (4.49)

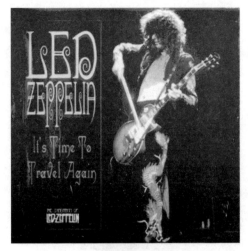

It's Time to Travel Again
Venue: Brussels
Date: 1/12/75
Cover: D4C
Recording: 7
Source: M - Aud
Company: Diagram's of Led Zeppelin
Matrix #: TDOLZ 419701/419702
Place Of Origin: Japan
Total Disc Time: 47.45 - 60.14
N.B. Apparently a new recording from the Voorst
National. Some minor quality fluctuations.

D1:
Rock and Roll
Sick Again
When the Levee Breaks
Over the Hills and Far Away
When the Levee Breaks
Song Remains the Same
The Rain Song
Kashmir
D2:
The Wanton Song
No Quarter
Trampled Underfoot
In My Time of Dying
Stairway to Heaven
Black Dog
Communication Breakdown

It's Been Great

Venue: Oakland
Date: 7/23/77
Cover: D2C
Recording: 8
Source: M -Aud
Company: Image Quality
Matrix #: IQ 0010/11/12
Place Of Origin: Japan
Total Disc Time: 61.57 - 61.25 - 45.55

N.B. Another release of the first night in Oakland. Also
available as "Confusion".

D1:
The Song Remains The Same (6:18)
The Rover - Sick Again (6:51)
Nobody's Fault But Mine (7:28)
Over The Hills And Far Away (8:36)
Since I've Been Loving You (9:40)
No Quarter (22:47)
D2:
Ten Years Gone (11 :34)
The Battle Of Evermore (7:13)
Going To California (6:04)
Black Country Woman (2:32)
Bron-y-Aur Stomp (7:06)
Trampled Underfoot (8:01)
White Summer - Black Mountain (9:16)
Kashmir (9:36)
D3:
Guitar Solo (10:17)
Achilles Last Stand (9:57)
Stairway To Heaven (12:12)
Whole Lotta Love (3:13)
Rock And Roll (4:15)
Black Dog (5:59)

Jazz

Venue: Newport
Date: 7/6/69
Cover: D4C
Recording: 7
Source: M -Aud
Company: n/a
Matrix #: NPJF 1001
Place Of Origin: Japan
Total Disc Time: n/a

N.B. The first time this has been available all in one
place. Previous releases either only included the encore
of Long Tall Sally or everything but the encore.
Several different tapes were available of this show.
The Tarantura title "Tales From 69"
also includes this tape in it's entirety.

D1:
Train Kept A Rollin (3.45)
I Can't Quit You (5.57)
Dazed &Confused (13.05)
You Shook Me (11.13)
How Many More Times (14.53)
Communication Breakdown (4.46)
Long Tall Sally (5.12)

Jimmy's Birthday Party

Venue: London
Date: 1/9/70
Cover: D4C in case
Recording: 7,5*
Source: St - SB, M - SB*
Company: Tarantura
Matrix #: RAH 1-2
Place Of Origin: Japan
Total Disc Time: 50.10 - 41.37

N.B. Another extraordinary package from Tarantura. Comes in a box which contains a poster with some spectacular on stage shots from the show. The contents of both discs are markedly improved on the competition. Unquestionably a "must-have".

D1:
Whole Lotta Love (6.52)
Communication Breakdown (6.06)
C'mon Everybody (2.44)
Something Else (2.16)
Bring It On Home (8.00)
How Many More Times Medley (25.17)
(Inc. The Hunter - Boogie Chillen - Move On Down The
Line - Bottle Up And Go - Leave My Woman Alone -
The Lemon Song - That's Alright)
D2:
We're Gonna Groove (3.42)
I Can't Quit You (5.03)
White Summer (3.51)
Black Mountain Side (8.20)
Whole Lotta Love (6.27)
Communication Breakdown (cut) (2.32)
C'mon Everybody (2.34)
Long Tall Sally Medley (7.38)
Incl. Great Balls Of Fire - Move On Down The Line

Jim's Picks

Venue: Hampton
Date: 9/9/71
Cover: D4C sleeve
Recording: 8
Source: M -SB
Company: Tarantura
Matrix #: HAMP-1,2
Place Of Origin: Japan
Total Disc Time: n/a

N.B. Also available as "Hampton '71" and "Inspired".

D1:
Immigrant Song (3:55)
Heartbreaker (7:41)
Since I've Been Loving You (8:24)
Out On The Tiles Intro, Black Dog (7:06)
Dazed And Confused (22:17)
D2:
Stairway To Heaven (10:49)
Celebration Day (5:43)
That's The Way (7:33)
Going To California (5:30)
What Is And What Should Never Be (5:26)
Moby Dick (11:44)

Join The Blimp

Venue: London
Date: 5/17/75
Cover: DBW sleeve
Recording: 7
Source: M - Aud
Company: Tarantura
Matrix #: UK 1-4
Place Of Origin: Japan
Total Disc Time: 54.47 - 50.59 - 29.00 - 58.56

N.B. Nicely packaged rare set from Japan of the first night at Earl's Court. Regrettably there don't seem to be any good tapes around of this show. This is unneccessarily split over four discs and could easily have fit on three.

D1:
Introduction (1.13)
Rock & Roll (4.20)
Sick Again (5.26)
Over The Hills & Far Away (8.06)
In My Time Of Dying (11.35)
The Song Remains The Same (6.08)
The Rain Song (8.02)
Kashmir (9.57)
D2:
No Quarter (22.58)
Tangerine (4.54)
Going To California (9.04)
That's The Way (6.47)
Bron-y-Aur Stomp (7.16)
D3:
Trampled Underfoot (9.19)
Moby Dick (19.41)
D4:
Dazed &Confused (27.32)
Stairway To Heaven (20.06)
Whole Lotta Love (5.13)
Black Dog (6.05)

Johnny Piston & The Moondogs

Venue: New Orleans
Date: 5/14/73
Cover: D4C
Recording: 8
Source: St -SB
Company: n/a
Matrix #: TM 005/006
Place Of Origin: Europe
Total Disc Time: 73.01 – 76.11

N.B. The Municipal Auditorium soundboard tape. Previously available as "Live & Led Live", "Longest Night" and "Whole Lotta Rock". The track listing has been shifted around to make it all fit on two discs.

D1:
Heartbreaker
Whole Lotta Love
Communication Breakdown
Rock And Roll (cut)
Celebration Day
Black Dog
Over The Hills And Far Away
Misty Mountain Hop
Since I've Been Loving You
No Quarter
D2:
The Song Remains The Same
The Rain Song (cut)
Dazed And Confused
Stairway To Heaven
Moby Dick (cut)

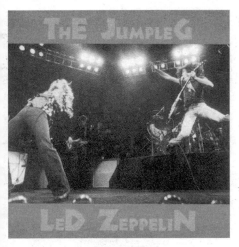

Jumpleg (The)

Venue: New York
Date: 2/12/75
Cover: D4C in cardboard case
Recording: 6 - 7
Source: St - Aud
Company: Tarantura
Matrix #: T3CD 7 1-3
Place Of Origin: Japan
Total Disc Time: 52.57 - 45.49 - 61.50
N.B. Powerful and confident sounding show. Nicely packaged by the boys at Tarantura.

D1:
Rock And Roll (3.46)
Sick Again (4:57)
Over The Hills And Far Away (8.57)
In My Time Of Dying (11.38)
The Song Remains The Same (6:28)
The Rain Song (7:42)
Kashmir (8:31)
D2:
No Quarter (18.08)
Trampled Underfoot (8:11)
Moby Dick (17.20)
D3:
Dazed And Confused (31.41)
Stairway To Heaven (11.57)
Whole Lotta Love (1:49)
Black Dog (5:33)
Heartbreaker (8:59)

KB

Venue: Copenhagen
Date: 5/3/71
Cover: D4C
Recording: 7
Source: M - Aud
Company: Image Quality
Matrix #: IQ-051/052
Place Of Origin: Japan
Total Disc Time: 66.55 - 57.10
N.B. The complete tape of the show at the KB Hallen in Copenhagen. Including all of the rare stuff. Gallow's Pole, Four Sticks, and the bizarre melding of Communication Breakdown with Celebration Day.

D1:
Immigrant Song (3.52)
Heart Breaker (7.28)
Since I've Been Loving You (8.21)
Dazed and Confused (19.13)
Black Dog (6.27)
Stairway to Heaven (9.35)
Going to California (4.35)
That's the Way (7.23)
D2:
What Is and What Should Never Be (5.43)
Four Sticks (6.02)
Gallow's Pole (6.14)
Whole Lotta Love Medley (21.09)
(Inc. Boogie Chillen-Trucking Little Mama-That's All Right- Mess of Blues- Honey Bee- The Lemon Song)
Communication Breakdown - Celebration Day (9.56)
Misty Mountain Hop (4.56)
Rock and Roll (4.04)

Kicks

Venue: Stockholm

Date: 3/14/69

Cover: D4C sleeve

Recording: 8

Source: M - SB

Company: Tarantura

Matrix #: K&S 974

Place Of Origin: Japan

Total Disc Time: 21:27

N.B. Tarantura knocks off the old K & S vinyl title.

D1:

I Can't Quit You Baby (5:34)

I Gotta Move (3:31)

Dazed And Confused (10:08)

How Many Times More (2:14)

Killer Missile

Venue: Tampa

Date: 6/3/77

Cover: D4C sleeve

Recording: 5

Source: M - Aud

Company: n/a

Matrix #: n/a

Place Of Origin: Japan

Total Disc Time: n/a

N.B. The show that was rained out and cancelled early. 500 Numbered copies.

D1:

Song Remains The Same

Sick Again

Nobody's Fault But Mine

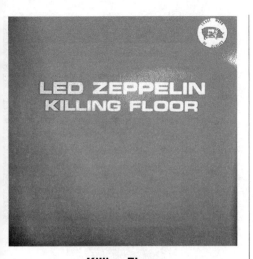

Killing Floor

Venue: Boston

Date: 1/26/69

Cover: D4C

Recording: 6

Source: M -Aud

Company: Cobra

Matrix #: 018

Place Of Origin: Japan

Total Disc Time: n/a

N.B. Another reissue of an old tape by Cobra using the vinyl title and packaging. This tape has also been available as "Tight But Loose".

D1:

Train Kept A Rollin

I Can't Quit You

Killing Floor

Dazed & Confused

You Shook Me

Communication Breakdown

D2:

White Summer

Black Mountain Side

Babe I'm Gonna Leave You

Pat's Delight

How Many More Times

Kinetic Circus

Venue: Ipswich

Date: 11/12/71

Cover: D4C sleeve

Recording: 7

Source: M -Aud

Company: Theramin

Matrix #: ARM171171

Place Of Origin: Europe

Total Disc Time: 58.22

N.B. This title also came out with a different cover under the name "Two Penny Upright". It is the same tape as the "Ipswich 1971" Cd but better quality and shorter. This is an Antrabata title with a Theramin sleeve, making it probably European manufactured for Japan. The cover says it is from the Birmingham Mayfair Suite and also lists the tracks wrong.

D1:

Introduction (1.02)

Immigrant Song (3.48)

Heartbreaker (7.51)

Black Dog (6.20)

Since I've Been Loving You (8.17)

Rock & Roll (3.52)

That's The Way (6.55)

Tangerine (6.52)

Dazed & Confused (13.26)

Kingdom Of Zep

Venue: Seattle
Date: 7/17/77
Cover: D4C in double case
Recording: 5
Source: M - Aud
Company: Silver Rarities
Matrix #: SIRA 131-132-133
Place Of Origin: Europe
Total Disc Time: 71:27 - 64:48 - 71:17
N.B. The first appearance of the legendary Seattle concert. Although this show is known to exist on video it has never seen a full release.
Unfortunately this is not the soundboard tape.

D1:
The Song Remains The Same (7.52)
Sick Again (8.03)
Nobody's Fault But Mine (7.55)
Over The Hills & Far Away (8.43)
Since I've Been Loving You (9.17)
No Quarter (29.35)
D2:
Ten Years Gone (14.35)
Battle Of Evermore (7.21)
Going To California (6.44)
Black Country Woman (1.48)
Bron-Y-Aur Stomp (12.21)
White Summer - Black Mountain Side (11.16)
Kashmir (10.41)
D3:
Moby Dick (25.56)
Page Solo (14.47)
Achilles Last Stand (10.52)
Stairway To Heaven (13.32)
Whole Lona Love - Rock & Roll (6.08)

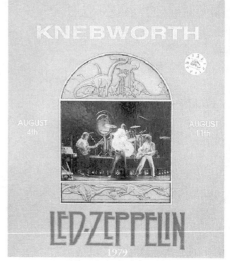

Knebworth 1979

Venue: Knebworth
Date: 8/4/79 - 8/11/79*
Cover: D4C gatefold book with hot foil stamp
Recording: 8
Source: St - Aud
Company: Tarantura
Matrix #: KNEB 04-1-3 KNEB 11-1-3
Place Of Origin: Japan
Total Disc Time: 59.45 - 64.20 - 48.45 - 53.18 - 48.06 - 39.05
N.B. This one takes packaging over the edge once again. A beautiful fold open book type cover 12" by 10" with a twenty page color booklet inside and a repro of the poster for the 11th. All six CD's actually show a slight improvement in quality over previous versions. Ridiculously limited and ridiculously priced.

D1:
The Song Remains The Same (5.09)
Celebration Day (3.03)
Black Dog (5.02)
Nobody's Fault But Mine (6.06)
Over The Hills & Far Away (6.37)
Misty Mountain Hop (4.24)
Since I've Been Loving You (8.00)
No Quarter (17.00)
D2:
Ten Years Gone (7.00)
Hot Dog (3.11)
The Rain Song (8.22)
White Summer - Black Mountain Side (6.26)
Kashmir (8.41)
Trampled Underfoot (6.56)
Sick Again (5.06)
Achilles Last Stand (8.54)
D3:
Guitar Solo - In The Evening (14.50)
Stairway To Heaven (9.21)
Rock & Roll (3.35)
You'll Never Walk Alone (0.30)
Whole Lotta Love (6.51)
Heartbreaker (5.43)
D4:
The Song Remains The Same (5.01)
Celebration Day (2.54)
Black Dog (5.14)
Nobody's Fault But Mine (5.44)
Over The Hills & Far Away (5.46)
Misty Mountain Hop (4.27)
Since I've Been Loving You (8.31)
No Quarter (13.47)
D5:
Hot Dog (4.03)
The Rain Song (7.42)
White Summer/ Black Mountain Side (5.59)
Kashmir (8.13)
Trampled Underfoot (6.20)
Sick Again (5.07)
Achilles Last Stand (8.58)
D6:
Guitar Solo - In The Evening (12.24)
Stairway To Heaven (9.29)
Rock & Roll (3.47)
Whole Lotta Love - Boogie Chillen (10.24)
Communication Breakdown (2.13)

Knees Up Mother Brown

Venue: Charlotte
Date: 6/9/72
Cover: D2C
Recording: 7
Source: M - Aud
Company: Image Quality
Matrix #: IQ 024/025
Place Of Origin: Japan
Total Disc Time: 60.45 - 66.07
N.B. The entire tape in better quality than previous releases such as "Acoustic Tales In Charlotte" and "Don't Do It If You Don't Want To".

D1:
Immigrant Song (3:40)
Heartbreaker (6:43)
Celebration Day (4:05)
Black Dog (6:06)
Since I've Been Loving You (8:12)
Stairway To Heaven (9:59)
Going To California (5:33)
That's The Way (6:54)
Tangerine (3:49)
Bron-Yr-Aur Stomp (6:08)
D2:
Dazed And Confused (25:07)
What Should Never Be (5:08)
Moby Dick (18:55)
Whole Lotta Love (7:29)
Rock And Roll (4:21)
Communication Breakdown (5:13)

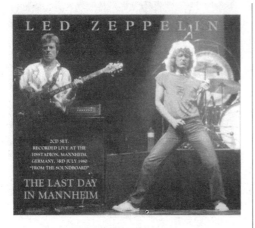

Last Day In Mannheim (The)

Venue: Mannheim

Date: 7/3/80

Cover: D4C in gatefold slipcase

Recording: 7 - 9

Source: M -SB

Company: Whole Lotta Live

Matrix #: WLL 024 - 025

Place Of Origin: Italy

Total Disc Time: 63.09 - 47.32

N.B. A straight knock off of discs one and two of the Tarantura title "Eye thank Yew".

D1:

Train Kept A Rollin' (3.58)

Nobody's Fault But Mine (5.20)

Black Dog (5.38)

In The Evening (9.13)

The Rain Song (9.07)

Hot Dog (4.03)

All My Love (5.47)

Trampled Underfoot 8.57)

Since I've Been Loving You (9.00)

D2:

Achilles Last Stand (10.04)

White Summer (6.51)

Black Mountain Side(1.41)

Kashmir (9.14)

Stairway To Heaven (10.58)

Communication Breakdown (2.48)

Rock And Roll (3.30)

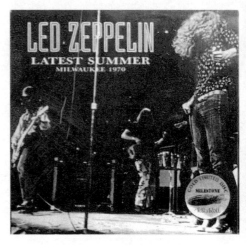

Latest Summer

Venue: Milwaukee

Date: 8/31/70

Cover: D2C

Recording: 6

Source: M -Aud

Company: Jelly Roll

Matrix #: JR 09

Place Of Origin: Japan

Total Disc Time: n/a

N.B. The first time that this has been released on bootleg. The version pictured above has a sticker which says "gold limited disc".

D1:

Immigrant Song

Heartbreaker

Dazed and Confused

Bring It on Home

That's the Way

Bron-y-Aur

Since I've Been Loving You

Led Zeppelin Lead poisoning Live in Vienna 73

Lead Poisoning

Venue: Vienna

Date: 3/16/73

Cover: D4C

Recording: 6

Source: M - Aud

Company: Cobra

Matrix #: 008

Place Of Origin: Japan

Total Disc Time: n/a

N.B. Not as good as the soundboard recording available from Tarantura as "Zig Zag Zep".

D1:

Rock And Roll

Over The Hills And Far Away

Black Dog

Misty Mountain Hop

Since I've Been Loving You

Dancing Days

Bron-Y-Aur Stomp

The Song Remains The Same

The Rain Song

D2:

Dazed And Confused

Stairway To Heaven

Whole Lotta Love

(Inc. Boogie Mama - Let's Have A Party -

I Can't Quit You - The Lemon Song)

Heartbreaker

Lead Set

Venue: San Francisco

Date: 4/26/69 - 4/27/69*

Cover: D4C Box **Recording:** 6

Source: M - Aud

Company: Tarantura

Matrix #: SF 26-4-69

Place Of Origin: Japan

Total Disc Time: n/a

N.B. Track times were not available at press time. Very nicely packaged four cd set from the Winterland and Fillmore shows.

D1: Communication Breakdown

I Can't Quit You

Dazed & Confused

You Shook Me

How Many More Times Medley (Inc. Smokestack Lightning - The Hunter - Girl From The North Country)

D2:

White Summer/ Black Mountain Side

Killing Floor

Babe I'm Gonna Leave You

Pat's Delight

As Long As I Have You Medley

(Inc. Fresh Garbage - Shake - Hush Little Baby)

D3:

Train Kept A Rollin'

I Can't Quit You

As Long As I Have You Medley

(Inc. Fresh Garbage - Shake - Cat's Squirrel - Cadillac No Money Down - I'm A Man)

You Shook Me

How Many More Times Medley (Inc. The Hunter - Babe I'm Gonna Leave You - Mulberry Bush)

Communication Breakdown

D4:

Killing Floor

Babe I'm Gonna Leave You

White Summer/ Black Mountain Side

Sitting & Thinking

Pat's Delight

Dazed & Confused

Led Astray

Venue: Baton Rouge

Date: 2/28/75

Cover: D4C

Recording: 7

Source: St - Aud

Company: Silver Rarities

Matrix #: SIRA 194/195/196

Place Of Origin: Europe

Total Disc Time: n/a

N.B. Another reissue of the Baton Rouge show. Also available as "Bon Soir Baton Rouge".

DI:

Intro

Rock & Roll

Sick Again

Over The Hills & Far Away

In My Time Of Dying

Song Remains The Same

Rain Song

Kashmir

D2:

No Quarter

Trampled Underfoot

Moby Dick

D3:

Dazed & Confused

Stairway To Heaven

Whole Lotta Love

Black Dog

Led Zeppelin

Venue: Various Studios

Date: Various

Cover: D4C gatefold sleeve

Recording: 7 - 9

Source: St - SB ,M - SB

Company: n/a

Matrix #: n/a

Place Of Origin: Europe

Total Disc Time: 70.53 - 71.50

N.B. A compilation of various studio outtakes. Some from Morgan Studios, some from Headley Grange, some from Olympic etc all available previously.

DI:

Babe I'm Gonna Leave You (6.36)

Babe I'm Gonna Leave You (Take 2) (6.12)

You Shook Me (7.46)

Tribute To Bert Berns (Takes 1-3) (8.22)

Instrumental Takes 4,5,7 (14.44)

We're Gonna Groove (2.37)

Jennings Farm Blues (various takes) (16.48)

Jennings Farm Blues (6.17)

Moby Dick Intro (1.40)

D2:

Poor Tom (3.03)

Immigrant Song (2.41)

Out On The Tiles (3.45)

That's The Way (various takes) (9.35)

Willow Tree (3.16)

Something Else (2.16)

Black Dog (Rehearsal) (6.56)

No Quarter (4.04)

Stairway To Heaven (instrumental takes) (7.01)

Stairway To Heaven (8.10)

Walter's Walk (4.30)

Friends (takes 1 & 2) (2.25)

Friends (Take 3) (4.46)

Led Zeppelin

Venue: Studio

Date: n/a

Cover: D4C

Recording: 10

Source: St - SB

Company: Lily

Matrix #: CE30

Place Of Origin: Japan

Total Disc Time: 58.05

N.B. A straight pirate knock off of various studio tracks.

D1:

Rock & Roll

Whole Lotta Love

Stairway To Heaven

Heartbreaker

Living Loving Maid

Song Remains The Same

Black Dog

Immigrant Song

Babe I'm Gonna Leave You

Rain Song

Good Times Bad Times

Battle Of Evermore

Led Zeppelin

Venue: Studio

Date: n/a

Cover: D4C

Recording: 10

Source: St - SB

Company: Lily

Matrix #: LC 51

Place Of Origin: Japan

Total Disc Time: 59.05

N.B. A straight pirate knock off of various studio tracks.

D1:

Rock & Roll

Whole Lotta Love

Stairway To Heaven

Heartbreaker

Living Loving Maid

Song Remains The Same

Black Dog

Immigrant Song

Babe I'm Gonna Leave You

Rain Song

Good Times Bad Times

Battle Of Evermore

Led Zeppelin

Venue: Studio

Date: n/a

Cover: D4C

Recording: 10

Source: St - SB

Company: Beautiful Pops Explosion

Matrix #: TNCD 1022

Place Of Origin: Japan

Total Disc Time: n/a

N.B. A straight pirate knock off of various studio tracks.

D1:

Whole Lotta Love

Stairway To Heaven

Heartbreaker

Living Loving Maid

Rock & Roll

Song Remains The Same

Good Times Bad Times

Battle Of Evermore

Black Dog

Immigrant Song

Babe I'm Gonna Leave You

Rain Song

Led Zeppelin Outtakes
(11 CD Box Set)

Venue: Various **Date:** Various

Cover: Deluxe grey box

Recording: Various **Source:** Various

Company: Antrabata

Matrix #: n/a

Place Of Origin: Europe

Total Disc Time: n/a

N.B. This is an extremely rare 11 CD box set made by European label Antrabata. Made to look Japanese or perhaps just made specifically for Japan. None of the material is particularly rare but it is all put together in a very conservatively decorated package. Most of the material is well distributed and available in many other places. The last disc includes the recording from the Rainbow Theatre in 1980 just before Bonham's death. Many of the discs have since been released in deluxe color covers. A real mish-mash of material. The first 20 came in a silver box the remainder of the reun of 325 copies came in a grey box.

D1 Tracks 1-4, Olympic Studios, London September 20 to October 10 1968. Tracks 5-6 Olympic Studios, London October '68? Track 7 Morgan Studios, London June 1969. **D2** track 1 Olympic Studios, London November 1969. Track 2 Electric Ladyland Studios, New York June 1972. Track 3-5 Headley Grange Studios, Hampshire, UK May-June 1970. **D3** track 1 Headley Grange Studios, Hampshire, UK May-June '70. Track 2-3 Mirror Sound Studios, Los Angeles May '69. Track 4-5, Bron-Yr-Aur Cottage, Wales, UK May '70. Tracks 5-6 Headiey Grange Studios, Hampshire, UK December 1970 and January 1971. **D4** track 1 unknown. Track 2 Olympic Studios, London June 5 1970. Track 3 Rolling Stones, Mobile Studio, Stargroves, UK May 1972. Track 4 unknown. **D5** tracks 1,7-15, Bron-Y-Aur Cottage, Wales May 1970. Tracks 2-6, Headley Grange Studios, Hampshire, UK May-June 1970. **D6** tracks 1-6 Headley Grange Studios, Hampshire, UK December 1970 and January 1971. Track 7 Headley

Grange, Hampshire, UK January 1971. Track 8 Jimmy Page's home studio, UK January 1972? Track 9 unknown. **D7**: Bombay, India April 1972. **D8** track 1 Southampton University, Southampton January 20 1973. Tracks 2-16 Chicago Auditorium, Chicago July 6 1973? **D9** tracks 1-9 Headley Grange Studios, Hampshire, UK November 1973 to May 1974. Track 10 WLIR 92.7 Radio Broadcast, Westbury, New York spring '75. **D10** Polar Studios, Stockholm, Sweden November to December 1978. **D11** tracks 1-5 Victoria Theatre, London May 1980. Tracks 6-7 Clearwell Castle, Forest Of Dean, Wales May 1978. Track 8 Boleskin House, Near Loch Ness, Scotland, UK November 1973. Tracks 9-11 Malibu, CA October to November 1975.

DI:
Babe I'm Gonna Leave You (7:01)
Babe I'm Gonna Leave You (6:16)
You Shook Me (7:56)
Baby Come On Home (8:53)
Guitar, Organ Instrumentals (15:53)
Guitar, Organ Instrumentals (21 :37)
Sugar Mama (2:58)
D2:
Jennings Farm Blues (24:53)
No Quarter (25:08)
That's The Way (5:37)
Feel So Bad, Fixin' To Die, That's Alright (7:06)
Since I've Been Loving You (7:34)
D3:
Since I've Been Loving You (vocal track) (3:06)
Moby Dick (1:41)
Drum Set (7:01)
I Wanna Be Her Man – Guitar Instrumentals Inc. Down
By The Seaside, Stairway To Heaven (Instrumental Take),
Blues Guitar Instrumentals (54:41)
Blues Guitar Instrumentals (0:28)
D4:
Guitar & Piano Instrumentals (42:59)
Poor Tom (3:21)
Walter's Walk (4:39)
Guitar Instrumentals (0:09)
D5:
Friends (3:28)
Immigrant Song (2:42)
Out On The Tiles (3:35)
Bron-Y-Aur (1:40)
Poor Tom (3:22)
Hey Hey What Can I Do (1:49)
Guitar Instrumentals (2:08)
Guitar Instrumentals (1:33)
That's The Way (9:10)
Friends (1 :22)
Bron-Y-Aur, Guitar Instrumentals (8:31)
Guitar Instrumentals (2:00)
D6:
Black Dog (6:59)
No Quarter (4:07)
Stairway To Heaven (Instrumental) (7:04)
Guitar Instrumentals (1:03)

Stairway To Heaven (6:10)
Stairway To Heaven (8:20)
The Battle Of Evermore (5:47)
Guitar Instrumentals (4:21)
Ten Years Gone (7:12)
D7:
Friends (31:42)
Four Sticks (5:18)
Friends (4:52)
Friends (4:40)
Four Sticks (2:1 7)
D8:
Frankfurt Special (Station Blues) (5:52)
Sugar Baby (5:07)
The Wanton Song (2:39)
The Rover (8:22)
Night Flight (11:04)
School Days (3:10)
Nadine (1:03)
Round And Round (3:25)
Move On Down The Line (2:54)
Love Me Like A Hurricane (2:43)
C'mon Pretty Baby (3:03)
Shakin' All Over (2:51)
Hungry For Love (2:27)
I'll Never Get Over You (2:13)
Reelin' And Rockin' (1:46)
Surrender (3:38)
D9:
The Wanton Song (5:35)
Take Me Home (4:45)
In The Morning (6:13)
Sick Again (3:49)
The Rover (1:21)
Jam (3:16)
In My Time Of Dying (12:59)
The Wanton Song (3:56)
D10:
Carouselambra (11:30)
Untitled, Wearing And Tearing (6:00)
Fool In the Rain (6:27)
Hot Dog (3:31)
In The Evening (6:39)
South Bound Suarez (4:20)
Darlene (5:21)
Fool In The Rain (6:21)
Carouselambra (8:48)
All My Love (7:55)
D11:
White Summer (2:26)
White Summer, Black Mountain Side (6:19)
Kashmir (8:35)/Achilles Last Stand (10:15)
Stairway To Heaven (10:11)
Say You're Gonna Leave Me (4:46)
Carouselambra (12:38)
Lucifer Rising (5:14)
Royal Orleans (0:21)
Tea For One (Hootchie Kootchie Version) (2:46)
Don't Start Me Talkin', Blues Medley, All My Lovin' (4:55)

Legendary End (The)

Venue: Los Angeles
Date: 6/27/77
Cover: D4C
Recording: 7 - 8
Source: St - Aud
Company: Silver Rarities
Matrix #: SIRA 206/207/208
Place Of Origin: Europe
Total Disc Time: 75.16 – 71.06 – 72.22
N.B. Another reissue of the last night in LA 1977.
Also available as "Farewell To LA".

D1:
Song Remains The Same
Sick Again
Nobody's Fault But Mine
Over The Hills & Far Away
Since I've Been Loving You
No Quarter
D2:
Ten Years Gone
Battle Of Evermore
Going To California
Going Down South
Black Country Woman
Bron-y-Aur Stomp
Dancing Days
White Summer
Black Mountain Side
Kashmir
Trampled Underfoot
D3:
Moby Dick
Guitar Solo
Achilles Last Stand
Stairway To Heaven
Whole Lotta Love
Rock & Roll

Legendary Fillmore Tapes Vol 1

Venue: New York

Date: 2/1/69

Cover: D4C

Recording: 4

Source: M -Aud

Company: Savege Beast Music

Matrix#: SB949629

Place Of Origin: Japan

Total Disc Time: 46.24

N.B. The recording is distant with lots

of ambient reverb.

D1:

White Summer/ Black Mountain Side (9.40)

Train Kept A Rollin' (2.52)

I Can't Quit Baby (5.59)

Pat'sDelight (7.54)

How Many More Times (16.29)

Communication Breakdown (3.30)

Legendary Fillmore Tapes Vol 2

Venue: New York

Date: 5/30/69

Cover: D4C

Recording: 3

Source: M -Aud

Company: Savege Beast Music

Matrix#: SB959630

Place Of Origin: Japan

Total Disc Time: 60.19

N.B. A really poor recording. Barely listenable.

D1:

Train Kept A Rollin' (3.07)

I Can't Quit You (6.27)

Dazed &Confused (11.38)

You Shook Me(9.53)

White Summer/ Black Mountain Side (9.57)

How Many More Times (15.42)

Communication Breakdown (3.30)

Let Me Get Back To 1972

Venue: Osaka

Date: 10/9/72

Cover: D4C

Recording: n/a

Source: n/a

Company: H Bomb

Matrix#: HBM95R01/02/03

Place Of Origin: Japan

Total Disc Time: n/a

N.B. All details are not available.

Another re-issue of the Osaka tape.

D1:

Rock & Roll

Black Dog

Over The Hills & Far Away

Misty Mountain Hop

Since I've Been Loving You

Dancing Days

The Song Remains The Same

The Rain Song

D2:

Dazed & Confused

Stairway To Heaven

Moby Dick

D3:

Whole Lotta Love

Stand By Me

Immigrant Song

Light & Shade

Venue: Tokyo
Date: 9/24/71
Cover: D4C gatefold sleeve
Recording: 7
Source: M - Aud
Company: Diagrams Of Led Zeppelin
Matrix #: TDOLZ 027/28/29
Place Of Origin: Japan
Total Disc Time: 52.03 – 61.29 – 48.18

N.B. This concert was previously available as "Pretty Woman" this however is a big improvement and is apparently from a new previously unbootlegged tape.

D1:
Immigrant Song
Heartbreaker
Since I've Been Loving You
Black Dog
Dazed And Confused
D2:
Stairway To Heaven
Celebration Day
That's The Way
Going To California
Tangerine
What Is And What Should Never Be
Moby Dick
D3:
Whole Lotta Love Medley
(Inc. Boogie Chillen – Cocaine - Rave On – Your Time Is Gonna Come – I'm A Man – The Hunter – Mary Lou – Pretty Woman – How Many More Times)
Organ Solo - Thank You
Communication Breakdown

Lighter Than Air

Venue: Studio - Cleveland* - Headley Grange
Date: 5/?/70 - 4/27/77*
Cover: D4C in case
Recording: 8 - 10
Source: St - SB
Company: Teddy Bear
Matrix #: TB 51
Place Of Origin: Italy
Total Disc Time: 60.20

N.B. A compilation of material from the third album sessions and from the Headley Grange rehearsals. tracks 3 - 6 are from the Cleveland 77 soundboard tape.

D1:
Blues Mama (6.33)
That's The Way (5.34)
The Battle Of Evermore (7.10)*
Going To California (4.24)*
Black Country Woman (5.44)*
Bron-y-Aur Stomp (5.11)*
Hey Hey What Can I Do (3.56)
Untitled Instrumental (3.58)
I Wanna Be Her Man (2.06)
Down By The Seaside (5.14)
Friends (3.13)
Poor Tom (2.55)
Stairway To Heaven (3.46)

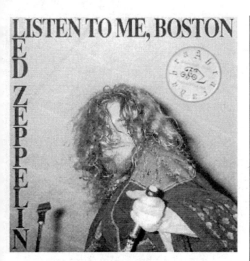

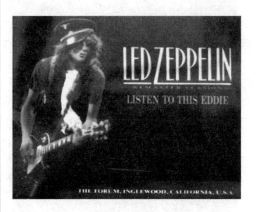

Listen To Me Boston

Venue: Boston

Date: 9/7/71

Cover: D4C

Recording: 5

Source: M - Aud

Company: Tarantura

Matrix #: BOS 1/2

Place Of Origin: Japan

Total Disc Time: 50:04 - 40:44

N.B. Another show is bootlegged for the first time. Not a great recording but it is a new show.

D1:

Immigrant Song (4:44)

Heartbreaker (7:43)

Since I've Been Loving You (8:32)

Out On The Tiles - Black Dog (6:34)

Dazed And Confused (22:31)

D2:

Stairway To Heaven (8:06)

The Lemon Song - Whole Lotta Love (7:44)

Communication Breakdown (8:14)

Organ Solo - Thank You (12:36)

Rock And Roll (4:04)

Listen to This Eddie

Venue: Los Angeles

Date: 6/21/77

Cover: D4C

Source: 8

Recording: St -Aud

Source: Jelly Roll

Matrix #: JR 06/07/08

Place Of Origin: Japan

Total Disc Time: n/a

N.B. Another reissue of the now legendary show from the Forum.

D1:

Song Remains the Same

Sick Again

Nobody's Fault the Mine

Over the Hills and Far Away

Since I've Been Loving You

No Quarter

D2:

The Rain Song

The Battle of Ever More

Going to California

Black Country Woman

Bron-y-Aur Stomp

White Summer-Black Mountain Side-Kashmir

D3:

Moby Dick

Heartbreaker

Guitar Solo

Achilles Last Stand

Stairway to Heaven

Whole Lotta Love

Rock and Roll

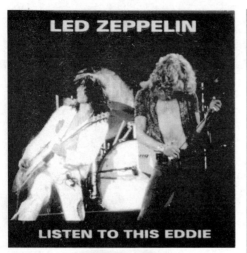

Listen To This Eddie

Venue: Los Angeles
Date: 6/21/77
Cover: D4C sleeve
Recording: 8
Source: St - Aud
Company: Diagrams of Led Zeppelin
Matrix #: Vol 050
Place Of Origin: Japan
Total Disc Time: n/a

N.B. Just another reissue of the forum tape. Obviously this one is destined to be reissued many times.

D1:
Song Remains the Same
Sick Again
Nobody's Fault but Mine
Over the Hills and Far Away
Since I've Been Loving You
No Quarter
D2:
Ten Years Gone
The Battle of Ever More
Going to California
Black Country Woman
Bron-y-Aur Stomp
White Summer
Black Mountain Side
Kashmir
Moby Dick
D3:
Heartbreaker
Guitar Solo
Achilles Last Stand
Stairway to Heaven
Whole Lotta Love
Rock and Roll

Listen To This Eddie Remastered

Venue: Los Angeles
Date: 6/21/77
Cover: D4C in double case
Recording: 9
Source: St - Aud
Company: Silver Rarities
Matrix #: SIRA 161 162 163
Place Of Origin: Europe
Total Disc Time: 68.47 - 70.41 - 55.58

N.B. Another re-issue of the amazing first night in L.A. 77. Perhaps the best sounding so far although it is clearly from the well circulated source tape.

D1:
The Song Remains The Same (6.18)
Sick Again (6.01)
Nobody's Fault But Mine (6.43)
Over The Hills & Far Away (6.04)
Since I've Been Loving You (8.06)
No Quarter (27.57)
D2:
Ten Years Gone (9.14)
Battle of Evermore (5.22)
Going To California (4.48)
Black Country Woman (1.42)
Bron-y-Aur Stomp (6.50)
White Summer - Black Mountain Side (8.24)
Kashmir (9.12)
Moby Dick (17.43)
D3:
Heartbreaker (8.34)
Guitar Solo (16.17)
Achilles Last Stand (8.57)
Stairway To Heaven (11.38)
Whole Lotta Love (1.24)
Rock & Roll (4.00)

Live At Leeds 1971

Venue: Leeds

Date: 3/9/71

Cover: D4C in double case

Recording: n/a

Source: n/a

Company:

Matrix#: ZA 61

Place Of Origin: Japan

Total Disc Time:

N.B. All details are not available the cover probably lists the date incorrectly.

D1:

Immigrant Song

Heartbreaker

Since I've Been Loving You

Black Dog

You Shook Me

Whole Lotta Love

Organ Solo/ Thank You

Live At Paris Theatre

Venue: London

Date: 3/25/71 – 6/27/69*

Cover: D4C

Recording: 9

Source: St – SB, M –SB*

Company: Black Panther

Matrix #: ABP 092

Place Of Origin: Italy

Total Disc Time: n/a

N.B. Another reissue of the BBC stuff from Italy. All track details not available at press time.

D1:

Immigrant Song (3.13)

Heartbreaker (5.18)

Dazed & Confused (16.04)

Going To California (4.00)

What Is & What Should Never Be (4.34)

Stairway To Heaven (8.40)

Black Dog (5.32)

Whole Lotta Love (10.14)

Communication Breakdown (3.20)*

I Can't Quit You (6.19)*

You Shook Me (10.06)*

Live at the Forum Inglewood California

1971

Venue: Los Angeles

Date: 8/21/71-8/22/71

Cover: D4C sleeve

Recording: 6

Source: M - Aud

Company: Diagrams of Led Zeppelin

Matrix #: Vol 038/039

Place of Origin: Japan

Total Disc Time: n/a

N.B. Gatefold 4 CD set featuring the complete tapes from both shows at the Forum. All track details not available at press time.

Live At The Lyceum In London

Venue: London

Date: 10/12/69

Cover: D4C sleeve

Recording: 4-5

Source: M - Aud

Company: Cobra

Matrix #: 016

Place Of Origin: Japan

Total Disc Time: 60.19

N.B. Another reissue of the recording from the Lyceum ballroom. Nothing special.

D1:

Good Times Bad Times/Communication Breakdown

I Can't Quit You

Heartbreaker

You Shook Me

What Is and What Should Never Be

Dazed and Confused

How Many More Times

Lived 1975 Part I

Venue: Unknown

Date: Unknown

Cover: D4C

Recording: n/a

Source: n/a

Company: Superstar

Matrix #: MON808/OSR

Place Of Origin: Japan

Total Disc Time: 75.18

N.B. A weird piece that looks like a pirate but includes all live material. Most information was not available at press time. One thing is for sure it's from 1973 not 1975.

D I:

Rock & Roll (4.32)

Celebration Day (3.43)

Black Dog (5.26)

Over The Hills & Far Away (6.05)

Misty Mountain Hop (4.55)

Since I've Been Loving You (8.00)

No Quarter (12.20)

Dazed & Confused (25.52)

Live From The Midnight Sun

Venue: Toronto
Date: 9/4/71
Cover: D4C
Recording: 7 - 8
Source: M -Aud
Company: Diagrams Of Led Zeppelin
Matrix #: TDOLZ 1899701/02
Place Of Origin: Japan
Total Disc Time: n/a

N.B. It would seem that Diagrams Of Led Zeppelin have set themselves the goal of getting the entire 1971 tape archive out on bootleg. Something which I have no problem with, even though most of the tapes aren't that great. This one however is good and I was wondering if at this point Peter Grant was still not allowed to enter Canada because of his altercation in Vancouver the previous year. Anyway, regardless someone got in with a good tape deck fortunately for us.

D I:
Immigrant Song (3:43)
Heartbreaker (7:09)
Since I've Been Loving You (7:04)
Out On The Tiles Intro, Black Dog (5:16)
Dazed And Confused (20:19)
Stairway To Heaven (9:05)
Celebration Day (4:23)
That's The Way (6:29)
Going To California (4 18)
D2:
What Is And What Should Never Be (4:20)
Moby Dick (14:09)
Good Times Bad Times Medley (20:12)
(Inc. Whole Lotta Love - Just A Little Bit - Boogie Chillen
My Baby Left Me - Mess O'Blues - You Shook Me)
Communication Breakdown (7:32)
Thank You (7:53)

Live In Copenhagen

Venue: Copenhagen
Date: 5/3/71
Cover: D4C
Recording: 6
Source: M - Aud
Company: Cobra
Matrix #: 012
Place Of Origin: Japan
Total Disc Time: 72.28 – 51.27

N.B. Another release of an old show. This being the legendary "testbed" concert. The band throw in almost the entire fourth album as well as material from the third not noted for it's frequent live appearance.

D1:
Immigrant Song
Heartbreaker
Since I've Been Loving You
Dazed And Confused
Black Dog
Stairway To Heaven
Going To California
That's The Way
What Is And What Should Never Be
D2:
Four Stick
Gallows Pole
Whole Lotta Love Medley
(Inc. Boogie Chillen - Trucking Little Mama -
That's Alright - Mess Of Blues - Lemon Song)
Communication Breakdown (Inc. Celebration Day)
Misty Mountain Hop
Rock And Roll

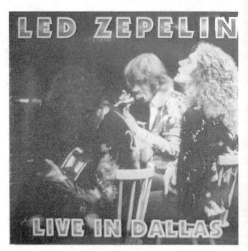

Live In Dallas

Venue: Dallas
Date: 3/5/75
Cover: D4C sleeve
Recording: 6
Source: M -Aud
Company: Diagrams Of Led Zeppelin
Matrix #: TDOLZ Vol 014
Place Of Origin: Japan
Total Disc Time: 57.24 – 65.03 – 61.45

N.B. The second night in Dallas.
An OK audience recording.

D1:
Rock & Roll
Sick Again
Over The Hills & Far Away
In My Time Of Dying
Song Remains The Same
Rain Song
Kashmir
D2:
No Quarter
Trampled Underfoot
Moby Dick
D3:
Dazed & Confused
Stairway To Heaven
Whole Lotta Love (Inc. The Crunge)
Black Dog

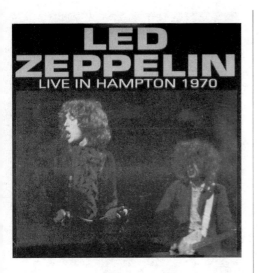

Live In Hampton 1970

Venue: Hampton
Date: 8/17/70
Cover: D4C sleeve
Recording: 3
Source: M -Aud
Company: Diagrams Of Led Zeppelin
Matrix #: TDOLZ 0469701-2
Place Of Origin: Japan
Total Disc Time: 61.04 - 61.21
N.B. A really awful recording from Hampton Virginia.

D1:
Immigrant Song (4.38)
Heartbreaker (7.49)
Dazed & Confused (19.31)
Bring It On Home (10.51)
That's The Way (7.29)
Bron-y-Aur Stomp (4.03)
Since I've Been Loving You (7.38)
D2:
Organ Solo - Thank You (14.00)
What Is & What Should Never Be (5.33)
Moby Dick (17.32)
Whole Lotta Love (15.47)
Communication Breakdown (8.29)

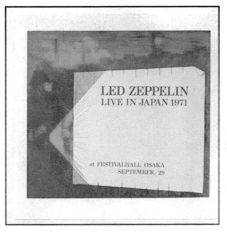

Live In Japan 1971

Venue: Osaka
Date: 9/29/71
Cover: D4C slipcase with insert
Recording: 8
Source: St - SB
Company: Rock Solid
Matrix #: RSR CD 1 2 3
Place Of Origin: Japan
Total Disc Time: n/a
N.B. Total disc times not available at press time.

D1:
Immigrant Song
Heartbreaker
Since I've Been Loving You
Black Dog
Dazed & Confused
D2:
Stairway To Heaven
Celebration Day
That's The Way
Going To California
Tangerine
Friends
Smoke Gets In Your Eyes
What Is & What Should Never Be
D3:
Moby Dick
Whole Lotta Love Medley
(Inc. Boogie Chillen-Tossin' And Turnin'-Twist & Shout-
Fortune Teller-Good Times Bad Times-You Shook Me)
Communication Breakdown
Thank You

Live in Kyoto

Venue: Kyoto

Date: 10/10/72

Cover: D4C

Recording: 6

Source: M - Aud

Company: n/a

Matrix #: n/a

Place Of Origin: Japan

Total Disc Time: n/a

N.B. Another reissue of the audience recording from Kyoto Japan. Slightly better than previous versions.

D1:

Rock and Roll

Black Dog

Misty Mountain Hop

Since I've Been Loving You

The Song Remains the Same

The Rain Song

D2:

Dazed and Confused

Stairway to Heaven

Over the Hills and Far Away

Whole Lotta Love

Immigrant Song

Live In Liverpool '73

Venue: Liverpool

Date: 1/15/73

Cover: D4C

Recording: 7 – 8

Source: St - SB

Company: Diagrams Of Led Zeppelin

Matrix #: TDOLZ 008/009

Place Of Origin: Japan

Total Disc Time: 74.27 – 50.16

N.B. Another new tape surfaces. Parts of this had been out before on the Ukinel title "Tangible Vandalism". This tape is much more complete.

D1:

Over the Hills And Far Away

Black Dog

Misty Mountain Hop

Since I've Been Loving You

Dancing Days

Bron-Yr-Aur Stomp

The Song Remains The Same

The Rain Song (cut)

Dazed And Confused (cut)

D2:

Stairway to Heaven

Whole Lotta Love (Inc. Everybody Needs Somebody To Love, Boogie Chillen, Baby I Don't Care (cut), Let's Have A Party, I Can't Quit You, Going Down Slow)

Heartbreaker

The Ocean

Live In Nagoya

Venue: Nagoya

Date: 10/5/72

Cover: D4C sleeve

Recording: 4

Source: M -Aud

Company: Smile

Matrix #: TOE 001

Place Of Origin: Japan

Total Disc Time: 45.06 – 53.41

N.B. A reissue of the Nagoya tape in poor quality. Nice cover though.

D1:

Rock & Roll

Black Dog

Over The Hills & Far Away

Misty Mountain Hop

Since I've Been Loving You

Dancing Days

Bron-y-Aur Stomp

Song Remains The Same

Rain Song

D2:

Dazed & Confused

Stairway To Heaven

Whole Lotta Love

Cherry Blossom (Organ solo)

Thank You

Live In San Francisco

Venue: San Francisco

Date: 1/10/69

Cover: D4C

Recording: 7

Source: M -Aud

Company: Black Panther

Matrix #: n/a

Place Of Origin: Italy

Total Disc Time: n/a

N.B. Another reissue of the Fillmore tape. Also available as "For Your Love" and "East West"

D1:

Dazed & Confused (10.24)

How Many More Times (5.31)

Tobacco Road (8.45)

White Summer (6.28)

You Shook Me (8.14)

Babe I'm Gonna Leave You (5.43)

Communication Breakdown (3.43)

For Your Love (7.47)

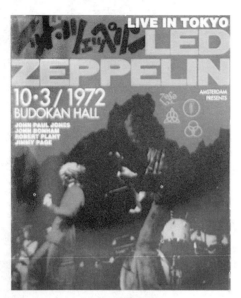

Live In Tokyo

Venue: Tokyo

Date: 10/3/72

Cover: D4C

Recording: 4 -5

Source: M - Aud

Company: AMSTERDAM

Matrix #: AMS 9609-3-1/2/3

Place Of Origin: Japan

Total Disc Time: n/a

N.B. Previously available as "2nd Night In A Judo Arena"

D1:

Rock And Roll

Black Dog

Over The Hills And Far Away

Misty Mountain Hop

Since I've Been Loving You

Dancing Days

Bron-Y-Aur Stomp

D2:

The Song Remains The Same

The Rain Song

Dazed And Confused

D3:

Stairway To Heaven

Whole Lotta Love

Immigrant Song

The Ocean

Live In USA 1977

Venue: Unknown

Date: ?/?/77

Cover: D4C

Recording: n/a

Source: n/a

Company: Apple House Music

Matrix #: ST23

Place Of Origin: Japan

Total Disc Time: 73.16

N.B. An unknown compilation of material from Japan

from the 1977 USA tour.

D1:

Sick Again (6.11)

Nobody's Fault But Mine (6.32)

In My Time Of Dying (10.54)

Since I've Been Loving You (8.23)

No Quarter (20.35)

Ten Years Gone (8.32)

Song Remains The Same (3.40)

Moby Dick (8.26)

D3:
Immigrant Song*
Heartbreaker*
Dazed and Confused*
Bring It on Home*
That the Way*
Bron-y-Aur*
Since I've Been Loving You*
Organ Solo*
Thank You*
D4:
What Is and What Should Never Be*
Moby Dick*
Whole Lotta Love*
Communication Breakdown Medley
(Inc. Good Times Bad Times - For What It's Worth)*
Out On the Tiles*
Blueberry Hill*

Live on Blueberry Hill

Venue: Los Angeles
Date: 9/4/70
Cover: D4C
Recording: 8
Source: M - Aud, St - Aud*
Company: Last Stand Disc
Matrix #: LSD 25/26/27/28
Place of Origin: Japan
Total Disc Time: n/a

N.B. This one is mastered from two different tape sources. Presumably the original TMQ tape and the Rubber Dubber tape. Although some people claim to be able to hear a marked improvement over previous versions, I can't tell the difference between this and the original Neutral Zone title and the Tarantura version of the Rubber Dubber tape.

D1:
Immigrant Song
Heartbreaker
Dazed and Confused
Bring It on Home
That the Way
Bron-y-Aur
Since I've Been Loving You
Organ Solo
Thank You
D2:
What Is and What Should Never Be
Moby Dick
Whole Lotta Love
Communication Breakdown Medley (Inc. Good Times Bad Times - For What It's Worth)
Out On the Tiles
Blueberry Hill

Live On Blueberry Hill

Venue: Los Angeles
Date: 9/4/70
Cover: D4C sleeve
Recording: 8
Source: M -Aud
Company: Cobra
Matrix #: 005
Place Of Origin: Japan
Total Disc Time: n/a

Now CPS001

N.B. Another re-issue of the widespread audience recording from the forum.

D1:
Immigrant Song
Heartbreaker
Dazed & Confused
Bring It On Home
That's The Way
Bron-y-Aur
Since I've Been Loving You

Organ Solo
Thank You
D2:
What Is & What Should Never Be
Moby Dick
Whole Lotta Love Medley
(Inc. Boogie Chillen - Some Other Guy - I've Got Girl -
I'm Moving On - Think It Over - Lemon Song)
Communication Breakdown
(Inc. Good Times Bad Times -
For What It's Worth - I Saw Standing There)
Out On The Tiles
Blueberry Hill

Live On Blueberry Hill

Venue: Los Angeles
Date: 9/4/70
Cover: D4C in case
Recording: 7
Source: M - Aud
Company: n/a
Matrix #: n/a
Place Of Origin: Japan
Total Disc Time: n/a
N.B. All track information not available at press time.

Immigrant Song (3.25)
Heartbreaker (6.27)
Dazed & Confused (16.42)
What Is & What Should Never Be (4.29)
Moby Dick (12.35)
Communication Breakdown Medley (10.12)
(Inc. Good Times Bad Times-For What It's Worth-
I Saw Her Standing There)
That's The Way (7.05)

Live On Blueberry Hill

Venue: Los Angeles
Date: 9/4/70
Cover: D4C in case
Recording: 7
Source: M - Aud
Company: n/a
Matrix #: n/a
Place Of Origin: Japan
Total Disc Time: n/a
N.B. All track information not available at press time.

D1:
Since I've Been Loving You (6.58)
Organ Improvisation (5.57)
Thank You (7.02)
Out On The Tiles (3.30)
Blueberry Hill (3.55)
Bring It On Home (9.30)
Whole Lotta Love Medley (17.24)
Incl. Boogie Chillen - Movin On - I've Got A Girl - Some
Other Guy - Think It Over - The Lemon Song
Bron-y-Aur (5.36)

Live On Blueberry Hill II
Venue: Oakland
Date: 9/2/70
Cover: D4C   sleeve
Recording: 7
Source: M - Aud
Company: Tarantura
Matrix #:   OAK1,2
Place Of Origin: Japan
Total Disc Time: n/a
N.B. The best version of this tape so far.

D1:
Immigrant Song
Heartbreaker
Dazed And Confused
Bring It On Home
That's The Way
Bron-Y-Aur Stomp
Since I've Been Loving You
Organ Solo/Thank You
D2:
What Is And What Should Never Be
Moby Dick
Whole Lotta Love Medley
(Inc. Let That Boy Boogie -Ju Ju Rhythm -Lawdy Miss
Clawdy - For What It's Worth - Honey Bee -
Moving On - Fortune Teller - That's All Right Mama)
Communication Breakdown - Good Times Bad Times
Train Kept A Rollin'
Blueberry Hill
Long Tall Sally

Long Beach Arena Complete
Venue: Long Beach
Date: 3/11/75
Cover: D4C
Recording: 9
Source: St - Aud
Company: Confusion
Matrix #: n/a
Place Of Origin: Japan
Total Disc Time: n/a
N.B. Another reissue of the Long Beach tape however
the speed is fixed and this runs correctly.

D1:
Rock & Roll
Sick Again
Over The Hills & Far Away
In My Time Of Dying
Song Remains The Same
Rain Song
Kashmir
D2:
No Quarter
Trampled Underfoot
Moby Dick
D3:
Dazed & Confused
Stairway To Heaven
Whole Lotta Love
Black Dog

Long Beach Arena Fragment

Venue: Long Beach

Date: 3/12/75

Cover: D4C

Recording: 7

Source: M - Aud

Company: HOLY

Matrix #: SH002-A

Place Of Origin: Japan

Total Disc Time: 34:01

N.B. Just like the title says, just a fragment.

D1:

Stairway To Heaven (9.09)

Whole Lotta Love Medley (7.54)

(Inc. The Crunge – Sex Machine)

Black Dog (5.49)

Heartbreaker Medley (11.09)

(Inc. I'm A Man)

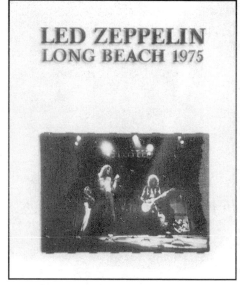

Long Beach 1975
Venue: Long Beach
Date: 3/11/75
Cover: D4C
Recording: 8
Source: St - Aud
Company: Last Stand Disc
Matrix #: LSD 31/32/33
Place Of Origin: Japan
Total Disc Time: n/a
N.B. A reissue of the well circulated audience recording from the Long Beach arena.

D1:
Introduction
Rock and Roll
Sick Again
Over the Hills and Far Away
In My Time of Dying
The Song Remains the Same
The Rain Song
Kashmir
D2:
No Quarter
Trampled Underfoot
Moby Dick
D3:
Dazed and Confused
Stairway to Heaven
Whole Lotta Love - The Crunge
Black Dog

Long Island Line

Venue: New York

Date: 6/15/72

Cover: D4C

Recording: 5

Source: M - Aud

Company: Image Quality

Matrix #: IQ 049/050

Place Of Origin: Japan

N.B. One of the less bootlegged tapes that are out there. A fairly reasonable recording from the Nassau County Coliseum.

D1:

Immigrant Song (4.08)

Heartbreaker (8.47)

Black Dog (6.07)

Since I've Been Loving You (8.46)

Stairway to Heaven (10.55)

Going to California (6.06)

That's the Way (7.13)

Tangerine (3.39)

Bron-y-Aur Stomp (4.54)

D2:

Dazed and Confused (27.40)

What Is and What Should Never Be (5.36)

Moby Dick (2.59)

Whole Lotta Love (23.18) (Inc. Boogie Chillen - Hello Mary Lou - Money Honey - Heartbreak Hotel - Trucking Little Momma - Going down Slow)

Luftschiffe

Venue: Chicago

Date: 1/20/75* -1/21/75

Cover: D4C

Recording: 6

Source: M -Aud

Company: Tarantura

Matrix #: CS-001/002

Place Of Origin: Japan

Total Disc Time: 63:00 - 64:35

N.B. A compilation of bits from the two shows at Chicago Stadium.

D1:

Rock And Roll *

Sick Again

Over The Hills And Far Away

When The Levee Breaks

In My Time Of Dying

The Song Remains The Same

The Rain Song

Kashmir

The Wanton Song

D2:

No Quarter

Trampled Underfoot

Moby Dick

How Many More Times *

Stairway To Heaven *

Whole Lotta Love

Black Dog

Communication Breakdown

Lunatics In Munich

Venue: Munich

Date: 3/17/73

Cover: D4C sleeve

Recording: n/a

Source: n/a

Company: Holy Grail

Matrix #: HGCD 102

Place Of Origin: Japan

Total Disc Time: n/a

N.B. All track information not available at press time. First release of this show on CD.

D1:

Rock & Roll

Over The Hills & Far Away

Black Dog

Misty Mountain Hop

Since I've Been Loving You

Dancing Days

Bron-y-Aur Stomp

The Song Remains The Same

The Rain Song

D2:

Dazed & Confused

Stairway To Heaven

Whole Lotta Love Medley

(Inc. Everybody Needs Someone To Love - Boogie Chillen - Baby I Don't Care - Let's Have A Party - I Can't Quit You - The Lemon Song - Going Down Slow)

Heartbreaker

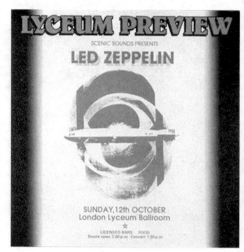

Lyceum Preview

Venue: London

Date: 10/12/69

Cover: D4C

Recording: 5

Source: M -Aud

Company: Immigrant

Matrix #: IM 009

Place Of Origin: Japan

Total Disc Time: n/a

N.B. Another reissue of the Lyceum gig although better quality than some. Nice cover too.

D1:

Good Times Bad Times

Communication Breakdown

I Can't Quit You

Heartbreaker

You Shook Me

What Is & What Should Never Be

Dazed & Confused

How Many More Times Medley (Inc. Over Under Sideways Down - The Hunter - Boogie Chillen)

LZ Rhoder

Venue: Providence
Date: 7/21/73
Cover: D4C sleeve
Recording: n/a
Source: n/a
Company: n/a
Matrix #: TM 007/LZ008
Place Of Origin: Europe
Total Disc Time:
N.B. 59.36 - 72.08

N.B. All details not available at press time. A European re-issue of the Japanese title LZ Rider.

D1:
Rock & Roll (4.20)
Celebration Day (3.28)
Black Dog (5.38)
Over The Hills & Far Away (6.24)
Misty Mountain Hop (7.08)
Since I've Been Loving You (8.10)
No Quarter (cut)(14.51)
The Song Remains The Same (cut) (1.14)
The Rain Song (8.18)
D2:
Dazed & Confused (27.13)
Stairway To Heaven (11.28)
Moby Dick (13.25)
Heartbreaker (7.53)
Whole Lotta Love (7.04)
The Ocean (5.03)

LZ Rider

Venue: Providence
Date: 7/21/73
Cover: D4C sleeve
Recording: n/a
Source: n/a
Company: Tarantura
Matrix #: LZ 1-2
Place Of Origin: Japan
Total Disc Time: 59.36 - 72.08
N.B. All details not available at press time. A previously unavailable show.

D1:
Rock & Roll (4.20)
Celebration Day (3.28)
Black Dog (5.38)
Over The Hills & Far Away (6.24)
Misty Mountain Hop (7.08)
Since I've Been Loving You (8.10)
No Quarter (cut)(14.51)
The Song Remains The Same (cut) (1.14)
The Rain Song (8.18)
D2:
Dazed & Confused (27.13)
Stairway To Heaven (11.28)
Moby Dick (13.25)
Heartbreaker (7.53)
Whole Lotta Love (7.04)
The Ocean (5.03)

Mad Dogs Box

Venue: San Diego - Los Angeles* - Baton Rouge# - New York^
Date: 9/3/70 - 8/21/71* - 2/28/75# - 6/7/77^
Cover: D2C velvet covered box
Recording: n/a
Source: n/a
Company: Mad Dogs
Matrix #: DX I-X
Place Of Origin: Japan
Total Disc Time: n/a
N.B. All track information not available at press time. Comes in a 12" by 12" box with a 69 tour booklet.

D1:
Immigrant Song
Heartbreaker
Dazed And Confused
Bring It On Home
That's The Way
Since I've Been Loving You

D2:
Organ Solo,
Thank You
What Is And What Should Never Be
Moby Dick
Whole Lotta Love
Communication Breakdown

D3:
Immigrant Song *
Heartbreaker *
Since I've Been Loving You *
Black Dog*
Dazed And Confused *
Stairway To Heaven *
That's The Way *
Going To Calitomia *

D4:
What Is and What Should Never Be *
Whole Lotta Love *

Weekend *
Rock And Roll *
Communication Breakdown *
Organ Solo - Thank You *

D5:
Rock And Roll #
Sick Again #
Over The Hills And Far Away #
In My Time of Dying #
The Song Remains The Same #
The Rain Song #
Kashmir #

D6:
No Quarter #
Trampled Underfoot #
Moby Dick #

D7:
Dazed And Contused (Inc. Woodstock) #
Stairway To Heaven #
Whole Lotta Love #
Black Dog #

D8:
The Song Remains The Same ^
The Rover - Sick Again^
Nobody s Fault But Mine ^
In My Time Of Dying ^
Since I ve Been Loving You ^

D9:
No Quarter (Inc. Nutcracker Suite)
Ten Years Gone ^
The Battle Of Evermore ^
Going To California ^
Low Hide ^
Black Country Woman ^
Bron-Yr-Aur Stomp ^
White Summer - Black Mountain Side - Kashmir ^

D10:
Out On The Tiles - Moby Dick^
Guitar Solo (Inc. Star Spangled Banner) ^
Achilles Last Stand ^
Stairway To Heaven ^
Whole Lotta Love ^
Rock And Roll ^

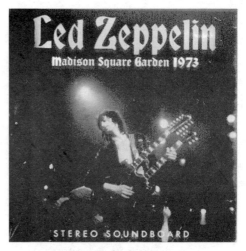

Made In England

Venue: Oxford

Date: 1/17/73

Cover: D4C sleeve

Recording:

Source: M- SB

Company: Tarantura

Matrix #: OX 73-1,2

Place Of Origin: Japan

Total Disc Time: n/a

N.B. The rest of the elusive Oxford soundboard finally emerges. Limited edition of 500 copies.

D1:

Rock And Roll (3:33)

Over The Hills And Far Away (5:12)

Out On The Tiles - Black Dog (5:32)

Misty Mountain Hop (5:04)

Since I've Been Loving You (7:44)

Dancing Days (4:25)

Bron-Y-Aur Stomp (6:12)

The Song Remains The Same (5:47)

The Rain Song (6:41)

D2:

Dazed And Confused (Inc. San Francisco, Walter's Walk) (27:59)

Stairway To Heaven (10:39)

Whole Lotta Love (4:30)

Madison Square Garden 1973

Venue: New York

Date: 7/29/73

Cover: D4C

Recording: 8

Source: St - SB

Company: Firepower

Matrix #: FP032

Place Of Origin: Japan

N.B. The unaltered sound board tape from the last show in New York in 1973.

D1:

Rock and Roll

Celebration Day

Black Dog

Over the Hills and Far Away

Misty Mountain Hop

Since I've Been Loving You

No Quarter

D2:

The Song Remains the Same

The Rain Song

Dazed and Confused

Mad Screaming Gallery

Venue: New York – Rochester*
Date: 9/3/71 – 9/14/71*
Cover: D4C sleeve
Recording: 4
Source: M -Aud
Company: Lemon Song
Matrix #: LS7203-5
Place Of Origin: Japan
Total Disc Time: 70.42 – 65.21 – 71.58
N.B. Parts of this are also available as "Hard Company" and "How've You Been". The last four tracks are credited to Rochester although I haven't actually heard it to be able to confirm.

D1:
Immigrant Song
Heartbreaker
Since I've Been Loving You
Black Dog
Dazed & Confused
D2:
That's The Way
Going To California
What Is & What Should Never Be
Moby Dick
D3:
Organ Solo - Thank You
Rock & Roll
Celebration Day
That's The Way*
Going To California*
What Is & What Should Never Be*
Moby Dick*

Magical Dreams 72

Venue: Osaka
Date: 10/9/72
Cover: D4C Sleeve
Recording: 8
Source: St - Aud
Company: Wyvern Legend
Matrix #: WLG 26561-3
Place Of Origin: Japan
Total Disc Time: 48.04 - 56.39 - 40.14
N.B. A new label reissues the Osaka tape. Nice cover.

D1:
Rock and Roll
Black Dog
Over the Hills and Far Away
Misty Mountain Hop
Since I've Been Loving You
Dancing Days
The Song Remains the Same
The Rain Song
D2:
Dazed and Confused
Stairway to Heaven
Moby Dick
D3:
Whole Lotta Love
Stand by Me
Immigrant Song

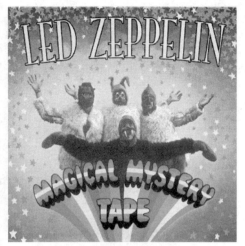

Magical Mystery Tape

Venue: Chicago
Date: 7/6/73
Cover: D4C sleeve
Recording: 8 - 9
Source: St - SB
Company: Tarantura
Matrix #: TMMT -1
Place Of Origin: Japan
Total Disc Time: 51.13
N.B. An interesting spoof of the Beatles using some of (Eric Idle's own spoof) The Rutles artwork. A very good quality re-issue of the Chicago soundcheck. Picture Disc.

D1:
Strawberry Jam #1 (2.57) (Sugar Baby)
Strawberry Jam #2 (1.40) (Sugar Baby)
The Wanton Song (2.10)
The Rover (4.29)
Studio Chatter (4.45)
Night Flight #1 (0.48)
Night Flight #2 (1.55)
Chatter (2.04)
Night Flight #3 (3.38)
Chatter (0.59)
Chatter (0.25)
Night Flight #4 (1.05)
Night Flight #5 (2.41)
Schooldays (Long Live Rock & Roll) (3.34)
Nadine (0.55)
Round & Round (3.16)
Move On Down The Line (2.32)
Love Me Like A Hurricane (2.43)
Move It (1.26)
Dynamite (1.10)
Shakin All Over (2.52)
Chatter (0.29)
Hungry For Love (1.30)
I'll Never Get Over You (2.20)
Reelin & Rockin (2.07)
Surrender (0.27)
Chatter (0.23)
Chatter (0.42)
Chatter (0.10)

Magick

Venue: London

Date: 11/20/71

Cover: D4C sleeve

Recording: 6

Source: M -Aud

Company: Tarantura

Matrix #: EM 001,2

Place Of Origin: Japan

Total Disc Time: n/a

N.B. Another reissue of the Empire Pool Wembley

show.

D1:

Heartbreaker

Black Dog

Since I've Been Loving You

Rock & Roll

Stairway To Heaven

Going To California

That's The Way

D2:

Dazed & Confused

What Is & What Should Never Be

Celebration Day

Moby Dick

Whole Lotta Love Medley (Inc. Boogie Chillen - Hello

Mary Lou - Mess Of Blues - Going Down Slow)

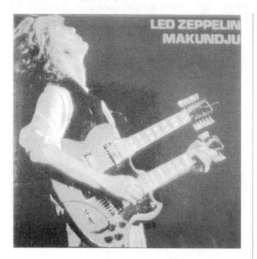

Makundju

Venue: Tampa

Date: 4/9/70

Cover: D4C

Recording: 5

Source: M - Aud

Company: Cobra

Matrix #: 021

Place Of Origin: Japan

Total Disc Time: n/a

N.B. Previously available only on vinyl. This recording from the Curtis Hickson Hall is incomplete and full of dropouts.

D1:

White Summer

Since I've Been Loving You

Whole Lotta Love

Moby Dick

How Many More Times Medley (Inc. Boogie Chillen - Traveling Momma - Mess of Blues - The Lemon Song)

Maple Leaf

Venue: Toronto

Date: 9/4/71

Cover: D4C

Recording: 7

Source: M - Aud

Company: Baby Face

Matrix #: 9601

Place Of Origin: Japan

Total Disc Time: 57.30 - 64.17

N.B. A good clear recording from Maple Leaf Gardens. Parts of the show have been available from a sound board recording.

D1:

Immigrant Song

Heart Breaker

Since I've Been Loving You

Black Dog

Dazed and Confused

Stairway to Heaven

Celebration Day

D2:

That's the Way

Going to California

What Is and What Should Never Be

Moby Dick (Cut)

Whole Lotta Love Medley (Inc. Boogie Chillen - My Baby Left Me -Mess of Blues -You Shook Me)

Communication Breakdown

Thank You (Cut)

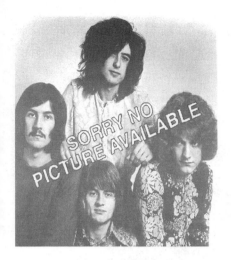

Maryland Deluxe

Venue: Landover

Date: 5/25/77 – 5/26/77* – 5/28/77^ – 5/30/77#

Cover: D4C deluxe Box

Recording: 6

Source: M -Aud

Company: Diagrams Of Led Zeppelin

Matrix #: TDOLZ 022 – 023 – 024 - 025

Place Of Origin: Japan

Total Disc Time: n/a

N.B. A 12 CD box set incorporating the titles "Running On Pure Heart & Soul", "Your Teenage Dream", "Tightest & Loosest" and "Thunderous Break". A compilation of the well circulated landover Maryland string of concerts. None of the tapes are very good. Always interesting to note how poor many of these 1977 tapes really are. The bigger the venue apparently the harder to get a decent tape.

Masters Of Excess

Venue: Boston

Date: 5/?/69

Cover: D4C

Recording: 6

Source: M -Aud

Company: The Symbols

Matrix #: n/a

Place Of Origin: Japan

Total Disc Time: n/a

N.B. Another re-issue of the mysterious Boston tape. In the book "Led Zeppelin – Live" it is pegged as May 19th. However I have no idea where that date comes from. Firstly they didn't play in Boston on the 19th. They played 27th – 29th . Having said that I have seen no evidence to support which night this may be from. Noise reduction on this CD virtually eliminates half the sonic range of the recording.

D1:
As Long As I Have You Medley
(Inc. Fresh Garbage, Shake, Hush Little Baby)
I Can't Quit You
Dazed And Confused
You Shook MeD2:
Pat's Delight
Babe I'm Gonna LeaveYou
How Many More Times Medley
(Inc. For Your Love, The Hunter, Improvisation)
Communication Breakdown

Melancholy Danish Page Boys

Venue: Copenhagen

Date: 7/24/79

Cover: D4C

Recording: 8

Source: St - Aud

Company: Cobra

Matrix #: 022

Place Of Origin: Japan

Total Disc Time: n/a

N.B. Another reissue of the audience recording. Packaged to look exactly like the original vinyl title. Full track details not available at press time

D1:

Song Remains the Same

Black Dog

Nobody's Fault But Mine

Over the Hills and Far Away

Misty Mountain Hop

Since I've Been Loving You

No Quarter

Hot Dog

The Rain Song

D2:

White Summer

Kashmir

Trampled Underfoot

Achilles Last Stand

Moby Dick

In the Evening

Stairway to Heaven

Rock and Roll

Melbourne Masters

Venue: Melbourne

Date: 2/20/72

Cover: D4C

Recording: 7

Source: M -Aud

Company: Immigrant

Matrix #: IM-035/036

Place Of Origin: Japan

Total Disc Time: 53:20 - 53:56

N.B. A slight improvement on previous versions of this tape.

D1:

Immigrant Song

Heartbreaker

Black Dog

Since I've Been Loving You

Stairway To Heaven

Going To California

That's The Way

Tangerine

Bron-Y-Aur Stomp

D2:

Dazed And Confused

Rock And Roll

Whole Lotta Love Medley

(Inc. Boogie Chillen - Let's Have A Party)

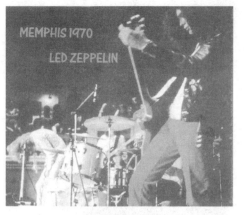

Memphis 1970

Venue: Memphis

Date: 4/17/70

Cover: D4C in double case

Recording: 5

Source: St - Aud

Company: Zoso **Matrix #:** 003-004

Place Of Origin: Japan

Total Disc Time: 74.54 - 59.45

N.B. A fairly clear audience recording with an introduction from the bootlegger which taken on face value would seem to confirm the recording date. An interesting medley during How Many More Times.

D1:

We're Gonna Groove (5.17)

Dazed & Confused (17.06)

Heartbreaker (6.37)

Bring It On Home (9.18)

White Summer - Black Mountain Side (12.51)

Since I've Been Loving You (7.10)

Organ Solo - Thank You (11.54)

What Is & What Should Never Be (4.35)

D2:

Moby Dick (19.55)

How Many More Times Medley (33.33) (Inc. I'm Going Down - Bolero - The Hunter - Boogie Chillen - Truckin Little Mama - My Baby Don't Love Me - Ramble On - Mess Of Blues - That's Alright Mama)

Whole Lotta Love (6.14)

Memphis

Venue: Memphis

Date: 4/17/70

Cover: D4C sleeve

Recording: 5

Source: St - Aud

Company: Neptune

Matrix #: NEP 001 - 002

Place Of Origin: Japan

Total Disc Time: 71.02 - 65.45

N.B. A fairly clear audience recording with an introduction from the bootlegger which taken on face value would seem to confirm the recording date. An interesting medley during How Many More Times.

D1:

We're Gonna Groove (5.17)

Dazed & Confused (17.06)

Heartbreaker (6.37)

Bring It On Home (9.18)

White Summer - Black Mountain Side (12.51)

Since I've Been Loving You (7.10)

Organ Solo - Thank You (11.54)

D2:

What Is & What Should Never Be (4.35)

Moby Dick (19.55)

How Many More Times Medley (33.33) (Inc. I'm Going Down - Bolero - The Hunter - Boogie Chillen - Truckin Little Mama - My Baby Don't Love Me - Ramble On - Mess Of Blues - That's Alright Mama)

Whole Lotta Love (6.14)

Merry Christmas Mr Jimmy

Venue: London
Date: 12/23/72
Cover: D4C sleeve
Recording: 7
Source: M - Aud
Company: Lemon Song
Matrix #: LS 7208/09
Place Of Origin: Japan
Total Disc Time: n/a

N.B. The complete show which until now has escaped the attention of the bootleggers. Also available as "The Titanic".

D1:
Rock And Roll
Over The Hills And Far Away
Black Dog
Misty Mountain Hop
Since I've Been Loving You
Dancing Days
Bron-Y-Aur Stomp
The Song Remains The Same
The Rain Song
Stairway To Heaven
D2:
Dazed And Confused
Whole Lotta Love, (Inc. The Crunge, Everybody Needs Someone To Love, Boogie Chillen, Let's Have A Party, Heartbreak Hotel, I Can't Quit You)
Heartbreaker

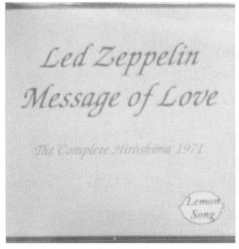

Message Of Love

Venue: Hiroshima
Date: 9/27/71
Cover: D4C
Recording: 4
Source: M -Aud
Company: Lemon Song
Matrix #: n/a
Place Of Origin: Japan
Total Disc Time: n/a

N.B. The Hiroshima tape emerges again from another Japanese label. Still crappy quality. Previously available as "Peace".

D1:
Immigrant Song
Heartbreaker
Since I've Been Loving You
Black Dog
Dazed And Confused
Stairway To Heaven
Celebration Day
D2:
That's The Way
Going To California
Tangerine
What Is And What Should Never Be
Moby Dick
Whole Lotta Love Medley (Inc. Boogie Chillen – Let's Have Fun – Be Bop A Lula)
Communication Breakdown

Midnight Rehearsals

Venue: Hollywood – Clearwell Castle# – Headley Grange^ –
Boleskine House? – Bron – y – Aur*
Date: 10-11/75 – 5/78# – 1/71^ – 11/73-5/74^ – 11/73? –
5/70* **Cover:** D4C **Recording:** 8 -9
Source: St - SB **Company:** n/a
Matrix #: n/a **Place Of Origin:** Japan
Total Disc Time: n/a

N.B. This is one of many releases to surface in late 1997 of
some amazingly clear recordings of various recording sessions.
The "Presence" rehearsals are probably recorded in Hollywood
California (although some have attributed them to Malibu). Plant
sequestered himself at a house in Malibu to recuperate from his
car accident that summer, however the band did commute into
Los Angeles to rehearse and as far as anyone knows the
rehearsals were either conducted in Hollywood or possibly Santa
Monica. The Clearwell Castle material is live in an apparently cav-
ernous room (judging by the echo). The "Swansong" demos are
early recordings made by Page, Jones and Bonham. At the time
Page talked extensively to the media about a guitar epic he was
constructing. As is evident by these recordings this was to finally
emerge about a decade later as "Midnight Moonlight" with the
Firm. The cover attributes the Lucifer Rising material to
Boleskine House in Scotland. As romantic a notion as this may be
there doesn't seem to be any direct evidence to support this.
Some of this material may have originated from Headley Grange
but then again….get at least one of the many versions of these
tapes that are floating around.

D1:
Royal Orleans (Inst.) (0.20),
Tea For One (1.55)
Don't Start Me Talking - All My Loving (4.35)
Fire (2.59)
Carouselambra #1 (3.01)
Carouselambra #2 (3.46)
Carouselambra #3 (3.56)
In the Evening intro (0.56)
The Battle of Evermore (5.44)
Swansong demo (Midnight Moonlight) (17.59)
Ten Years Gone demo (7.58)
Night Flight (alt. mix) (3.43)
Lucifer Rising (4.03)
Acoustic guitar demo #1 (2.36)
Acoustic guitar demo #2 (0.31)

Missing Sailor

Venue: San Diego
Date: 9/3/70
Cover: D4C in double case
Recording: n/a
Source: n/a
Company: Immigrant
Matrix #: IM 031 - 032
Place Of Origin: Japan
Total Disc Time: n/a

N.B. All track information not available at press time.
Previously unreleased show.

D1:
Immigrant Song
Heartbreaker
Dazed & Confused
Bring It On Home
That's The Way
Since I've Been Loving You
D2:
Organ Solo - Thank You
What Is & What Should Never Be
Moby Dick
Whole Lotta Love Medley (Inc. Boogie Chillen - I've Got
A Girl - Killing Floor - Two And One To Three - Crosscut
Saw - Honey Bee - The Lemon Song - Needle Blues -
Since My Baby's Been Gone - Lawdy Miss Claudie)
Communication Breakdown

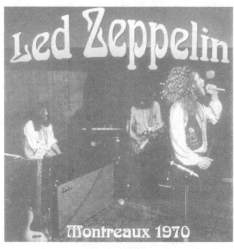

Monsters Of Rock

Venue: Seattle - Detroit*
Date: 7/17/73 - 7/13/73*
Cover: D4C folding slipcase
Recording: 8
Source: St - SB
Company: Tarantura
Matrix #: T3CD-9
Place Of Origin: Japan
Total Disc Time: 64.32 - 48.14 - 54.41
N.B. Another delightful package from
Tarantura with an accordion type fold out cover.
Each disc is housed in it's own printed sleeve.
Sound quality is extremely good.

D1:
Rock And Roll (4.05)
Celebration Day (3.43)
Bring It On Home- Black Dog (5.54)
Over The Hills And Far Away (6.45)
Misty Mountain Hop (5.29)
Since I've Been Loving You (7.56)
No Quarter (13.54)
The Song Remains The Same (6.04)
The Rain Song (8.03)
D2:
Dazed And Confused (34.15)
Stairway To Heaven (10.54)
D3:
Moby Dick (24.35)*
Heartbreaker (7.34)*
Whole Lotta Love (15.12)*
Dancing Days (1.16) (cut)*.

Montreaux 1970

Venue: Montreux
Date: 3/7/70
Cover: D4C in case
Recording: 7
Source: M - Aud
Company: Live Storm
Matrix #: LSCD 51525
Place Of Origin: Italy
Total Disc Time: 71.08
N.B. Another Italian re-issue of the
well-known audience tape.

D1:
We're Gonna Groove (3.52)
I Can't Quit You (5.45)
White Summer (10.17)
Dazed & Confused (15.07)
Heartbreaker (6.20)
Since I've Been Loving You (6.02)
Thank You (8.02)
What Is & What Should Never Be (4.21)
How Many More Times (cut) (9.50)

Motor City Daze

Venue: Detroit - London*
Date: 7/12/73 - 3/19/69*
Cover: D4C in double case
Recording: 7,3*
Source: M - Aud ,M - SB*
Company: ANTRABATA
Matrix #: ARM 120773
Place Of Origin: Japan
Total Disc Time: 46.43 - 46:38 - 54:18.
N.B. Fairly good recording from Cobo Hall in a
nice package. Comes with a bonus track of the
missing song from the BBC sessions.
Poor quality but interesting none the less.

D1:
Rock and Roll (Fades In) (1.05)
Celebration Day (3.38)
Black Dog (6.07)
Over The Hills And Far Away (7.13)
Misty Mountain Hop (5.06)
Since I ve Been Loving You (10.15)
No Quarter (12.49)
D2:
The Song Remains The Same (6.13)
The Rain Song (9.27)
Dazed And Confused (30.55)
D3:
Stairway To Heaven (12.57)
Moby Dick (Edit) (3.35) Heartbreaker (7.05)
Whole Lotta Love (16.28)
Communication Breakdown (5.05)
The Ocean (5.58)
Sunshine Woman * (3.05)

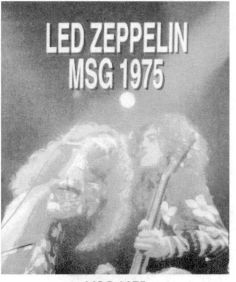

MSG 1975

Venue: New York
Date: 2/12/75
Cover: D4C
Recording: 7
Source: M - Aud
Company: Last Stand Disc
Matrix #: LSD 12/13/14
Place Of Origin: Japan
Total Disc Time: n/a
N.B. A slightly better than average recording from
Madison Square Gardens.

D1:
Rock and Roll
Sick Again
Over the Hills and Far Away
In My Time of Dying
The Song Remains the Same
The Rain Song
Kashmir
D2:
No Quarter
Trampled Underfoot
Moby Dick
D3:
Dazed and Confused
Stairway to Heaven
Whole Lotta Love
Black Dog
Heartbreaker

Mystery European Gig

Venue: Hamburg
Date: 3/10/70
Cover: D4C
Recording: 6
Source: M - Aud
Company: The Symbols
Matrix #: n/a
Place Of Origin: Japan
Total Disc Time: n/a

N.B. Another seemingly unreleased show. There is some dispute over whether this is the Frankfurt or Hamburg show. Luis Rey in his book "Live" attributes this to Frankfurt on March 10th 1970 however in Hot Wacks Supplement 5 it is attributed to Hamburg on March 11th 1970. Just to throw another wrench in the works how about this?? I reckon it was Hamburg on March 10th. Both Melody Maker and Billboard announced that the band would play Frankfurt on March 10th. On February 28th 1970 New Musical Express reported that the Led Zeppelin show slated for Frankfurt was cancelled due to riots at a Jethro Tull concert the previous week. On March 7th Disc reported that the band would add an extra show in Hamburg. The band were originally scheduled to play Hamburg on March 11th so the extra date would make the most sense the day before (i.e. when Frankfurt was originally scheduled). If you can figure that lot out - not only are you loonier than I must be, but you get a badge too!

D1:
We're Gonna Groove
I Can't Quite You Baby
Dazed And Confused
Heartbreaker
White Summer, Black Mountain Side
Since I've Been Loving You
Organ Solo - Thank You
D2:
What Is And What Should Never Be
Moby Dick
How Many More Times Medley
(Inc. The Hunter - Boogie Chillen -Truckin' Little Mama -
Ramblin - Down By The Riverside- Travelling Riverside Blues -
Long Distance Call Blue - The Lemon Song)
Whole Lotta Love

Nasty Music

Venue: Stoke - Oxford - Berlin - Dundee - Liverpool
Date: 1/15/73 - 1/7/73 - 3/19/73 - 1/27/73 - 1/14/73
Cover: D2C cover in plastic case with DBW inserts
Recording: 7
Source: St - SB
Company: Tarantura
Matrix #: T3CD- 011-1-2-3
Place Of Origin: Japan
Total Disc Time: 52.59 - ??? - ???

N.B. Limited edition of 300 copies in plastic case.

D1:
Rock & Roll (3.45)
Over The Hills & Far Away (5.45)
Black Dog (6.18)
Misty Mountain Hop (5.20)
Since I've Been Loving You (8.02)
Dancing Days (4.48)
Bron-y-Aur Stomp (5.44)
The Song Remains The Same (5.58)
The Rain Song (5.53)
D2:
Dazed & Confused
Stairway To Heaven (9.59)
D3:
Whole Lotta Love
Heartbreaker (7.06)
Communication Breakdown (4.31)
The Ocean (4.03)

Newcastle Symphony
Venue: Newcastle
Date: 11/30/72
Cover: D2C
Recording: 4 - 6
Source: M -Aud
Company: Image Quality
Matrix #: IQ 022/23
Place Of Origin: Japan
Total Disc Time: n/a

N.B. This tape did the rounds for some time with the date and venue disguised as other shows.
Parts of it have been available before as "Nice Starter" and "Stepmother's Club".

D1:
Rock And Roll (3:50)
Over The Hills And Far Away (5:59)
Black Dog (5:46)
Misty Mountain Hop (5:34)
Since I've Been Loving You (7:43)
Dancing Days (5:28)
Bron-Y-Aur Stomp (5:20)
The Song Remains The Same (5:26)
The Rain Song (8.17)
D2:
Dazed And Confused (Inc.The Crunge) (23:16)
Stairway To Heaven (10:05)
Whole Lotta Love Medley (20:23)
(Inc. Everybody Needs Somebody To Love, Boogie
Chillen, Let's Have A Party, Going Down Slow)
Immigrant Song (4:12)
Heartbreaker (5:54)
Mellotron Solo - Thank You (8:42)

Nice Opening Night
Venue: London
Date: 5/17/75
Cover: D4C
Recording: 7
Source: M - Aud
Company: Image Quality
Matrix #: IQ 028/029/030
Place Of Origin: Japan
Total Disc Time: n/a

N.B. An above average recording from this first gig at Earl's Court. For some reason this first show has not been bootlegged very often.

D1:
Rock and Roll (3.47)
Sick Again (6.38)
Over the Hills and Far Away (8.57)
In My Time of Dying (11.49)
The Song Remains the Same (5.19)
The Rain Song (9.40)
Kashmir (9.00)
D2:
No Quarter
Tangerine (5.31)
Going to California (6.59)
That's the Way (6.23)
Bron-y-Aur Stomp (8.06)
Trampled Underfoot (8.07)
D3:
Moby Dick (20.31)
Dazed and Confused (27.37)
Stairway to Heaven (8.29)
Whole Lotta Love (5.15)
Black Dog (6.08)

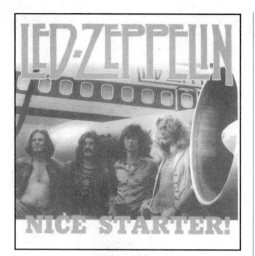

Nice Starter

Venue: Newcastle
Date: 11/30/72
Cover: D2C
Recording: 6
Source: M -Aud
Company: The Symbols
Matrix #: n/a
Place Of Origin: Japan
Total Disc Time: n/a

N.B. This tape did the rounds for some time with the date and venue disguised as other shows. Parts of it have been available before as "Newcastle Symphony" and "Stepmother's Club".

D1:
Rock And Roll (3:50)
Over The Hills And Far Away (5:59)
Black Dog (5:46)
Misty Mountain Hop (5:34)
Since I've Been Loving You (7:43)
Dancing Days (5:28)
Bron-Yr-Aur Stomp (5:20)
The Song Remains The Same (5:26)
The Rain Song (8.17)
D2:
Dazed And Confused (Inc. The Crunge) (23:16)
Stairway To Heaven (10:05)
Whole Lotta Love Medley (20:23)
(Inc. Everybody Needs Somebody To Love, Boogie
Chillen, Let's Have A Party, Going Down Slow)
Immigrant Song (4:12)
Heartbreaker (5:54)
Mellotron Solo - Thank You (8:42)

1980

Venue: Various

Date: Various

Cover: D4C folder

Recording: 9

Source: St - SB - M - SB

Company: Tarantura

Matrix #: n/a

Place Of Origin: Japan

Total Disc Time: n/a

N.B. Another super deluxe package from Tarantura. A binder which holds several multiple CD sets documenting the soundboard recordings from Brussels, Bremen, Zurich and Hannover in 1980. These titles were then released individually as "Hannover 1980", "Zurich 1980", "Bremen 1980", and "Brussels 1980".

1970 Studio Works

Venue: London-New York-Bron-y-Aur-Headley Grange
Date: Various 1969-1970
Cover: D4C gate fold sleeve
Recording: 8 Source: St- SB
Company: Theramin **Matrix #:** n/a
Place Of Origin: Japan **Total Disc Time:** n/a
N.B. Another compilation of various studio material. Some taken from Olympic Studios, some from Mystic studios in New York, some from Headley Grange, and some from Bron-y-Aur.

D1:
Jennings Farm Blues (Various Takes)
No Quarter
That's the Way
Feel so Bad
Since I've Been Loving You
D2:
Since I've Been Loving You (Vocal)
Moby Dick
Moby Dick Drum Fill
I Want to Be Her Man
Guitar Jam
Down by the Seaside
D3:
Guitar Improvisations
Poor Tom
Walters Walk
D4:
Friends
Immigrant Song
Out on the Tiles
Bron-y-Aur
Poor Tom
Hey Hey What Can I Do
The Rover
Instrumental
Poor Tom
Instrumental
Instrumental
That's the Way (Five Takes)
Friends
Bron-y-Aur (Three Takes)
Instrumentals

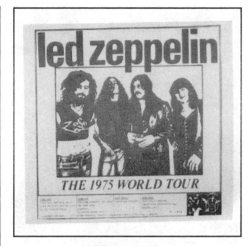

1975 World Tour

Venue: Montreal
Date: 2/6/75
Cover: D2C
Recording: 7
Source: St - Aud
Company: Cobra
Matrix #: 020
Place Of Origin: Japan
Total Disc Time: n/a
N.B. Another Cobra reissue of an old vinyl title. This one complete with all of the bizarre stereo tricks that were on the original tape.

D1:
Rock and Roll
Sick Again
Over the Hills and Far Away
The Song Remains the Same
The Rain Song
Kashmir
No Quarter
Trampled under Foot
D2:
Moby Dick
Dazed and Confused
Stairway to Heaven
Whole Lotta Love - Black Dog
Heartbreaker

929

Venue: Osaka
Date: 9/29/71
Cover: D4C sleeve
Recording: 5
Source: M -Aud
Company: H Bomb
Matrix#: HBM9510/11/12
Place Of Origin: Japan
Total Disc Time: 58.36 – 64.16 – 55.17
N.B. All details are not available. Another re-issue of the Osaka tape.

D1:
Immigrant Song
Heartbreaker
Since I've Been Loving You
Black Dog
Dazed & Confused
D2:
Stairway To Heaven
Celebration Day
That's The Way
Going To California
Tangerine
Friends
Smoke Gets In Your Eyes
D3:
Whole Lotta Love Medley (Inc. Boogie Chillen – Tossin & Turnin – Twist & Shout – Fortune Teller – Good Times Bad Times – You Shook Me)
Communication Breakdown
Organ Solo - Thank You
Rock & Roll

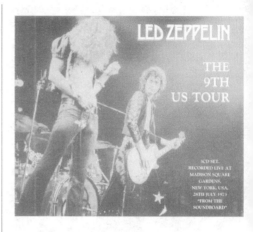

Ninth US Tour (The)

Venue: New York
Date: 7/28/73
Cover: D4C in double case
Recording: 9
Source: St - SB
Company: Whole Lotta Live
Matrix #: WLL 004-005-006
Place Of Origin: Italy
Total DiscTime: 63.36 - 70.31 - 29.13
N.B. A knock off of the Tarantura title "Tour De Force".

D1:
Opening (1.36)
Rock & Roll (3.57)
Celebration Day (3.27)
Black Dog (5.45)
Over The Hills & Far Away(6.13)
Misty Mountain Hop (4.56)
Since I've Been Loving You (8.17)
No Quarter (12.43)
The Song Remains The Same (5.43)
The Rain Song (7.59)
D2:
Dazed & Confused (29.11)
Stairway To Heaven (11.28)
Moby Dick (28.10)
D3:
Heartbreaker Medley (20.38)
(Inc. Whole Lotta Love - Boogie Chillen)
The Ocean (4.30)

No License No Festival

Venue: Boston
Date: 9/9/70
Cover: D4C in case
Recording: 4
Source: M -Aud
Company: Silver Rarities
Matrix #: SIRA 164 165
Place Of Origin: Europe
Total Disc Time: n/a

N.B. Another re-issue of the Boston tape which partially emerged years ago on the vinyl titles "207.19" Also available as "Come Back To Boston".

D1:
Introduction (3.11)
Immigrant Song (5.41)
Heartbreaker (6.29)
Dazed & Confused (16.42)
Bring It On Home (9.20)
That's The Way (7.14)
Bron-y-Aur (5.03)
Since I've Been Loving You (12.15)
D2:
Thank You (11.03)
What Is & What Should Never Be (4.48)
Moby Dick (12.40)
Whole Lotta Love Medley (18.27) (Inc. Boogie Chillen - Ramble On - For What It's Worth - Some Other Guy - Honey Bee - The Lemon Song)
Communication Breakdown (5.44)

Not Authorised

Venue: n/a
Date: n/a
Cover: D4C in case
Recording: n/a
Source: n/a
Company: Mainline
Matrix #: SW 39
Place Of Origin: Australia
Total Disc Time: n/a

N.B. All track information not available at press time.

D1:
The Battle Of Evermore
Going To California
Black Country Woman
Bron - y - Aur Stomp
White Summer
Kashmir
Stairway To Heaven
Rock And Roll
Trampled Underfoot

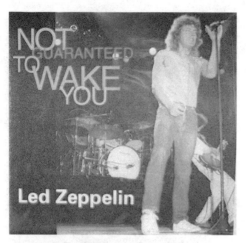

Not Guaranteed To Wake You

Venue: Rotterdam
Date: 6/21/80
Cover: D4C
Recording: 7, 8
Source: St - Aud, St - SB
Company: Diagrams Of Led Zeppelin
Matrix #:
Place Of Origin: Japan
Total Disc Time: 65.01 – 42.16

N.B. Apparently partly from an audience recording from the Rotterdam show. This makes it an oddity as since all those soundboards emerged there has been almost no audience releases from that tour.

D1:
The Train Kept A Rollin'
Nobody's Fault But Mine
Black Dog
In The Evening
The Rain Song
Hot Dog
All My Love
Trampled Underfoot (cut)
Since I've Been Loving You
Achilles Last Stand
D2:
White Summer, Black Mountain Side (cut)
Kashmir
Stairway To Heaven
Rock And Roll
Heartbreaker

Nutty and Cool

Venue: Baltimore
Date: 6/11/72
Cover: D4C sleeve
Recording: n/a
Source: M -Aud
Company: Baby Face
Matrix #: 9604
Place of Origin: Japan
Total Disc Time: n/a

N.B. Seemingly a new show on bootleg. All track details not available at press time.

D1:
Immigrant Song
Heartbreaker
Black Dog
Since I've Been Loving You
Stairway to Heaven
Going to California
That's the Way
Tangerine
Bron-y-Aur Stomp
Dazed and Confused
D2:
What Is and What Should Never Be
Moby Dick
Whole Lotta Love Medley
(Inc. Boogie Chillen - Hello Mary Lou - Heartbreak
Hotel - I'm Going Down - Going Down Slow)
Rock and Roll
Communication Breakdown

One Day After Eddie

Venue: Los Angeles
Date: 6/25/77
Cover: D4C
Recording: 7 - 8
Source: M -Aud
Company: Immigrant
Matrix #: 054 - 056
Place Of Origin: Japan
Total Disc Time: 77.20 – 51.01 – 70.15

N.B. An above average audience recording from the string of LA dates. Available multiple times before.

D1:
The Song Remains The Same
Sick Again
Nobody's Fault But Mine
In My Time Of Dying
Since I've Been Loving You
No Quarter
D2:
Ten Years Gone
The Battle Of Evermore
Going To California
Black Country Woman
Bron-Y-Aur Stomp
White Summer
Kashmir
D3:
Moby Dick
Over The Hills And Far Away
Guitar Solo
Achilles Last Stand
Stairway To Heaven
Whole Lotta Love
Rock And Roll

Olympiahalle

Venue: Munich
Date: 3/17/73
Cover: D4C in double slimline case
Recording: 6
Source: St - Aud
Company: Immigrant
Matrix #: IM 022 -023
Place Of Origin: Japan
Total Disc Time: 57.26 - 73.59

N.B. A fairly average audience recording from the Olympiahalle gig.

D1:
Rock And Roll (4.00)
Over The Hills And Far Away (7.20)
Black Dog (6.18)
Misty Mountain Hop (4.39)
Since I've Been Loving You (9.06)
Dancing Days (5.39)
Bron-Y-Aur Stomp (5.18)
The Song Remains The Same (5.42)
The Rain Song (9.24)
D2:
Dazed And Confused (28.43)
Stairway To Heaven (11.42)
Whole Lotta Love (25.57)
Heartbreaker (7.37)

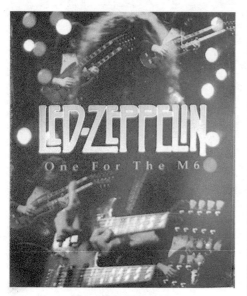

One For The M6

Venue: Liverpool
Date: 1/14/73
Cover: D2C
Recording: 8
Source: M - SB
Company: Crazy Dream
Matrix #: CDZ 73001/002
Place Of Origin: Japan
Total Disc Time: n/a
N.B. Also available as "The Fabulous Four".

D1:
Over The Hills And Far Away (5.28)
Black Dog (5.52)
Misty Mountain Hop (5.00)
Since I've Been Loving You (7.36)
Dancing Days (4.24)
Bron-Y-Aur Stomp (6.02)
The Song Remans The Same (5.49)
The Rain Song (5.38)
Dazed And Confused (22.50)
D2:
Stairway To Heaven (10.51)
Whole Lotta Love Medley (Inc. Everybody Needs
Someone To Love - Boogie Chillen - Baby I Don't Care -
Shape I'm In) (23.20)
Heartbreaker (7.02)
The Ocean (4.29)

One More For The Road

Venue: Milwaukee
Date: 7/10/73
Cover: D4C in double case
Recording: 4 - 6
Source: St - Aud
Company: RED HOT
Matrix #: RH-012013
Place Of Origin: Japan
Total Disc Time: 64.05 - 52.01
N.B. A new recording of the Milwaukee show.
Previously unavailable but not great quality.

D1:
Rock & Roll (4.16)
Celebration Day (3.35)
Black Dog (5.43)
Over The Hills And Far Away (6.22)
Misty Mountain Hop (4.55)
Since I ve Been Loving You (8.39)
No Quarter (13.00)
The Song Remains The Same (5.46)
The Rain Song (8.19)
D2:
Dazed And Confused (29.38)
Stairway To Heaven (11.11)
Moby Dick (10.33) (cut)

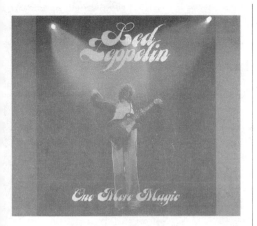

One More Magic

Venue: New York
Date: 7/28/73
Cover: D4C in double case
Recording: 7 - 8
Source: St - SB
Company: Immigrant
Matrix #: IM 019-021
Place Of Origin: Japan
Total Disc Time: 50.05 - 45.38 - 70.21

N.B. The entire show which comprised the bulk of the movie soundtrack. This features almost an hour of music cut from the movie and soundtrack album.
Good quality recording.

D1:
Rock & Roll (5.33)
Celebration Day (3.43)
Bring It On Home - Black Dog (6.42)
Over The Hills & Far Away (7.13)
Misty Mountain Hop (4.49)
Since I've Been Loving You (9.44)
No Quarter (12.36)
D2:
The Song Remains The Same (6.35)
The Rain Song (9.27)
Dazed & Confused (29.36)
D3:
Stairway To Heaven (12.47)
Moby Dick (28.11)
Heartbreaker Medley (24.50)
(Inc. Whole Lotta Love - Boogie Chillen)
The Ocean (4.33)

Ooh My Ears Man

Venue: Adelaide
Date: 2/19/72
Cover: D4C
Recording: 8
Source: M -Aud
Company: Diagrams Of Led Zeppelin
Matrix #: TDOLZ 034
Place Of Origin: Japan
Total Disc Time: 51.31 - 42.35

N.B. A reissue of the great Adelaide audience tape. Previously available as "Voodoo Drive" on Tarantura.

D1:
Immigrant Song
Heartbreaker
Black Dog
Since I've Been Loving You
Stairway To Heaven
Going To California (cut)
That's The Way (cut)
Tangerine (cut)
Bron-Y-Aur Stomp (cut)
D2:
Dazed And Confused (cut)
Moby Dick (cut)
Whole Lotta Love Medley (Inc. Boogie Chillen – Mary
Lou – Let's Have A Party – That's Alright Mama - Going
Down Slow)

Operation Moonbeam

Venue: Brussels

Date: 1/12/75

Cover: D4C sleeve

Recording: 4

Source: M - Aud

Company: Tarantura

Matrix #: BELGIUM1,2

Place Of Origin: Japan

Total Disc Time: n/a

N.B. An infrequently bootlegged show from the 1975 warm up date in Belgium. Not a great recording.

D1:

Rock & Roll

Sick Again

Over The Hills & Far Away

When The Levee Breaks

Song Remains The Same

Rain Song

Kashmir

D2:

The Wanton Song

No Quarter

Trampled Underfoot

In My Time Of Dying

Stairway To Heaven

Whole Lotta Love - Black Dog

Communication Breakdown

Orlando Madness Vol. I

Venue: Orlando

Date: 8/31/71

Cover: DBW slick

Recording: n/a

Source: n/a

Company: n/a

Matrix #: n/a

Place Of Origin: Japan

Total Disc Time: n/a

N.B. All track information not available at press time.

Previously unreleased show.

D1:

Immigrant Song

Heartbreaker

Since I've Been Loving You

Dazed & Confused

Black Dog

Orlando Madness Vol. 2

Venue: Orlando

Date: 8/31/71

Cover: DBW slick

Recording: n/a

Source: n/a

Company: n/a

Matrix #: n/a

Place Of Origin: Japan

Total Disc Time: n/a

N.B. All track information not available at press time.

Previously unreleased show.

D1:

Stairway To Heaven

Celebration Day

That's The Way

Going To California

What Is & What Should Never Be

Moby Dick

Osaka Tapes

Venue: Osaka
Date: 10/4/72
Cover: D4C
Recording: 4 -5
Source: M -Aud
Company: Amsterdam
Matrix #: AMS 9610-2
Place Of Origin: Japan
Total Disc Time: n/a

N.B. Also available as "Dancing Geisha" and "Stand By Me" "Second Daze". This box set was also released individually as "Connexion" and "Raw Tapes Pt 1 and 2". The cover claims it is the same tape three times but the first two discs (Connexion) are cleaned up whereas the third through sixth discs are not. Beats me what the point of that exercise is. Suffice to say that discs three through six have the same track listings as one and two.

D1:
Rock & Roll
Black Dog
Over The Hills & Far Away
Misty Mountain Hop
Since I've Been Loving You
Dancing Days
Bron-y-Aur Stomp
Song Remains The Same
Rain Song
D2:
Dazed & Confused
Stairway To Heaven
Whole Lotta Love
Heartbreaker
Immigrant Song

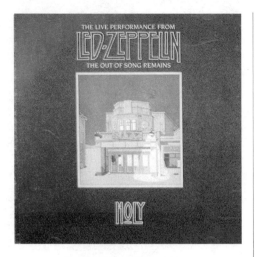

Out Of Song Remains

Venue: New York

Date: 7/27/73

Cover: D4C

Recording: 8

Source: St - SB

Company: Holy

Matrix #: SH003

Place Of Origin: Japan

Total Disc Time: n/a

N.B. Soundboard bits and pieces from the first night in New York. Parts of this may have been used in the movie soundtrack.

D1:

The Rain Song (7:47)

Dazed And Confused (Inc. San Francisco) (30:42)

Stairway to Heaven (11:18)

D2:

Moby Dick (19:40)

Heartbreaker (7:03)

Whole Lotta Love Medley (Inc. Boogie Chilen) (15:42)

The Ocean (5:16)

Out Of The Way

Venue: Birmingham
Date: 5/18/77
Cover: D4C sleeve
Recording: 6
Source: M - Aud
Company: Diagrams Of Led Zeppelin
Matrix #: TDOLZ 0036/37/38
Place Of Origin: Japan
Total Disc Time: n/a

N.B. Previously available as the title "Dixie" which I erroneously pegged as an excellent soundboard recording. This is audience and as much as it is better than "Dixie" it certainly isn't soundboard.

D1:
The Song Remains The Same (6:17)
The Rover Intro, Sick Again (6:42)
Nobody's Fault But Mine (7:30)
In My Time Of Dying (12:09)
Since I've Been Loving You (9:23)
No Quarter (21:06)
D2:
Ten Years Gone (13:41)
The Battle Of Evermore (6:18)
Going To California (4:54)
Black Country Woman (1:48)
BronY-Aur Stomp (6:11)
White Summer – Swansong/Midnight Moonlight - Black Mountainside (6:03)
Kashmir (9:49)
Out On The Tiles, Moby Dick (20:26)
D3: Guitar Solo (Inc. Star Spangled Banner (9:45)
Achilles Last Stand (10:27)
Stairway To Heaven (11:27)
Rock And Roll (4:44)

Out On The Tiles

Venue: Los Angeles
Date: 6/21/77
Cover: D4C deluxe sleeve
Recording: 8
Source: St - Aud
Company: Tarantura
Matrix #: T19CD 1-3-RE
Place Of Origin: Japan
Total Disc Time: n/a

N.B. A really nicely packaged re-release of the now legendary "Listen To This Eddie" tape.

D1:
Song Remains The Same
Sick Again
Nobody's Fault But Mine
Over The Hills & Far Away
Since I've Been Loving You
No Quarter
D2:
Ten Years Gone
Battle Of Evermore
Going To California
Black Country Woman
Bron-y-Aur Stomp
White Summer - Black Mountain Side
Kashmir
D3:
Moby Dick
Hearbreaker
Guitar Solo
Achilles Last Stand
Stairway To Heaven
Whole Lotta Love
Rock & Roll

Over The Garden

Venue: New York
Date: 6/13/77
Cover: D4C
Recording: 4
Source: M -Aud
Company: Diagrams Of Led Zeppelin
Matrix #: TDOLZ-0039/0041
Place Of Origin: Japan
Total Disc Time: 65:24 - 54:41 - 68:48

N.B. Another previously unbootlegged show.

D1:
The Song Remains The Same
The Rover Intro / Sick Again
Nobody's Fault But Mine
Over The Hills And Far Away
Since I've Been Loving You
No Quarter
D2:
Ten Years Gone
The Battle Of Evermore
Going To California
Black Country Woman
Bron-Y-Aur Stomp
White Summer - Black Mountain Side
Kashmir
D3:
Out On The Tiles / Moby Dick
Heartbreaker
Guitar Solo
Achilles Last Stand
Stairway To Heaven
Whole Lotta Love
Black Dog

Over the Twelve Foot End

Venue: Ipswich
Date: 11/16/71
Cover: D4C sleeve
Recording: 6
Source: M -Aud
Company: n/a
Matrix #: n/a
Place of Origin: Japan
Total Disc Time: n/a

N.B. I believe that this was the first release of this tape. However I may be wrong on that score. Regardless this concert has surfaced several times on bootleg in the last twelve months.

D1:
Immigrant Song
Heartbreaker
Black Dog
Since I've Been Loving You
Rock and Roll
Stairway to Heaven
Going to California
D2:
That's the Way
Tangerine
Dazed and Confused
What Is And What Should Never Be
Celebration Day
Whole Lotta Love (Cut)

Persistence Kezar

Venue: San Francisco
Date: 6/2/73
Cover: D4C
Recording: 6
Source: M -Aud
Company: Holy
Matrix #: SH 004-A
Place Of Origin: Japan
Total Disc Time: n/a

N.B. Previously only available on vinyl under the same title. In fact the last three tracks are from the vinyl album.

D1:
Introduction (2:36)
Rock And Roll (3:50)
Celebration Day (2:39)
Bring It On Home - Black Dog (6:09)
Over The Hills And Far Away (7:00)
Misty Mountain Hop (5:10)
Since I've Been Loving You (8:20)
No Quarter (10:08)
The Song Remains The Same (6:23)
The Rain Song (8.17)
D2:
Dazed And Confused (Inc. San Francisco) (30:31)
Stairway To Heaven (10:54)
Moby Dick (4:28)
D3:
Heartbreaker (8:02)
Whole Lotta Love Medley (Inc Boogie Chillen) (12:25)
Communication Breakdown (4:09)
The Ocean (5:31)
Heartbreaker (7:52)
Whole Lotta Love Medley (Inc Boogie Chillen) (12:25)

Philadelphia Special

Venue: Philadelphia

Date: 2/8/75

Cover: D4C

Recording: 7

Source: M -Aud

Company: n/a

Matrix #: LZ 001/002

Place Of Origin: Japan

Total Disc Time: 75.45 – 75.37

N.B. Another previously unbootlegged show. An acceptable audience recording typical of tapes from that tour.

D1:

Rock And Roll (cut)

Sick Again

Over The Hills And Far Away (cut)

In My Time of Dying

The Song Remains The Same

The Rain Song

Kashmir

No Quarter (cut)

Trampled Underfoot

D2:

Moby Dick (cut)

Dazed And Confused (Inc. San Francisco)

Stairway To Heaven (cut)

Whole Lotta Love

Black Dog

Heartbreaker

Physical Geography

Venue: Headley Grange-Island Studios

Date: 1973-1974

Cover: D4C

Recording: 9

Source: St - SB

Company: n/a

Matrix #: n/a

Place Of Origin: Japan

Total Disc Time: n/a

N.B. Another reissue of the amazing new soundboard recordings which are also available as the titles Brutal Artistry and Alternative Physical.

D1:

Trampled Underfoot

Kashmir

Custard Pie

In the Light

Midnight Moonlight

Midnight Moonlight

The Wanton Song

Take Me Home

Take Me Home

In the Light

Sick Again

In My Time of Dying

In My Time of Dying

Physical Graffiti Alternative Trax

Venue: Studio (Headley Grange?)

Date: 1973-1974

Cover: D4C sleeve

Recording: 9

Source: St - SB

Company: n/a

Matrix #: PA2

Place Of Origin: Europe

Total Disc Time: 58.36

N.B. Another release of the amazing new Physical Graffiti tapes. This one ostensibly features two 10" mixes of Trampled Underfoot and Black Country Woman although I can't tell them apart from the final album mix.

D1:

Trampled Underfoot (Alternative Mix) (5.40)

Trampled Underfoot (Live) (9.02)

Trampled Underfoot (10" 45 rpm mix) (5.34)

Kashmir (instrumental) (8.42)

Custard Pie (Alternative take) (4.19)

Custard Pie (Live) (4.25)

In The Light (different take) (7.14)

Swansong (Take One) (1.23)

Swansong (Take two) (3.37)

Ten Years Gone (No lyrics) (4.13)

Black Country Woman (10" 45 rpm mix) (4.27)

Physically Present

Venue: Island Studios-Headley Grange

Date: 1973-1974

Cover: D4C

Recording: 9

Source: St - SB

Company: House of Elrond

Matrix #: n/a

Place Of Origin: Japan

Total Disc Time: n/a

N.B. One of many releases of this material. Also available as Alternative Physical Graffiti, and Brutal Artistry.

D1:

Custard Pie

The Rover

In My Time of Dying

Trampled under Foot

Kashmir

In the Light

Bron-y-Aur

Down by the Seaside

Ten Years Gone

Night Flight

The Wanton Song

Swan Song

Swan Song (2)

Sick Again

Physical Vancouver Farewell

Venue: Vancouver **Date:** 3/19/75 - 3/20/75*
Cover: D4C   **Recording:** 7 **Source:** M -Aud
Company: Tarantura **Matrix #:** PV-001/006
Place Of Origin: Japan
Total Disc Time: 54:38 - 35:52 - 38:29 - 52:38 - 36:12 -
73:23 **N.B.** Seemingly the complete performances from
the two shows in Vancouver. Not bad quality and another
worthwhile compilation from Tarantura.
D1: Rock And Roll
Sick Again
Over The Hills And Far Away
In My Time Of Dying
The Song Remains The Same
The Rain Song
Kashmir
D2:
No Quarter
Trampled Underfoot
Moby Dick
D3:
Dazed And Confused
D4:
Rock And Roll
Sick Again
Over The Hills And Far Away
In My Time Of Dying
The Song Remains The Same
The Rain Song
Kashmir
D5:
No Quarter
Trampled Underfoot
Moby Dick
D6:
Dazed And Confused
Stairway To Heaven
Whole Lotta Love
Heartbreaker

Plays Pure Bob

Venue: Dallas

Date: 8/31/69

Cover: D4C

Recording: 5

Source: Aud

Company: Tarantura

Matrix#: BOB 001

Place Of Origin: Japan

Total Disc Time: 63.35

N.B. Apparently an audience recording from the legendary Dallas Pop Festival.

D1:

Train Kept A Rollin' (2.59)

I Can't Quit You (6.03)

Dazed & Confused (14.21)

You Shook Me (10.27)

How Many More Times Medley (cut) (21.18)

(Inc. The Hunter - Suzie Q - The Lemon Song -

Eyesight To The Blind - Boogie Chillen)

Communication Breakdown (4.22)

Please Please Me
Venue: Osaka
Date: 9/28/71
Cover: D4C sleeve
Recording: 9
Source: St - Aud
Company: Tarantura
Matrix #: T3CD-4
Place Of Origin: Japan
Total Disc Time: 68.30 - 31.07 - 52.10
N.B. An unusual set of material with an amusing spoof
of the Beatles album of the same name.
Tarantura's usual tasteful packaging.
D1:
Immigrant Song (3.55)
Heartbreaker (6.45)
Since I've Been Loving You (7.23)
Black Dog (5.40)
Dazed And Confused (25.52) (cut)
Stairway To Heaven (8.20)
Please Please Me (.23)
From Me To You (.29)
Celebration Day (3.23)
D2:
Bron-Y-Aur Stomp (3.18)
That's The Way (6.43)
Going To California (6.20)
We Shall Overcome (1.12)
Tangerine (3.29)
Down By The Riverside (2.20)
What Is And What Should Never Be (5.02)
D3:
Moby Dick (18.44)
Whole Lotta Love Medley: (17.43) (cut)
(Inc. Boogie Chillen - Dear Love - Bachelor Boy -
C'mon Baby - Maybelline - Mary Lou)
Come On Everybody (3.29)
High Heeled Sneakers (3.48)
Communication Breakdown (7.45)

Pleeease!
Venue: Vancouver
Date: 3/20/75
Cover: D4C double case
Recording: 5
Source: M - Aud
Company: Silver Rarities
Matrix #: SIRA 126127128 3
Place Of Origin: Europe
Total Disc Time: 52:29 - 50:04 - 68:55
N.B. Not from the 19th this is the second night.

D1:
Rock And Roll (3.49)
Sick Again (5.59)
Over The Hills And Far Away (8.24)
In My Time Of Dying (11.59)
The Song Remains The Same (5.12)
The Rain Song (8.49)
Kashmir (8.15)
D2:
No Quarter (23.45)
Trampled Underfoot (8.15)
Moby Dick (18.02)
D3:
Dazed And Confused (39.48)
Stairway To Heaven (11.39)
Whole Lotta Love (6.50)
Heartbreaker (10.35)

Polished Performance

Venue: New York - Tampa * - Cleveland# - Fort Worth^

Date: 6/11/77 - 6/3/77* - 4/28/77# - 5/22/77^

Cover: D4C in double case

Recording: n/a

Source: n/a

Company: POT

Matrix #: POT 004 005

Place Of Origin: Japan

Total Disc Time: n/a

N.B. All track information not available at press time.

DI:

Ten Years Gone (9.00)

Battle Of Evermore (4.43)

No Quarter (5.15)

Song Remains The Same-Sick Again (11.19)*

Nobody's Fault But Mine (3.18)*

D2:

No Quarter (17.13)#

Achilles Last Stand (9.22)^

Whole Lotta Love-Rock & Roll (5.07)^

Stairway To Heaven (11.11)^

It'll Be Me (3.52)^

Power and Glory (The)

Venue: Los Angeles
Date: 6/21/77-6/22/77-6/23/77-6/25/77-6/26/77-6/27/77
Cover: D4C
Recording: 7-8
Source: St - Aud
Company: Diagrams of Led Zeppelin
Matrix #: TDOLZ 509701-3/ 519701-4/ 529701-3/539701-3/549701-3/559701-4
Place Of Origin: Japan
Total Disc Time: 68.15 - 71.31 -55.41 -45.30 -46.11 - 61.39 -54.16 -69.16 -62.03 -63.11 -73.11 -62.52 -73.47 - 73.08 -65.23 -52.13 -40.26 -60.07 -63.47 -57.33
N.B. Another of those absurd 20 CD box sets from Japan. Once again this one is from the string of Los Angeles concerts held in 1977. The quality is about what you would expect from these recordings, no surprises. There are many other ways of getting this material but much like the title Week for Badge Holders this certainly makes it convenient.

DI:
Song Remains the Same
Sick Again
Nobody's Fault but Mine
Over the Hills and Far Away
Since I've Been Loving You
No Quarter
D2:
Ten Years Gone
The Battle of Ever More
Going to California
Black Country Woman
Bron-y-Aur Stomp
White Summer/Black Mountain Side
Kashmir
Moby Dick
D3:
Heartbreaker
Guitar Solo

Achilles Last Stand
Stairway to Heaven
Whole Lotta Love-Rock and Roll
D4:
Song Remains the Same
Sick Again
Nobody's Fault But Mine
In My Time of Dying
Since I've Been Loving You
D5:
No Quarter
Ten Years Gone
D6:
The Battle of Ever More
Going to California
Black Country Woman
Bron-y-Aur Stomp
White Summer/Black Mountain Side
Kashmir
Moby Dick
D7:
Over the Hills and Far Away
Guitar Solo
Achilles Last Stand
Stairway to Heaven
Whole Lotta Love-Rock and Roll
D8:
Song Remains the Same
Sick Again
Nobody's Fault but Mine
Over the Hills and Far Away
Since I've Been Loving You
No Quarter
D9:
Ten Years Gone
The Battle of Ever More
Going to California
Black Country Woman
Bron-y-Aur Stomp
White Summer/Black Mountain Side
Kashmir
Trampled under Foot
D10:
Moby Dick
Guitar Solo
Achilles Last Stand
Stairway to Heaven
Whole Lotta Love-Rock and Roll
D11:
Song Remains the Same
Sick Again
Nobody Fault But Mine
In My Time of Dying
Since I've Been Loving You
No Quarter
D12:
Ten Years Gone
The Battle of Ever More
Going to California

Bron-y-Aur Stomp
White Summer/Black Mountain Side
Kashmir
Trampled under Foot
D13:
Moby Dick
Guitar Solo
Achilles Last Stand
Stairway to Heaven
Whole Lotta Love-Rock and Roll
D14:
Song Remains the Same
Sick Again
Nobody's Fault But Mine
Over the Hills and Far Away
Since I've Been Loving You
No Quarter
D15:
Ten Years Gone
The Battle of Ever More
Going to California
That's All Right
Black Country Woman
Bron-y-Aur Stomp
White Summer/Black Mountain Side
Kashmir
Moby Dick
D16:
Guitar Solo
Achilles Last Stand
Stairway to Heaven
It'll Be Me
D17:
Song Remains the Same
Sick Again
Nobody's Fault but Mine
Over the Hills and Far Away
Since I've Been Loving You
D18:
No Quarter
Ten Years Gone
The Battle of Ever More
Going to California
D19:
Going Down South
Black Country Woman
Bron-y-Aur Stomp
Dancing Days
White Summer/Black Mountain Side
Kashmir
Trampled Under Foot
Moby Dick
D20:
Guitar Solo
Achilles Last Stand
Stairway to Heaven
Whole Lotta Love-Rock and Roll

Psychedelic Explosion

Venue: San Francisco

Date: 4/26/69

Cover: D4C

Recording: 6

Source: M - Aud

Company: Diagrams Of Led Zeppelin

Matrix #: TDOLZ0006/7

Place Of Origin: Japan

Total Disc Time: n/a

N.B. An excellent version of this show. Previously available as the title "Smokestack Lightning".

D1:

Communication Breakdown (4:18)

I Can't Quit You Baby (7:01)

Dazed And Confused (16:17)

You Shook Me (11:07)

How Many More Times Medley (19:35)

(Inc. Smoke Stack Lightning - The Hunter -

Girl From The North Country)

D2:

White Summer, Black Mountain Side (11:50)

The Lemon Song - That's Alright (9:15)

Babe I'm Gonna Leave You (7:16)

Pat's Delight (6:40)

As Long As I Have You Medley (Inc. Fresh Garbage,

Shake, Hush Little Baby) (18:20)

Whole Lotta Love (8:55)

Pure Nostulgia

Venue: Cologne

Date: 6/18/80

Cover: D4C sleeve

Recording: n/a

Source: n/a

Company: Neptune

Matrix #: n/a

Place Of Origin: Japan

Total Disc Time: n/a

N.B. All track information not available at press time.

D1:

Train Kept A Rollin' (3.00)

Nobody's Fault But Mine (4.37)

Black Dog (4.51)

In The Evening (7.23)

The Rain Song (cut) (6.31)

Hot Dog (3.25)

All My Love (5.24)

Trampled Underfoot (6.52)

Since I've Been Loving You (8.35)

D2:

Achilles Last Stand (7.13)

White Summer - Black Mountain Side (7.10)

Kashmir (8.30)

Stairway To Heaven (9.47)

Rock & Roll (3.12)

Communication Breakdown (2.22)

Push Push
Venue: Oakland
Date: 7/24/77
Cover: D4C
Recording: 7-8
Source: M -Aud
Company: Image Quality
Matrix #: 026/027
Place Of Origin: Japan
Total Disc Time: 72.14 - 73.18
N.B. The last American show previously available as the title "Fighting Finish".

D1:
The Song Remains The Same (5:30)
The Rover, Sick Again (7:17)
Nobody's Fault But Mine (6:23)
Over The Hills And Far Away (5:32)
Since I've Been Loving You (9:05)
No Quarter (23:13)
Ten Years Gone (9:49)
The Battle Of Evermore (5:34)
D2:
Going To California (6:19)
Mystery Train (0:54)
Black Country Woman (1 :52)
Bron-Yr-Aur Stomp (6:24)
Trampled Underfoot (7:40)
White Summer, Black Mountain Side (7:37)
Kashmir (10:39)
Guitar Solo (Inc. Star Spangled Banner) (7:11)
Achilles Last Stand (9:26)
Stairway To Heaven (10:56)
Whole Lotta Love (1:11)
RockAnd Roll (4:18)

Quantient
Venue: Tampa
Date: 5/5/73
Cover: D4C box set
Recording: 6
Source: M - Aud
Company: Cobra
Matrix #: 023
Place Of Origin: Japan
Total Disc Time: n/a
N.B. A re-issue of the vinyl title of the same name. Apparently numbered and limited. Full track details were not available at print time. This also came in two different colored boxes. The promo version was a silver box while the retail version was in a black box.

D1:
Rock and Roll
Celebration Day
Black Dog
Over the Hills and Far Away
Misty Mountain Hop
Since I've Been Loving You
No Quarter
Song Remains the Same
The Rain Song
D2:
Dazed and Confused
Stairway to Heaven
Moby Dick
Heartbreaker
Whole Lotta Love
The Ocean

Rare Broadcasts

Venue: n/a
Date: n/a
Cover: D4C in double case
Recording: n/a
Source: n/a
Company: n/a
Matrix #: n/a
Place Of Origin: Italy
Total Disc Time: n/a

N.B. All track information not available at press time. Probably BBC and 1980 board stuff.

D1:
Communication Breakdown
You Shook Me
I Can't Quit You
Heartbreaker
What Is & What Should Never Be
How Many More Times
Whole Lotta Love
Immigrant Song
That's The Way
Going To California
Black Dog
D2:
Trampled Underfoot
Kashmir
Achilles Last Stand
Nobody's Fault But Mine
All My Love
Train Kept A Rollin'
In The Evening
Stairway To Heaven

Rare Short Party

Venue: New Haven
Date: 8/15/70
Cover: D4C
Recording: 4
Source: M -Aud
Company: Image Quality
Matrix #: IQ003/004
Place Of Origin: Japan
Total Disc Time: 44.00 – 41.38

N.B. The Yale Bowl concert previously an unknown show which was identified on paper and then miraculously a tape appears! Not great though.

D1:
Immigrant Song (3:45)
Heartbreaker (6:18)
Dazed And Confused (17:25)
Bring It On HOme (9:43)
Since I've Been Loving You (6:52)
D2:
What Is And What Should Never Be (4:16)
Moby Dick (15:34)
Whole Lotta Love Medley (12:58)
(Inc. Boogie Chillen - Shake - Move On Down
The Line - Honey Bee - The Lemon Song)
Communication Breakdown (8:49)
(Inc. Good Times Bad Times)

Rarities

Venue: Various
Date: Various
Cover: n/a
Recording: n/a
Source: n/a
Company: Fire Power
Matrix#: FP-2
Place Of Origin: n/a
Total Disc Time: n/a

N.B. Apparently a combination of various pirate sources knocked off from the Westwood One legit radio disc of the same name.

The Yardbirds
I'm Confused - Train Kept A Rollin' - Think About It - Goodnight Sweet Josephine - Psychodaisies - Happenings Ten Years Time Ago - Stroll On
Jimmy Page
She Just Satisfies - Keep Movin' My Baby (Dave Berry) A Certain Girl - Leave My Kitten Alone (First Gear) - Surprise Surprise (Lulu) How Do You Feel (The Primitives)
Robert Plant
You'd Better Run - Everybody's Gonna Say - Our Song - Long Time Coming - I've Got A Secret
Led Zeppelin
Travelling Riverside Blues
Jim's Blues (PJ Proby)

Rave On

Venue: Manchester
Date: 11/24/71
Cover: D4C
Recording: 4
Source: M - Aud
Company: Diagrams Of Led Zeppelin
Matrix #: TDOLZ 029
Place Of Origin: Japan
Total Disc Time: 61.05 - 45.54

N.B. Another previously unreleased show. The tape is listenable but lots of hiss.

D1:
Immigrant Song
Heartbreaker
Black Dog
Since I've Been Loving You
Celebration Day
Stairway To Heaven
Going To California
That's The Way
Tangerine
Bron-Y-Aur Stomp
D2:
Dazed And Confused
What Is And What Should Never Be
Rock And Roll
Whole Lotta Love
Thank You

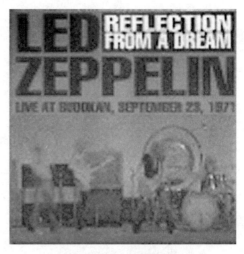

Red Snapper Deluxe

Venue: Montreal - Wallingford^ - Columbia*
Date: 6/7/72 - 8/17/69^ - 5/25/69*
Cover: D4C
Recording: 5
Source: m -Aud
Company: Balboa
Matrix #: BP95010/11
Place Of Origin: Europe
Total Disc Time: 60.36 - 67.13

N.B. A nice compilation of otherwise difficult to acquire
bits and pieces. The Montreal tape is distant but listenable. The cover doesn't mention Going To California.

D1:
Immigrant Song (4.52)
Heartbreaker (7.50)
Black Dog (6.35)
Since I've Been Loving You (8.19)
Stairway To Heaven (11.09)
Going To California (6.42)
That's The Way (6.30)
Tangerine (8.33)
D2:
Dazed & Confused (25.32)
What Is & What Should Never Be (4.31)
Moby Dick (15.27)
Whole Lotta Love (5.21)
Train Kept A Rollin' (2.25)^
I Can't Quit You (6.32)^
Whole Lotta Love (7.25)*

Reflection From A Dream

Venue: Tokyo
Date: 9/23/71
Cover: D4C gatefold sleeve
Recording: 7
Source: M -Aud
Company: Diagrams Of Led Zeppelin
Matrix #: TDOLZ 026
Place Of Origin: Japan
Total Disc Time: n/a

N.B. New tapes of the two 1971 Tokyo shows recently
surfaced and this is one of them. Much better quality
than the previous versions.

D1:
Immigrant Song
Heartbreaker
Since I've Been Loving You
Black Dog
Dazed And Confused
Stairway To Heaven
D2:
Celebration Day
Bron-Y-Aur Stomp
That's The Way
Going To California
What Is And What Should Never Be
Moby Dick
D3:
Whole Lotta Love Medley
Communication Breakdown

Reflections On My Mind

Venue: Miami

Date: 2/14/69

Cover: D2C

Recording: 7

Source: M -Aud

Company: Image Quality

Matrix #: IQ 005/6

Place Of Origin: Japan

Total Disc Time: n/a

N.B. From the now well documented show in Miami. No one has really determined for sure whether this is the first or second night but since there doesn't appear to be two tapes perhaps that's academic.

D1:

The Train Kept A Rollin' (3:08)

I Can't Quit You (5:47)

Dazed And Confused (10:58)

Killing Floor (Inc. Lemon Song, Needle Blues) (6:07)

Baby I'm Gonna Leave You (6:45)

How Many More Times (cut) (11:14) D2:

White Summer, Black Mountain Side (9:50)

As Long As I Have You Medley (13:22)

(Inc. Fresh Garbage - Shake - Hush)

You Shook Me (9:06)

Pat's Delight (12:31)

Return Of The Auschwitz

Venue: Dortmund

Date: 7/17/80

Cover: D4C sleeve

Recording: n/a

Source: n/a

Company: Neptune

Matrix #: n/a

Place Of Origin: Japan

Total Disc Time: n/a

N.B. All track information not available at press time.

D1:

Train Kept A Rollin' (2.34)

Nobody's Fault But Mine (4.27)

Black Dog (4.42)

In The Evening (7.27)

The Rain Song (7.18)

Hot Dog (3.41)

All My Love (5.38)

Trampled Underfoot (7.01)

Since I've Been Loving You (8.40)

D2:

Achilles Last Stand (9.24)

White Summer - Black Mountain Side (6.08)

Kashmir (8.00)

Stairway To Heaven (8.40)

Whole Lotta Love - Heartbreaker (6.36)

Whole Lotta Love

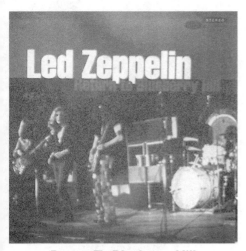

Return To Blueberry Hill

Venue: Los Angeles
Date: 9/4/70
Cover: D4C
Recording: 8
Source: M -Aud
Company: n/a
Matrix #: n/a
Place Of Origin: Europe
Total Disc Time: n/a

N.B. Another reissue of the LA show. Nothing special. The songs are in the original order.

DI:
Immigrant Song (3.25)
Heartbreaker (6.27)
Dazed & Confused (16.42)
Bring It On Home (9.30)
That's The Way (7.05)
Bron-y-Aur (5.36)
Since I've Been Loving You (6.58)
Organ Improvisation (5.57)
Thank You (7.02)
D2:
What Is & What Should Never Be (4.29)
Moby Dick (12.35)
Whole Lotta Love Medley (17.24) (Inc. Boogie Chillen - Movin On - I've Got A Girl - Some Other Guy - Think It Over - The Lemon Song)
Communication Breakdown Medley (10.12) (Inc. Good Times Bad Times-For What It's Worth- I Saw Her Standing There)
Out On The Tiles (3.30)
Blueberry Hill (3.55)

Return To Blueberry Hill

Venue: Los Angeles
Date: 9/4/70
Cover: D4C sleeve
Recording: 8
Source: M - Aud
Company: Immigrant
Matrix #: IM 033-034
Place Of Origin: Japan
Total Disc Time: n/a

N.B. All track information not available at press time. Show restored to original running order.

DI:
Immigrant Song (3.25)
Heartbreaker (6.27)
Dazed & Confused (16.42)
Bring It On Home (9.30)
That's The Way (7.05)
Bron-y-Aur (5.36)
Since I've Been Loving You (6.58)
Organ Improvisation (5.57)
Thank You (7.02)
D2:
What Is & What Should Never Be (4.29)
Moby Dick (12.35)
Whole Lotta Love Medley (17.24)
(Inc. Boogie Chillen - Movin On - I've Got A Girl - Some Other Guy - Think It Over - The Lemon Song)
Communication Breakdown Medley (10.12)
(Inc. Good Times Bad Times - For What It's Worth - I Saw Her Standing There)
Out On The Tiles (3.30)
Blueberry Hill (3.55)

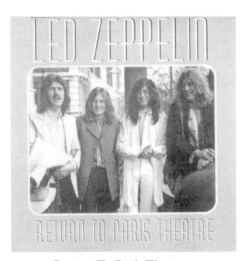

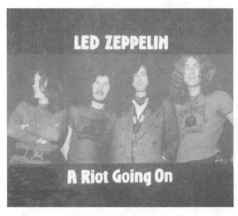

Riot Going On

Venue: Copenhagen

Date: 2/28/70

Cover: D4C in double case

Recording: n/a

Source: n/a

Company: POT

Matrix #: POT 006 - 007

Place Of Origin: Japan

Total Disc Time: n/a

N.B. All track information not available at press time.

D1:

Dazed And Confused (16.28)

Heartbreaker (6.24)

White Summer (4.21)

Black Mountain Side (7.58)

Since I've Been Loving You (8.57)

Organ Solo (1.26)

Thank You (6.11)

Moby Dick (16.57)

D2:

How Many More Times Medley (21.35)

(Inc. The Hunter - Move On Down The Line -

Trucking Little Mama

Whole Lotta Love (6.46)

Communication Breakdown (5.05)

Come On Everybody (3.24)

Something Else (2.06)

Bring It On Home (8.15)

Long Tall Sally (5.56)

Return To Paris Theatre

Venue: London

Date: 3/25/71

Cover: D4C sleeve

Recording: 9

Source: St - SB

Company: n/a

Matrix #: n/a

Place Of Origin: Europe

Total Disc Time: 53.03 - 53.21

N.B. No label identified. The cover claims this is from the Stereo pre-broadcast reels. It is the nearest thing I have heard to a good uncut clean version of the show complete with chatter etc. Comes with deluxe color deust sleevs for each CD.

D1:

Intro (1.13)

Immigrant Song (3.10)

Heartbreaker (5.39)

Since I've Been Loving You (7.23)

Black Dog (6.07)

Dazed & Confused (20.44)

Stairway To Heaven (8.47)

D2:

Going To California (6.02)

That's The Way (6.57)

What Is & What Should Never Be (5.46)

Whole Lotta Love Medley (22.07)

Thank You (6.32)

Communication Breakdown (5.57)

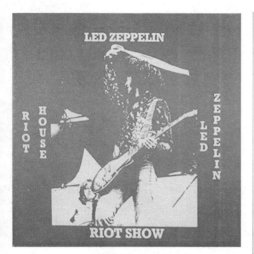

Riot House

Venue: Riot House
Date: 12/22/72
Cover: D2C sleeve
Recording: 7
Source: M -Aud
Company: Cobra
Matrix #: 006
Place Of Origin: Japan
Total Disc Time: n/a
N.B. Another Cobra reissue of an old vinyl piece but a more complete tape.

D1:
Rock & Roll
Over The Hills & Far Away
Black Dog
Misty Mountain Hop
Since I've Been Loving You
Dancing Days
Bron-y-Aur Stomp
Song Remains The Same
Rain Song
Stairway To Heaven
D2:
Dazed & Confused
Whole Lotta Love Medley (Inc. Everybody Needs
Someone To Love - Boogie Chillen - Let's Have A Party -
Heartbreak Hotel - I Can't Quit You)
Immigrant Song
Heartbreaker
Organ Solo
Thank You

Rip It Up

Venue: Los Angeles
Date: 6/25/77
Cover: D4C in double case
Recording: 6
Source: M - Aud
Company: Silver Rarities
Matrix #: SIRA 200/201/202
Place Of Origin: Europe
Total Disc Time: 68.03 - 57.00 - 67.50
N.B. Clear audience recording but tons of wow and flutter on the tape. Not as well known as some of the shows from this series of gigs in Los Angeles but this is the one to include the impromptu performance of Rip It Up at the end of In My Time Of Dying. It also includes the unusual pairing of Whole Lotta Love and Communication Breakdown as the encores. The tape appears to run a bit fast.

D1:
The Song Remains The Same (5.31)
Sick Again (7.14)
Nobody's Fault But Mine (6.57)
In My Time Of Dying (11.56)
Since I've Been Loving You (8:29)
No Quarter (27.53)
D2:
Ten Years Gone (9.40)
Battle Of Evermore (6.13)
Going To California (5.35)
Black Country Woman (2.04)
Bron-y-Aur Stomp (7.34)
White Summer - Black Mountain Side (8.21)
Kashmir (10.19)
Trampled Underfoot (7.14)
D3:
Moby Dick (27.29)
Guitar Solo (14.42)
Achilles Last Stand (9:18)
Stairway To Heaven (11.36)
Whole Lotta Love (1.48)
Communication Breakdown (2.58)

Rock Hour

Venue: London

Date: 6/27/69

Cover: D4C

Recording: 9

Source: M - SB

Company: Antrabata

Matrix #: ARM 270669

Place Of Origin: Europe

Total Disc Time: n/a

N.B. The cover claims this is from the BBC master tapes. It's possible but unlikely. Excellent quality none the less. Limited edition of 325 copies.

D1:

Intro

Communication Breakdown

I Can't Quit You

Interview

Dazed And Confused

Liverpool Scene Sketch

White Summer / Black Mountain Side

You Shook Me

How Many More Times Medley

Rocking in Chicago

Venue: Chicago

Date: 7/6/73

Cover: D4C

Recording: 8

Source: St - SB

Company: Moonlight

Matrix #: ML 9643

Place Of Origin: Japan

Total Disc Time: n/a

N.B. Another reissue of the rehearsal recording. Previously available multiple times. Nothing special.

D1:

The Rover (4 Takes)

Night Flight (Two Takes)

Hail Hail Rock and Roll

Nadine

Round and Round

Move on down the Line

Love Me like a Hurricane

Move It

Dynamite

Shaking All over

Hungry for Love

I'll Never Get over You

Reeling and Rocking

Surrender

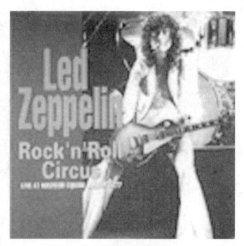

Rock 'N Roll Circus

Venue: New York
Date: 6/10/77
Cover: D4C
Recording: 7
Source: M -Aud
Company: Diagrams Of Led Zeppelin
Matrix #: TDOLZ0012/13/14
Place Of Origin: Japan
Total Disc Time: n/a
N.B. Another show previously unavailable. This one from Madison Square Gardens.

D1:
The Song Remains The Same,
The Rover - Sick Again,
Nobody's Fault But Mine,
Over The Hills And
Far Away,
Since I've Been Loving You,
No Quarter
D2:
Ten Years Gone,
The Battle of Evermore,
Going to California,
Black Country Woman,
Bron-Y-Aur Stomp,
White Summer -Black Mountain Side,
Kashmir,
Out On Tiles - Moby Dick,
D3:
Heartbreaker,
Guitar Solo,
Achilles Last Stand,
Stairway to Heaven,
Whole Lotta Love,
Rock And Roll

Rock N' Roll Spring Time

Venue: Nagoya
Date: 10/5/72
Cover: D4C
Recording: 7
Source: M - Aud
Company: Image Quality
Matrix #: IQ-053/054
Place Of Origin: Japan
Total Disc Time: 49.54 - 74.04
N.B. A new source recording of the Nagoya concert. Considerably better than previous versions.

D1:
Rock and Roll (5.39)
Black Dog (6.15)
Misty Mountain Hop (4.32)
Since I've Been Loving You (8.34)
Dancing Days (5.25)
Bron-y-Aur Stomp (5.53)
Song Remains the Same (5.19)
The Rain Song (8.15)
D2:
Dazed and Confused (27.22)
Stairway to Heaven (9.50)
Whole Lotta Love Medley (23.12) (Inc. Every Body
Needs Somebody to Love - Boogie Chillen - Feel so
Good - Let's Have a Party - You Shook Me)
Organ Solo – Sakura (4.58)
Thank You (8.41)

Room 2/3

Venue: San Francisco
Date: 11/6/69 – 11/7/69*
Cover: D4C
Recording: 4 – 5*
Source: M -Aud
Company: Image Quality
Matrix #: IQ 019/20/21
Place Of Origin: Japan
Total Disc Time: 64.36 - 63.33 - 56.07

N.B. Both nights at the Winterland Ballroom. The first night is not as clear as the second. Overall about the best you can expect to get of these two shows for now.

D1:
Good Times Bad Times, Communication Breakdown (5:04)
I Can't Quite You (6:41)
Heartbreaker (5:45)
Dazed And Confused (17:14)
White Summer - Black Mountain Side (17:14)
What Is And What Should Never Be (4:56)
Moby Dick (11 :47)
D2:
How Many More Times (21 :25)
C' Mon Everybody (3:15)
Something Else (2:19)
Good Elmes Bad Times - Communication Breakdown (4:33)*
I Can't Quite You (6:58)*
Heartbreaker (38:44)*
Dazed And Confused (18:45) *
D3:
White Summe -, Black Mountain Side (14:47)*
Babe I'm Gonna Leave You (6:34)*
What Is And What Should Never Be (5:04)*
Moby Dick (17:30)*
How Many More Times (12:09)*

Rotterdum 1980

Venue: Rotterdam

Date: 6/21/80

Cover: D4C Sleeve

Recording: 8

Source: St-Aud

Company: Tarantura

Matrix #: 1980-007,8

Place Of Origin: Japan

Total Disc Time: n/a

N.B. Tarantura puts together the two tapes from the show for the first time. Still not the complete show but the most that you can get in one place.

D1:
The Rain Song
Hot Dog
All My Love
Trampled Underfoot
since I've Been Loving You
D2:
Achilles Last Stand
White Summer-Black Mountain Side
Kashmir
Stairway to Heaven
Rock and Roll
Heartbreaker

Royal Albert Hall

Venue: London

Date: 1/9/70

Cover: DBW in case

Recording: 7 - 8

Source: M - SB

Company: Monada

Matrix #: PX 4307

Place Of Origin: Europe

Total Disc Time: 52.17

Historical Buthday STTP 034 ✓

N.B. Finally part of the amazing performance at the Royal Albert Hall appears from a good soundboard tape. Although this is far from complete it qualifies as a must-have by anyone's standards if only to hear the lyrics for "Bottle Up & Go" clearly and the extra stuff during the medley. Runs slow compared to the video.

D1:

Whole Lotta Love (6.52)

Communication Breakdown (6.06)

C'mon Everybody (2.44)

Something Else (2.16)

Bring It On Home (8.00)

How Many More Times Medley (25.17)

(Inc. The Hunter - Boogie Chillen - Move On Down the Line - Bottle Up And Go - Leave My Woman Alone - The Lemon Song - That's Alright)

Running On Pure Heart And Soul

Venue: Landover

Date: 5/30/77

Cover: D4C

Recording: 6

Source: M -Aud

Company: Diagrams Of Led Zeppelin

Matrix #: TDOLZ 259701/2/3

Place Of Origin: Japan

Total Disc Time: n/a

N.B. Also available as part of the box set Maryland Deluxe. Not a great recording (the best from this string of shows) but not available on bootleg CD before.

D1:

The Song Remains The Same

Sick Again

Nobody's Fault But Mine

In My Time Of Dying

Since I've Been Loving You

No Quarter

D2:

Ten Years Gone

The Battle Of Evermore

Going To California

Surrender - Black Country Woman - Bron-Y-Aur Stomp

White Summer - Black Mountain Side - Kashmir

Out On The Tiles - Moby Dick

D3:

Guitar Solo

Achilles Last Stand

Stairway To Heaven

Whole Lotta Love

Rock And Roll

Safecrackers Show (The)

Venue: New York

Date: 7/27/73

Cover: D4C

Recording: 8

Source: M -SB

Company: MIDAS TOUCH

Matrix #: 62211

Place Of Origin: Japan

Total Disc Time: 64.02

N.B. Not a particularly well balanced

soundboard recording.

D1:

Dazed And Confused (cut)(1.50)

Stairway To Heaven (12.01)

Moby Dick (21.40)

Heartbreaker (6.19)

Whole Lotta Love (15.18)

The Ocean (4.40)

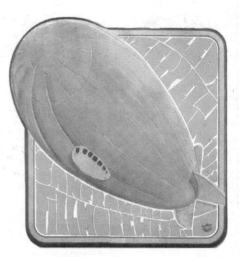

San Francisco Fillmore West 1969

Venue: San Francisco
Date: 4/27/69
Cover: D4C fold out cardboard jacket
Recording: 9
Source: M - SB
Company:
Matrix #: LZ 01/1 01/2
Place Of Origin: Italy
Total Disc Time:
N.B. A repackaging of the Kaleidoscopic versions of
this show. A very unique cover which
opens out on a swivel hinge.

D1:
Train Kept A Rollin' (2.56)
I Can't Quit You (5.59)
As Long As I Have You Medley (19.37)
(Incl. Fresh Garbage- The Lemon Song- Cat's Squirrel-
I'm A Man- Cadillac No Money Down)
You Shook Me (9.38)
How Many More Times Medley (19.19)
(Inc. The Hunter- Here We Go Round
The Mulberry Bush)
D2:
Killing Floor (cut) (7.31)
Babe I'm Gonna Leave You (7.00)
Sitting & Thinking (7.33)
Moby Dick (7.17)
Dazed & Confused (12.19)
Communication Breakdown (4.10)

San Francisco '69

Venue: San Francisco

Date: 1/9/69

Cover: D2C in case

Recording: 8 - 9

Source: St - SB

Company: AULICA

Matrix #: A137

Place Of Origin: Italy

Total Disc Time: 41.42

N.B. The well circulated soundboard recording of the
band's first performance at the Fillmore West.

D1:

As Long As I Have You (17.57)

Killing Floor (6:50)

White Summer (9:38)

Babe I'm Gonna Leave You (6:44)

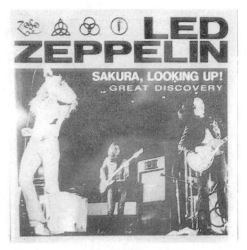

Sakura Looking Up! Great Discovery

Venue: Nagoya

Date: 10/5/72

Cover: D4C

Recording: 6

Source: M - Aud

Company: Jelly Roll

Matrix #: JR 10/11

Place Of Origin: Japan

Total Disc Time: n/a

N.B. Another re-issue of the well circulated Nagoya
audience recording.

D1:

Rock and Roll

Black Dog

Misty Mountain Hop

Since I've Been Loving You

Dancing Days

Bron-y-Aur Stomp

The Song Remains the Same

The Rain Song

D2:

Dazed and Confused

Stairway to Heaven

Whole Lotta Love Medley (Inc. Everybody Needs
Somebody - Boogie Chillen - Feel so Good - Let's Have
a Party - You Shook Me)

Sakura Sakura

Thank You

Satisfaction

Venue: London

Date: 3/25/71

Cover: D4C

Recording: 9

Source: St - SB

Company: NDM

Matrix #: n/a

Place Of Origin: Europe

Total Disc Time: n/a

N.B. Another compilation of BBC stuff.

D1:

Communication Breakdown (5.08)

Going To California (4.07)

Dazed & Confused (18.18)

Stairway To Heaven (8.10)

What Is & What Should Never Be (4.40)

Whole Lotta Love Medley (13.36)

(Inc. Boogie Chillen - Fixin To Die - That's Alright -

For What It's Worth - Mess Of Blues)

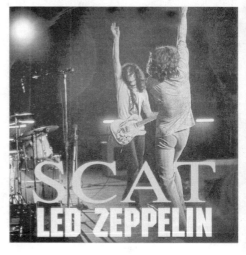

Scat

Venue: Milwaukee

Date: 8/31/70

Cover: D4C

Recording: 5

Source: M -Aud

Company: Diagrams Of Led Zeppelin

Matrix #: TDOLZ 056

Place Of Origin: Japan

Total Disc Time: 55.42

N.B. A new show to CD.

Also known as "Milwaukee 1970".

D1:

Immigrant Song (3.25)

Heartbreaker (6.35)

Dazed & Confused (16.31)

Bring It On Home (12.31)

That's The Way (6.11)

Bron-y-Aur (2.57)

Since I've Been Loving You (7.32)

Schaefer Music Festival

Venue: New York

Date: 7/21/69

Cover: D4C in case

Recording: 7

Source: M - Aud

Company: Rock Calendar

Matrix #: RC 2107

Place Of Origin: Europe

Total Disc Time: 63.55

N.B. Taken from the well known audience recording.

DI:

The Train Kept A Rollin' (2.33)

I Can't Quit You (6.11)

Dazed & Confused (12.22)

You Shook Me (10.02)

White Summer/ Black Mountain Side (8.11)

How Many More Times Medley (15.50)

(Inc. The Woody Woodpecker Song -

For What It's Worth - The Lemon Song)

Communication Breakdown (3.12)

Seattle Daze

Venue: Seattle

Date: 7/17/73

Cover: D4C

Recording: St - Aud

Source: 8 - 9

Company: Image Quality

Matrix #: IQ 007/8/9

Place Of Origin: Japan

Total Disc Time: n/a

N.B. The complete show from an audience tape.

DI:

Introduction (1 :50)

Rock And Roll (4:41)

Celebration Day (3:22)

Black Dog (5:55)

Over The Hills And Far Away (6:40)

Misty Mountain Hop (5:06)

Since I've Been Loving You (8:22)

No Quarter (12:57)

The Song Remains The Same (5:38)

The Rain Song (8:36)

D2:

Dazed And Confused (Inc. San Francisco) (33:51)

Stairway To Heaven (12:29)

D3:

Moby Dick (31 :44)

Heartbreaker (8:00)

Whole Lotta Love (Inc. Boogie Chillen) (14:55)

The Ocean (6:01)

Seattle Won't You Listen

Venue: Seattle
Date: 3/17/75
Cover: D4C
Recording: 7
Source: M -Aud
Company: Diagrams Of Led Zeppelin
Matrix #: TDOLZ 0022/23/24
Place Of Origin: Japan
Total Disc Time: n/a

N.B. A good clean recording from Seattle.
As complete as the tape that has been circulating
amongst the traders.
Also available as "Two Days In Seattle" and "The
Hammer Of The Gods".

D1:
Rock & Roll
Sick Again
Over The Hills & Far Away
In My Time Of Dying
Song Remains The Same
Rain Song
Kashmir
D2:
No Quarter
Trampled Underfoot
Moby Dick
D3:
Dazed & Confused
Stairway To Heaven
Whole Lotta Love (Inc. The Crunge)
Black Dog

Second City Showdown

Venue: Chicago
Date: 7/6/73
Cover: D4C sleeve
Recording: 8
Source: St - SB
Company: MIDAS TOUCH
Matrix #: 61831/2/3
Place Of Origin: Japan
Total Disc Time: n/a

N.B. Not sure if this is the entire show from a soundboard tape as it wasn't available for review at
press time. If it is the entire show then
it's the first time it has come out complete.

D1:
Rock And Roll (4:32)
Celebration Day (3:34)
Bring It On Home Intro, Black Dog (6:32)
Over The Hills And Far Away (6:51)
Misty Mountain Hop (4:45)
Since I've Been Loving You (9:18)
No Quarter (11 :44)
The Song Remains The Same (6:23)
The Rain Song (8:29)
D2:
Dazed And Confused (Incl. San Francisco) (29:48)
Stairway To Heaven (11 :16)
D3:
Moby Dick (24:54)
Heartbreaker (6:07)
Whole Lotta Love Medley (16:59)
(Inc. Boogie Chillen)
Communication Breakdown (5:35)

2nd European Tour (The)
Venue: Copenhagen
Date: 6/3/71
Cover: D4C in double case
Recording: 6
Source: M - Aud
Company: Whole Lotta Live
Matrix #: WLL 011/012
Place Of Origin: Italy
Total Disc Time: 72.36 - 52.47
N.B. A very nice reproduction of the famous concert which featured the two rare live performances of Gallow's Pole and Four Sticks.

D1:
Immigrant Song (4.00)
Heartbreaker (7.04)
Since I've Been Loving You (8.27)
Dazed & Confused (18.55)
Black Dog (6.25)
Stairway To Heaven (10.29)
That's The Way (8.24)
What Is & What Should Never Be (4.27)
D2:
Four Sticks (6.59)
Gallow's Pole (6.13)
Whole Lotta Love Medley (21.12)
(Inc. Boogie Chillen - Trucking Little Mama -
Mess Of Blues - The Lemon Song)
Communication Breakdown -
Celebration Day (8.05)
Misty Mountain Hop (4.25)
Rock And Roll (4.01)

Second Night in the Garden
Venue: New York
Date: 6/8/77
Cover: D4C
Recording: 4
Source: M - Aud
Company: Diagram's of Led Zeppelin
Matrix #: Vol 021
Place Of Origin: Japan
N.B. A new release for bootleg. Sound quality is pretty poor. Several cuts and dropouts during the course of the show.

D1:
The Song Remains the Same
Sick Again
Nobody's Fault But Mine
In My Time of Dying
Since I've Been Loving You
No Quarter
D2:
Ten Years Gone
The Battle of Ever More
Going to California
Black Country Woman
Bron-y-Aur Stomp
White Summer-Black Mountain Side
Kashmir
D3:
Moby Dick
Achilles Last Stand
Stairway to Heaven
Whole Lotta Love
Rock and Roll

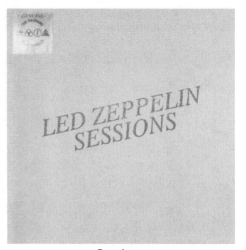

Sessions

Venue: Headley Grange - Bombay
Date: 1/?/71 – 3/?/72
Cover: D4C
Recording: 7 - 8
Source: St - SB
Company: Diagrams Of Led Zeppelin
Matrix #: TDOLZ 499701-2
Place Of Origin: Japan
Total Disc Time: n/a

N.B. Another reissue of studio outtakes. This one ostensibly includes further versions of Battle Of Evermore. All details not available at press time.

D1:
Stairway To Heaven (instrumental version 1)
Guitar Instrumental (Down By The Seaside early version)
Guitar Instrumental1 (Bron-Yr-Aur early version)
Guitar Instrumental2 (Bron-Yr-Aur early version)
Black Dog (rehearsal take)
No Quarter (rehearsal take)
Stairway To Heaven (instrumental version 2-4)
Guitar Instrumental
Stairway To Heaven (take 1)
Stairway To Heaven (take 2)
Battle Of Evermore (acoustic intro fragment)
Battle Of Evermore (alternate stereo take, different lyrics with Plant only)
Battle Of Evermore (alternate stereo mix, echoed harmonies and choruses only)
Battle Of Evermore (alternate stereo mix, higher main vocals)
Battle Of Evermore (alternate final stereo mix version 1)
Battle Of Evermore (alternate final stereo mix version 2)
D2:
Friends (studio rehearsal session)
Four Sticks (instrumental version 1)
Friends (final version 1)
Friends (final version 2)
Four Sticks (instrumental version 2)

Seventh American Tour (The)

Venue: Los Angeles
Date: 8/21/71
Cover: D4C in double case
Recording: 4 - 5
Source: M - Aud
Company: Whole Lotta Live
Matrix #: WLL 022 -023
Place Of Origin: Italy
Total Disc Time: 65.43 - 59.13

N.B. Another new show to CD. Not a great recording and it runs too fast but worth while for the startling performances.

D1:
Immigrant Song (4.01)
Heartbreaker (6.22)
Since I've Been Loving You (8.49)
Black Dog (6.38)
Dazed & Confused (19.38)
Stairway To Heaven (9.05)
That's The Way (6.36)
Going To California (4.34)
D2:
What Is & What Should Never Be (5.25)
Whole Lotta Love Medley (27.57)
(Inc Boogie Chillen - I'm Moving On -
That's Alright - Mess Of Blues -
Got A Lot Of Living To Do - Long Distance Call)
Weekend (4.08)
Rock & Roll (3.52)
Communication Breakdown (7.56)
Organ Solo (2.08)
Thank You (7.47)

79

Venue: Copenhagen - Knebworth^#
Date: 7/23/79 - 7/24/79* - 8/4/1979^ - 8/11/1979#
Cover: Hard binder with hot foil stamp
Recording: 8 - 9
Source: St - Aud
Company: Antrabata
Matrix #: ARM 237779, ARM 247779, ARM 4879, ARM 11879
Place Of Origin: Europe
Total Disc Time: 62.26 – 68.54 – 68.06 – 75.43 – 60.46 – 54.30 – 58.29 – 67.31 – 77.35
N.B. Each concert was released as part of the box set and also available separately as individual sets. Supposedly only 325 copies of this one in a deluxe hard binder.

WARM UP NIGHT ONE
D1:
The Song Remains The Same,
Celebration Day,
Black Dog,
Nobody's Fault But Mine,
Over The Hills And Far Away,
Misty Mountain Hop,
Since I've Been Loving You,
No Quarter,
Hot Dog
D2:
The Rain Song,
White Summer / Black Mountain Side,
Kashmir,
Trampled Underfoot,
Achilles Last Stand,
Page's Solo,

In The Evening,
Stairway To Heaven,
Rock And Roll

WARM UP NIGHT TWO
D3: The Song Remains The Same,*
Celebration Day,*
Black Dog,*
Nobody's Fault But Mine,*
Over The Hills And Far Away,*
Misty Mountain Hop,*
Since I've Been Loving You,*
No Quarter,*
Ten Years Gone,*
Hot Dog 8
D4:
The Rain Song,*
White Summer / Black Mountain Side,*
Kashmir,*
Trampled Underfoot,*
Sick Again,*
Achilles Last Stand,*
Guitar Solo,*
In The Evening,*
Stairway To Heaven,*
Whole Lotta Love *

KNEBWORTH FESTIVAL / NIGHT ONE
D5:
The Song Remains The Same,^
Celebration Day,^
Black Dog,^
Nobody's Fault But Mine,^
Over The Hills And Far Away,^
Misty Mountain Hop,^
Since I've Been Loving You,^
No Quarter,^
D6:
Ten Years Gone,^
Hot Dog,^
The Rain Song,^
White Summer - Black Mountain Side,^
Kashmir,^

Trampled Underfoot, ^

Sick Again, ^

Achilles Last Stand ^

D7:

Guitar Solo, ^

In The Evening, ^

Stairway To Heaven, ^

Rock And Roll, ^

Whole Lotta Love, ^

Heartbreaker ^

KNEBWORTH FESTIVAL / NIGHT TWO

D8:

The Song Remains The Same, #

Celebration Day, #

Black Dog, #

Nobody's Fault But Mine, #

Over The Hills And Far Away, #

Misty Mountain Hop, #

Since I've Been Loving You, #

No Quarter #

D9:

White Summer - Black Mountain Side, #

Kashmir, #

Trampled Underfoot, #

Sick Again, #

Achilles Last Stand, #

Guitar Solo, #

In The Evening, #

Stairway To Heaven, #

Rock And Roll, #

Whole Lotta Love, #

Communication Breakdown #

Sex Machine

Venue: Los Angeles

Date: 3/25/75

Cover: D4C gatefold sleeve

Recording: 7

Source: M -Aud

Company: Lemon Song

Matrix #: LS 7212-13

Place Of Origin: Japan

Total Disc Time: n/a

N.B. A reissue of the audience tape from the Forum. Nothing special.

D1:

Rock & Roll

Sick Again

Over The Hills & Far Away

In My Time Of Dying

Song Remains The Same

Rain Song

Kashmir

D2:

No Quarter

Trampled Underfoot

Moby Dick

Dazed & Confused (Inc. Spanish Eyes - Woodstock)

Stairway To Heaven

Whole Lotta Love (Inc. Sex Machine - The Crunge)

Black Dog

Short Cut

Venue: Gladsaxe Copenhagen – Milan*

Date: 3/15/69 – 7/3/71*

Cover: D4C

Recording: 6

Source: M -Aud

Company: Image Quality

Matrix #: IQ 035

Place Of Origin: Japan

Total Disc Time: n/a

N.B. A compilation of the Teen Clubs gig and the Milan
riot tape. All deatls not available at press time.

D1:

Train Kept A Rollin'

I Can't Quit You

As Long As I Have YouMedley

You Shook Me

Communication Breakdown

Since I've Been Loving You*

Black Dog*

Dazed & Confused*

Silently Ravaging America

Venue: Los Angeles

Date: 6/25/72

Cover: D4C double case

Recording: 6 -7

Source: M - Aud

Company: Whole Lotta Live

Matrix #: WLL 016 - 017

Place Of Origin: Italy

Total Disc Time: 73.49 - 73.09

N.B. Re-issue of discs three and four of the Tarantura
title "Route 66".

D1:

Immigrant Song (5.01)

Heartbreaker (7.45)

Over The Hills And Far Away (5.34)

Black Dog (5.58)

Since I've Been Loving You (8.00)

Stairway To Heaven (9.47)

Going To California (5.39)

That's The Way (5.52)

Tangerine (4.01)

Bron-Y-Aur Stomp (5.23)

What Is & What Should Never Be (4.11)

Dancing Days (4.00)

D2:

Dazed And Confused (25.50)

Incl. The Crunge

Moby Dick (19.21)

Whole Lotta Love Medley (22.50) Incl. Boogie Chillen -
Let's Have A Party - Mary Lou - Heartbreak Hotel -
Going Down Slow

Rock And Roll (3.58)

Sizzles In Seattle
Venue: Seattle
Date: 6/19/72
Cover: D4C
Recording: 4
Source: M -Aud
Company: Lemon Song
Matrix #: LS-7215/7217
Place Of Origin: Japan
Total Disc Time: 63:57 - 54:59 - 72:55
N.B. A poor audience recording from the Seattle show.

D1:
Immigrant Song
Heartbreaker
Black Dog
The Ocean
Since I've Been Loving You
Stairway To Heaven
Going To California
Black Country Woman
That's The Way
Tangerine
Bron-Y-Aur Stomp
D2:
Dazed And Confused
What Is And What Should Never Be
Dancing Days
Moby Dick
D3:
Whole Lotta Love (Inc.Boogie Chillen)
Rock And Roll
Organ Solo / Thank You
Money
Over The Hills And Far Away
Dancing Days

Smoke Gets In Your Eyes
Venue: Osaka
Date: 9/29/71
Cover: D4C slick on white sleeve
Recording: 7 - 8
Source: St - SB
Company: Rock Solid
Matrix #: RSR CD001
Place Of Origin: Japan
Total Disc Time: n/a
N.B. A really rare Japanese piece comes with an insert
listing all the tracks.

D1:
Immigrant Song
Heartbreaker
Since I've Been Loving You
Black Dog
Dazed & Confused (Inc. Pennies From Heaven)
Stairway To Heaven
Celebration Day
That's The Way
D2:
Going To California
Tangerine
Friends
Smoke Gets In Your Eyes
What Is & What Should Never Be
Moby Dick
Whole Lotta Love Medley (Inc. Boogie Chillen – Tossing
& Turning – Twist & Shout – Fortune Teller – Good Times
Bad Times – You Shook Me)

Solid Guitar

Venue: Dallas

Date: 3/4/75

Cover: Screen printed die cut wooden box

Recording: 8

Source: M -SB

Company: Tarantura

Matrix #: PRCD1,2

Place Of Origin: Japan

Total Disc Time: n/a

N.B. Another outrageous package from Tarantura. This is a hinged wooden box similar to the grey market wooden box that came out in the USA of the 2CD remasters package. Not the most practical of storage mediums but undeniably this is the kind of thing that makes bootlegs so collectable.

D1:

Rock & Roll

Sick Again

Over The Hills & Far Away

In My Time Of Dying

Song Remains The Same

Rain Song

D2:

Kashmir

No Quarter

Trampled Underfoot

Moby Dick

Sometime In New York City

Venue: New York

Date: 6/14/72

Cover: D4C

Recording: 4

Source: M -Aud

Company: Image Quality

Matrix #: IQ 043-45

Place Of Origin: Japan

Total Disc Time: 60.48 – 49.12 – 42.38

N.B. The show at the Nassau Coliseum in Uniondale New York. Barely listenable..

D1:

Immigrant Song (4.17)

Heartbreaker (8.16)

Black Dog (6.50)

Since I've Been Loving You (8.37)

Stairway To Heaven (11.05)

Going To California (5.50)

That's The Way (7.25)

Tangerine (3.09)

Run Around Sue (0.42)

Bron-y-Aur Stomp (4.40)

D2:

Dazed & Confused (26.37)

What Is & What Should Never Be (5.07)

Moby Dick (17.29)

Whole Lotta Love (25.17)

Rock & Roll (4.05)

Communication Breakdown (5.19)

Weekend (3.38)

Bring It On Home (4.21)

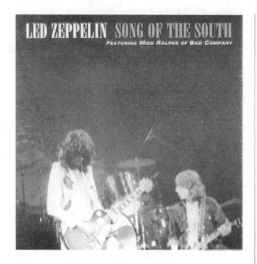

Song Of The South

Venue: Fort Worth

Date: 5/22/77

Cover: D4C in case

Recording: 8

Source: St - Aud

Company: Capricorn

Matrix #: CR-2036

Place Of Origin: USA

Total Disc Time: 60.37

N.B. Bright crisp stereo audience recording. Features the rare encore of It'll Be Me with Bad Company guitarist Mick Ralphs joining the very exclusive club of people to play on stage with Led Zeppelin.

D1:

Moby Dick (15.23)

Guitar Solo - Achilles Last Stand (20.24)

Stairway To Heaven (13.01)

Whole Lotta Love - Rock &Roll (6.59)

It'll Be Me (4.49)

Spitfire

Venue: Hannover

Date: 6/24/80

Cover: D4C sleeve

Recording: 8

Source: St - SB

Company: Theramin

Matrix #: n/a

Place of Origin: Japan

Total Disc Time: n/a

N.B. I'm not sure if the Theramin label is European or Japanese. This is the sound board recording from the Messehalle.

D1:

Train Kept a Rolling

Nobody's Fault but Mine

Black Dog

In the Evening

The Rain Song

Hot Dog

All My Love

Trampled Underfoot

D2:

Since I've Been Loving You

Achilles Last Stand

White Summer-Black Mountain Side

Kashmir

Stairway to Heaven

Rock and Roll

Communication Breakdown

Stairway To Heaven

Venue: London
Date: 3/25/71
Cover: D4C sleeve
Recording: 9
Source: St - SB
Company: Cobra
Matrix #: 014
Place Of Origin: Japan
Total Disc Time: n/a

N.B. Another in Cobra's series of reissues of famous bootlegs. This one featuring the omnipresent BBC tape and the cover of an old Italian bootleg.

D1:
Immigrant Song
Heartbreaker
Since I've Been Loving You
Black Dog
Stairway To Heaven
D2:
Going To California
That's The Way
What Is & What Should Never Be
Whole Lotta Love Medley
(Inc. Boogie Chillen - Fixin To Die - That's Alright - For What It's Worth - Mess Of Blues - The Lemon Song)
Thank You
Communication Breakdown

Stairway To Heaven Sessions 1970-1971

Venue: Headley Grange
Date: 1/?/71
Cover: D4C
Recording: 9
Source: St - SB
Company: ZOSO
Matrix #: 9301/2
Place Of Origin: Japan
Total Disc Time: n/a

N.B. Another reissue of the Headley Grange (Island?) tapes. Nothing new or special going on here that hasn't been out a million times before.

D1:
Stairway To Heaven
Untitled (Take One)
Untitled (Take Two)
Black Dog
No Quarter
Stairway To Heaven (Take Two)
Untitled (Take Three)
Stairway To Heaven (Take Four)
Stairway To Heaven (take Five)
Stairway To Heaven (Live)
Friends
D2:
Immigrant Song
Out On The Tiles
I Wanna Be Her Man
Acoustic Instrumentals (Six takes)
Down By The Seaside (Three Takes)
Acoustic Instrumentals (Take Seven)
Bron-y-Aur Stomp
Poor Tom
Hey Hey What Can I Do

Stairway To Heaven Sessions 1970-1971

Venue: Bron-Yr-Aur Cottage, Headley Grange, Olympic
Studios (?) **Date:** May 1970, Jan 1971
Cover: D4C in slimline double case
Recording: 7-8 **Source:** St - SB
Company: Live Storm
Matrix: #LSCD 52631
Country: Italy
Total Time: 55:39 - 57:05

D1:
Stairway take 1 (3.42)
Untitled 1 (3.56)
Untitled 2 (1.52)
Black Dog (6.46)
No Quarter (5.41)
Stairway take 2 (5.51)
Untitled 3 (1.50)
Stairway take 3 (6.01)
Stairway take 4 (8.08)
Stairway (live) (8.39)
Friends (4.29)
D2:
Immigrant Song (2.35)
Out on the Tiles (3.39)
I Wanna Be Her Man   (1.50)
Acoustic Jam take 1   (2.40)
Acoustic Jam take 2   (6.01)
Acoustic Jam take 3   (2.09)
Acoustic Jam take 4   (6.17)
Acoustic Jam take 5   (4.11)
Acoustic Jam take 6   (11.24)
Down By the Seaside take 1   (3.19)
Down By the Seaside take 2   (2.16)
Down By the Seaside take 3   (1.50)
Acoustic Jam take 7 (2.01)
Bron-Yr-Aur Stomp (1.49)
Poor Tom (2.48)
Hey, Hey What Can I Do (1.49)

Standing in the Shadow

Venue: Long Beach
Date: 3/12/75
Cover: D4C
Recording: 7
Source: St - Aud
Company: Diagram's of Led Zeppelin
Matrix #: TDOLZ 379701/379702/379703
Place Of Origin: Japan
Total Disc Time: 74.33 -56.24 - 39.39
N.B. This recording was previously available as the title
"Trampled Under Jimmy's Foot" . This one however runs
at the correct speed.

D1:
Rock and Roll
Sick Again
Over the Hills and Far Away
In My Time of Dying
Song Remains the Same (Cut)
The Rain Song
Kashmir
No Quarter
D2:
Trampled under Foot
Moby Dick
Dazed and Confused
D3:
Stairway to Heaven
Whole Lotta Love
Black Dog
Heart Breaker (Inc. I'm a Man)

Stepmothers Club

Venue: Newcastle - Milan*

Date: 11/30/72 - 7/14/71*

Cover: D4C in double case

Recording: 5 - 6

Source: M - Aud

Company: Mad Dogs

Matrix #: Mad Dogs 027-028

Place Of Origin: Japan

Total Disc Time: 44.04 - 42.12

N.B. Not from Stepmothers this is from
the gig in Newcastle.

D1:

Immigrant Song (4.04)

Heartbreaker (6.28)

Dazed And Confused (24.18)

Stairway To Heaven (9.10)

D2:

Thank You (8.25)

Whole Lotta Love Medley (23.16)

(Inc. Everybody Needs Someone To Love - Boogie

Chillen - Let's Have A Party - Going Down Slow)

Since I've Been Loving You (6.22)*

Black Dog (4.53)*

Stepmothers Return To The Club Tour 1971

Venue: Newcastle - Vienna*

Date: 11/30/72 - 3/9/70*

Cover: D4C in double case

Recording: 5 - 6

Source: M - Aud

Company: ZEPPELIN LIVE ARCHIVES

Matrix #: ZLA-93145

Place Of Origin: USA

Total Disc Time: 52.25 - 63.34

N.B. Not from Stepmothers this is from
the gig in Newcastle.

D1:

Immigrant Song (4.04)

Heartbreaker (6.28)

Dazed And Confused (24.18)

Stairway To Heaven (9.10)

Thank You (8.25)

D2:

Whole Lotta Love Medley (23.16)

(Inc. Everybody Needs Someone To Love - Boogie

Chillen - Let's Have A Party - Going Down Slow)

I Can't Quit You Baby * (5.24)

White Summer - Black Mountain Side * (12.37)

How Many More Times * Medley (22.15)

(Inc .The Hunter - Boogie Chillen -

Truckin' Little Mama - The Lemon Song

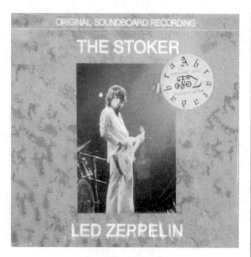

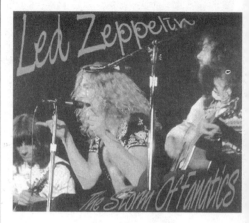

Stoker (The)

Venue: Stoke
Date: 1/15/73
Cover: D4C
Recording: 8
Source: St - SB
Company: Tarantura
Matrix #: STOKE 1,2
Place Of Origin: Japan
Total Disc Time: n/a

N.B. All details not available at press time. Presumably the soundboard tape again.

D1:
Rock & Roll
Over The Hills & Far Away
Black Dog
Misty Mountain Hop
Since I've Been Loving You
Dancing Days
Bron-y-Aur Stomp
Song Remains The Same
Rain Song
D2:
Dazed & Confused
Stairway To Heaven(cut)
Whole Lotta Love(cut)

Storm Of Fanatics

Venue: Tokyo
Date: 9/23/71
Cover: D4C in double case
Recording: 7
Source: St - Aud
Company: Mud Dogs
Matrix #: 016 - 017
Place Of Origin: Japan
Total Disc Time: 65.03 - 71.51

N.B. Bass is a bit distorted otherwise not too bad a recording.

D1:
Immigrant Song (4.17)
Heartbreaker (7.30)
Since I ve Been Loving You (7.16)
Black Dog (5.41)
Dazed And Confused (22.18)
Stairway To Heaven (9.14)
Celebration Day (4.07)
D2:
Bron-Yr-Aur Stomp (0.56)
That s The Way (6.29)
Going To California (6.04)
What Is And What Should Never Be (4.28)
Moby Dick (16.30)
Whole Lotta Love (27.04)
(Inc. Good Times Bad Times -
How Many More Times - You Shook Me)
Communication Breakdown (3.32)

Stormy Blues

Venue: Vancouver - Studio*

Date: 3/21/70 - ?/68*

Cover: D4C in case

Recording: 8

Source: M - SB, St - SB

Company: Joker

Matrix #: TR-11 - JOK 008

Place Of Origin: Australia

Total Disc Time: 44.54

N.B. A direct re-issue from the original glass master of
"Whole Lotta Zep".

D1:

Heartbreaker (6.32)

Thank You (8.10)

What Is & What Should Never Be (4.21)

Communication Breakdown -

Ramble On (4.56)

We're Gonna Groove (3.45)

Since I've Been Loving You (7.01)

Whole Lotta Love (2.44)

We're Gonna Groove (3.45)

Operator (4.13)*

Stroll On

Venue: West Allis

Date: 7/25/69

Cover: D4C sleeve

Recording: 7

Source: M -Aud

Company: Diagrams Of Led Zeppelin

Matrix #: TDOLZ 179701

Place Of Origin: Japan

Total Disc Time: 52.52

N.B. A new source tape from the state
fair show in Wisconsin.

This one is considerably clearer than previous tapes.

D1:

Train Kept A Rollin'

I Can't Quit You

Dazed & Confused

White Summer, Black Mountain Side

How Many More Times

Communication Breakdown

St. Tangerine's Day

Venue: New York
Date: 2/14/75
Cover: D4C
Recording: 5
Source: M - Aud
Company: Image Quality
Matrix #: IQ-040/41/42
Place Of Origin: Japan
Total Disc Time: 67.23 - 43.36 - 69.51

N.B. Once again Image Quality has made an effort to reconstruct a recording. This version is more complete than a version that was released as Saint Valentine's Day Massacre. Various bits in pieces from at least two different sources have been put together to create this three CD set.

D1:
Rock and Roll (5.38)
Sick Again (7.10)
Over the Hills and Far Away (9.30)
In My Time of Dying (11.33)
Since I've Been Loving You (9.30)
Song Remains the Same (5.28)
The Rain Song (9.45)
Kashmir (cut) (8.46)
D2:
No Quarter (12.13)
Trampled under Foot (9.43)
Moby Dick (cut) (10.37)
D3:
Dazed and Confused (cut) (32.07)
Tangerine (0.38)
Stairway to Heaven (13.27)
Whole Lotta Love-Black Dog (13.38)
Heartbreaker (10.00)

Stuck On You

Venue: Glasgow
Date: 12/4/72
Cover: D4C gatefold sleeve
Recording: 4
Source: M -Aud
Company: Diagrams Of Led Zeppelin
Matrix #: TDOLZ Vol 30
Place Of Origin: Japan
Total Disc Time: n/a

N.B. Another new show from the Diagrams label in Japan. Never out on bootleg before. Not great quality though.

D1:
Rock And Roll
Over The Hill And Far Away
Black Dog
Misty Mountain Hop
Since I've Been Loving You
Dancing Days
Bron-Y-Aur Stomp
The Song Remains The Same
The Rain Song
D2:
Dazed And Confused
Stairway To Heaven
Whole Lotta Love
Heartbreaker

Studio Daze Revisited

Venue: Headley Grange* - Polar, Stockholm§ - Long
Beach† - Island Studio+

Date: 5/70* - 12/78§ - 6/27/72† - 5/72+

Cover: D4C in case

Recording: 10

Source: St - SB

Company: TMQ **Matrix #:** n/a

Place Of Origin: Japan

Total Disc Time: n/a

N.B. Not all details available at press time. Basically
"Studio Daze" with the addition of the Moby Dick out
take.

DI:

That's The Way* (5.30)

Blues Medley* (7.02)

Since I've Been Loving You* (7.26)

All My Love§ (7.41)

What Is & What Should Never Be† (4.42)

Dancing Days† (4.25)

No Quarter (Instr)+ (7.24)

No Quarter (Instr)+ (8.41)

No Quarter + (7.16)

Moby Dick

Summer Of '69

Venue: San Bernadino

Date: 8/8/69

Cover: D4C sleeve

Recording: 5

Source: M -Aud

Company: Rubber Dubber

Matrix #: RD 001

Place Of Origin: Japan

Total Disc Time: 54.42

N.B. Previously unreleased show, also available as a very
limited edition 10" acetate with deluxe sleeve, only five
copies! Page is obviously having trouble with his guitar
again. A rare blues jam is played while the rest of the
band wait. It isn't the song listed on the
Cover. A very distorted and obviously loud recording. A
nice repro of the concert poster inside and some attention to detail in the liner notes. Limited to 750 numbered copies. Very worthwhile.

DI:

Train Kept A Rollin' (3.07)

I Can't Quit You (6.55)

Blues Jam (3.02)

Dazed & Confused (11.02) (cut)

White Summer (2.17) (cut)

You Shook Me (8.26)

How Many More Times (19.08)

Sundazed

Venue: Los Angeles
Date: 6/26/77
Cover: D4C
Recording: 8
Source: M -Aud
Company: Silver Rarities
Matrix #: SIRA 203/4/5
Place Of Origin: Europe
Total Disc Time: 77.14 - 51.34 - 50.26
N.B. Another reissue of the Forum show.
Nothing different or special.
Also available as part of "Week For Badgeholders".

Sunset

Venue: Los Angeles
Date: 6/27/77
Cover: D4C sleeve
Recording: 7-8
Source: M - Aud
Company: Diagrams of Led Zeppelin
Matrix #: Vol 055
Place Of Origin: Japan
Total Disc Time: n/a
N.B. Just another reissue of the forum tape. Part of a
series by Diagrams of Led Zeppelin re-issuing the entire
Los Angeles concert series.

DI:
Song Remains The Same
Sick Again
Nobody's Fault But Mine
Over The Hills & Far Away
Since I've Been Loving You
No Quarter
Ten Years Gone
D2:
Battle Of Evermore
Going To California
That's Alright
Black Country Woman
Bron-y-Aur Stomp
White Summer Black Mountain Side
Kashmir
Moby Dick
D3:
Guitar Solo
Achilles Last Stand
Stairway To Heaven
It'll Be Me

DI:
The Song Remains the Same
Sick Again
Nobody Fault but Mine
Over the Hills and Far Away
Since I've Been Loving You
D2:
No Quarter
Ten Years Gone
The Battle of Ever More
Going to California
D3:
Going Down South
Black Country Woman
Bron-y-Aur Stomp
Dancing Days
White Summer-Black Mountain Side
Kashmir
Trampled under Foot
Moby Dick
D4:
Guitar Solo
Achilles Last Stand
Stairway to Heaven
Whole Lotta Love
Rock and Roll

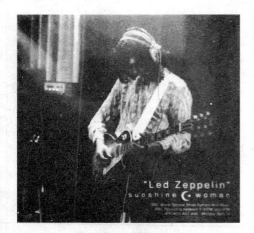

Sunshine Woman

Venue: London-Montreux*
Date: 3/3/69-3/7/70*
Cover: D4C
Recording: 7
Source: St- SB, St -Aud
Company: n/a
Matrix #: n/a
Place Of Origin: Japan
Total Disc Time: n/a

N.B. Inevitably this tape would finally surface on bootleg. The legendary missing BBC session. Even the band couldn't get their hands on this one to include on the official BBC album. The tape popped up somewhere in Poland where a collector apparently found it in a tape archive. The balance of this piece is completed with part of the Montreux tape.

D1:
Alexis Korner Introduction
What Is and What Should Never Be
Alexis Korner
I Can't Quit You
Alexis Korner
You Shook Me
Sunshine Woman
We're Gonna Groove*
I Can't Quit You*
White Summer*
Dazed and Confused*

Sweet at Night

Venue: Offenbach
Date: 3/24/73
Cover: D4C sleeve
Recording: 8
Source: M - Aud
Company: Diagrams of Led Zeppelin
Matrix #: Vol 040 TDOLZ 409701/409702
Place of Origin: Japan
Total Disc Time: n/a

N.B. From the same recording as the title Custard Pie. One of my favorites.

D1:
Rock and Roll
Over the Hills and Far Away
Black Dog
Misty Mountain Hop
Since I've Been Loving You
Bron-y-Aur Stomp
The Song Remains the Same
The Rain Song
D2:
Dazed and Confused
Stairway to Heaven
Whole Lotta Love
Heartbreaker

Takka Takka

Venue: San Francisco
Date: 6/2/73
Cover: D4C
Recording: 7
Source: St - Aud
Company: Tarantura
Matrix #: KEZAR 1/2
Place Of Origin: Japan
Total Disc Time: 60.52 - 75.34

N.B. I suspect that this is just another re-issue of the Kezar Stadium tape. Longer than the title "The Vibes Are Real". This recording is also availabe as "Who's Next". However there is some rumour that this is a board tape.

D1:
Rock And Roll (6:26)
Celebration Day (3:28)
Bring It On Home Intro, Black Dog (5:50)
Over The Hills And Far Away (6:34)
Misty Mountain Hop (5:36)
Since I've Been Loving You (7:59)
No Quarter (10:17)
The Song Remains The Same (6:13)
The Rain Song (8:29)
D2:
Dazed And Confused (Inc. San Francisco) (29:33)
Stairway To Heaven (11:01)
Moby Dick (4:28)
Heartbreaker (8:01)
Whole Lotta Love (Inc. Boogie Chillen) (12:34)
Communication Breakdown (3:38)
The Ocean (6:19)

Tales From 69

Venue: Kansas City - Newport* - Wallingford+
Date: 11/5/69 - 7/6/69* - 8/17/69+
Cover: D4C fold out digipak
Recording: 6,5*,4+
Source: M -Aud
Company: Tarantura
Matrix #: NO 69-3-1~3.
Place Of Origin: Japan
Total Disc Time: 39.11 - 58.51 - 9.03

N.B. A nice triple package of three different shows. For the price charged they could have left out the nine minute third disc and made this a double. A variety of sound sources, mostly passable.

D1:
Communication Breakdown (3.51)
I Can't Quit You (5.27)
Heartbreaker (5.20)
Dazed & Confused (12.16)
How Many More Times (12.17)
D2:
Train Kept A Rollin (3.45)*
I Can't Quit You (5.57)*
Dazed &Confused (13.05)*
You Shook Me (11.13)*
How Many More Times (14.53)*
Communication Breakdown (4.46)*
Long Tall Sally (5.12)*
D3:
Train Kept A Rollin' (2.35)+
I Can't Quit You (6.28)+

Tampa Stadium

Venue: Tampa

Date: 5/5/73

Cover: D4C sleeve

Recording: 7

Source: M -Aud

Company: Tarantura

Matrix #: TAMP-1,2.

Place Of Origin: Japan

Total Disc Time: 53:27 - 68:22

N.B. An average audience recording
from Tampa Stadium.

D1:

Rock And Roll,

Celebration Day,

Black Dog,

Over The Hills And Far Away,

Misty Mountain Hop,

Since I've Been Loving You,

No Quarter,

The Song Remans The Same,

The Rain Song

D2:

Dazed And Confused,

Stairway To Heaven,

Moby Dick,

Heartbreaker,

Whole Lotta Love,

The Ocean,

Communication Breakdown.

Tangerine

Venue: New York

Date: 6/15/72

Cover: D4C

Recording: 5

Source: M -Aud

Company: Mud Dogs

Matrix #: 020/021

Place Of Origin: Japan

Total Disc Time: n/a

N.B. Another new show to CD. This has all kinds of
annoying chatter over the tape and includes many cuts
but as far as I know this is the only tape of this show.

D1:

Immigrant Song

Heartbreaker

Black Dog

Since I've Been Loving You

Going To California

Tangerine

Bron-y-Aur Stomp

D2:

Dazed & Confused

What Is & What Should Never Be

Moby Dick

Whole Lotta Love Medley

(Inc. Boogie Chillen - Hello Mary Lou - Money Honey -

Heartbreak Hotel -

Millionaire Blues - Going Down Slow)

Tapes From The Darkside

Venue: Osaka
Date: 10/9/72
Cover: D4C in double case
Recording: n/a
Source: n/a
Company: H- Bomb
Matrix #: HB 9301-3
Place Of Origin: Japan
Total Disc Time: n/a

N.B. All track information not available at press time.

DI:
Rock & Roll (4.01)
Black Dog (5.28)
Over The Hills & Far Away (5.50)
Misty Mountain Hop (5.12)
Since I've Been Loving You (7.34)
Dancing Days (4.02)
The Song Remains The Same (5.50)
The Rain Song (7.29)
D2:
Dazed & Confused (26.42)
(Inc.The Crunge
Stairway To Heaven (10.52)
Moby Dick (16.10)
D3:
Whole Lotta Love Medley
(cut) (28.30)
(Inc. Everybody Needs Someone To Love - Leave My
Woman Alone - All Shook Up - Lawdy Miss Clawdy -
Heartbreak Hotel - Going Down Slow)
Stand By Me (6.13)
Immigrant Song (3.35)

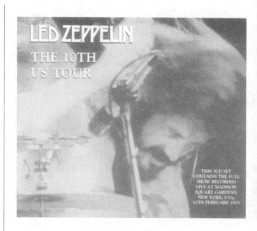

Tenth US Tour (The)

Venue: New York
Date: 2/12/75
Cover: D4C in double case
Recording: 6 - 7
Source: St - Aud
Company: Whole Lotta Live
Matrix #: WLL 001/02/03
Place Of Origin: Italy
Total Disc Time: 52.45 - 45.46 - 61.50

N.B. A knock off of the Tarantura title "The Jumpleg".

DI:
Rock And Roll (3.46)
Sick Again (4:57)
Over The Hills And Far Away (8.57)
In My Time Of Dying (11.38)
The Song Remains The Same (6:28)
The Rain Song (7:42)
Kashmir (8:31)
D2:
No Quarter (18.08)
Trampled Underfoot (8:11)
Moby Dick (17.20)
D3:
Dazed And Confused (31.41)
Stairway To Heaven (11.57)
Whole Lotta Love (1:49)
Black Dog (5:33)
Heartbreaker (8.59)

Texas International Pop Festival

Venue: Dallas

Date: 8/31/69

Cover: D4C Sleeve

Recording: 9

Source: St - SB

Company: Last Stand Disc

Matrix #: LSD 19

Place Of Origin: Japan

Total Disc Time: n/a

N.B. Another reissue of the now well-circulated Dallas soundboard tape. Nice rubber stamp cover!

D1:

Train Kept a Rolling

I Can't Quit You

Dazed and Confused

You Shook Me

How Many More Times

Communication Breakdown

Texas Two Steps

Venue: Dallas - Houston*

Date: 3/28/70 - 3/29/70*

Cover: D4C

Recording: 5-6

Source: M - Aud

Company: Diagram's of Led Zeppelin

Matrix #: TDOLZ 359701/359702

Place Of Origin: Japan

Total Disc Time: 64.23 - 58.27

N.B. These are new recordings to bootleg. One from the Dallas Memorial Auditorium and the other from the University of Houston Hofheinz Pavilion. The Houston material is slightly better than the Dallas material although neither are very good they are still interesting nonetheless. Despite the audience noise and cuts and dropouts it's still neat to hear these two shows.

D1:

We're Gonna Groove

Dazed and Confused

Heartbreaker

Bring It on Home

White Summer/Black Mountain Side

Since I've Been Loving You

Thank You

D2:

What Is and What Should Never Be

Moby Dick

White Summer - Black Mountain Side*

For What It's Worth - How Many More Times*

Three Days After

Venue: Los Angeles
Date: 6/3/73 - 9/4/70*
Cover: D4C sleeve
Recording: 5 - 7*
Source: M -Aud
Company: Cobra
Matrix #: 013
Place Of Origin: Japan
Total Disc Time: n/a

N.B. Another in Cobra's series of reissues of classic vinyl bootlegs, however this one doesn't use the original 2LP set as a template instead opting for the more complete but inferior audience recording.

D1:
Rock & Roll
Celebration Day
Black Dog
Over The Hills & Far Away
Misty Mountain Hop
Since I've Been Loving You
No Quarter
Song Remains The Same
Rain Song
D2:
Dazed & Confused
Stairway To Heaven
Moby Dick
D3:
Heartbreaker - Whole Lotta Love Medley
(Inc. Going Down - I'm A Man -
The Hunter - Boogie Chillen)
The Ocean
Communication Breakdown
Organ Solo
Thank You
That's The Way*
Bron-y-Aur*

Thunderous Break

Venue: Landover
Date: 5/26/77
Cover: D4C
Recording: 6
Source: M -Aud
Company: Diagrams Of Led Zeppelin
Matrix #: TDOLZ 239701/2/3
Place Of Origin: Japan
Total Disc Time: n/a

N.B. Also available as part of the box set "Maryland Deluxe". Another mediocre audience recording.

D1:
The Song Remains The Same
The Rover, Sick Again
Nobody's Fault But Mine
In My Time Of Dying
Since I've Been Loving You
No Quarter
D2:
Ten Years Gone
The Battle Of Evermore
Going To California
Dancing Days,
Black Country Woman,
Bron-Y-Aur Stomp
White Summer - Black Mountain Side
Kashmir
D3:
Out On The Tiles - Moby Dick
Guitar Solo
Achilles Last Stand
Stairway To Heaven
Whole Lotta Love
Rock And Roll

Thunderstorm

Venue: London
Date: 5/23/75
Cover: D4C fold out sleeve
Recording: 6 - 7
Source: M - Aud
Company: Tarantura
Matrix #: T4 - CD5
Place Of Origin: Japan
Total Disc Time: 48.12 - 63.52 - 31.26 - 58.53
N.B. Fairly distorted audience recording in a typically
lavish Tarantura package.

D1:
Intro - Opening (1 :25)
Rock And Roll (3:55)
Sick Again (6:03)
Over The Hills And Far Away (7:34)
In My Time Of Dying (13:22)
The Song Remains The Same (6:23)
The Rain Song (9:35)
D2:
Kashmir (9:12)
No Quarter (28:12)
Tangerine (5:02)
Going To California (5:34)
That s The Way (7:43)
Bron-Y-Aur Stomp (7:30)
D3:
Trampled Underfoot (6:30)
Moby Dick (23:45)
D4:
Dazed And Contused (31.12)
Stairway To Heaven (11 :37)
Whole Lotta Love (13:02)
(Inc .The Crunge - Black Dog)

Tight But Loose

Venue: New York
Date: 2/1/69
Cover: D4C sleeve with hot foil
Recording: 7
Source: M - Aud
Company: Tarantura
Matrix #: T2CD-2
Place Of Origin: Japan
Total Disc Time: 45.31 - 45.53
N.B. Nice packaging of a show not available before. The
band play an unusual and exceptional set.

D1:
The Train Kept A Rollin' (3.21)
I Can't Quit You (5.28)
Killing Floor (6.30)
Dazed And Confused (12.15)
(Inc. Shapes of Things)
You Shook Me (12.35)
Communication Breakdown (2.55)
D2:
White Summer - Black Mountain Side (9.08)
Babe I'm Gonna Leave You (7.27)
Pat's Delight (13.58)
How Many More Times Medley (15.22) (cut)
(Inc. For Your Love - Over Under Sideways Down)

Tightest & Loosest

Venue: Landover
Date: 5/28/77
Cover: D4C
Recording: 6
Source: M -Aud
Company: Diagrams Of Led Zeppelin
Matrix #: TDOLZ 249701/2/3
Place Of Origin: Japan
Total Disc Time: n/a
N.B. The third night in Landover Maryland. Mediocre
quality recording. Part of the 12 CD box set "Maryland
Deluxe". Another new show to bootleg CD.

DI:
The Song Remains The Same
The Rover, Sick Again
Nobody's Fault But Mine
In My Time Of Dying
Since I've Been Loving You
No Quarter
Ten Years Gone
D2:
The Battle Of Evermore
Going To California
Black Country Woman,
Bron-Y-Aur Stomp
White Summer - Black Mountain Side
Kashmir
Out On The Tiles - Moby Dick
D3:
Guitar Solo
Achilles Last Stand
Stairway To Heaven
Whole Lotta Love
Rock And Roll

Time Traveller

Venue: Los Angeles
Date: 6/22/77
Cover: D4C sleeve
Recording: 7-8
Source: St - Aud
Company: Diagrams of Led Zeppelin
Matrix #: Vol 051
Place Of Origin: Japan
Total Disc Time: n/a
N.B. Just another reissue of the forum tape. Part of a
series by Diagrams of Led Zeppelin reissuing the entire
Los Angeles concert series.

DI:
Song Remains the Same
Sick Again
Nobody's Fault but Mine
In My Time of Dying
Since I've Been Loving You
D2:
No Quarter
Ten Years Gone
D3:
The Battle of Ever More
Going to California
Black Country Woman
Braon-y-Aur Stomp
White Summer
Black Mountain Side
Kashmir
Moby Dick
D4:
Over the Hills and Far Away
Guitar Solo
Achilles Last Stand
Stairway to Heaven
Whole Lotta Love
Rock and Roll

Titanic (The)

Venue: London
Date: 12/23/72
Cover: D4C sleeve
Recording: 7
Source: M - Aud
Company: Image Quality
Matrix #: IQ 016/17/18
Place Of Origin: Japan
Total Disc Time: n/a
N.B. The complete show.
Also available as "Merry Christmas Mr Jimmy".
Moby Dick is introduced by Plant as "The Titanic".
This one maintains the original song order.

D1:
Rock And Roll
Over The Hills And Far Away
Black Dog
Misty Mountain Hop
Since I've Been Loving You
Dancing Days
Bron-Y-Aur Stomp
The Song Remains The Same
The Rain Song
Stairway To Heaven
D2:
Dazed And Confused
Whole Lotta Love Medley
(Inc. The Crunge - Everybody Needs Someone To Love -
Boogie Chillen - Let's Have A Party -
Heartbreak Hotel - I Can't Quit You)
Heartbreaker

Tocatta & Fugue

Venue: Helsinki
Date: 2/24/70
Cover: D4C gatefold sleeve
Recording: 5
Source: M -Aud
Company: Tarantura
Matrix #: TF-001-002
Place Of Origin: Japan
Total Disc Time: 58:40 / 49:14
N.B. Tarantura reissues the well
circulated audience tape.

D1:
We're Gonna Groove,
I Can't Quit You,
Dazed And Confused,
Heartbreaker,
White Summer--Black Mountain Side,
Since I've Been Loving You,
Thank You
D2:
Moby Dick,
How Many More Times,
Whole Lotta Love

Touch & Go

Venue: Toronto – London* - Brussels^

Date: 9/4/71 – 3/19/69* - 1/12/75^

Cover: D4C sleeve

Recording: 9,4*,5^

Source: M – SB,M –Aud^

Company: Antrabata

Matrix #: TG3

Place Of Origin: Europe

Total Disc Time: 61.43

N.B. The version of Sunshine Woman is from the original flexidisc and is not from the much better tape which popped up in early 1998.The version of Train is by the Scotty McCabe Quintet and is really great.

D1:

Stairway To Heaven (9.32)

Celebration Day (5.15)

That's The Way (7.57)

Going To California (4.48)

What Is & What Should Never Be (4.54)

Moby Dick (15.13)

Sunshine Woman (3.10)*

Train Kept A Rollin' (2.15)

When The Levee Breaks (8.39)^

Tour De Force LA 1975

Venue: Los Angeles
Date: 3/27/75
Cover: D4C
Recording: 8
Source: St - Aud
Company: Rabbit
Matrix #: RR 005/6/7
Place Of Origin: Japan
Total Disc Time: 68.04 - 66.31 - 74.13
N.B. This recording was previously available as the titles "Cosmic Crazy" and "Electric Orgasm". Some consider this to be a better recording than either of those titles.

D1:
Rock and Roll
Sick Again
Over the Hills and Far Away
In My Time of Dying
Song Remains the Same
The Rain Song (Cut)
Kashmir
Since I've Been Loving You
D2:
No Quarter
Trampled Under Foot
Moby Dick
D3:
Dazed and Confused (cut)
Stairway to Heaven
Whole Lotta Love
Black Dog

Tour Over Europe 1980

Venue: Zurich

Date: 6/29/80

Cover: D4C in case

Recording: 8

Source: M - SB

Company: Joker

Matrix #: JOK 008-D

Place Of Origin: Australia

Total Disc Time: 42.18

N.B. Another re-issue from down under.

Nothing noteworthy.

D1:

Train Kept A Rollin' (3.24)

Nobody's Fault But Mine (5.30)

Black Dog (5.27)

In The Evening (9.01)

The Rain Song (8.53)

Hot Dog (4.02)

All My Love (6.13)

Tour Over Europe 1980
Venue: Frankfurt
Date: 6/30/80
Cover: D4C
Recording: 8
Source: St - SB
Company: Last Stand Disc
Matrix #: LSD 29/30
Place Of Origin: Japan
Total Disc Time: n/a

N.B. Another reissue of one of the board tapes from the 1980 European tour. The cover claims that this is digitally re-mastered from the master tapes.

D1:
Train Kept a Rolling
Nobody Fault but Mine
Black Dog
In the Evening
The Rain Song
Hot Dog
All My Love
Trampled under Foot
Since I've Been Loving You
D2:
Achilles Last Stand
White Summer-Black Mountain Side
Kashmir
Stairway to Heaven
Rock and Roll
Money
Whole Lotta Love

Trampled Underfoot

Venue: New York

Date: n/a

Cover: D4C

Recording: n/a

Source: M - Aud

Company: Cobra

Matrix #: 028

Place Of Origin: Japan

Total Disc Time: n/a

N.B. All of the details of this piece were not available at press time. However if it is the same as the title that came out on the vinyl then it is not a very good recording. However this is purely conjecture.

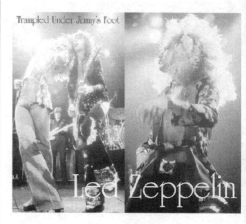

Trampled Under Jimmy's Foot

Venue: Long Beach

Date: 3/12/75

Cover: D4C in double case

Recording: 7

Source: M - Aud

Company:
Silver Rarities

Matrix#: SIRA 168/169/170

Place Of Origin: Europe

Total Disc Time: 55.20 - 46.49 - 74.47

N.B. Finally the second night from Long Beach surfaces thanks to the persistence of the folks at Silver Rarities. An unusual and amusing intro to Song Remains The Same which collapses into laughter.

D1:
Rock & Roll (4.31)
Sick Again (6.12)
Over The Hills & Far Away (8.01)
In My Time Of Dying (11.56)
The Song Remains The Same (6.53)
The Rain Song (8.31)
Kashmir (9.16)
D2:
No Quarter (22.31)
Trampled Underfoot (8.21)
Moby Dick (15.57)
D3:
Dazed & Confused (34.43)
Stairway To Heaven (13.09)
Whole Lotta Love (15.11)
Heartbreaker (11.44)

Trampled Underwood

Venue: New York
Date: 2/13/75
Cover: D4C
Recording: 7-8
Source: M - Aud
Company: Image Quality
Matrix #: IQ-046/47/48
Place Of Origin: Japan
Total Disc Time: 66.52 -75.54 -34.57

N.B Recorded at the Nassau County Coliseum in Uniondale New York. All in all a very listenable recording, despite all the cuts in the tape. Includes a very rare performance of Roll Over Beethoven.

D1:
Rock and Roll (4.26)
Sick Again (6.32)
Over the Hills and Far Away (8.33)
In My Time of Dying (cut) (11.12)
Song Remains the Same (Cut) (4.52)
The Rain Song (cut) (7.50)
Kashmir (cut) (6.04)
No Quarter (17.19)
D2:
Trampled under Foot (9.12)
Moby Dick (25.59)
Dazed and Confused (39.57)
D3:
Stairway to Heaven (13.14)
Whole Lotta Love - Black Dog (5.53)
Roll over Beethoven (7.53)
Communication Breakdown (7.54)

Trentham Gardens

Venue: Stoke – Studio*
Date: 1/15/73 – 1960's*
Cover: D2C
Recording: 8
Source: St - SB
Company: n/a
Matrix #: MWL 009-010
Place Of Origin: Japan
Total Disc Time: n/a

N.B. The soundboard from Stoke On Trent along with a batch of miscellaneous Yardbirds sessions.

D1:
Rock & Roll (3:45)
Over The Hills And Far Away (5:45)
Black Dog (6:18)
Misty Mountain Hop (5:20)
Since I've Been Loving You (8:02)
Dancing Days (4:48)
Dazed And Confused (29:23)
Stairway To Heaven (11:20)
D2:
Bron-Y-Aur Stomp (5:44)
The Song Remains The Same (5:31)
The Rain Song (5:18)
Whole Lotta Love Medley (Inc. Everybody Needs
Someone To Love - Boogie Chillen - Baby I Don't Care -
Let's Have A Party)
Hang On Sloopy *
Smokestack Lightning *
You're A Better Man Than I *
The Train Kept A Rollin' *
Shapes Of Things *
Dust My Broom*
Scratch My Back *
Over Under Sideways Down *
The Sun Is Shining *
Shapes Of Things *

Tribute To Bert Berns

Venue: Olympic Studios

Date: 1968 - 1969

Cover: D4C

Recording: 9

Source: St - SB

Company: n/a

Matrix #: n/a

Place Of Origin: Japan

Total Disc Time: n/a

N.B. Another compilation of the studio outtakes previously available on "Babe I'm Gonna Leave You" and "Jennings Farm Blues".

D1:

Babe I'm Gonna Leave You (Take One)

Babe I'm Gonna Leave You Ttake Two)

You Shook Me

Tribute To Bert Berns (Take One)

Tribute To Bert Berns (Take Two)

Tribute To Bert Berns (Take Three)

Instrumental

Instrumental

Moby Dick

Jennings Farm Blues

Jennings Farm Blues

Tune Up

Venue: Detroit

Date: 1/31/75

Cover: D4C

Recording: 6

Source: M -Aud

Company: Immigrant

Matrix #: IM052-53

Place Of Origin: Japan

Total Disc Time: n/a

N.B. First time on CD. This show was out on vinyl many years ago as "Detroit Just About Back".

D1:

Rock And Roll

Sick Again

Over The Hills And Far Away

In My Time Of Dying

The Song Remains The Same

The Rain Song

Kashmir

No Quarter

D2:

Trampled Underfoot

Moby Dick

How Many More Times

Stairway to Heaven

Whole Lotta Love

Black Dog

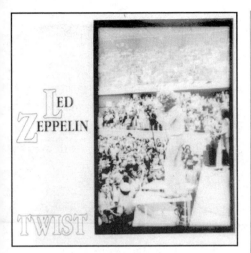

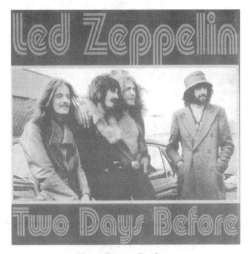

Twist

Venue: New York

Date: 7/21/69

Cover: D4C

Recording: 7

Source: M - Aud

Company: Diagrams of Led Zeppelin

Matrix #: n/a

Place Of Origin: Japan

N.B. This Disc features a more complete tape. Includes

Train Kept a Rollin'.

D1:

Train Kept A Rolling

I Can't Quit You

Dazed and Confused

You Shook Me

White Summer

Black Mountain Side

How Many More Times

Communication Breakdown

Two Days Before
Venue: Oakland
Date: 9/2/70
Cover: D4C in double slimline case
Recording: 5 - 6
Source: M - Aud
Company: Silver Rarities
Matrix #: SIRA 129/130
Place Of Origin: Europe
Total Disc Time: 71.07 - 72.38
N.B. Great medley. Slightly distant recording but worth
having for the unusual encore of Train Kept A Rollin'.

D1:
Immigrant Song (4.15)
Heartbreaker (6.11)
Dazed & Confused (16.24)
Bring It On Home (10.08)
That's The Way (5.20)
Bron-y-Aur (2.01)
Since I've Been Loving You (6.53)
Thank You (13.14)
D2:
What Is & What Should Never Be (4.54)
Moby Dick (21.55)
Whole Lotta Love Medley (23.08)
(Inc. Boogie Chillen - For What It's Worth -
Lawdy Miss Clawdy - Honey Bee - Long Distance Call -
Moving On - That's Alright)
Communication Breakdown (6.36)
Train Kept A Rollin' (2.37)
Blueberry Hill (3.12)
Long Tall Sally (4.51)

Two Days After

Venue: San Francisco
Date: 6/2/73
Cover: D4C
Recording: 6
Source: M -Aud
Company: Immigrant
Matrix #: IM 037-039
Place Of Origin: Japan
Total Disc Time: n/a

N.B. Just another reissue of the Kezar Stadium gig. Also available as "Persistance Kezar".

D1:
Rock And Roll (3:50)
Celebration Day (2:39)
Bring It On Home Intro, Black Dog (6:09)
Over The Hills And Far Away (7:00)
Misty Mountain Hop (5:10)
Since I've Been Loving You (8:20)
No Quarter (10:08)
D2:
The Song Remains The Same (6:23)
The Rain Song (8.17)
Dazed And Confused (Inc. San Francisco) (30:31)
Stairway To Heaven (10:54)
D3:
Moby Dick (4:28)
Heartbreaker (8:02)
Whole Lotta Love Medley (Inc Boogie Chillen) (12:25)
Communication Breakdown (4:09)
The Ocean (5:31)

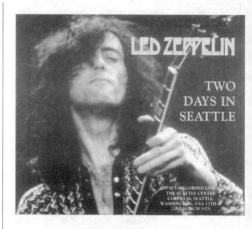

Two Days In Seattle

Venue: Seattle
Date: 3/21/75* - 3/17/75
Cover: D2C triple gatefold sleeve
Recording: 7* - 6
Source: M - Aud
Company: Whole Lotta Live
Matrix #: WLL 013 - 014 - 015
Place Of Origin: Italy
Total Disc Time: 58.59 - 58.08 - 66.53

N.B. A straight knock off of the Tarantura title "Hammer Of The Gods".

D1:
Opening (1.53)
Rock & Roll (4.09)*
Sick Again (5.22)*
Over The Hills & Far Away (7.22)*
In My Time Of Dying (11.26)*
The Song Remains The Same (5.46)
The Rain Song (8.30)
Kashmir (9.17)
D2:
No Quarter (26.07)
Trampled Underfoot (8.30)
Moby Dick (22.10)
D3:
Dazed & Confused (34.52)
Stairway To Heaven (12.33)
Whole Lotta Love - The Crunge (10.50)
Black Dog (5.48)

207.19

Venue: Seattle - Boston *

Date: 3/21/75 - 9/9/70 *

Cover: D4C

Recording: 8,5*

Source: M - Aud

Company: COBRA

Matrix #:011

Place Of Origin: Japan

Total Disc Time: 56:07 - 50:58

N.B. An exact duplicate of the vinyl title of the same name. An amazingly long version of Dazed.

D1:

Dazed And Confused

Stairway To Heaven

D2:

Whole Lotta Love (Inc.The Crunge)

Black Dog

Communication Breakdown

Heartbreaker

Whole Lotta Love *

Communication Breakdown *

214

Venue: Seattle

Date: 3/21/75

Cover: D4C

Recording: 8

Source: M - Aud

Company: COBRA

Matrix #:011

Place Of Origin: Japan

Total Disc Time: 58:26 - 72:23

N.B. An exact duplicate of the vinyl title of the same name.

D1:

Rock And Roll

Sick Again

Over The Hills And Far Away

In My Time Of Dying

The Song Remains The Same

The Rain Song

Kashmir

D2:

No Quarter

Since I've Been Loving You

Trampled Underfoot

Moby Dick

Two Originals

Venue: Studio

Date: n/a

Cover: D4C

Recording: 10

Source: St - SB

Company: n/a

Matrix #: 2511

Place Of Origin: Japan

Total Disc Time: n/a

N.B. A straight pirate of the rare European legit double

album of Led Zeppelin 1 and 2.

Limited to 500 numbered copies.

Two Penny Upright

Venue: Ipswich – Vancouver* - Berlin^
Date: 11/16/71 – 7/18/73* – 3/19/73^
Cover: D4C
Recording: 7 ,8^
Source: M –Aud, M – SB^
Company: Antrabata
Matrix #: ARM 171171/ARM 180773/ARM 190373
Place Of Origin: Europe
Total Disc Time: 58.27 - ? - ?
N.B. All details not available at press time. This set
includes three tapes not readily available before. The
Ipswich disc was sold separately as "Kinetic Circus".

D1:
Intro
Immigrant Song
Heartbreaker
Black Dog
Since I've Been Loving You
Rock & Roll
That's The Way
Tangerine
Dazed & Confused (cut)
D2:
Rock & Roll*
Celebration Day*
Black Dog*
Over The Hills & Far Away*
Misty Mountain Hop*
Since I've Been Loving You*
No Quarter*
Dazed & Confused (cut)*
D3:
Whole Lotta Love Medley^

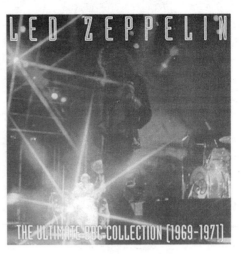

Tympani For The Butterqueen

Venue: Fort Worth

Date: 5/19/73

Cover: D4C

Recording: 8

Source: St - SB

Company: MIDAS TOUCH

Matrix #: 62021/2

Place Of Origin: Japan

Total Disc Time: n/a

N.B. The ubiquitous soundboard tape surfaces again.

D1:

Rock And Roll (4:42)

Celebration Day (3:53)

Bring It On Home - Black Dog (6:39)

Over The Hills And Far Away (7:09)

Misty Mountain Hop (4:48)

Since I've Been Loving You (8:48)

No Quarter (11 :51)

The Song Remains The Same (5:35)

The Rain Song (8:47)

D2:

Dazed And Confused (Inc. San Francisco) (32:31)

Stairway To Heaven (11 :54)

Ultimate BBC Collection
1969-1971 (The)

Venue: London

Date: 6/27/69 - 4/1/71*

Cover: D4C in case

Recording: 9

Source: M - SB, St - SB*

Company: Home

Matrix #: HR 6033-7

Place Of Origin: Germany

Total Disc Time: 68.31

N.B. Just another re-issue of the BBC stuff from the two live concerts.

D1:

Communication Breakdown (3.22)

I Can't Quit You (6.18)

You Shook Me (10.15)

Immigrant Song (3.17)*

Heartbreaker (5.07)*

Dazed & Confused (16.19)*

Going To California (4.03)*

Stairway To Heaven (8.43)*

Black Dog (5.17)*

Whole Lotta Love (4.37)*

Ultra Rare Trax Pt 2

Venue: Headley Grange
Date: Various
Cover: D4C
Recording: 8
Source: St - SB
Company: Savege Beast Music
Matrix #: SB 969631
Place Of Origin: Japan
Total Disc Time: n/a

N.B. Another compilation of outtakes from the various sessions at Headley Grange/ Bron-y-Aur/ Island.

D1:
Ten Years Gone (Take One)
Ten Years Gone (Take Two)
Ten Years Gone (Take Three)
Boogie With Stu (Five Takes)
Night Flight (Five Takes)
Bron-y-Aur (Three Takes)
Acoustic Demos (Six Takes)
Since I've Been Loving You (Accapella) (Two takes)
Hey Hey What Can I Do
Poor Tom
Immigrant Song
Out On The Tiles
Bron-y-Aur

Ultraviolence

Venue: Cleveland
Date: 1/24/75
Cover: D4C
Recording: 4
Source: M -Aud
Company: SH
Matrix #: OF5ABC
Place Of Origin: Japan
Total Disc Time: n/a

N.B. Another new show to bootleg. Barely worth exhuming. Really crappy quality. Does feature one of the rare 1975 performances of How Many More Times.

D1:
Rock And Roll
Sick Again
Over The Hills And Far Away
In My Time Of Dying
The Song Remains The Same
The Rain Song
Kashmir
D2:
The Wanton Song
No Quarter
Trampled Underfoot
Moby Dick
D3:
How Many More Times (Inc. The Hunter)
Stairway To Heaven
Whole Lotta Love - Black Dog
Communication Breakdown (Inc. The Lemon Song)

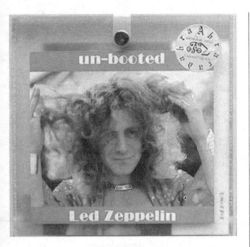

Un-booted

Venue: Seattle - New York* - Fort Worth^

Date: 7/17/77 - 6/11/77* - 5/22/77^

Cover: D4C in plastic carrying case

Recording:

Source:

Company:

Matrix #: UN-77-1~3

Place Of Origin:

Total Disc Time:

N.B. Limited to only 300 copies.

Mick Ralphs joins the band for It'll Be Me.

D1:

Stairway To Heaven,

Whole Lotta Love,

Rock And Roll

D2:

No Quarter*,

Ten Years Gone*,

The Battle Of Evermore*

D3:

Guitar Solo^,

Achilles Last Stand^,

Stairway To Heaven^,

Whole Lotta Love^,

Rock And Roll^,

It'll Be Me ^

Unlicensed Live Vol 2.

Venue: n/a

Date: n/a

Cover: D4C in case

Recording: n/a

Source: n/a

Company: Mainline

Matrix #: SW

Place Of Origin: Australia

Total Disc Time: n/a

N.B. All track information not available at press time.

D1:

Going To California

Stairway To Heaven

Whole Lotta Love

What Is & What Should Never Be

Dazed & Confused

Communication Breakdown

Vienna 1980

Venue: Vienna

Date: 6/26/80

Cover: D4C

Recording: 7

Source: St - Aud

Company: Tarantura

Matrix #: 1980 13,14

Place Of Origin: Japan

Total Disc Time: n/a

N.B. This is one of the few audience recordings from the 1980 tour to make it to CD.

D1:

Train Kept A Rolling

Nobody's Fault But Mine

Black Dog

In The Evening

The Rain Song

Hot Dog

All My Love

Trampled Underfoot

D2:

Since I've Been Loving You

White Summer

Kashmir

Stairway To Heaven

Rock & Roll

Whole Lotta Love

Vienna 1973

Venue: Vienna

Date: 3/16/73

Cover: D4C

Recording: 7

Source: M - Aud

Company: Diagrams of Led Zeppelin

Matrix #: TDOLZ 489701/02

Place Of Origin: Japan

Total Disc Time: 56.57 - 70.13

N.B. An audience recording previously available on CD as the title Led Poisoning. Not bad quality.

D1:

Rock and Roll

Over the Hills and Far Away

Black Dog

Misty Mountain Hop

Since I've Been Loving You

Dancing Days

Bron-y-Aur Stomp

Song Remains the Same

The Rain Song

D2:

Dazed and Confused

Stairway to Heaven

Whole Lotta Love Medley

(Inc. Boogie Chillen - Baby I Don't Care - Let's Have a Party - I Can't Quit You - The Lemon Song)

Heartbreaker

Viva La France

Venue: Paris
Date: 4/1/73
Cover: D4C
Recording: 5
Source: M -Aud
Company: Diagrams Of Led Zeppelin
Matrix #: TDOLZ Vol 028
Place Of Origin: Japan
Total Disc Time: n/a
N.B. A much more complete version of this tape. Basically only fragments of this have been available before. Very poor quality though.

D1:
Rock And Roll
Over The Hills And Far Away
Black Dog
Misty Mountain Hop
Since I've Been Loving You
Dancing Days
Bron-Y-Aur Stomp
The Song Remains The Same
The Rain Song
Dazed And Confused
D2:
Moby Dick
Stairway To Heaven
Whole Lotta Love Medley (Inc. Everybody Needs Somebody To Love - Boogie Chillen - Baby I Don't Care - Let's Have A Party - I Can't Quit You - Lemon Song)

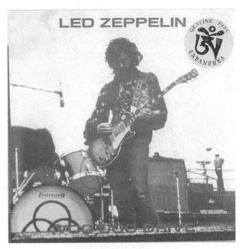

Voodoo Drive

Venue: Adelaide
Date: 2/19/72
Cover: D4C in vinyl gatefold
Recording: 7
Source: St - Aud
Company: Tarantura
Matrix #: T2CD 16-1-2
Place Of Origin: Japan
Total Disc Time: 52.56 - 43.44
N.B. A bit rumbly but otherwise a nice document. Includes material previously unavailable. Page plays about three notes of Voodoo Chile before Dazed which seems hardly worth mentioning.

D1:
Immigrant Song (3.51)
Heartbreaker (6.39)
Out On The Tiles Intro. (0.08)
Black Dog (4.58)
Since I've Been Loving You (7.47)
Stairway To Heaven (9.00)
Going To California (5.31)
That's The Way (6.36)
Tangerine (cut) (0.50)
Bron-y-Aur Stomp (4.35)
D2:
Voodoo Chile (0.04)
Dazed & Confused (20.48)
Moby Dick (cut) (3.45)
Whole Lotta Love Medley (cut) (18.14) (Inc. Boogie Chillen - Mary Lou - Let's Have A Party - That's Alright Mama - Going Down Slow)

Week For Badge Holders (A)

Venue: Los Angeles - New York*
Date: 6/21/77 - 6/22/77# - 6/23/77+ - 6/25/77^ - 6/26/77† - 6/27/77‡ - 6/14/77*
Cover: D3C box set with D4C sleeves and posters
Recording: 7 - 8
Source: St - Aud
Company: Tarantura
Matrix #: Tarantura T 19
Place Of Origin: Japan
Total Disc Time: 67.06 - 50.33 - 73.15 - 73.49 - 43.13 - 71.36 - 69.12 - 52.01 - 71.25 - 73.12 - 62.57 - 74.28 - 66.54 - 59.09 - 55.35 - 40.33 - 45.54 - 60.02 - 72.15

N.B. An outrageously lavish packaging of the entire string of shows in LA 77. Although once again the exchange rate with the yen results in an exorbitant price, this is one of those bootlegs that make you remember why you started collecting in the first place. All of the tapes are as good as I have heard them and the pictures are almost worth the price. Limited to 150 copies the first few with two posters. A very important addition to the Zeppelin pantheon.

Walk Don't Run

Venue: Los Angeles
Date: 8/22/71 - 8/21/71*
Cover: D2C sleeve
Recording: 5 - 6
Source: M -Aud
Company: Tarantura
Matrix #: n/a
Place Of Origin: Japan
Total Disc Time: n/a
N.B. A double package in nice slipcase featuring both audience tapes from the summer LA Forum shows.
D1:Walk Don't Run
Immigrant Song
Heartbreaker
Since I've Been Loving You
Black Dog
Dazed & Confused
Stairway To Heaven
Celebration Day
That's The Way
D2:What Is & What Should Never Be
Moby Dick
Whole Lotta Love Medley (Inc.Boogie Chillen - Think I'm Crazy - My Baby Left Me - Mess Of Blues - You Shook Me)
Communication Breakdown
Organ Solo
Thank You
D3: Immigrant Song*
Heartbreaker*
Since I've Been Loving You*
Black Dog*
Dazed & Confused*
Stairway To Heaven*
That's The Way*
Going To California*
D4:What Is & What Should Never Be*
Whole Lotta Love Medley (Inc.Boogie Chillen - I'm Moving On - That's Alright - Mess Of Blues)
Weekend*
Rock & Roll*
Communication Breakdown*
Organ Solo*
Thank You*

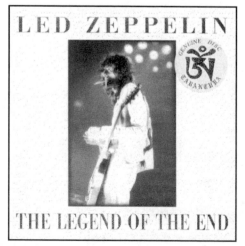

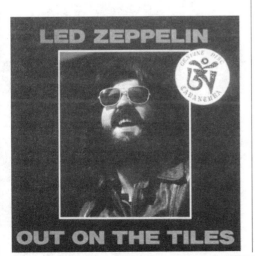

D1:
Intro - The Song Remains The Same (6:15)
The Rover Intro, Sick Again (6:01)
Nobody s Fault But Mine (6:42)
Over The Hills And Far Away (6:02)
Since I ve Been Loving You (7:55)
No Quarter (26:43)

D2:
Ten Years Gone Bad (8:44)
Battle Of Evermore (5:21)
Going To California (4:43)
Black Country Woman (1:41)
Bron-Y-Aur Stomp (6:43)
White Summer (7:33)
Black Mountain Side (2:12)
Kashmir (9:11)

D3:
Out On The Tiles - Moby Dick (17:23)
Heartbreaker (8:33)
Guitar Solo (Inc. Star Spangled Banner) (16:12)
Achilles Last Stand (8:55)
Stairway To Heaven (11:23)
Whole Lotta Love (1:24)
Rock And Roll (3:57)

D4:
The Song Remains The Same (6:17) *
The Rover Intro, Sick Again (6:02) *
Nobody's Fault But Mine (6:44) *
Over The Hills And Far Away (6:02) *
Since I've Been Loving You (8:01) *
No Quarter (Includes Sakura) (26:55) *
Ten Years Gone (8:06) *

D5:
The Battle Of Evermore (5:22) #
Going To California (4:44) #
Black Country Woman (1:40) #
Bron-Y-Aur Stomp (6:55) #
White Summer (7:39) #
Black Mountain Side (2:07) #
Kashmir (9:11) #

D6:
Out On The Tiles Intro, Moby Dick (17:44) #
Over The Hills And Far Away (6:03) #
Guitar Solo (Inc. Star Spangled Banner) (14:33) #
Achilles Last Stand (8:55) #
Stairway To Heaven (11:02) #
Whole Lotta Love (1:17) #
Rock And Roll (3:55) #

D7:
The Song Remains The Same (6:18) +
The Rover Intro, Sick Again (6:11) +
Nobody's Fault But Mine (6:44) +
Over The Hill And Far Away (6:03) +
Since I've Been Loving You (7:56) +
No Quarter (26:44) +

D8:
Ten Years Gone (9:12) +
Battle of Evermore (5:23) +
Going To California (4:48) +
Black Country Woman (1:39) +
Bron-Y-Aur Stomp (6:50) +
White Summer (7:28) +
Black Mountain Side (2:07) +
Kashmir (9:14) +

D9:
Trampled Underfoot (8:44) +
Out On The Tiles Intro, Moby Dick (17:43) +
Guitar Solo (Inc. Star Spangled Banner) (15:56) +
Achilles Last Stand (8:55) +
Stairway To Heaven (11:23) +
Whole Lotta Love (1:25) +
Rock And Roll (4:01) +

D10:
The Song Remains The Same (6:16) ^
The Rover Intro, Sick Again (6:03) ^
Nobody's Fault But Mine (6:45) ^
In My Time Of Dying - Rip It Up (10:55) ^
Since I've Been Loving You (7:56) ^
No Quarter (27:55) ^

D11:
Ten Years Gone (9:02) ^
The Battle Of Evermore (5:33) ^
Going To California (5:21) ^
Black Country Woman (2:21) ^
Bron-Y-Aur Stomp (6:55) ^
White Summer (7:35) ^
Black Mountain Side (2:23) ^
Kashmir (9:25) ^
Trampled Underfoot (7:42) ^

D12:
Out On The Tiles Intro, Moby dick (26:33) ^
Guitar Solo (Inc. Star Spangled Banner) (14:35) ^ Achilles
Last Stand (8:35) ^
Stairway To Heaven (11:25) ^
Whole Lotta Love (2:27) ^
Communication Breakdown (3:23) ^

D13:
The Song Remains The Same (1:15 Cut) †
The Rover Intro, Sick Again (5:59) †

Nobody s Fault But Mine (6:45) †
Over The Hills And Far Away (6:02) †
Since I ve Been Loving You (8:05) †
No Quarter (26:55) †

D14:
Ten Years Gone (9:12) †
The Battle Of Evermore (5:24) †
Going To California (4:48) †
That's Alright (1:44) †
Black Country Woman (1:44) †
Bron-Y-Aur Stomp (6:55) †
White Summer (7:55) †
Black Mountain Side (2:40) †
Kashmir (9:14) †

D15:
Out On The Tiles Intro, Moby Dick (4:44 Cut) †
Guitar Solo (Inc. Star Spangled Banner) (21:23) † Achilles
Last Stand (8:44) †
Stairway To Heaven (11:23) †
It 'll Be Me (2:54) †

D16:
The Song Remains The Same (6:15) ‡
The Rover Intro, Sick Again (5:58) ‡
Nobody's Fault But Mine (6:45) ‡
Over The Hills And Far Away (6:05) ‡
Since I 've Been Loving You (8:02) ‡

D17:
No Quarter (27:44) ‡
Ten Years Gone (9:02) ‡

D18:
The Battle Of Evermore (5:26) ‡
Going To California (4:46) ‡
Going Down South (1:02) ‡
Black Country Woman (1:45) ‡
Bron-Y-Aur Stomp (6:55) ‡
Dancing Days (3:45) ‡
White Summer (7:25) ‡
Black Mountain Side (2:32) ‡
Kashmir (9:03) ‡
Trampled Underfoot (7:44) ‡

D19:
Out On The Tiles - Moby Dick (16:02) ‡
Guitar Solo (Inc. Star Spangled Banner) (24:55) ‡ Achilles
Last Stand (8:55 cut) ‡
Stairway To Heaven (11:12) ‡
Whole Lotta Love (1:45) ‡
Rock And Roll (3:55) ‡

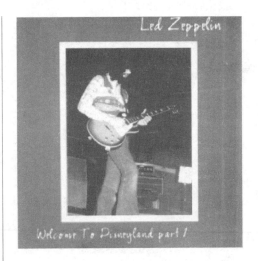

Welcome Back

Venue: New York

Date: 6/15/72

Cover: D4C gate fold sleeve

Recording: n/a

Source: M - Aud

Company: Tarantura

Matrix #: NCNY 001-2

Place Of Origin: Japan

Total Disc Time: 60.10 - 61.51

N.B. Another previously unavailable show surfaces on Tarantura. No doubt this will touch off a series of clone titles. Full details not available at press time.

D1:

Immigrant Song

Heartbreaker

Black Dog

Since I've Been Loving You

Stairway to Heaven

Going to California

That's the Way

Tangerine

Brian R. Stomp

D2:

Dazed and Confused

What Is and What Should Never Be

Moby Dick

Whole Lotta Love Medley (Inc. Boogie Chillen -You Don't Let Me Stop - Hand Jive - Hello Mary Lou - Money Honey - Heartbreak Hotel - Trucking Little Mama - Millionaire Blues - Going down Slow)

Welcome To Disneyland Part 1

Venue: Orlando

Date: 8/31/71

Cover: DBW slick

Recording: 4

Source: M -Aud

Company: Lemon Song

Matrix #: 7201

Place Of Origin: Japan

Total Disc Time: 53:37

N.B. Also available as "Orlando Madness"

D1:

Immigrant Song

Heartbreaker

Since I've Been Loving You

Dazed & Confused

Black Dog

Welcome To Disneyland Part 2

Venue: Orlando

Date: 8/31/71

Cover: DBW slick

Recording: 4

Source: M -Aud

Company: Lemon Song

Matrix #: 7202

Place Of Origin: Japan

Total Disc Time: 50:42

N.B. Previously unreleased show. Also available as

"Orlando Madness Vol 2"

DI:

Stairway To Heaven

Celebration Day

That's The Way

Going To California

What Is & What Should Never Be

Moby Dick

We're Gonna Groove

Venue: Vancouver

Date: 3/21/70

Cover: D4C

Recording: 8

Source: St - SB

Company: Black Panther

Matrix #: ABP 093

Place Of Origin: Italy

Total Disc Time: n/a

N.B. Another reissue of the Vancouver Mudslide tape.

DI:

Heartbreaker (6.13)

Thank You (8.03)

That's The Way (6.38)

What Is & What Should Never Be (4.15)

Communication Breakdown (5.03)

We're Gonna Groove (3.55)

Since I've Been Loving You (6.57)

Whole Lotta Love (2.47)

Stairway To Heaven (9.01)

We're Gonna Rock

Venue: Raleigh

Date: 4/8/70

Cover: D4C

Source: 5-6

Recording: M - Aud

Source: Blimp

Matrix #: n/a

Place Of Origin: Japan

Total Disc Time: n/a

N.B. Another reissue of the tape from the Dorten

Auditorium.

The cover lists the date incorrectly.

D1:

We're Gonna Groove

Dazed and Confused

Heartbreaker

Bring It on Home

White Summer-Black Mountain Side

Since I've Been Loving You

Thank You

What Is and What Should Never Be

Moby Dick

Where The Zeppelin Roam

Venue: Buffalo

Date: 7/15/73

Cover: D4C

Recording: 8

Source: St - SB

Company: MIDAS TOUCH

Matrix #: 62121/2

Place Of Origin: Japan

Total Disc Time: n/a

N.B. The umpteenth release of the Buffalo soundboard.

D1:

RockAnd Roll (5:10)

Celebration Day (3:35)

Black Dog (7:07)

Over The Hills And Far Away (7:02)

Misty Mountain Hop (4:58)

Since I've Been Loving You (9:32)

No Quarter (14:03)

The Song Remains The Same (5:38)

The Rain Song (9:08)

D2:

Dazed And Confused (Inc. San Francisco) (33:41)

Stairway To Heaven (11 :25)

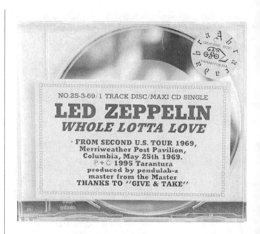

Whole Lotta Landover

Venue: Landover
Date: 5/26/77
Cover: D4C
Recording: 7
Source: M -Aud
Company: Immigrant
Matrix #: n/a
Place Of Origin: Japan
Total Disc Time: n/a
N.B. A reissue of one of the Landover Maryland con-
certs. Also available as "Thunderous Break".

D1:
The Song Remains The Same
The Rover, Sick Again
Nobody's Fault But Mine
In My Time Of Dying
Since I've Been Loving You
No Quarter
D2:
Ten Years Gone
The Battle Of Evermore
Going To California
Dancing Days,
Black Country Woman,
Bron-Y-Aur Stomp
White Summer - Black Mountain Side
Kashmir
Out On The Tiles - Moby Dick
D3:
Guitar Solo
Achilles Last Stand
Stairway To Heaven
Whole Lotta Love
Rock And Roll

Whole Lotta Love

Venue: Columbia

Date: 5/25/69

Cover: Sticker on single CD case

Recording: 5

Source: M - Aud

Company: Tarantura

Matrix #: 25-3-69

Place Of Origin: Japan

Total Disc Time: 7.15

N.B. CD single featuring an extraordinary rendition of
Whole Lotta Love. The disc has the wrong
Date this is from May not March. A gem.

D1:

Whole Lotta Love (7.15)

Who's Birthday

Venue: Tampa
Date: 4/9/70
Cover: D4C sleeve
Recording: 6 - 7
Source: St - Aud
Company: Tarantura
Matrix #: T2CD 15 1-2
Place Of Origin: Japan
Total Disc Time: 60.46 - 30.54

N.B. There are some problems with the source tape including drop-outs etc but overall it has that "Blueberry Hill" feel to the sound

D1:
Intro - Bring It On Home (2:42 Cut)
White Summer (5:44)
Black Mountain Side (6:34)
Since I've Been Loving You (7:12)
Organ Solo(3:34)
Thank You (5:45)
What Is And What Should Never Be (1 :44 cut)
Moby Dick (18:12)
D2:
How Many More Times Medley: (22:18)
(Inc. Ravels Bolero -The Hunter - Boogie Chillen -
Trucking Little Mama - Mess O' Blues -
My Baby Don't Love Me - Lemon Song
Whole Lotta Love (7:44)

Who's Next

Venue: San Francisco
Date: 6/2/73
Cover: D4C sleeve
Recording: 7
Source: M -Aud
Company: Diagrams Of Led Zeppelin
Matrix #: TDOLZ 329701/2
Place Of Origin: Japan
Total Disc Time: 61.36 - 75.51

N.B. Also available as "Persistence Kezar", "Takka Takka" and a shorter version was available as "The Vibes Are Real"

D1:
Rock And Roll
Celebration Day
Black Dog
Over The Hills And Far Away
Misty Mountain Hop
Since I've Been Loving You
No Quarter
The Song Remains The Same
The Rain Song
D2:
Dazed & Confused
Stairway To Heaven
Moby Dick (cut)
Heartbreaker
Whole Lotta Love (Inc. Boogie Chillen)
Communication Breakdown
The Ocean

Wizardry

Venue:
New York
Date: 7/28/73
Cover: D4C in case
Recording: 8
Source: M - SB
Company: Joker **Matrix #:** JOK 008-A
Place Of Origin: Australia
Total Disc Time: 47.13
N.B. Another re-issue from down under of the sound-board from Madison Square Gardens.

D1:
Rock & Roll   (3.57)
Celebration Day   (3.27)
Black Dog   (5.45)
Over The Hills & Far Away   (6.13)
Misty Mountain Hop   (4.56)
Since I've Been Loving You   (8.17)
No Quarter (12.43)

Yellow Zeppelin

Venue: Miami
Date: 2/14/69
Cover: D4C sleeve in boxset
Recording: 6- 7
Source: M - Aud
Company: Tarantura
Matrix #: T2 CD 011 1 -2
Place Of Origin: Japan
Total Disc Time: 44.15 - 45.37
N.B.   Quite nice quality
Recording of the gig at Thee Image club in Miami. I suspect this is the first night. The cover has the wrong date. Comes in a boxset with a T-shirt. The cover art is by Bill Stout and is a very good parody of the Beatles Yellow Submarine art. Picture discs.

D1:
The Train Kept A Rollin' (3:12)
I Can't Quit You (5:29)
Dazed And Confused (11 :05)
Killing Floor Medley (5:58)
(Inc. The Lemon Song - Needle Blues)
Babe I'm Gonna Leave You (6:44)
How Many More Times (11 :05)
D2:
White Summer - Black Mountain Side (9:44)
As Long As I Have You Medley: (13:24)
(Inc. Fresh Garbage - Shake - Hush)
You Shook Me (8:54)
Pat's Delight (13:12)

You Gotta Be Cool

Venue: Tulsa
Date: 8/21/70
Cover: D4C in double case
Recording: 3 - 5
Source: M - Aud
Company: Whole Lotta Live
Matrix #: WLL 009 -010
Place Of Origin: Italy
Total Disc Time: 72.25 - 65.54

N.B. A straight knock off of the title
"Bottle Up And Go". The cover incorrectly
lists track six as Bron-y-Aur Stomp.

D1:
Immigrant Song (3.38)
Heartbreaker (7.56)
Dazed & Confused (Inc. White Summer) (18.37)
Bring It On Home (10.52)
That's The Way (6.52)
Bron-y-Aur (5.10)
Since I've Been Loving You (7.38)
D2:
Organ Solo - Thank You (13.00)
What Is & What Should Never Be (4.26)
Moby Dick (18.34)
Whole Lotta Love (18.34)
(Inc. Boogie Chillen - Bottle Up And Go - Shake Rattle &
Roll - I'll Be Yours You Be Mine Heartbeat - The Lemon
Song - My Baby Left Me - That's Alright Mama)
Communication Breakdown (5.33)

Your Teenage Dreams

Venue: Landover
Date: 5/25/77
Cover: D4C
Recording: 6
Source: M -Aud
Company: Diagrams Of Led Zeppelin
Matrix #: TDOLZ 229701/2/3
Place Of Origin: Japan
Total Disc Time: n/a

N.B. Another set extracted from the "Maryland Deluxe"
12 CD set.

D1:
The Song Remains The Same
Sick Again
Nobody's Fault But Mine
In My Time Of Dying
Since I've Been Loving You
No Quarter
D2:
Ten Years Gone
The Battle Of Evermore
Going To California
Black Country Woman
Bron-Y-Aur Stomp
White Summer - Black Mountain Side
Kashmir
Out On The Tiles, Moby Dick
D3:
Guitar Solo
Achilles Last Stand
Stairway To Heaven
Whole Lotta Love
Rock and Roll

Zig Zag Zep

Venue: Vienna

Date: 3/16/73

Cover: D2C gatefold sleeve

Recording: 7 - 8

Source: M - SB

Company: Tarantura

Matrix #: T3CD 013-1-3

Place Of Origin: Japan

Total Disc Time: 40.22 - 48.09

N.B. The first appearance of a decent soundboard recording from the Vienna gig. The tape reverts to the old audience recording about eleven minutes through Whole Lotta Love.

D1:

Intro - Rock And Roll (3:38)

Over The Hills And Far Away (5.25)

Black Dog (6.06)

Misty Mountain Hop (5.10)

Since I've Been Loving You (7:38)

Dancing Days (4:35)

Bron-Y-Aur Stomp (7.05)

D2:

The Song Remains The Same (2:14) (Cut)

Dazed And Contused (21:33) (cut)

Stairway To Heaven (10:44)

Whole Lotta Love Medley: (12.46)

(Inc .Boogie Chillen - Baby I Don't Care -

Let's Have A Party - I Can't Quit You - Lemon Song)

Zurich 1980

Venue: Zurich

Date: 6/29/80

Cover: D4C gatefold sleeve

Recording: 9

Source: St - SB

Company: Tarantura

Matrix #: 1980-17,18

Place Of Origin: Japan

Total Disc Time: n/a

N.B. Part of the deluxe set "1980" and also available separately as this two CD set. Nothing special it is the well documented soundboard tape.

D1:

Train Kept A Rollin'

Nobody's Fault But Mine

Black Dog

In The Evening

Rain Song

Hot Dog

All My Love

Trampled Underfoot

Since I've Been Loving You

D2:

Achilles Last Stand

White Summer - Black Mountain Side

Kashmir

Stairway To Heaven

Rock & Roll

Heartbreaker

Led Zeppelin Concert Itinerary
(Revised June 1998)

September 7th, 1968 Gladsaxe Teen Clubs Box 45 Copenhagen
September 7th, 1968 Brondby Pop Club Norregard Hallen Copenhagen
September 8th, 1968 Fjordvilla Roskilde
September 8th, 1968   Nykøbing Raventlow Park Falster Island
September 12th, 1968 Gronalund Tivoli Stockholm
September 13th, 1968 Inside Club Stockholm
September 14th, 1968 Angby Parkdans Show, Knivsta
September 15th, 1968 Liseburg Amusement Park Gotëborg
September 27th, 1968 Olympic Studio
October 1968 Olympic Studio Sessions
October 18th, 1968 London Marquee
October 19th, 1968 Liverpool University
October 25th, 1968 Surrey University
November 9th, 1968 London Chalk Farm Roundhouse
November 16th, 1968 Manchester College Of Science & Technology
November 23rd, 1968 Sheffield
November 29th, 1968 Richmond Athletic Club
December 10th, 1968 London Marquee
December 13th, 1968 Canterbury Bridge Country Club
December 16th, 1968 Bath Pavilion
December 19th, 1968 Exeter City Hall
December 20th, 1968 Wood Green Fishmongers Hall
December 26th, 1968 Denver Auditorium
December 27th, 1968 Seattle Center Arena
December 28th, 1968 Vancouver Pacific Coliseum
December 30th, 1968 Spokane Gonzaga University
December 31st, 1968 Portland
January 2nd, 1969 Los Angeles Whisky a Go Go
January 3rd, 1969 Los Angeles Whisky a Go Go
January 4th, 1969 Los Angeles Whisky a Go Go
January 5th, 1969 Los Angeles Whisky a Go Go
January 9th, 1969 San Francisco Fillmore West
January 10th, 1969 San Francisco Fillmore West
January 11th, 1969 San Francisco Fillmore West
January 12th, 1969 San Francisco Fillmore West
January 15th, 1969 Iowa City Iowa University
January 17th, 1969 Detroit Grande Ballroom
January 18th, 1969 Detroit Grande Ballroom
January 19th, 1969 Detroit Grande Ballroom
January 23rd, 1969 Boston Tea Party
January 24th, 1969 Boston Tea Party
January 25th, 1969 Boston Tea Party
January 26th, 1969 Boston Tea Party
January 31st, 1969 New York Fillmore East
February 1st, 1969 New York Fillmore East
February 2nd, 1969 Toronto Rockpile
February 3rd, 1969 New York Steve Paul's Scene Club?
February 4th, 1969 New York Steve Paul's Scene Club?
February 5th, 1969 New York Steve Paul's Scene Club?
February 6th, 1969 New York Steve Paul's Scene Club?
February 7th, 1969 Chicago Kinetic Playground
February 8th, 1969 Chicago Kinetic Playground
February ??, 1969 Memphis
February 14th, 1969 Miami Thee Image Club
February 15th, 1969 Miami Thee Image Club

March 1st, 1969   Plymouth Van Dyke Club
March 3rd, 1969   London Maida Vale BBC Studios
March 5th, 1969   Cardiff
March 7th, 1969   London Hornsey Wood Tavern
March ??, 1969   Bolton
March ??, 1969   Stoke
March 12th, 1969   Leicester
March 13th, 1969   Brondby Pop Club Norregard Hallen
March 13th, 1969   Gladsaxe TV-Byen
March 14th, 1969   Stockholm Concerthouse
March 14th, 1969   Uppsala University Lecture Hall
March 15th, 1969   Gladsaxe Teen Clubs Box 45
March 16th, 1969   Copenhagen Tivolis Koncertsal
March 19th, 1969   BBC Studio Session London
March 21st, 1969   How Late It Is BBC TV
March 22nd, 1969   Birmingham Mother's
March 25th, 1969   Staines Super Session
March 28th, 1969   London Marquee
March 30th, 1969   Southall Northcote Arms Farx
March 31st, 1969   London Cooks Ferry Inn
April 1st, 1969   London Hampstead Klook's Kleek
April 5th, 1969   London Dagenham Roundhouse
April 8th, 1969   Welwyn Garden City Cherry Tree
April 9th, 1969   London Tolworth Toby Jug
April 14th, 1969   Stoke ?
April 17th, 1969   Sunderland ?
April 24th, 1969   San Francisco Fillmore West
April 25th, 1969   San Francisco Winterland
April 26th, 1969   San Francisco Winterland
April 27th, 1969   San Francisco Fillmore West
May 1st, 1969   UC Urvine
May 2nd, 1969   Pasadena Rose Palace
May 3rd, 1969   Pasadena Rose Palace
May 1969   Mirror Sound Studio Sessions
May ??, 1969   Portland
May 9th, 1969   Edmonton Gardens
May 10th, 1969   Vancouver PNE Agrodome
May 11th, 1969   Seattle Green Lake Aquatheatre
May 13th, 1969   Honolulu Civic Auditorium
May 16th, 1969   Detroit Grande Ballroom
May 17th, 1969   Athens Ohio University
May 18th, 1969   Minneapolis Guthrie Memorial Theatre
May 23rd, 1969   Santa Clara Pop Festival
May 23rd, 1969   Chicago Kinetic Playground
May 24th, 1969   Chicago Kinetic Playground
May 25th, 1969   Columbia Merriweather Post Pavilion
May 27th, 1969   Boston Tea Party
May 28th, 1969   Boston Tea Party
May 29th, 1969   Boston Tea Party
May 30th, 1969   New York Fillmore East
May 31st, 1969   New York Fillmore East
June 1969   Morgan Studio Session
June 13th, 1969   Birmingham Town Hall
June 15th, 1969   Manchester Free Trade Hall
June 16th, 1969   London Dave Symonds Show BBC
June 19th, 1969   Paris Tous En Scene TV
June 20th, 1969   Newcastle City Hall
June 21st, 1969   Bristol Colston Hall
June 24th, 1969   London John Peel's Top Gear BBC

June 26th, 1969 Portsmouth Guild Hall
June 27th, 1969 London BBC Playhouse Theatre
June 28th, 1969 Bath Festival
June 29th, 1969 London Royal Albert Hall
July 5th, 1969 Atlanta Pop Festival
July 6th, 1969 Newport Jazz Festival
July 11th, 1969 Baltimore Jazz Festival
July 12th, 1969 Philadelphia Spectrum Jazz Festival
July 18th, 1969 Chicago Kinetic Playground
July 19th, 1969 Chicago Kinetic Playground
July 20th, 1969 Cleveland Musicarnival
July 21st, 1969 New York Central Park
July 25th, 1969 West Allis Milwaukee State Fair
July 26th, 1969 Vancouver PNE Agrodome
July 27th, 1969 Woodinville Goldcreek Park Seattle Pop Festival
July 29th, 1969 Edmonton Kinsmen Field House
July 30th, 1969 Salt Lake City Terrace Ballroom
July 31st, 1969 Eugene
August 1st, 1969 Santa Barbara Fairgrounds
August 3rd, 1969 Houston Music Hall
August 4th, 1969 Dallas State Fair Coliseum?
August 6th, 1969 Sacramento Memorial Auditorium
August 7th, 1969 Berkeley Community Theatre
August ??, 1969 Mystic Studio Session
August 8th, 1969 San Bernadino Swing Auditorium
August 9th, 1969 Anaheim Convention Centre
August 10th, 1969 San Diego Sports Arena
August 16th, 1969 Asbury Park Convention Hall
August 17th, 1969 Wallingford Oakdale Theatre
August 18th, 1969 Toronto Rockpile
August 21st, 1969 Framingham Carousel Theatre
August 22nd, 1969 Dania Pirates World
August 23rd, 1969 Dania Pirates World
August 24th, 1969 Jacksonville Veterans Memorial Coliseum
August 29th, 1969 New York Singer Bowl
August 30th, 1969 New York Singer Bowl
August 31st, 1969 Dallas Pop Festival
October 10th, 1969 Paris Olympia
October 12th, 1969 London Lyceum Ballroom
October 13th, 1969 Haarlem Holland
October 17th, 1969 New York Carnegie Hall
October 18th, 1969 Detroit Olympia
October 19th, 1969 Chicago Kinetic Playground
October 24th, 1969 Cleveland Public Auditorium
October 25th, 1969 Boston Gardens
October 26th, 1969 Charlotte Independence Coliseum
October 30th, 1969 Buffalo Kleinhan's Music Hall
October 31st, 1969 Providence
November 1st, 1969 Syracuse Onadaga War Memorial
November 2nd, 1969 Toronto O'Keefe Centre
November 4th, 1969 Kitchener Memorial Auditorium
November 5th, 1969 Kansas City
November 6th, 1969 San Francisco Winterland
November 7th, 1969 San Francisco Winterland
November 8th, 1969 San Francisco Winterland
December 6th, 1969 Paris L'Ecole Centrale Chatenay Lamabry
November ??, 1969 Olympic Studio Session
January 7th, 1970 Birmingham Town Hall
January 8th, 1970 Bristol Colston Hall

January 9th, 1970 London Royal Albert Hall
January 13th, 1970 Portsmouth Guild Hall
January 15th, 1970 Newcastle City Hall
January 16th, 1970 Sheffield City Hall
January 24th, 1970 Leeds Town Hall
February 17th, 1970 Edinburgh Usher Hall
February 24th, 1970 Helsinki
February 25th, 1970 Goteborg Konserthuset
February 26th, 1970 Stockholm Konserthuset
February 28th, 1970 Copenhagen K.B.Hallen
March 7th, 1970 Montreux Casino
March 8th, 1970 Munich
March 9th, 1970 Vienna Konserthaus
March 10th, 1970 Frankfurt
March 11th, 1970 Dusseldorf
March 12th, 1970 Hamburg Musikhalle
March 21st, 1970 Vancouver Pacific Coliseum
March 22nd, 1970 Seattle Center Arena
March 23rd, 1970 Portland Memorial Coliseum
March 25th, 1970 Denver Coliseum
March 26th, 1970 Salt Lake City Salt Palace
March 27th, 1970 Los Angeles Forum
March 28th, 1970 Dallas Memorial Auditorium
March 29th, 1970 Houston Hofheinz Pavilion
March 30th, 1970 Pittsburgh Civic Centre
March 31st, 1970 Philadelphia Spectrum
April ??, 1970 Dayton
April 2nd, 1970 Charleston
April 3rd, 1970 Macon Coliseum
April 4th, 1970 Indianapolis ?
April 5th, 1970 Baltimore Civic Center
April 7th, 1970 Charlotte Independence Coliseum
April 8th, 1970 Raleigh Dorten Arena
April 9th, 1970 Tampa Curtis Hixon Hall
April 10th, 1970 Miami Convention Hall
April 11th, 1970 St. Louis Kiel Auditorium
April 12th, 1970 St.Paul Minnesota
April 13th, 1970 Montreal Forum
April 14th, 1970 Ottawa Civic Centre
April ??, 1970 Rochester
April 16th, 1970 Evansville Indiana Roberts Stadium
April 17th, 1970 Memphis Mid-South Coliseum
April 18th, 1970 Phoenix Arizona Coliseum
April 26th, 1970 Julie Felix TV Appearance
May 1970 Bron-y-Aur Rehearsals
May 1970 Headley Grange Studio sessions
May 19th, 1970 Olympic Studios
June 22nd, 1970 Rejkyavik Laugardalsholl Sports Center
June 28th, 1970 Bath Festival
July 16th, 1970 Cologne
July 17th, 1970 Essen Grugahalle
July 18th, 1970 Frankfurt Festhalle
July 19th, 1970 Berlin Deutschlandhalle
August 15th, 1970 New Haven Yale
August 17th, 1970 Hampton Beach Coliseum
August 20th, 1970 Oklahoma City Coliseum Fairgrounds
August 21st, 1970 Tulsa
August 22nd, 1970 Fort Worth Tarrant Convention Centre
August 23rd, 1970 San Antonio Hemisphere Arena

August 25th, 1970 Nashville
August 26th, 1970 Cleveland Public Hall
August 28th, 1970 Detroit Olympia
August 29th, 1970 Winnipeg Arena
August 31st, 1970 Milwaukee Arena
September 1st, 1970 Seattle Center Coliseum
September 2nd, 1970 Oakland Coliseum
September 3rd, 1970 San Diego Sports Arena
September 4th, 1970 Los Angeles Forum
September 6th, 1970 Honolulu International Center
September 9th, 1970 Boston Gardens
September 19th, 1970 New York Madison Square Garden
December 1970 - January 1971 Headley Grange Studio Session
March 5th, 1971 Belfast Ulster Hall
March 6th, 1971 Dublin Boxing Stadium
March 9th, 1971 Leeds University
March 10th, 1971 Canterbury University
March 11th, 1971 Southampton University
March 13th, 1971 Bath Pavilion
March 14th, 1971 Stoke Hanley Place
March 18th, 1971 Newcastle Mayfair
March 19th, 1971 Manchester University
March 20th, 1971 Sutton Coldfield Belfry
March 21st, 1971 Nottingham Rowing Club
March 23rd, 1971 Marquee London
April 1st, 1971 London BBC Paris Theatre
May 3rd, 1971 Copenhagen K.B.Hallen
May 4th, 1971 Odense Fyns Forum
May 10th, 1971 Liverpool University
July 5th, 1971 Milan Vigorelli Stadium
August 7th, 1971 Montreux Casino
August 8th, 1971 Montreux Casino
August 19th, 1971 Vancouver Pacific Coliseum
August 20th, 1971 Seattle Center
August 21st, 1971 Los Angeles Forum
August 22nd, 1971 Los Angeles Forum
August 23rd, 1971 Fort Worth Tarrant Convention Center
August 24th, 1971 Dallas Memorial Aud
August 25th, 1971 Houston Hofheinz
August 26th, 1971 San Antonio Municipal Auditorium
August 27th, 1971 Oklahoma City
August 28th, 1971 St. Louis Arena
August 29th, 1971 New Orleans Municipal Auditorium
August 31st, 1971 Orlando Civic Auditorium
September 1st, 1971 Hollywood Florida Sportatorium
September 3rd, 1971 New York Madison Square Gardens
September 4th, 1971 Toronto Maple Leaf Gardens
September 5th, 1971 Chicago Amphitheatre
September 6th, 1971 Boston Gardens
September 9th, 1971 Hampton Beach Coliseum
September 10th, 1971 Syracuse Onadaga War Memorial
September 11th, 1971 Rochester Memorial Auditorium
September 13th, 1971 Berkeley Community Theatre
September 14th, 1971 Berkeley Community Theatre
September 16th, 1971 Honolulu International Center
September 17th, 1971 Honolulu International Center
September 23rd, 1971 Tokyo Budokan Hall
September 24th, 1971 Tokyo Budokan Hall
September 27th, 1971 Hiroshima Shiei Taiikukan

September 28th, 1971   Osaka Festival Hall
September 29th, 1971   Osaka Festival Hall
November 11th, 1971   Newcastle City Hall
November 12th, 1971   Newcastle Mecca Ballroom
November 13th, 1971   Dundee Caird Hall
November 16th, 1971   Ipswitch St Matthew's Baths
November 17th, 1971   Birmingham Kinetic Circus
November 18th, 1971   Sheffield University
November 20th, 1971   Wembley Empire Pool
November 21st, 1971   Wembley Empire Pool
November 23rd, 1971   Preston Town Hall
November 24th, 1971   Manchester Free Trade Hall
November 25th, 1971   Leicester University
November 29th, 1971   Liverpool University
November 30th, 1971   Manchester Kings Hall Belle Vue
December 2nd, 1971   Bournemouth Starkers
December 9th, 1971   Coventry Locarno?
December 15th, 1971   Salisbury
February 16th, 1972   Perth Subiaco Oval
February 19th, 1972   Adelaide Memorial Drive
February 20th, 1972   Melbourne Kooyong Tennis Courts
February 24th, 1972   Auckland Western Spring Stadium
February 27th, 1972   Sydney Showgrounds
February 29th, 1972   Brisbane Festival Hall
March ??, 1972   Bombay Session with Orchestra
May ??, 1972   Olympic Studio Session
May ??, 1972   Stargroves Studio Session
May ??, 1972   Island Studio Session
May 27th, 1972   Amsterdam R.A.I. Oude Rai
May 28th, 1972   Brussels Forest National
June 6th, 1972   Detroit Cobo Hall
June 7th, 1972   Montreal Forum
June 8th, 1972   Boston Gardens
June 9th, 1972   Charlotte Coliseum
June 10th, 1972   Buffalo Memorial Auditorium
June 11th, 1972   Baltimore Civic Centre
June 13th, 1972   Philadelphia Spectrum
June 14th, 1972   Hempstead Nassau County Coliseum
June 15th, 1972   Hempstead Nassau County Coliseum
June 17th, 1972   Portland Memorial Coliseum
June 18th, 1972   Seattle Coliseum
June 19th, 1972   Seattle Coliseum
June 21st, 1972   Denver Coliseum
June 22nd, 1972   San Bernadino Swing Auditorium
June 23rd, 1972   San Diego Sports Arena
June 25th, 1972   Los Angeles Forum
June 27th, 1972   Long Beach Arena
June 28th, 1972   Tucson Community Centre
October 2nd, 1972   Tokyo Budokan Hall
October 3rd, 1972   Tokyo Budokan Hall
October 4th, 1972   Osaka Festival Hall
October 5th, 1972   Nagoyashi Kokaido
October 9th, 1972   Osaka Festival Hall
October 10th, 1972   Kyoto Kaikan #1 Hall
October 27th, 1972   Montreux The Pavilion
October 28th, 1972   Montreux The Pavilion
November 30th, 1972   Newcastle City Hall
December 1st, 1972   Newcastle City Hall
December 3rd, 1972   Glasgow Green's Playhouse

December 4th, 1972   Glasgow Green's Playhouse
December 7th, 1972   Manchester Hardrock
December 8th, 1972   Manchester Hardrock
December 11th, 1972   Cardiff Capitol
December 12th, 1972   Cardiff Capitol
December 16th, 1972   Birmingham Odeon
December 17th, 1972   Birmingham Odeon
December 20th, 1972   Brighton Dome
December 22nd, 1972   London Alexandra Palace
December 23rd, 1972   London Alexandra Palace
January 2nd, 1973   Sheffield City Hall
January 7th, 1973   Oxford New Theatre
January 14th, 1973   Liverpool Empire
January 15th, 1973   Stoke Trentham Gardens
January 16th, 1973   Aberystwyth King's Hall
January 18th, 1973   Bradford St George's Hall
January 20th, 1973   Southampton University
January 21st, 1973   Southampton Gaumont
January 25th, 1973   Aberdeen Music Hall
January 27th, 1973   Dundee Caird Hall
January 28th, 1973   Edinburgh King's Theatre
January 30th, 1973   Preston Guild Hall
March 2nd, 1973   Copenhagen K.B. Hallen
March 4th, 1973   Goteborg Scandinavium Arena
March 6th, 1973   Stockholm   Royal Tennis Arena
March 7th, 1973   Stockholm   Royal Tennis Arena
March 10th, 1973   Oslo
March 11th, 1973   Rotterdam
March 12th, 1973   Brussels
March 13th, 1973   Munich
March 14th, 1973   Nuremburg Messehalle
March 16th, 1973   Vienna Concert House
March 17th, 1973   Munich Olympiahalle
March 19th, 1973   Berlin Deutschlandhalle
March 21st, 1973   Hamburg Musichalle
March 22nd, 1973   Essen Grughalle
March 24th, 1973   Offenburg Orthenau Halle
March 26th, 1973   Lyons Palais Des Sports
March 27th, 1973   Nancy Parc Des Expositions
April 1st, 1973   Paris Palais De Sports De St Ouen
April 2nd, 1973   Paris Palais De Sports De St Ouen
May 4th, 1973   Atlanta Braves Stadium
May 5th, 1973   Tampa Stadium
May 7th, 1973   Jacksonville Civic Centre
May 10th, 1973   Tuscaloosa University Of Alabama
May 11th, 1973   St Louis Kiel Aud.
May 13th, 1973   Mobile City Aud.
May 14th, 1973   New Orleans Mun.Aud.
May 16th, 1973   Houston Sam Houston Arena
May 18th, 1973   Dallas Memorial Auditorium
May 19th, 1973   Fort Worth Tarrant Con. Centre
May 22nd, 1973   San Antonio Hemisphere Arena
May 23rd, 1973   Albuquerque University Of New Mexico
May 25th, 1973   Denver Coliseum
May 26th, 1973   Salt Lake City Salt Palace
May 28th, 1973   San Diego Sports Arena
May 31st, 1973   Los Angeles Forum
June 2nd, 1973   San Francisco Kezar Stadium
June 3rd, 1973   Los Angeles Forum

July 6th, 1973   Chicago Aud.
July 7th, 1973   Chicago Aud.
July 8th, 1973   Indianapolis Arena
July 9th, 1973   St Paul Civic Centre
July 10th, 1973   Milwaukee Arena
July 12th, 1973   Detroit Cobo Hall
July 13th, 1973   Detroit Cobo Hall
July 15th, 1973   Buffalo Auditorium
July 17th, 1973   Seattle Coliseum
July 18th, 1973   Vancouver PNE Coliseum
July 21st, 1973   Providence Civic Centre
July 23rd, 1973   Baltimore Civic Centre
July 24th, 1973   Pittsburgh 3 Rivers Stadium
July 25th, 1973   Boston Gardens
July 27th, 1973   New York M.S.G.
July 28th, 1973   New York M.S.G.
July 29th, 1973   New York M.S.G.
December 1973 - June 1974   ?? Headley Grange Session
January 11th, 1975   Rotterdam Ahoy
January 12th, 1975   Brussels Forest Nationale
January 18th, 1975   Minneapolis Met Centre
January 20th, 1975   Chicago Stadium
January 21st, 1975   Chicago Stadium
January 22nd, 1975   Chicago Stadium
January 24th, 1975   Cleveland Coliseum
January 25th, 1975   Indianapolis Arena
January 29th, 1975   Greensboro Coliseum
January 31st, 1975   Detroit Olympia Stadium
February 1st, 1975   Pittsburgh Civic Arena
February 2nd, 1975   Pittsburgh Civic Arena
February 3rd, 1975   New York M.S.G.
February 4th, 1975   New York Nassau Coliseum
February 6th, 1975   Montreal Forum
February 7th, 1975   New York M.S.G.
February 8th, 1975   Philadelphia Spectrum
February 10th, 1975   Washington Capitol Centre
February 12th, 1975   New York M.S.G.
February 13th, 1975   New York Nassau Coliseum
February 14th, 1975   New York Nassau Coliseum
February 16th, 1975   St Louis Missouri Arena
February 27th, 1975   Houston Coliseum
February 28th, 1975   Baton Rouge L.S.U.
March 3rd, 1975   Fort Worth Tarrant Con.Centre
March 4th, 1975   Dallas Memorial Auditorium
March 5th, 1975   Dallas Memorial Auditorium
March 7th, 1975   Austin Events Centre
March 10th, 1975   San Diego Sports Arena
March 11th, 1975   Long Beach Arena
March 12th, 1975   Long Beach Arena
March 17th, 1975   Seattle Coliseum
March 19th, 1975   Vancouver Coliseum
March 20th, 1975   Vancouver Coliseum
March 21st, 1975   Seattle Coliseum
March 24th, 1975   Los Angeles Forum
March 25th, 1975   Los Angeles Forum
March 27th, 1975   Los Angeles Forum
May 17th, 1975   London Earl's Court
May 18th, 1975   London Earl's Court
May 23rd, 1975   London Earl's Court

May 24th, 1975 London Earl's Court
May 25th, 1975 London Earl's Court
October 10th, 1975 St. Helier Jersey Behan West Park
April 1st, 1977 Dallas Memorial Auditorium
April 3rd, 1977 Oklahoma City Myriad
April 6th, 1977 Chicago Stadium
April 7th, 1977 Chicago Stadium
April 9th, 1977 Chicago Stadium
April 10th, 1977 Chicago Stadium
April 12th, 1977 Minneapolis Met Centre.
April 13th, 1977 St Paul Civic Centre
April 15th, 1977 St Louis Missouri Arena
April 17th, 1977 Indianapolis Market Square Arena
April 19th, 1977 Cincinnatti Riverfront Coliseum
April 20th, 1977 Cincinnatti Riverfront Coliseum
April 23rd, 1977 Atlanta The Omni
April 25th, 1977 Louisville Kentucky Fairgrounds
April 27th, 1977 Cleveland Richfield Coliseum
April 28th, 1977 Cleveland Richfield Coliseum
April 30th, 1977 Pontiac Silverdome
May 18th, 1977 Birmingham Coliseum
May 19th, 1977 Baton Rouge LSU Assembly Cent.
May 21st, 1977 Houston The Summit
May 22nd, 1977 Fort Worth Convention Centre
May 25th, 1977 Washington Largo Capitol Centre
May 26th, 1977 Washington Largo Capitol Centre
May 28th, 1977 Washington Largo Capitol Centre
May 30th, 1977 Washington Largo Capitol Centre
May 31st, 1977 Greensboro Coliseum
June 3rd, 1977 Tampa Stadium
June 7th, 1977 New York Madison Square Gardens
June 8th, 1977 New York Madison Square Gardens
June 11th, 1977 New York Madison Square Gardens
June 12th, 1977 New York Madison Square Gardens
June 13th, 1977 New York Madison Square Gardens
June 14th, 1977 New York Madison Square Gardens
June 19th, 1977 San Diego Sports Arena
June 21st, 1977 Los Angeles Forum
June 22nd, 1977 Los Angeles Forum
June 23rd, 1977 Los Angeles Forum
June 25th, 1977 Los Angeles Forum
June 26th, 1977 Los Angeles Forum
June 27th, 1977 Los Angeles Forum
July 17th, 1977 Seattle Kingdome
July 20th, 1977 Tempe Activities Centre
July 23rd, 1977 Oakland Coliseum
July 24th, 1977 Oakland Coliseum
May ??, 1978 Clearwell Castle Rehearsals
November - December ??, 1978 Polar Studio Session
July 23rd, 1979 Copenhagen Falkoner Theatre
July 24th, 1979 Copenhagen Falkoner Theatre
August 4th, 1979 Knebworth
August 11th, 1979 Knebworth
June 17th, 1980 Dortmund Westfalenhalle
June 18th, 1980 Cologne Sportshalle
June 20th, 1980 Brussels Forest National
June 21st, 1980 Rotterdam Ahoy
June 23rd, 1980 Bremen Stadthalle
June 24th, 1980 Hanover Messehalle

June 26th, 1980 Vienna Stadthalle
June 27th, 1980 Nuremburg Messezentrum Halle
June 29th, 1980 Zurich Hallenstadion
June 30th, 1980 Frankfurt Festhalle
July 2nd, 1980 Mannheim Eisstadium
July 3rd, 1980 Mannheim Eisstadium
July 5th, 1980 Munich Olympichalle
July 7th, 1980 Berlin Eissporthalle
September 24th , 1980 Windsor Rehearsal
July 13th, 1985 Philadelphia JFK Stadium
May 14th, 1988 New York Madison Square Garden
May 12, 1990 Bewdley Heath Hotel
January 15, 1995 New York Waldorf Astoria

Other Led Zeppelin bootlegs known to exist include:
After The Crash ("XYZ" Demos & Shaken Outtakes, Rude World Demos) 1CD Midas Touch
Artwork! 2 CD $47
Complete Geisha Tape (9/29/71 2 CD) Memphis Label
The Crunge (Pittsburgh 73)
Dinosaurs in the Park (8/11/79 Knebworth) - TDOLZ 3 CD
Four for Texas (5/18/73 Dallas) - TDOLZ 2 CD
Front Row (9/23/71 2 CD) Memphis Label
Harper Live! 1 CD Tarantura Label
Heavy Metal Hullabaloo (2/3/75 MSG) 3 CD TODLZ Label
Houses Of The Holy Revised Versions (Megamixes of all HOTH tracks) HF10191 1CD
I Can't Get No Satisfaction (3/6/73 Stockholm 3 CD
It's Good to Be Seen (6/18/80) 2 CD TDOLZ Label
It's Time to Travel Again (1/12/75 Brussels) 2 CD TDOLZ
LA Jive & Rambling Mind (3/27/70 LA) 2 CD Holy Grail Label
Let's Have That Party 2/20/72 Ltd to 200 2CD Gold Series
Listen To This Eddie Original Master Recording - 6/21/77 3CD
MSG '77 (6/13/77) 3 CD
Mudslide (Vancouver 3/21/70) 1 CD TDOLZ Label
Munich 80 2CD Tarantura
Nassau '75 3 CD
No Quarter - Japanese Paper Sleeve CD Matrix # PHCR 1592
Osaka Woman - 9/28/71 3CD
Peerless Performance (6/29/80) Theramin ARM 2906801-2 2CD
Rockpile Canada 2/2/69 Totonka Label 1CD
Rotterdam '73 TDOLZ Label
Short Cuts (3/15/69 Afternoon Show! & Milan '71) 1 CD IQ Label
Studio Gems(Proby, 1st album demos , Jennings Farm & BBC) 1CD Kobra KRLZ01
Studio Gems 2 (Julie Felix Show, 3rd Album outtakes) Kobra 1CD KRLZ02
Studio Haze Vol 1 (1st & 3rd album demos, Headley and Bombay) Laughing Skull T331/2 2 CD
Swansong (New Phys Graff Sessions) 1 CD Tarantura Label
Wanderers (The) 2/29/72 Ltd to 200 2CD Gold Series

**Also in Japan all ten Led Zeppelin albums were re-issued in cardboard replica
sleeves. Each one was identical to the original album jacket but CD sized.**
Led Zeppelin I   AMCY-2431
Led Zeppelin II   AMCY-2432
Led Zeppelin III AMCY-2433
Led Zeppelin IV AMCY-2434
Houses Of The Holy AMCY-2435
Physical Graffiti AMCY-2436~7
Presence AMCY-2438
Song Remains The Same   AMCY-2439~40
In Through The Out Door AMCY-2441
Coda AMCY-2442

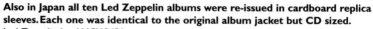

Look for these other books from

Collector's Guide Publishing Inc.

Available in all good book stores.

LED ZEPPELIN
The Press Reports

In "Led Zeppelin - The Press Reports...." noted Led Zeppelin expert Robert Godwin has collected and reviewed over a thousand articles from around the globe. Reports of the band's activities from Tokyo to New York and from Sydney to London are compiled and collated in chronological order.

"...outrageously exhaustive..." Guitar World

"....exceptional... a marvel of meticulous research.." FMQB

"The Press Reports...." includes an exclusive interview compact disc with Jimmy Page from 1977 in which he discusses his amazing career as one of the world's top rock musicians.

New 2nd Printing
Features
pre-Zep section
1963-1968

THE COLLECTOR'S GUIDE TO HEAVY METAL

....for who can resist the unswerving majesty of the power chord? read about it, as we batter, praise, and otherwise penetrate the essence of over 3,300 bruising records comprising a large wedge of the world's Most Powerful Music. Designed to guide the discerning fan through the jungle of releases competing for your CD dollar. Hard Rock, Heavy Metal, Grunge, Thrash, Funk Metal, Black Metal, Death Metal, Euro Metal, Prog Metal, Punk, etc etc.

Includes an exclusive nineteen track Heavy Metal sampler compact disc.

"....Martin Popoff is to heavy metal what Hunter S. Thompson was to politics...this is a completists guide to Heavy Metal. By any definition...."
Lollipop Magazine

THE PROGRESSIVE ROCK FILES

If you've ever listened to bands like Yes or Genesis and liked what you heard...
If you've ever felt you had to hide your purchase of the latest Emerson Lake & Palmer CD...
If you've ever wondered how many other progressive rock bands are out there...

...The Progressive Rock Files is the book you've been looking for! After years of research, musicologist and radio personality **Jerry Lucky** has created a definitive guide to Progressive Rock music.

Everything from the history and the critical thrashing, to the complex development this musical genre has gone through from it's beginnings in 1967 to the present day.
Included are definitions of virtually all popular musical styles and for the first time a definition of what Progressive Rock actually is...and it's probably not what you think.

Also included is a comprehensive **A-Z listing of over 1400 Progressive Rock bands** each with a brief musical description and recored discography to aid in your discovery of this challenging and adventurous musical art-form.